Anpu

By P Fontanouie

Proem

This tale, when a queen had died, across realms and spectrums much sadness was felt. "it was anyone's game," Pam just stood quietly after, thinking, we were all there, wondering whether it is okay to give a plain tangerine as a gift. Did the assassin turn, was he pushed, had the tempter Pam managed to swing the whole thing around, was she really an actor, or grateful, for the opportunity to be trained. What and who were they protecting, you, from whom, why, since when?

Disclaimer; Legal and Otherwise.

This book, is formed of two-halves, two books, named 'Anpu Jaffa 1 & 11.' Scale-wise the book was unable to be downloaded on some devices, hence the measure taken. Still grateful to have got it uploaded, printable etcetera, and available. Thank you!

GSTK.

Chapter One

72 Luxton Court

Lovers And an Easier Sceptic

It was 08.30AM, or so thereabouts, Pamela heard what sounded like a real heavy thud from the floor of one of the flats above, realizing that her mind was still closed, as though to reduce interruption or risk before, to shut it all out, for various reasons, probably to include insanity after what we seem to have been through. Noise, not the flat immediately above though, 'Dung Beetle paradise, where they were kicking a ball around much of the day, it sounded as though someone, - or something, very hefty-footed had stamped down extremely hard and deliberately on a wooden, carpeted floor. Then, as though everything that was surrounding, an energy almost, as the weight of the culprit, or whatever was responsible seemed to shake it and was forming what was visible to Pamela a cascade, then as it disappeared from that apartment and into the flat directly above Pamela's and then somehow, it then levelled back into her own flat. The thought of the wick to her oil lamp, coiled then, as though waiting to be used, it was on a shelf of a corner unit that had belonged to her father. It was to that coiled wick, that whatever it was, certainly a kind of energy force, went directly to, it returned to there, only to then become absorbed totally, yes in that small candle wick, until no doubt Pamela would eventually decide to use it for what purpose and when. She was thinking of silver birch trees and of a woodland, but at that moment she did not know exactly why? An image appeared from behind one of those trees, then it disappeared as quickly, yes, just like a small rabbit might well down a hole, a second later it appeared again, as though peeking from the other side of the tree, it was Chimook, she knew them from before, but why here, and why now she wondered. Then afraid to walk too far into the forest, as beautiful as it looked, she thought the Chimook had wanted to play a game but wanted to think first, or was Pamela too pre-occupied anyway really, she had other things on her mind, and was just observing how beautiful the trees looked then and especially from where she stood. The forest didn't look green, it was very much like something you might imagine on a tinted greetings card, maybe even a Christmas Card, and it looked as though it glistened somehow, but it was not a wet looking damp moist looking forest, but clean and sharp, and all a colour of light faun but with reflective light then against the bark of the very many trees. She did think it was quite beautiful, afraid though, only because it was a woodland forest, despite one of her trusted friends the Chimook, being seen there. Some would say, 'oh it's one of Pamela's imaginary friends,' we've all been there, or some have, but there was a reason that she had seen her so called 'imagined,' friend and friends, if it or they were 'imagined,' at all. She noticed some cord had tied her hair behind, but didn't remember tying it herself, she thought this as she leaned forward and almost so quietly knelt down, or crouched, so politely to look at what was probably the smallest of daisy-like flowers on the ground that she had ever seen before. Although pre-occupied, yes there was something on her mind indeed, you see, two of the stones that protruded just enough that the Wibbly Wobbly river could be walked across safely and that had been placed there by none other than The King and Queen of Pasturelands themselves, had gone missing, so you'd only ever now get half-way across there. It was to cause terrible noise issues throughout the kingdom, and grumpiness, such noise would keep others awake, this also in turn would mean that the littler people who weren't so little really in many ways, those with huge hands and feet and noses almost like Pamela's had looked for a while after she was born, until it corrected itself in more recent times, for many years after, some wouldn't understand some things straight away then, they or some of them couldn't, maybe because they'd never thought about it, maybe they never found time or needed to. Some of their tummies were a little larger than some could suggest was 'average,' too, but they didn't mind, because those there really didn't know any different, but most of all, what seemed to annoy often, was the tickling, if they tried to swim too deep in Tepetape' that was the real name for Wibbly Wobbly River, their noses would feel tickly, 'so much,' that it would become quite unbearable for them, and that would make the soles of their feet tickle and they'd never get anything done, and they'd laugh a lot, but it wasn't a real laugh, not like being touched with a feather. As for the bridge, all guessed, by the stones having vanished, full access particularly for some, most, had now been prevented. When anyone walked, or tried to walk across, there were strong currents and winds sometimes, well not much of a wind, but if the stones were slippery a little, or if your feet were too big or sometimes even too small, you'd have to hold onto the ropes on either side and thinner ones beneath, ropes that had been then put there temporarily, to attempt to help those who needed desperately to cross to the other riverbank, they'd always seemed content with just slightly carefully, very soberly or cautiously jumping from one stone onto another, even although not like in other places possibly, it was what they knew, and whatever the weather was like, - and even if and as when it rained there, it really did rain.

Quite often, where the rope bridge now was, whether before or after the stones had vanished, you'd stand there if it wasn't so windy and if it hadn't rained, and when you looked around, would be just amidst the birch trees, on some days if the moment was precisely right, and it was worth waiting for, and again and again but not to rush time, just to enjoy it when it did happen, glistening at you, and when it did, and if the sunlight was shining through the trees too, and those in-turn had their seeds hanging in thin furry silvery envelopes amidst their long baby leaves you knew it did and that it had. You were never quite alone there, but it would make you think sometimes, and often, to be careful who you travel with, as sad as it might be to need ever to think that, and not just because the river had five exits and only one of them good. Some birds of an unusual kind were heard along near so often the good exit, that was helpful, especially if heading downstream if on a log and if it was windy and in a strong current, because you couldn't paddle quick enough in time after hearing the birds, if you were there at the right moment anyway, and it was a very long and very steep walk back, but only at certain times of the year would that usually happen and some even thought it was funny when that happened too. No-one knew why it was known as Wibbly-wobbly River though, maybe because some could not say Tepetape' properly, who named it that too, we'll never know, but the beauty of that moment there, whether with those new ropes or not, and however slippery the stones, superseded it. On the bridge, or thereabouts or at that place and from where, was to be seen, if there at the right moment, or depending on who you were, or even whether you knew it or not, why you were, or might have been, or may be, - was a clockface of light. Was this one of those days, or did it really happen ever anyway, and what only if after other points had been accomplished? It fitted from beneath what was the pandoras box itself, and the clockface moved, because it clicked into place on its own now, upon the top of that extremely safely positioned box. Those on the bridge with you, were, none of them had reason to be afraid, even as that clock-face or locking device, started, or seemed to turn, from left to right, and then back again, and then forward a little and back further again, forth and back, sometimes fast and sometimes not, moving the locking device, as though it was trying to crack open the combination of a safe. It then clicked and then it beeped twenty-three times, and then sixteen times, then suddenly it stopped. Of course, it would not be able 'presumably,' to further, because the combination had been sealed long before and by one of those who was then on that bridge, at that very moment in time. Then, 'almost' as though from within it, a golden creature-like character emerged, yes, it seemed to come from within the box, but how could it, it was not unlocked, because that had been correctly achieved, then the character, whilst as soon on that bridge, from that day on, for a while would remain totally invisible to, and totally odourless to predators, and their children, or anyone associated to them, they or theirs, or them in any way, any shape, or in any form, too, it could and would and did, have them believe that all, and any of their own known and arranged subsequent or even thought of, routines, would remain exactly as they always were, had they been, or even if they were not, and there was nothing, they could do about it, they'd not understand it anyway, neither fathom, to ever become or that then became, as invisible as those on the bridge would become, to possibly even the wind itself.

However strangely or however odd it may seem, 'to some,' at around this same time, dear Pamela had been asked to collect a prescription after various consultations with a couple of medical professionals, with Pamela able to refer to incidences of the past that were thankfully on file, none where drug use had been permanently arranged, in the form of a prescription from one of the doctors then. To gain some clarification and a level of safety and a sanctity of a kind, Pamela on this occasion was so thankful that her request could under those circumstances and was met, whereby a prescription was written for her. First there had been a period of reading the information on the medicine, and then to decide whether it was a correct decision, but Pamela seemed quite sure. She went to collect the prescription and then had to get on a bus to locate a pharmacist. There was a pharmacist close to where she lived and so she went there. Much to her horror, the pharmacist said that they did not have that medication in stock and that it could be a while, she was annoyed, but not for so obvious reasons, and thought about the situations happening generally and presumed that they must have ran out, she didn't ask, but she did ask, hypothetically, thinking of some she had worked with in the past, and how some of them might have responded there, she asked, "you are aware what this medication is and its use and purpose," the pharmacist said yes. For Pamela, who felt as though she herself then was being challenged and that it could somehow delay, irritate, or hinder recovery, it was difficult. Asking this question, for her, created for her, his level of expertise as a pharmacist, in order that she could then feel safe to ask a further or next question. Feeling safe to, because of how he responded, she then asked politely, "If I were to leave here and harm someone, or worse, what would you do"? He quibbled, and she then said, 'seriously, it's a serious question, you are a pharmacist, you do not have this medicine in stock, we are amidst a pandemic situation and neither can you give reassurance as to when you can supply or have a supply ready," he threw Pamela out of the pharmacy and shouted that it was his reaction to Covid-19 and told her loudly to stay away. She ignored his remark, and dismayed, went elsewhere instead. There, the prescription was dispensed to her, she was sad that the pharmacist was afraid because of all that had been happening, and. or feeling fears of so many, it did though re-assure her, that his professionalism was on track, as she moved forward more confidently after that experience and with a clearer personal directive in mind.

#

Unfortunately, it was and so very sadly, within days that news would be heard across then the whole of the Kingdom of Pasturelands that His most extreme eminence, His Royal Highness, The King of Pasturelands had passed away. It was a sad and dark sombre moment-in-time for some, not dark like a dark forest, but as though you'd been forced to wear sunglasses all of the time, even when it was not sunny, it might even make it difficult for some to notice white flowers or even pink ones or red or any, however fragrant any might have tried so hard to be, if they'd felt able to sometimes, respectfully it was for Pamela and in her emotional and somewhat bullied hurt position, as though then, even the flowers just couldn't. The King was a kind man Pamela thought, and because of his kindness, he was considered a consort, Pamela had always thought of him as kind, but she didn't understand what a consort was then, she had thought he was much more gentlemanly than as a king could, she'd imagined, - be.

Those on the bridge then, still in shock, and some because of the terrible plague that had hit Pasturelands since more than a year before, so there were other reasons now too, why many would think of those closer to them and theirs, and to some, whether directly or not, those and those considered, even the imaginary friends? The Queen of Pasturelands and not a soul or person could intervene or know, what their thoughts or misunderstandings were, neither could they presume to be near that bridge, only the person who was there, and she knew every and anyone who too was. When they'd started to walk across, there were strong currents and winds, so yes, it was still important to hold on tight to the ropes, it was then, precisely then, that the huge pale pink and lightest lime green clock face did surprisingly actually appear. Simultaneously it was to turn around onto its back and face upward beneath the feet of those on the bridge at that time, 'as though' a light that had surrounded it, so yes, if on the bridge right then, whilst it seemed, beneath nutlets of the silver birch trees as though surrounded by them there, an idea somehow formed. Neither could anything that others, - or friends, or some might say, impact on anyone on that bridge. For sure, a star then appeared in the nutlets, on and to, only the minds of those on that bridge at that moment then, a golden star shape, with and whilst and as, squirrels, grey squirrels who were busy eating, holding and gnawing the sides or acorns, although none were afraid at all, around acorns, their tails bushed and twitching only with a real excitement. The nutlet fruits of the birch are some two or three millimetres across, and with two wings each, their flowers, - catkins, the wings allow the seeds to travel on a nice wind, even a mile or so from the parent tree. How long though, those on the bridge that day would remain there, was not known to them, or certainly what may lie ahead. With no idea either, that there could have been more to it, certainly that some, or even they, - could have contemplated to understand fully then, if they knew of course? Those were kind and thinking of preservation and in a safe way, however 'unconventionally,' quite conventionally too? Whilst there, away from the riverbanks, they could also hear elephants, some could, although none could be seen, all of the time and each movement was being carefully monitored by Pamela, and she didn't even realise she was doing it, she wasn't being forced to do it, it was quite instinctive for her, would all be revealed in due course, if none knew, what could there ever actually become, to be revealed? Some could hear car horns, or 'a' car horn, it was feeding time in some way, for the elephants possibly, but from which side of the bridge were the noises coming from, and how and what sound from which side? It too, was all unknown, as to whether the lovely elephants that could obviously be heard, whether they were the big-eared or the smaller-eared kind? Then within a second, before any could question further, they might wonder what could happen next, as they then found themselves perched on top of a flower, having hovered somehow to the very top of a stem, their own wings were invisible, and everything was or became then, so very quiet, there as they waited, and as strange as it could seem to some, and despite loving elephants, they and maybe for them too, just waited there, and to just simply for a while be in the quiet. Also floating in the air, as though in what to them looked like being in space, were steam irons, metal ironing boards, rugs, filing cabinets and yellow, red, and grey plastic washing-up bowls. One of them mentioned 'rat noises,' but they all, even if they could work out why, if, whether, or not, just stared at each other and shrugged their shoulders as if to say, what?

So, The King of Pasturelands had passed away on the day before, or the day after moving onto what could only ever really have been considered 'a magic bridge.' To be seen too, were people although they were busy, now at either side of the ends of the bridge, was the very reason those on the bridge, or who had been, were there at all. If the bridge were to release itself from the edges, it would form a rope raft at first of a kind, but which way, if it did, would the, or such a raft go, upstream or down? Fortunately, that had not happened, not yet. It was pretty much at that absolute moment that the ropes between the two banks glowed an orange and silver-grey, those on the bridge let go of the ropes, the platform separated from the banks cleanly and had risen, to some twelve feet, very slowly, - in the meantime, like a horses' blinkers, panels formed down both sides, behind where the ropes were and met beneath, - those on the 'platform' on a flower, were now inside a capsule.

It was not scary at all, for any of them, it was air-conditioned, and you could see out of it as though there was a window all around, you could even see a person, or Pamela could, a giant, trying to catch it in a net, but however he tried, he could not, he waved his arms about so much, and the largest butterfly net Pamela had ever seen, that you could see his frustration, or Pamela could, she just looked on, certainly as though quite disinterested, and thankful, especially then, that he never would. He had become one of the 'not so nice' giants of Pasturelands, and had been known to enjoy catching some, yes, indeed he was quite known.

Some shapes appeared on a window, right angles, three and then two more to make it five, one of those on the platform now within a capsule touched it but didn't know why, and the capsule turned around 270 degrees, so they were now facing going with the flow of the water, it stopped briefly and so slowly, then it turned further, a further 180 degrees. So now they were facing against the tide or upstream. No-one could harm any of them, no-one at all. The platform had obviously flown quite briefly and then landed right on the very tip of the tongue of the now open-mouthed giant, - that was or had been the reason he'd tried then to catch it, it must have stung him maybe like tiny mouth-ulcer on the tongue, he tried to wipe his mouth and stuck his tongue out as he then bit the head of the tiny ulcer completely off between his incisor teeth and could feel it then sore as though oozing fluid, but much quicker than he'd recover from biting the head off the tiny ulcer, was the capsule to evade him, even spinning slightly, it was just way too fast for him. And if that wasn't enough, but for some strange reason, in that moment, biting the head from the mouth ulcer, had disrobed him, it was not a pleasant sight at all, also it was noticed just how very dirty their feet were, or his. Many had often thought that the reason things rarely grew for a long time once a giant had walked there was because of their size, to have walked there with such weight and force, but often they were so busy playing and eating and escaping the gazes of their wives and friends, who'd be wondering what they were doing, that they just didn't have time to wash their feet and to wash their toenails, certainly not properly anyway, what would be left for the bees if so much apart from lovely trees was lost, or would the bees have to tread in what the dirtier feet types might sometimes leave behind too? It became noticeable that somehow a clearing of a kind should be considered, but with not much time, how could such be achieved without any, or required approvals in place? Maybe such a clearing would become a kind of cleaner direction? It was difficult to say and really for then, very early days. Of course, it was known only to some too, that dragon's spit if smelled could help, and that a hair from a dragons' chin would or could cause if it touched a giant's feet or hands, and that the itching was so intense that it would be enough to make the giant run screaming to put his, or her, if it was a lady giant, their foot or feet into water quickly, but where were they possibly going to find dragon's spit, or notice a hair from a dragon's chin, stuck, there where they were, would they forget anyway and if they did, would it be not so much like 'some cannot copy what some cannot see,' or that some would make noises or call names or throw very floury rock cake balls secretly at the back of your head when you are not looking, as though trying to crack open eggs to create an omelette, but more like flipping a coin but not gambling on an outcome, but trusting somehow, because a sincere hope in a way, had somehow seemed all that may remain, and dragon's spit from within a capsule, even though the windows were so very clean?

It soon became evening and was quite dark outside, - although there were stars twinkling in the sky outside above, all in the capsule apart from myself, were fast asleep, on blow- up cushions that appeared, and there was even a pump to pump them up. Everything in the capsule must have shrunk but in different degrees, I looked at even my shoes and my feet were smaller too or was it that my shoes got bigger, I could not be totally sure? Whilst laying down, an elephant-shape face pressed against the capsule from the outside, so from inside, it looked like an elephant head on a wall, its trunk moved, and its eyes did too. I decided that I preferred to see elephants and the eyeball that also appeared from no-where – also 'peering' in, - where they should be. It was for a moment that somewhere, something did not like the fact that I was not being looked at, or stared at, from outside, even by elephants, not even in a place that was a private space.

Then was heard, a ball of scrunched paper being thrown across the capsule space and a large foot banging down from above, as though it was a giant calling out for food or something like that. Then I saw a cat I'd once had and said to it, 'I'll feed you fresh food very soon.' This served well as it took my mind away from where it had been focused on the scrunched paper that had mysteriously been heard as it had seemingly been thrown across the length of space, to where it had obviously or supposedly landed. This was very frightening for me, I decided to investigate it anyway, and why. Too afraid to move though, I focused on my cat, a cat I had not actually seen for a very long time, despite the fact that the particular lovely, beautiful cat had gone off to visit other plains some time before, it was not behaving strangely at all, and was none the wiser, even that a scrunched paper ball had been seemingly thrown across the room. That was odd, but I decided even though I could not physically move then, not to attempt it anyway. Of course, too I could see what looked like white flashes, and I wondered if I needed a coat, but it was close somehow, and somehow dare I say 'fresh' in such, - that would to many have been considered a confined space, though the dynamics of it gave a different impression and feel and was not cold at all. The elephant heads and other faces turned their gaze and their ears, so they then faced outward, so they could neither see nor hear us, but I guess we, or I, could see and hear, presumably? The giant foot that was heard again to stamp on the ground from above, somehow, I moved it, or did I, was it I that moved it, or another intrusion, now the capsule had at least one leg, but it was attached to the outside. We all were, and now remained safe, and safer within the capsule. As if anything stranger than a stranger thing could happen, but a strange thought did occur, in that, what happens to some who may not, or were not quite so innocent really, or so well behaved, if a person comes along who is or could be? Would that give a reason why some seem to enjoy being horrid and cruel and saying unpleasant things to others, because it takes or removes that type or a particular type of attention from themselves? A strange thought indeed, and what to do with it, what if anything was to be done about it? Should an attempt be made at all? It was then, whilst looking out of a window, I saw the smaller, it must surely have been the tiniest of tiniest small creatures I thought, with the most beautiful of small clear, long- pointed wings, land on a wonderful cornflower, its body was so transparent that it looked quite almost as blue as the cornflower itself, now that is a wonderful sight I thought. Rather than pushing down as some giants could, not that the small creature there, would have been afraid, or would even have noticed a giant, or been bothered, however big its stompy-stamping-feet or foot, as sometimes the case might seem, sounded, - to those who might hear them. The image of that creature seemed to pull me out and upward as though I'd myself, and nothing to do with those I knew well or those I cared obviously about and who cared, been covered in horridness for such a long time, or had been forced to hear it, still inside the capsule with friends and those close, but unapproachable from those outside. The capsule changed shape and an arm appeared and then another leg, and suddenly it was not so much like a capsule, but an odd capsule, almost like a kind of body, if legs and arms only denoted that, or those types of legs and arms anyway. The disease that had plagued the land, then slipped from the outer skin of the capsule and dropped to the ground as though no more a problem. Of course, I worried whether it would affect skin, but no, it slid off from the capsule and to the ground, as though it could not affect now at all. The lovely creature was like a hummingbird somehow, but it was not, and its wings very pointed and narrow thin, and I'd like to say still it was tiny, because of its transparency, but I could not really tell, as much seemed then, all just slightly odd. It was very clever and yes with a very long beak, it had six transparent legs, like thin hairs, and tiny feet or what looked like shoes, like droplets of water. It had followed the trail of pink petals that could be seen from above and those too, just like tiny, small droplets of water, maybe it was just a droplet of water or dew I wondered? I certainly did, and it was early enough. Then, with its thin narrow beak inside the neck of a flower, it pulled, - its wings flapped about very quickly at first and then as though in quite slow motion, it pulled and pulled and pulled and didn't look at all stressed or bothered, and as it did, what resembled a large curtain appeared just beyond it, and that opened, like a pair of curtains with their tops remaining closed together, they were definitely and unmistakeably opening. Those, or some inside the capsule behaved as though they felt a shunting, and then another shunt, and then another, something was happening, none grabbed their seats, it wasn't like that at all, but none moved, as the capsule started to rise, and then further, it seemed almost dark for some reason, with light shining through an opening, and with the tiny creature still holding so tightly, what then looked like a cord. They in the capsule were then moving toward the opening between those two curtains, but instead of flying through, they seemed to hit the side of the curtain and then drop slightly, and then rise again and hit the curtain again and then once more, it was a Dum Dum bird, it had obviously landed at some point near the top of the capsule by mistake, or flown by, but where it was dark, it seemed, and where we were focused on the light seen through the gap in the curtains, none hadn't realised then that the capsule somehow was stuck on its feathers and especially as the Dum Dum birds themselves were notoriously clumsy, again it focused so carefully and flew toward the opening between the curtains, after flying around and thankfully successfully this time, a whole 360 degrees just to focus, then with anticipation and with its every squawk as the gap drew closer, it then got completely stuck between the curtains. It was squawking and pulling so hard and its small feet, not that you could see those, were obviously moving as though some birds might paddle very quickly at a quickened pace of ten-to-the-dozen, because it caused a vibration heard only within the squawking and that was only heard by lucky Pamela, who sat waiting, wondering and wondering too, too stunned, what this was all about? As she hadn't been aware and was doing this instinctively, she stared on and thought, 'what have I done to deserve this, please, please I implore you, please be so extremely kind somewhere and do tell me.' All she could hear in response though, was the continued squawking, as though the greater or lesser Dum Dum bird was quite disgruntled and not happy at all, trying to pull and push, push, shove and pull its way through the gap, and with what obviously was the small capsule stuck to it, then with its neck totally outstretched as far as it could go, the Dum Dum bird pulled the body of its whole plumage through the curtain, and then at last they were away. What was beyond, and would they ever be able to return, one of the other occupants of the capsule then woke up and they both stared to the sides and back as the curtain closed behind them.

The greater or lesser Dum Dum bird eventually did land, and the hand of the arm of the capsule that had held on so tightly, let go, there was no indication then as to where they were, Pamela decided to remain as calm as she could as she carefully wondered what the next move might be and whether it, - whether any of it, not that she was afraid or unconfident, but whether any such moves would be of their own choosing, or of something else. Everything remained silent for much of the rest of the day and evening, because of course on the other side of the curtain and without the plumage, they were in what to her, certainly looked like daylight anyway and despite the fact that one of the angled shapes, again on the monitor screen or window, seemed to be rotating anti-clockwise, she stared at it again, it did look as though it was rotating, backwards, but was it really? Again, she stared at it, almost slightly unsure, and said 'no,' but then noticed it was not at all, she shook her head very slightly. Then a voice was heard by Pamela only, others were napping or asleep. It was the voice of a person she thought, the person said, "is that where they all live, in there," but there was no-one around. A fly then swallowed the capsule that then flew and whether it went back through the curtain or not - was not known, it was so fast, but they whilst inside the body of the fly, were flown outside a building of a kind, then inside another building, where it flew then through another open door and up to the top of another building on the outside and in through a window then it landed on a sausage on a plate of the person who'd asked 'is that where they live,' and threw up all over a part of his sausage. He was making a cup of tea at the time, so he didn't notice anyway. Then because that's how a fly eats, it licked his sausage and mashed potato and thick onion gravy, and it really did have a big lick of that, especially the mash, then it flew away. The capsule though, did not affect him, he didn't even see it, it had become so small, but those inside could not be interfered with at all, don't ask how, but Pamela somehow, as though watching an experiment, although too unaware, oblivious, if anyone could be like that really, knew this? Or that was how it looked, she just stared then, in such a way that you could easily have been mistaken to believe and as she felt herself squinting in a disbelief of a kind, they were truly stuck, and as though to ask, 'come on then, boy, am I just waiting for this darling.' As much what happened next, was not something she'd require her crystal ball for, with the capsule and, now in the regurgitated fly-vomit on the sausage and mash gravy passed through his body and then was flushed down the toilet, by him certainly, and fortunately, 'unnoticed.' Then yes, The Greater, or Lesser Dum Dum Bird known for its locational skills and clumsiness had found the exact pipe the capsule was travelling through, and although a few metres above the pipe, perched but on a small twig-like thing on the ground, drew it up through the pipe without affecting the pipe and then through the soil, and to where it attached itself to its plumage feathers, now cleaner than ever before even, because all of the, or any other dust or residue of any kind, presumably from where other maybe unsavoury things had dropped from it, such as ill feeling and bad thoughts directed, any filth greasiness of any kind, was removed by the elements within the soil from the pipe that went for miles and miles, and even more miles beneath the ground. The capsule found itself within another capsule, - a silver coloured capsule, it was round. Some of the silver globe locked itself into place around the capsule and bolted then, what had been heard out, locks were heard sealing down hard the silver ball, the door then was certainly closed, as it had been before, although they, those inside the capsule/s had not realized anyway, but this time, yes, for sure, closed. Arm-like structures then formed onto the outside of the globe-like structure, only a few of them, but to push and keep away and at bay, those, or any possible intruders, then the arms closed neatly away again inside the capsule shape. It had resembled image depictions of what the disease that had plagued Pasturelands had looked like or been presented as looking- like microscopically, although only a few arms and where the arms on those had in such depictions, clung to anything they could- the arms of the globe only pushed away and would not permit attempts to re-enter. It was so shiny it glistened like highly polished steel, although it was not steel, not of any substance known to humanity, anywhere. A single numeric code of some six hundred numbers was them impressed and not to harm, onto the arm of one of those inside the capsule, from then, until advised not to, no-one would be able to access or intervene or enter the mind-sets of those 'within' the capsule, unless ever number of the code was first said before them, and in accurate order. None inside the capsule could see what sequence the numbers were, apart from one of them in the capsule-. And that was nothing to do with those, them, or anyone outside. The curtains had re-opened; the globe rested on the stem of a flower. More of the winged creatures flew in from beyond the curtain and each attached their beaks to the inside of the flower and simultaneously pulled, the stem of the flower under the pressure then bent itself like bamboo, but it did not break. They then let go of the pulleys, the globe flew out through the curtains. It was being kind to anyway, to have allowed them, to propel. It knew it could trust them, or that they would be harmed, or their lives end. By that practice too, it would help spread seed from that flower for miles around, the globe, before the curtain closed, was seen to stop, and as though to look back through the curtains. It wasn't as if you'd know if it did or not, because it was perfectly round, but it did. And it smiled, but you would not have seen that either, it smiled back at those who'd helped.

It landed, in a clearing behind some properties, near some trees. Playing there was a person named 'Judd,' he was with some other children, The globe changed by then to resemble a leathery type of football, it was a brownish colour, he picked it up and said to his friends, 'look, we found a ball, let's play,' none of his friends seemed interested in that type of game, not kicking a ball around, or even playing catch. One of his friends was some twenty yards away and had his back to Judd, he hadn't noticed that Judd had even asked, the others were sitting and laying on the grass. Judd then kicked the ball, he must have kicked it very hard because it went way past his friend metres away and over the nearest first few trees, he was surprised. The idea was that it might encourage his friend to go to the trees and inside the woodlands to search for it, but Judd alone saw that the ball did not stop, he moved backwards a few paces in utter disbelief, as the ball then stopped above the trees, and was there only visible to him, and as though it had stopped as if to turn and smile- that it did, then it turned again and continued on its journey beyond those trees, his friends disinterested, he would never see that ball again, not ever. Neither would it atter what garden he climbed into after, in search quietly of it.

It would be many years after, and in Pasturelands, he would realise that someone did own that ball, they had then too, that persons' name was known only to him. She was one of the persons in the capsule, and a capsule he would not now be welcomed by, in or at, because of how things were and are.

Although years later, yes, the King of Pasturelands had died, remained was his Queen, a lovely lady, that within the capsule knew the pain of intense loss that day, when he kicked that ball so far and so very hard. There was much to be done, although it would not then be his concern, or business, he would realise yes, but he was no longer a priority. Not even a bad, an inconsiderate, or even a kind thought. Whether below or higher, greatly thankfully it would always now be too, a hill for him to climb if somehow even slightly of a mind to be in pursuit. The globe could become with a head shaped like an animal, a wolf even, but flying through the wind as though at him, and then land, as if being tested, as a rug at his feet, where it would wait, smiling as he just walked over it without even noticing. But neither he, or his, or his friends would be able to interfere or infiltrate. Then once he'd passed, up would stand that and those he'd walked on, he would never know, neither would his friends, or theirs, or those he knew or became, or were acquainted to. There was nothing he could do about it, how could he, or his, they didn't know, and if they found out, they did not know the code, and neither could they discover it or learn it, or effect. Of course, they could copy what they could see, but only what they were purposely shown, it was important and for reasons selfless, reasons they would never understand anyway, and neither would or could for the precise reasons stipulated, would it become a plausible, or reckoned, recognised, or made up, or imagined, or guessed reason or excuse to try? And especially with much or Pasturelands still effected by the death of King and some still in mourning.

Why or how could a silver globe know the feeling of loss, maybe because long ago, some in some lands had chosen to worship some as only manifestations of things they only tried to explain or gain experience of. Whether by fear or pressure, that in their furtherance, they failed to see that rug or carpet they themselves had flown around on? But the of course surely could become a question, as to the recognised power and effect of worship, and an understanding of its diversity and the, or an importance of, and of a rug with a head shaped like an animal? As an example of how deep or how shallow some water can get and how hot or how cold some winds can be or could, even I was perplexed, because presumably not much was known then? Stumped at first base with only a hint of a smile you could say. So, what next? And what good is a not so lonely now Princess with scraggly hair and slightly larger than what could be considered the supposed average hands and feet, if there were such a thing? But shoes were produced long before I'd recently bought some, she thought to herself, and in sizes required then- and ladies' gloves too. Of course, the thought hadn't occurred to her that maybe a bigger man, or partner, or a real partner, might be worth considering. One thing she did realise was that if you use a red bar of soap for long enough, and a blue bar of soap too, or yellow, that if you didn't pay attention, a cream or white coloured bar of soap could look quite anaemic, and princesses in some places were said to be ten a gilder now anyway, but were they? To a real Princess it wouldn't matter, but would the same be for a Prince, or did that not matter too? The fact became that there were and would be more important things to be concerned by, certainly by the capsule occupants.

The silver sphere for generations in past times had been able to travel freely between time-zones, and atmosphere and climatic changes without hindrance and often with things to remedy even if unaware of it, this time would be no different. The underneath of the silver sphere without warning opened and the capsule seemed to just float to the ground as though attached or held by a parachute, but really it was four Bakewell tart looking umbrellas that sprung from the top of it. Obviously, on the way down to the ground, those on board were worried because they could not see what was preventing them from just falling and hitting the ground and creating what to some of them could have seemed a terrible mess, they were also unaware of changes that were potentially about to happen that would affect them from a perspective of noise and worry, the sound of what could only be compared to two boys kicking hard a metal bucket with handle around could be quite deafening to them. The sphere had hit a wall you see, this was why it opened from beneath and as a safety precaution those inside, were immediately thrown into evacuation measures, where the wall appeared from had not been a consideration or thought, because the capsule occupants weren't aware of that, they didn't feel a thing. The remaining inner contents of the sphere went up to the sky as the capsule moved to the ground. At no point though, would the workings of the sphere lose contact with the capsule, just as the greater or lesser Dum Dum Bird had skills, so does and did this. Beyond the earth as it was known, the sphere contents rose above with a protective, impenetrable and indecipherable, invisible, covering to prevent any form of intrusion or interaction or interference, the workings would rise above the earth such that the earth could have been viewed and so many smaller lit up globes, all of which were identical to each other, like quite motionless fireflies, there was also, above the earth, what looked like another planet, as shiny and as smooth as a billiard ball it stood there, quite totally black in colour. By the side of that, there was a white cloud, the white cloud seemed to drift to not so far from it, almost as though an unwanted guest or a guard of some kind. The earth below that with its primaries and secondaries of blues and greens, although it would be difficult to tell if you didn't know, such was their intensity and clarity and vibrance, did look considerably by quite far, much bigger comparatively. The contents of the sphere though were to travel even higher, with the earth South Easterly and the black billiard ball looking planet above it, slightly North-West or thereabout of that and the dinky white cloud West of that. The sphere content seemed, although invisible and non-interactional by way of being unchallenging, to enjoy an amusement somehow, as it had become almost of an electrified content, maybe that was all it was, and it would have been easy to surmise that possibly if then it did not join forces with another of its own kind, and when then, it changed colour to the same colour that its own kind was, as though a lost sheep having found again its own kind, and there were so many of them, they lit up and seemed to all be joined and became as one, not in a way that was encompassing but rather like beams and streaks of light, they witheringly formed around all of the planetary aspects, none were overlooked, it seemed to be definitely joining and growing more until it was just there, something was about to happen. The content of the sphere that had joined with its counterpart, as though somehow, they had not so much waited such a long time, but were just overwhelmingly aware of their meeting again, had to relocate the earth by just the almost tiniest fraction in a further South Westerly direction. This was done. There was no question of why, only the knowledge that for some reason, it was important, maybe somehow even an exercise in trust? No, that was doubtful, it had been meant to happen and that those components at that specific and very precise moment in time, were where they were and were meant to occur and we may never know why. There was concern that those inside the capsule might now be feeling some slight anxiety or pressure as result, it was a concern to the occupant of the sphere components. A spring shifting sound was then heard, as though beneath a seat, like a prong sound, not like that of a tuning fork, it was definitely a coiled spring sound, as though tweaked, and concern then was, would those in the capsule cope with the possible changes that may then happen to them with the slight change in circumstances with what was possibly, for security reasons too even, an quite unprecedented event. How to get back to them had become, only then, certainly for myself, a slightly more worrying concern. After all, there was certainly one real dignitary without doubt, in that capsule, it was quite scary, and the very reason for the lovely, tasselled cushions inside it, and would there be time, with the effects potentially of changes that 'may' occur to them. I had to feel and did as though they would be very and unquestionably fine anyway, but if with such certainty, if I didn't need to return to them now because of that certainty that they would be fine, should I want to, if I knew they would be safe. So, was whether there would be enough time more about myself, than them? And yes indeed, what changes may occur? I was now the colour of a very pale sunflower petal but somehow less and too, quite astonishingly vivid all at the same time.

An arm, yes it was an arm, but a very immensely thin arm, like a strand with a small hand at the end of it, of the same joined light, then reached down and brought the capsule up from the ground. Then it was as though the capsule became as large as the forearm of a human, it was then held, unbeknown to the occupants who themselves were being held for their own safety and unaware that anything was happening at all.

Some hours later, with that particular work having been accomplished and with that seen within only a few hours, it would be important for the integral safety of my associates, for that brief moment and my own peers known to me, that a code be formed to warn them of dangers that not only they had demonstrated potential of risk concerning, but also of risk that I was aware of and that they very probably would not be. Within moments by default, in this space, I was fairly much I believe, alone, and whilst some could continue to attempt intervention at me, or myself, they could not penetrate now from other systems, not unless I believed it totally safe that they could successfully consider to attempt, although to be very honest, there was nothing really apart from to fool and hoodwink that they really could do. They could mimic, yes, but such attempts would never carry any weight of credibility or have sufficient even miniscule degree of hold to bring any further or more damage than had already been encountered or that had already been caused. Whilst apportionment of blame was to be expected, it would only or inevitably be their frugal attempts to see what they could catch in their so–called, or so they, would consider - or believe possibly, net of chance, not of accomplishment, but of force and greed and selfishness. Another part of the code origination would be a constellational series itself, though which precisely would remain, and for the reasons as aforementioned of my own understanding, interpretation, and structure of design. - And for reasons known where it was integrally and known to me instinctively.

I was now thinking how much and at what point an oppressive and pressurising set of circumstances can not necessarily make you bend so far that you cannot anymore, to the point where you snap back into your original shape or position. Or of how it could with so much pressure, cause a skipping on, or change and an adapting to meet demands of the directives being how others can perceive their and life generally to be and forcefully slowly, to at what point do you realise that you yourself have had quite enough and have contended to and with all or any of their notions as far as you possibly could be pushed and prodded and that compliance, not to how they consider themselves to be or be capable of, but of how you really are- given the right circumstances, and how challenging it can be, once accepting such challenges personally, to attempt to re-gain a level of control over your own situation again, and in compliance with your own directive, and not that imposed by others not authorised, destined, or entitled to, even by way of extending or mind or intuition of a tolerance. Yes, the sky even around that black billiard-ball looking shiny planet, where light seemed to reflect from it or be deflected, or absorbed sometimes, like some huge eyeball, that it was not, and if it was, it was shut at this moment, was a darker but greyer not so deeper blue hue, and it was a ball shape, and not a hole, I was also quite aware that I was being overtly considerate in that evaluation. True, with mind to other past issues, I had not been 'black-balled,' as such by anyone, neither had I considered 'potting the black,' but there had been a reason for the degree shift, of that there was no doubt. More importantly, I had only just begun to consider thinking, however briefly for that moment then, about what had brought me to think of this and to that point? I was also considering that it was too good an opportunity to waste. It would be important that the scourge that had plagued the planet in recent years would be removed somehow, and as quickly as possible somehow indeed. An intent became, to appoint some helpers, but who, what or why, and for what areas of their expertise that would have been witnessed, was it though necessary? Should the main concern be about how to attempt to do something to achieve it, or was it about somehow, those in that capsule, and what about the dear lovely Queen of Pasturelands? Having decided that there were various and many reasons again, to want to see better achieved and to do, the prospect seemed less perilous and not so disenchanting, but first, 'oops,' how to get back to earth and when exactly? And what day and time would it be, would it be the same as it was, would it be the same as it was before and what might we find there? A few days ago, too, I was told by a member of my family that a day after I visited there, on a low wall outside the property, someone, not an animal, had been naughty and done a huge poop on the wall and left it there. As disgusting behaviour as it was, and as easy as it now was to ignore that and think of my immediate family instead and that location and thereabouts too, this certainly, and other factors, would make me not want to stay away for too long, as disgusting as it was.

I felt as though I'd spent e night for security reasons, seated on a central mechanism of a wheel of an oscillating paddle-steamer, first I'd had to walk toward the wheel that had been rotating away from me, and through it, to the very centre of it, and to one of four seats positioned for the very purpose within the structure of the stars themselves, as though then inside one of the two wheels that would then be rotating on either side of me as then at that moment seated. It would prevent from that day forward, any forced unwanted attention where some believed they had a right somehow to impose their circumstances uninvited upon me. Acceptance of their existence is not and can never constitute an open invitation, that door now closed, and firmly and in kindness. They could not claim to have pushed or brought me or guided or placed me- at or to this place, because they would have no idea that I had taken action, none whatsoever, neither would they or could they do anything but guess, however realistic or accurate, or 'conserving,' or seeming to want to preserve, such guesswork could adroitly allude to. Sat on central axel point of paddle steamer, where that comprised of three main parts, two wheels and a central axel. Another thing during that past week, considering food in a conventional way, other than that provided whilst in the capsule was rather scarce, was 'weight-gain,' some, including myself had encountered or observed body weight increases and especially a bloated feeling and appearance. Or was it to mark a further change with regard to eating structures and a greater depth of thinking around need and want or desire regarding food. Whatever it was, another opportunity, depending on how you viewed it, was being presented, and where opportunities for exercise weren't as forthcoming during even an unnoticeable duration, was it really help to be ignored? So, attention was now being presented, help, with that could there also be the beginnings of an excitement and how could it be utilised positively by way of constructiveness and good attitudes generally, although as they in the capsule were isolated, surely another means to generate and radiate back and forth had to somehow be discovered. But why? Why bother? Would, or could it ever become noticeable, that a few had been on such a journey, or had been cared for in such a way; And by whom, why, and by what? It should not become like being tap-dancers or anything like that, as great as they so often are, but surely, to have taken steps forward, and to be able to look back somehow, or with more than a pleasant and a loving smile or thought, had to play a part and despite what would launch with the recovery from the health situation as it had been and as it could be, the ravages and the difficulties that would now inevitably be presented, by the cost in having got through these days and time that were and was.

A belief momentarily was that for myself, became then observed, what resembled a half-man and half-animal, possibly a horse, it would with a bow and arrow it held, then fire a golden arrow straight through the black planet that had for also a so brief moment resembled a slowly winking eye, although very and quite obviously it certainly was not and never really had been, it looked like a billiard ball, there was no escaping that, not an eye that could then certainly at all be recognised as. The arrow did then pierce it and then went straight through it, and with a golden ornateness then its farther side, as though to, if chosen, to pull it closer. At first it was difficult to comprehend that such would happen or could, or did, and that the act would not somehow be harmful, so yes, it was easier to dismiss the thought completely. True, had the shinier black billiard- ball resemblant planet, if within our own galaxy been Antares, the bright red heart of Scorpius, The Scorpion, then such or the archer could have indeed been avenging Orion, or mimicking or re-enacting or playing, Orion who was slain by the Scorpion sting, so were some being given a light show or a lesson in behaviour or al opportunity to place before the gods a strategy concept for consideration, or were they themselves enjoying putting before a few a unique test, or could and could such have played any part at all in an opportunity to change destiny, whether now, in ahead times or maybe in past times, to save time maybe, or what if to alter a destiny somehow? And would it be right if it were so? he golden clasping threadlike grip that passed through the shiny black planet, and then formed so beautifully ornately behind it, with its grip, did look aesthetically beautiful, and appealing and very attractive, but was I right to suggest or then certainly think that no, it did not happen, if by it happening it should harm that planet. Orion it as said having been a great huntsman, some legends have him killed by Artemis for trying to rape her, others of the jealousy of Apollo because of the love of Artemis to Orion. Also, it the mythical hunter facing The Star of Taurus, The Bull, for certain it was April twenty first, The Bull had been chasing The Pleiades Sisters, those represented by the open cluster, and with his two hunting dogs represented by the constellation Canis. Aries, symbolised as a Ram, or The Ram, usually ends around nineteenth of April, to then become or enter into Taurus, symbolised by The Bull. The realisation too then that an infamous dictator had been born within or within these, the very cusp itself of these dates, was to leave a very bitter taste upon the back of my throat, not like I'd accidentally swallowed a small fly and then had to apologise, and not like I had not brushed my teeth, but just a sour taste, and it was far from pleasant. It was enough for me to sit up sharp, pull in my tummy and then very slightly clear my throat and think 'let's move on.' Whether from Germany or not, it had reminded only of the destruction and hurt that can be caused when power is used incorrectly and of how wrong they or those are, to believe that there could be a place for such unkindness and cruelty, under whatever guises may have been presented, and that should they believe there was a game to win, that 'in kindness,' there was not. But why should all this resurface now and for us, or for me? Certainly, in Greek Mythology, The Pleiades were The Seven Daughters of The Titan Atlas, who was forced to hold up the sky for eternity and was therefore unable to protect his daughters. To save the sisters from being raped by the hunter Orion, Zeus turned them into stars. Orion was the demi-god son of Poseidon, after his death he was placed among the stars. He was later brought back from the underworld to become The God of Hunting. For myself, aware that The Pleiades were an example of an open cluster, a group, stars born around the same time from a gigantic cloud of gas. What was to happen next, I had no idea, of that I was certain. On my mind though, for some strange reason then, was yogurt. Just yogurt. And that if you are trying to reduce food intake, and having say, four small meals daily, which I was not and hadn't, none of us were or had been, so why was I wondering about it? I was also thinking about a 375g yogurt pot and that if it says on the pot that 100g is 81 calories, then surely that pot of yogurt must present as for some a meal in itself? I hadn't considered that before, neither had I tasted yogurt for a while, and yes, I could almost then taste it. Then my mind or my imagination skipped onto, almost as though reading maybe another page, whether backward or forward I do not know, Palaeontology, and of how it had been suggested that at The Rainbows and Unicorns Quarry, Tyrannosaurs may have hunted in packs like wolves, and that it was possible that such animals may have lived in the same vicinity to each other, without travelling as a social group, and that they came together when resources and times got tougher. I was amazed to think it through, especially as it had been presumed, they were solitary predators, will wonders never cease I asked myself. Then came a thought, that if say Earth had indeed been moved or relocated slightly south westerly, and the black billiard- ball resemblant planet had not been moved at all, although now with an arrow shot through it, it could be being reigned in, or so to speak, was that, should an asteroid hurtle to where Earth had been? And had the arrow not then subsequently been shot, would such an asteroid have hit that planet and not Earth where it had been moved, or would such an asteroid pass straight through in between both planets and for example, then cause or create a vacuum, that would or could cause both planets to crash into each-other? Or that psychologically, was it about severing ties and simply cutting the cord, was that what all of this somehow was actually all about? But ties were being severed for accurate and good reasons. So, was it about my trusting my own decisions implicitly? And what if ties were severed and I liked it? What would that say about how things had been and how potentially unfair so much had been because I was too trusting. And now I seem to be or am requesting to be trusted to counter-balance fears that others may sub-consciously have. To quell, where others who had no right in the first instance, to pry directly anyway into the personal affairs or business of others. If "a road less travelled," constituted then two different paths, maybe it wasn't about how things had been and the choices held within that moment of time, but more-so of how things were and were now becoming where the better of the choices may lend a helping hand. But, as a friend often had said, and says, and fortunately for them, 'never a beggar or a borrower be,' would there actually be choices involved at all?

#

It would be some hours, maybe four or five, when I would wake up from a sleep, everything was then and seemed quite still. That day though would, because when or after waking, the thoughts were of connections, very much so, and of strange misdemeanours in the past and analytically and of how some might still attempt to manipulate and further those as though from afar, even of 'reeling in,' and how one connection certainly knowledge of quite particular individuals, who usually might not be as 'approachable,' how such other or associative connections might be abused whereby to extract from another and where the sole beneficiary, or beneficiaries, of that 'extracted,' that force, or energy, as though 'tapping into,' rather like a shooting range, but where poachers only have access to weapons, where the initial contact were left completely depleted or drained too, and if it were say to eventually relieve the initial contact completely, who might be aware of these availabilities and why, what if it were only myself, until now I thought, and that was how it would indeed remain. As if to stand up to it, and without an exorbitant resource, but because I knew only then, at that moment, how some were playing, 'potentially,' and why. It ceased to be a challenge for me, only a means for others and it was not even June yet, for those greedy and vindictive and selfish, playing at cruel, to merely take and spread around what they had not even a rightful claim to. Then, should the original source become further 'extracted' from, by some of those residing close to, those who pertained to be 'closer,' neighbourly, and who would dance in a circle in the back garden around their coloured tissue paper streamers and balloons blowing in the breeze, 'unknowingly,' as to the facts, yes, an innocent act of neighbour-ness, but on their parts, worthless now, totally worthless. It seemed cruel that in their minds could have dwelled a prospect or notion that the original source, might become obsolete, or might or may have, and that they would not care at all, as long as they are all okay, them and their somewhat smaller 'brood,' but I was glad to have fathomed it.

It would be at that moment a warrior I recognised would then be seen to jump down from the heavens, and yes, block any asteroid that may choose to fall in between the black billiard ball resemblant planet and Earth. It would also prevent from that day forth, the black planet resemblant of a billiard ball from extracting resources from Earth and those who presumably choose to live kindly there. So yes, a day of, and indeed a future of needs where warranted, being met, and a quiet feasting in accomplishment were to be considerably and favourably welcomed. - And with a gratitude that the perpetrator had been caught and would never be able to move, to do the same again from then after.

One of the sisters it seemed, had been observed by myself although I said nothing, as drawing some young, slightly too young toward Orion, I presumed this because only of, how they seemed to shine when together, although Orion possibly, though I couldn't be certain, not totally for sure, was in charge, it did look that way, or was presented that way. Was it nothing more than a bag snatch in an unlit alley by a confidence trickster? That sister though did seem to shine so much and became or was so extremely accommodating in the furtherance of what could to some, have been considered or compared to, 'leading some astray,' or was it called grooming these days, and without a marriage or wedding band ever seen, after all it was sometimes a road to no recovery, and as the perils could be unfathomable and harsh and indeed cruel, perhaps even cruel in a way that they would or could never ever really appreciate. I knew this very well. In 2002, a friend had published a book, and a copy landed on the floor of a home in Matlin, it involved Hermes, this was who was being thought of in recent years, that but I was uncertain as to the context with so much mimicking happening. It was never that I was reluctant to give, but more that for myself I was sure to give correctly. I treasured information entrusted to myself and the kindness and generosity behind the trust of and relating to acts.

I had been worried and afraid that the mimicking had taken off in leaps and bounds, I did look at Orion from where I was. Still with a foot of a warrior giant, now on the arrow stream that did pierce and hold so delightfully. I wondered about attempting to move or relocate the beam or strand of light where at that end there was caught and ornately that shiny black planet. Wondering if it could be somehow hooked and gradually by the acts that put it there then, whether it could be too, 'reeled' in somehow and then just as neatly fall into a black hole somewhere in the galaxy and become lost forever. But no, instead I remembered thirteen years ago, or was fourteen, I wasn't confused as such, It was thirteen, I thought about if further, another friend of mine had been working in a shop at Braithfurling, they were actually in the process of closing the premises down then, as after consideration and observance of trends there, it proved to be not such a viable concern, despite in their acquisition so much work done and a new premises now totally ready and waiting having been created there. As they'd been cleaning the floor, in an old cardboard box, was found some photos of cats and of a lady with a brooch, there was something instantly recognisable as something nice, that was given to me by that person as a gift, something that was going to be thrown out, or instead of selling it for a miniscule amount or giving it away, as was or had been often the case there then, I put a British five pound note I had into a collecting tin, realising that their bank would have changed it up.

I gazed across at Orion, and sucked on my lower lip and with almost a sadness, or what could have become the beginnings of, tears had started to rise in the back of my eyes and said, 'soon I must return to earth,' then tears in both eyes just reached the very edges of my eyelids, I had to blink to prevent further, then there was a slight pain in my forehead, just for a few moments, replaced by the wet feeling of where part of a tear or tears now rested. My thought obviously too was of the capsule and those who too were safe. It was as though Orion smiled at me in a way that I knew so well, and of course with utter unbridled satisfaction, - to have been recognised in such a way by myself, - and untouchable by me it seemed, not that I had any intentions of wanting to. Then I found myself dressed in regular clothes, and slowly moving toward earth, it all happened within seconds, and I soon realised I was laying on my bed and but imagining I was standing. I know I had brown clothes on, this was unusual for me, I had a brown outfit, but somehow not, brown ladies' trousers and a light brown blouse, they were neatly pressed and clean. Of course, not around my neck, but in my right hand that then was closed, was that gift from that day, it was the real Orion. I knew it was in my hand- and that those whose attempts were to deceive and mislead would end up remaining where they were and unable to be brought back, and it was there where ultimately, they would destroy only each other. With Earth now having moved slightly, the Earth was now safe again. - And so were the real sisters Pleiades, and of course, knowing their ambition, she remembered only what happened to Icarus, so if he that revelled about being Orion-like, didn't by default end up killing his accomplice or acquaintance, the Sun surely would destroy them both and it didn't even need to do anything, other than to be itself.

#

So, within what seemed twenty-four hours, I'd gone from being inside a sarcophagus of a silver filigree, with the only one thing keeping my motionless body alive, presumably being the very tip of my tongue pressing gently o my lips because my mouth was so dry, it kept my lips open very slightly, just enough to create a kind of airway channel to breathe. It was as though I could see myself too, or the sarcophagus, a huge thing and some referring to "he," but of course it was not a 'he,' but a she, although astonished at the detail or amount of detailing on the sarcophagus, It was a really huge thing size wise, and no yellow gold on it at all, none that I recalled, maybe there were traces, but I could not say for certain, had there been, they would not have been a darker gold coloured shade. It looked bigger than the Tutankhamun Sarcophagus I'd seen in photos, or slightly differently shaped, and somehow not as bold, but neater, or even smaller really, much smaller, but what could you really tell from photos, so there was no way of knowing really? And eventually that, as big as it may have seemed, could have constituted as nothing more than a white cloth and a quick burial at sea in remotest of waters. Some around though, had said, "it's not the first time she has been here,' it was though the second time, certainly by my then known personal understanding interpretationally maybe, and knowledge that somehow my past had come in contact with the known King or Queen or family of, of the person, 'at the top,' and I don't mean in a top or penthouse flat necessarily, or anyone pertaining to be, on that planet, I guess Earth somehow, The last time I estimated it to have been or may have been eighty seven or so generations earlier. This time it was kind of different. With a pressed pair of brown slacks and a light brown blouse I guess it somehow was. The main thing was that everything was fine or would become so. But hey, we didn't need to tell anyone did we? Or do we? No, we don't.

So, what to happen next? The capsule now in the pocket of my blouse, or was it my trousers, I really must try to be more careful I thought to myself, but I knew it was on my person so if I keep out of mischief or trouble, or harm's way, it should all be very fine, so I knew it was safe for sure, the main thing! And it was so refreshing to be away from unsavoury influences, and knowing that before I'd left them, they even recognised that it would be best or better to think of me with kindness from then on, with or regarding any interaction or thought be between them, or at each other, and maybe if somewhere a kind watchful eye we could be certain of somehow, should odd things happen, who could argue with that, in principle anyway, a nicer thought then and regarding I could not imagine, and where based upon trust, incredible. And as I had stipulated that I wanted no interaction with that who mimicked whose responsibility or job it was not to do so, or who did so for unfair and unjust or cruel, selfish means or intent, certainly with none who might consider themselves without merit, akin to or with a Pleiades sister or certainly even similar, to reach or be put or place with so called- 'Orion.' Such were seemingly the sycophants they are, as was an acceptability of any kind of arrangement even if their decision in the excitement of it all. How amazing I thought, well it is, isn't it? Now with smiles all around, and presumably genuine smiles, how now do I deal with this other issue, not the blessed virgin, but the virgin born a virgin and who knew others could benefit from the remaining of, - so and because of issues around such a birth and not so much that mistakes had happened or occurred, none did, but what steps had to be taken then to keep me alive. There was a place somewhere. I just didn't know where it was yet, but you know, somehow, I am kind of happy with how some things seem to be moving at last, and it seems nicely, or that it could. Maybe somehow, I just had to apply or involve myself in other matters or with, I cannot say 'new' friends, but friends and those I know already. To be honest, I am bewildered by it all and do not know exactly what to do? And then there is the thought of course, and amidst a subtly placed or found sense of trepidation, almost as if to say, 'she must be a friend of Dorothy's surely' before I even walked quietly out of the door onto the street to go to the shop, what to do with 'Orion'? Some would say and do, things like that, and often, they always do, I don't understand what some say, but I'll try. So often I think, this 'Dorothy,' must be such a big person really.

The amazing fact was that irrespective of who I am or may be known to some, or by what name, is not for me to say or imply, but all too often some do seem with peculiar motives often unfounded or despicable, to interfere with or get involved with the affairs of others and without so much of a hint of an invitation to do so. Genuine caring and care thoughtfully is recognised, or when know of or understood, and can be deemed appreciated Where in circumstances, it is quite the reverse, I find myself considering that when the King of Pasturelands died, it was indeed a very sad day for many. No invitations were sent to third parties to travel with The Queen of Pasturelands in her carriage, and unlike the carriage that transported her husband, the doors on her carriage were closed quite firmly. Be I a virgin or not, but yes, as I am, I hope you understand and comprehend fully, do not interfere in the business of others 'uninvited,' and neither presume that even if some of us were born in stables or barns that an open or ajar door or an unsettled room, is an or such an invite. Very much henceforth, you'll be a fool to, without reasons of only unquestionable kindness as regarding, or you may find yourself very quickly in the land of spirit and without so much of a tiniest of handles to hold onto or to prevent, inexplicable behaviour shall not be tolerated, or upheld by others. Though, do try or continue with unpleasantness for as long as it shall be permitted, or one day you may find yourselves going outside your door and never returning. Now isn't that a little horn to be heard sounding from those pursed lips I thought, lips of yours. Friendship and genuineness are exactly that, cruelty is precisely that and we'd all be considerably wiser not to forget it. Yes, even in a place that boasts Christianity or diversity, or diversity disguised, can be found evil without a cure, though do not believe you can precipitate that, or yours, and especially with your ways known and all so often and importantly, to yourself. I bid you a good day, and before you think or ask yourself, what planet is she from, maybe we should not go there so hastily, or maybe you or some because of not being a virgin of a particular and slightly peculiar kind, cannot. With more than sufficient time within that given day to consider your future, the or a future before you, particularly if to remain beneath a hearthrug over the dark. You might also be wise to at least remember she said that a half dozen eggs certainly still is six eggs, it is here presently, not five or seven eggs kindly. I could ask in some situations, especially where you blame, or think, 'if I hadn't been like this, you'd never be where you are now,' what better way to guarantee a success for your offspring than to blame others from the outset? So yes, thank you for I guess the warning is now, heeded. Maybe some could indeed consider themselves a catalyst, if they were to look it up as to what it means, or maybe they, just as they won't be aware of my plans now, never 'correctly,' or estimated other possibilities or prospects other than those propelled it seems, with their selfishness, mindlessly and into the lives of others, and inconsiderately indeed, into the quite private lives of others. The then thought, especially with examples shown, 'I could strip earrings from 'Pleiades,' take offs, if they had them, just by squeezing gently their abdominals or their internals. - Or I could learn from them? Why stop there when I can give a real big pull out on their internals.

Whether the last few moments or sentences it seemed, had been part of some nightmare on my part, or not, was indeterminable, I did realise that a Mr. Mainewafter from some years earlier who might usually have recommended a spring-clean even if it were Autumn, or Summer, was not here, or maybe somehow, thankfully he had been and maybe not so eagerly explainable because, only a few hours after I woke up. When I woke up, there was a quite fat-bodied smallish spider with legs of three-quarters of an inch approximately in circumference, that ran down the length of my right arm, a very black spider, now walking past my wrist and onto the back of my hand. I placed it on the floor rather than putting it outside, maybe because I had just woken up and despite various accusations as to my countenance generally by some, I was not thinking straight then for this purpose and reason. I know I'd had a dream, and, in that dream, I had drunk alcohol, and had unusually not been affected by it, although of course too, acutely aware that I had not drank alcohol at all, because I do not, or had not. Then as well, I was in what certainly looked like my own kitchen, but rather than cupboards next to a gas stove cooker, there were just two stoves, or ovens or cookers. I recall that the stove on the right side had four rings on it, a gas cooker with electric ignition, was the cooker I was apparently using then, at that moment, but it seemed to catch on fire somehow and was burning beneath some of the rings, and so I tried to squirt water on it to extinguish the flames that were getting then about ten inches above the cooker, so quite high, but there was nothing on the cooker that could have caused the flames, nothing had been left there, there was nothing there that would burn, I switched off the gas supply to the cooker but parts of the cooker itself were still ablaze, I noticed that above the cooker was a fume extractor hood and that was, because of the height, and because I wasn't able to determine a source of the flames, and how things looked or seemed, at risk of catching light or carrying flames somehow too, connected to a chimney type of thing, presumably it was all a risk situation. Then I saw my father walk in, he smiled, he somehow thought that maybe I'd been drinking alcohol, although I had not, and was glad that I was okay, even though I knew I had not been drinking alcohol really at all. Maybe it was a moral somehow, that maybe I could have dreams of it but, but if I did, I must be aware too that because I hadn't really, the effect could be quite severe for me, especially concerning my consciousness and coordination emotionally, my stability maybe? I was happy obviously to have seen my father in such a way, I'd remembered too, that I did have a cooker like that some years earlier, and of the same make, but that the cooker I'd had then had six rings, so where the idea of two cookers had come from, was inexplainable. It was or could only have been that where I had been, 'with the stars,' or so to speak, as there would be nothing to talk about regarding it, my father having seen me, he was not in the land of living as such, but I was glad and thankful that somehow, I was visible to him, it had all seemed somehow, however crass potentially as if almost a golden kind of pond, it was not pondering, that's for sure, because for myself, it was all quite real, despite being then quite asleep, not so exhausted 'this time,' that it could have seemed it. Pleased and thankful whether having consumed alcohol or not, and I know I hadn't, despite catching the cooker on fire, and that it was not my cooker, I concluded that it could only have been a dream.

It would not be long before a message was received on my phone, it said, 'we tried to call you today, can you call us back.' I'd for some strange reason been thinking of honey and on a chalk board in my mind was scrawled wording, 'collecting and eating honey from far away.' I couldn't make head or tail of it, but it was normal, another of those odd happenings, it was a call from an investigation team, they had been investigating a medical compliance team investigator who was a clinician too. It was concerning an allegation of misconduct of an adult nature against my younger sister of a year before, but it seemed very odd. Then I found myself sitting with my sister on a hill and there were, on that plateau of that not too steep hill, many persons. I was chatting to my sister as I too were happy that throughout the investigation, the claim brought had been upheld, yes, I telephoned them and hence I presume was why my sister was sitting with me as we discussed it. I could see a person some eight yards away with others, it was a person, a transexual kind, that stood up and walked toward myself and my sister, we were just sitting quietly. Apparently, that person had overheard the conversation and was a willing 'friendlier type,' regarding the said clinician, and had taken badly that we had brought a case against someone he/she obviously cared about. Because I was not completely sure whether the person had surgery or not was male or female, but they did have female looking clothes on, so maybe it was rude, but in fairness they could have been a transvestite or a cross-dresser, in which case, to then suggest or imply that they were male, or female, or transwoman could have presented as upsetting either way, to both groups, or individually to others. The person put something in front of my face, it looked to me like a robin with a worm in its mouth, this was all I saw. Whatever it was, I wondered why a person was holding a Robin anyway, in such a way, as though amidst a ball of soil. Immediately though, and before they had a chance to walk toward us, I saw the person stand, my only thought was, 'you will not do that to my sister,' I stood up, yes there was a slightly steep part of the hill to the left, where there was too a fourteen-foot ravine, something of what very much looked at that moment to be a kind of dug- out cattle-run, although none visible. I myself had not ever seen any, cattle, but somehow I knew, - I glanced at the person who had by then just started to think to walk toward us, my eyes must have changed suddenly then, as though we were inside a much deeper and dark forest, all I saw was that looking at me through many trees, and as if from a considerably far and greater distance than it was, however far away though, they weren't trees, they were people, I observed how I was being watched very carefully indeed by that person, as though we were unaware, my sister and I, and as suddenly they became recognised to me, as like a person might lurk in bushes and maybe take photos of say others bathing, I saw light as it just in that brief, so brief second- in the shadows, touched upon that so small camera lens, then just as quickly I was out of their view completely. In that millisecond then, I became as standing immediately in front of them. In the meantime, a man I'd been seeing for about a year having recognised that look in my eye tried to wedge himself in between us, and wanted to now 'get close,' I told him swiftly and quietly, 'get out of my way,' my thought with regard to that person was, 'I will eat your face off,' the person then tried to run away shouting 'that's a woman,' but it would be too late. With only the safety of my sister on my mind, they found themselves not only down the hill but in the raveen, on the ground with my foot on top of them, it was only then I could hear the sound of cattle, there were lots of them, I could hear their every hoof beating down on that dirt as they, huge things, charged ever closer from somewhere easterly, then I saw them, only out of the corner of my eye, within a second again, just as they were within feet of us, like an icicle on a leaf, and as sad as it was with the planet seemingly getting warmer where apparently it shouldn't be, unless commensurately, or normal for the time of year, I vanished, they too were now no more. Then I actually did wake up and thought only that a clinician wouldn't do things like that anyway, or those responsible as investigators for complaints. Cattle wouldn't have been treated in a cattle-run such as the likes in my dream, they'd be herded, and not such a confined space that was even less a gully than a ravine, - And neither would I, or my sister or my family have cause to bring such complaint anyway, not at all. As for the man I'd been seeing, he would always, as would 'his kind,' remain supportive for the rest of his days, although he'd never realise it. As with, or like a wild animal that had never seen a human being the stare, similar to a smile, where all you instantly see is prey, and not even competitive prey, was I to ever wonder whether Pamela herself had been preyed upon, or were they prey to each other but in different degrees? Although with Pinto, more about what you do not see, and as a defence mechanism, because she would not ever really know it presumably, that as obvious as with a charlatan and his own however dubious associates, colleagues, or looser partners. Pinto had been at that time; gone from the chap she'd been seeing and before he would even have realised. Then, at that moment, it was as though heard from somewhere, one of her own protagonists saying, "come on," but in a highly prevocational way, she was planning to move home anyway, and saw a package on top of a wall unit in her kitchen, she placed a stool and reached up, it contained a signed script of 'The Elephant Man,' so thrilled was she to see it, because she'd forgotten it was there, not that she'd read it, but she'd watched the film, then she stared at it quizzically, and thought how she had no idea why she'd actually acquired it at all in the first place however many years before. She did decide to do some research on it but after getting some porridge and a small apple, - for a moment as she walked out from her kitchen Pinto felt as though somehow she could hear her sister laughing, or at least believed she would have laughed over it somehow, had she not been at her own home then instead, Pinto imagined her sister saying to her, 'they must have seen you coming,' regarding the script. Quietly Pinto sat down and thought only 'you really think you know a lot don't you,' not of her sister, but of some others, her thought was quite vindictive in its way but then she opened the front part of a Grundig record player, it was an old model of a record player, she placed on it, a 78 record and slipped the arm with the needle across and as doing so brushed across the needle with a finger slightly to remove any dust residue that may have formed there, then she pressed the play button and whilst listening to some initial surface scratches as the record started to turn on the turntable, thought, not only of how she'd just woken up, but that 'they would have ever, and never shall they ever be or be considered by anyone as that lucky. The record started to play, the song was 'she wears red feathers (and a hooly hooly skirt),' written by songwriter Bob Merrill in 1952 and released in 1953. Who was she thinking of when she thought 'you have no idea,' I either do not know or cannot say for certain, then she walked across listening to the music to her quite damaged French Bergere chair and thought only how very pleased she was to have acquired that and that she'd contacted a company regarding a repair to it, or at least the starting somehow of? She adores that seat and would like to get a few more or at least one more but was complacent to the realism that without a van or a driving license it made things a little difficult regarding. Thinking about how she would like to have the seat repaired before she had dozed off, it is a black painted seat and not mahogany coloured as some she'd seen were. Quietly it was that yes, she had discovered a lost love, a love for pretty, with an elegance, and steadfast furniture being one of them. That morning as she dismantled some shelving in her kitchen, as fine as it could be to consider that she may have heard from somewhere a voice of a kind saying, 'she won't forgive them for what they did,' all she could think in response to it, to drown it out, was, 'if you don't have principles, you don't have anything.' and meaning of course, to say regarding, 'nothing.'

She then watched the news on television and attempted a slight clear up amidst the boxes in her room, she noticed that her black imitation small ostrich feather hair clip had fallen on the floor as well as a plastic tray of medications where they'd accidentally been knocked somehow from what they'd been positioned on. She tidied up what she could and cleaned a few items with apple scented anti-bacterial spray, then quite tiredly she placed her hairpiece on top of a smallish bookshelf to prevent it from becoming soiled. She'd inadvertently left it on the plastic tray whilst sorting out her wardrobe and attempting to get some things packed earlier, while or during those few moments when she could, and breaking most of her fingernails in the process, rather than trying to do it after.

That day was April 26th and she was aware that she had medical appointments to keep, on one of those days, two appointments, she'd not, despite them being hours apart considered what a logistical nightmare it might or could present, and possible implications, as innocent and minor to many, such circumstances may indeed seem, or what was happening to her possibly, as before such would not have presented as quite such a difficulty? We must only consider the work she had been doing to fully appreciate, or maybe 'comprehend' that. She'd been too busy trying to ward off annoyances from some neighbours, it was at that moment she found some black pvc ankle straps purchased some months before online, intended to keep her somewhat loose high heels firmly on, should she alone, decide to ever wear them again, not that she'd peen prompted to think that way when just moments later she was waving around in her right hand a broken at one end camera holding selfie stick, as though somehow and whilst giggling about it, thinking to consider whether she hadn't totally lost the plot.

Pinto had got up early, and because she had two hospital appointments, when she arrived at the hospital, she was told that she had to go across to another department, because now she was to be telephoned three days after concerning a mental health medication prescription. She'd now reached the end of her tether; she broke down in the hospital. She was advised that they may be able, when they telephoned, to send the prescription, but then, would it arrive in enough time, so it was then yet another inevitable journey she would have to plan for to hospital again, then she was told that her actual appointment was the following day anyway, in such a mess was she that she'd even got the days mixed up, she was certain she'd got it right, this meant that the tow appointments were the following day not just one. She was happier though to have whilst on that journey that day, purchased an Alpine plant, and particularly as it had, that night been the coldest in April frost-wise, for sixty years. On her mind though was that she questioned the differences between men and women clothed and of make-up. She wondered whether there were not too many differences, not seen evident differences, or vocal tones, in some, etc, so for some it could seem unfair. Then she heard what sounded like a cackling sort of laughter from somewhere again, she looked around her room and under hear bed, in the gaps between suitcases and at the window and even on the packed boxes and in-between, but from where, she could not fathom. It would or could have been easy for her to attribute it to the problem or to those who had become problematic as she believed, some she was wearisome of, although not afraid of, despite her realisation that she was in fact quite a withdrawn reserved type of girl, a realisation that would not surface until 15th June. It hadn't been though, until 14th June that she made what was very possibly to have become a somewhat after hidden and final 'adjustment ,' regarding the chap she'd met, shed sent him a message exactly a week earlier saying to him, 'you do realise that if thy have you working for them, in whatever capacity, and "helping out" that it's as good as nailing you to the boards through maintenance courts and without even need for a child, they'd nailed that good and proper, she told him. And if they are with so many anyway, without a DNA test, you know that a cat can have a kitten but because it has many partners in one night often, it would not be possible to prove without a test that parentage and they would often be so packed with testosterone anyway presumably because they are probably unlikely to be safe.' His response was short, "ok darling." That was the last time she would hear from him, she hoped somehow. What she'd said, was certainly not said by way of a tease, and she never would want to now. He'd been not a gigolo, or a confidence trickster, or even what some might consider a lovable rogue, but merely a petty scammer. She knew the signs, she just couldn't believe it, all she, 'Pinto,' did, was to make him look extremely good when he visited her, because she wanted to and to disguise him and his tracks, quietly hoping, and fragrance his actions with something that could seem to many, more appealing, she knew absolutely what he really was, deep in his heart, and now what they are who would have wanted him. And to there, his known destiny as a scammer, he now had that, his own unique quite non-refundable, paid in full, and not so, 'mission accomplished,' ticket. They were all virgins to him, each a new experience, it was never that how Pinto was mattered more, and never to him, because he could rub it in her face just as easily. A liar who associated with liars. Maybe he had found his matches, Pinto hoped so, but they would never become the type of people she would want to or could associate to or with, if asked, she would think 'definitely not,' as far as she was concerned, they too had been given an opportunity, but she was not saying anything about it. She, Dear, dear Pinto, well, who knows exactly what the future holds there? She smiled and thought of him with his supposedly newly found matches and imagined how some, and theirs might attempt to cackle as though akin almost to witches, and whilst professing to hold a bible in one hand, her only thought and it seemed to make her quite purple eyes, although she disputed this in her own mind often, when it was said of her, go almost red, was that she hoped he used them extremely well and demonstrating whilst doing so, the exact same mercies they'd shown her and wouldst no doubt certainly attempt to, others.

Instead, she decided or chose to think of problems and difficulties that some women must face and endure over generations. Pinto then thought how she would not today buy the coffees for her and the consultant she was to and was grateful and thankful to be able to visit on this day. As she'd slept, and usually did, or seemed to somehow, and had the day before, it seemed? But she was rarely exactly quite sure, especially during recent times, or was it? Maybe it had always been like that, but she'd never thought about it, her thoughts now were of a person whose mother was diagnosed with having Charles Bonnet Syndrome, - and too, about her personal decision regarding coffees, with a hopeful heart. She'd also the day before examined as much as possible the fauteuil chair, and had, now decided to tackle its repair herself, eventually, but from her room? Her porridge came out of the microwave like a bowl of thick gloopy glue, she remembered how some she'd had recently must have gone slightly off where it was the residue of an almost empty bag of porridge, but she still sat there and ate it, thinking of what an idiot she must be and where a person said to her in a street, 'you'll earn more money if you stay around here,' all she could do then was to make out she didn't her it at all and attempt to maintain a responsible looking if not 'unhearing,' composure. Yes, leaving the porridge in the microwave a little too long was often an issue, because she could not wait around twiddling her thumbs waiting, it wasn't like standing in front of a cooker or stove with a lovely saucepan and a wooden spoon, not at all, that was often a pleasure to do, or was once. She put a little milk onto the gloopy mixture and dug a spoon in and started to stir it, she thought of cows kindly and of so- called 'women,' some who had not been kind to her at all, not recently. 'Not that they were cows of the moo-moo kind,' she thought to herself, though they'd for certain like to consider themselves as in some ways productively as, she was quite sure of that and whilst she wanted to think of prunes with regard to their very probable 'insipid' nipples, that might be so unpleasant that it would stain a blouse, would not, because some including her, actually liked prunes a lot, and especially if it was to become - or was then the tail end of the covid pandemic? Some might think, 'oh well there's nothing wrong with that,' we've been making out to be being animals since being taught at school, and no doubt she thought, that would be the level of their biology lesson that they could have been bothered to listen to. They may have been in plays and taught assumptively, presumably in an attempt regarding as to the differences yes, but their mental aptitude had already been formed and based upon sole greed, and unadulterated. Now, she thought of the purchased Alpine plant and of whether she should or might give it a better chance or start, indoors by a window.

#

Whilst questioning some of what was being endured, initially the psychotic medication that was prescribed, in the past two weeks alone until then had tripled in dosage amount prescribed, and with a further increase to be applied after a further scheduled discussion within days. It was, and had been like it was all a kind of bombing raid or a shelling for dear Pinto, and something sadly that some would have thought was fun to watch or be a part of or believe that they were somehow influential in such, without wanting to seem condescending or disrespecting to anyone in normal acceptable terms by recognised professional standards, deserving who had been through those awful times, and theirs, but if it was anything to do with he who was Pintos' ex, surely, or a person she'd been seeing, surely his or his ancestors would have been involved more with the allied forces, she knew this, even if it was not really a thought but more as a knowledge-based whisper in her mind somewhere? The fact was, much of it had been confusing, something though had caused, because of the continual bombardment of abuses and interference, so was it all to only reiterate the importance keeping the appointments today? Whereas usually it might or could have seemed as just too exhaustive to consider travelling again, and sometimes there were days when it just did not happen anyway, there would be a telephone call on the day from the person waiting to enquire simply, "are you still coming today," then apologies as the whole exercise had been wiped from Pintos' memory and she then had to sleep it off to recover, and for what? To be able to predict outcomes. Was or had that been really it she thought, although again, this would be itself 'remembered,' within the earliest hours of 16th June. In the meantime, and email had been received and a replacement passport was to be sent to Pinto, but by the 16th of June, there would be no money to travel anywhere anyway, but she was still happy to receive her passport, very happy, and they were so kind, so very kind indeed, and amazingly professional she thought, she knew they were, of this there was absolutely no doubt at all. It meant staying indoors much again regarding the delivery dates etc from despatch, a hope was that it would arrive earlier. Was I correct to wonder whether it was a possible technique being observed, was there any merit then in the cliché, where even a part of a history somehow, was repeating itself, and was it equally as possible then, especially after today and appointments that were to be kept, and with all that had happened, for there to result in a satisfaction but of a different and unaccounted, underestimated, not anticipated wholly unknown, unprecedented kind? It would make her smile if she knew, if there was, this was for sure. If so, what could that be, and what of consequences, how and when? Maybe we would never know? And to serve what purpose, if any, and or was, or were they all just doing their jobs anyway? And with some involved then, only just eligible for the covid jab, would there be only possible implications, but hope had to, especially if non intrusively, play a part too, somewhere or everywhere presumably, I was concerned as to how Pinto was dealing with this, almost as listening to a pianist, or listening to a heartbeat gently knowing there was something more than a heart in there, something incapable of loathing, and kind, but at the same time, I was unafraid, and could there, if at that time, had or were recently about to have their first jabs, of those who believed or thought there was merit in it, whether they felt legally forced or unhappy to have it, or not. Or was everything totally 'in hand,' who could gain from it, and why, and could there be a more accurate campaign being played out? I had no idea myself, - so who if anyone, would know?

#

A few days had passed, yes, the new passport arrived. It didn't say Mr, or Miss on it, only an 'F' indicating gender/sex under headings in French and English, or English and French, either way, she thought it was genuinely nice. In though, considerable pain, I'd 'suffered a long time, so it wasn't always so confusing, but in a way, I should be slightly by it. I was thinking about a guy I'd met, especially as then, it was presumed that Covid restrictions would be relaxed considerably within the month to follow, he'd been homeless, it was a while back or ago, and nothing happened between us, but there was I'd thought at least, more potential than with if compared to what I had already been through, I wondered if he'd got to know what I had been through, then what his reaction to everything might be? Of course, though, I knew too how untidy carrying that much baggage could be, so in a suitcase 'beneath' the bed was where it remained. Obviously then, there was no question as to what his reaction could be, enthusiastic now yes, and loving and caring, but still, then once he had his coffee with honey and cooked breakfast, he'd have departed quickly, just no doubt as he and many would or might or could and had done so before. It wasn't such an alarming thought, and not a realisation then, again, that thought was to 'come up to the table,' in so many words, or as it were, on the 16th of June. Back then though I was thinking of that how some of my neighbours and during the crisis had worked out how to prize a pearl from the oyster, sure, they already knew, I thought pearls were to be adorned, loved, and given, not stolen. Would they be in the same business to open and scoop out a double pearl, to scoop without a thought its interior, it was doubtful I thought that they would ever really know the existence of such, and because of their perceptions of. So how were they ever to navigate biology anyway? That was a thought to be considered only a day before the purchasing of some gold earrings, having never worn gold before, apart from one ring that was lost many years earlier, as in yellow gold, she was uncertain as to whether it would look right on her. It was neither nine, eighteen or twenty-four carats, but of another composition, but they were small gold Honora freshwater pearl earrings and set in gold. She'd at first thought they were like some she'd dreamed of and just couldn't refuse them when they came up for sale, and because she'd never worn gold pearls before, whether small or not. She did think too of her other tiny pale pink pearl earrings set in silver, and had imagined, although it hadn't actually been, only in a vision of the beholder, no-one else, as though a small segment of the pearl, out of view by anyone else had opened, like a doorway, with the capsule, she opened it just a tiny bit more, and inside she then went, it was from that moment somehow and for whatever reason then she chose, to become a sanctuary. She trusted her own decision making and those of some others in their astuteness and non-defamatorily appreciated- and the accuracy in the deliverance of. A then hiding place, the pearl was then filled to the outside from in, and to in just as carefully further, and would not be noticeable to anyone else, not at all, or guessed, by prowess, association, by fishers' net, neighbourhood, or by anyone being near or close in any way to the possessor of this then, such knowledge. - pertaining to be existence of such. It would be within the double pink pearl that the found refuge for a while would remain, to and including all those cared for. And especially with two days earlier, all appointments now having been kept, and having had the second and final part of the Covid 19 vaccine. They could no longer penetrate, this did not prevent them from trying though, Pinto was to be reminded the day before again of how "she won't forgive them," she'd overheard somebody saying this. And no, she had no intention of that, neither was it important now for her or a concern for her, or them within the pearl. As far as the holder of the capsule was concerned and not that she could now give too much emphasis to it, though the repeated provocation did not help to move forward, they had abused the man she fell in love with or believed she did, and mutilated their existence, and her relationship in that as was at those times, their act of process. The matter was now out of their hands. Expecting to see trees or something, inside the double pearl, double, only something known then from within the/a business, 'they' would not now, and never would be involved in, as the pie-chart that grew and the tiniest slither removed, that being their lives and existences, certainly for a while, it was hoped. And as their existences were to break down around them further. There was nothing there now to be concerned with or about now anyway. It was then again as though her pupils seemed to move or dilate, at the very thought or prospect. It was strange because some had been saying days earlier which she thought was strange, how some kinds of persons must "avoid looking into her eyes," because she could see right through them. the fact was they were, and Pinto knew it, only attempting to steal even that by intimation as a useable prospect too. Another deceptive intrusion attempt. So, they were now behind the pearl and could, if they could see it, only admire it, but they would never know. And besides, they wouldn't see it, because the beholder was hidden, and the beholder had it on, even the toughest of chisels and the hardest of mallets would slip from it, if they ever did start to realise somehow, and for those reasons nether could they try. If they attempt to 'scale,' around it to give the impression that they were aware, even by saying things loudly like, 'we're here,' or, 'we gave you that,' or however, even with certainties not to quote such in many situations, however their games would attempt, the fact was, they could not. She even said to herself that if any of them had a problem with that, that they should quite confidently, in her own opinion, consult a psychiatrist for sure, or a lawyer.

#

She knew when she casually looked out through the peephole in the door, into the hallway, days before, and saw a lank dark haired child walking down the stairs opposite, and then suddenly stop a third way down and stare at her door, then quickly turn and walk back up the stairs out of sight for a moment as though afraid, only to then walk down the stairs again with neighbours from the other top flat and some from a flat on the second floor, that this was at that time, during those days, being all somehow strangely observed for some far odder reason, no doubt. And that which may have begun to have witnessed something somehow of this, and how swiftly as a group they shunted and scuttled quickly past her door as though passing by a noxious odour, or a very cold breeze had caught them from behind and their hair, hats and a scarf almost flying ahead of them. No time to take a glance at the mirror in the hallway on the wall this time. Pamela smile remembering that, but oh no, not until 16th June. She did think back then though how she was aware, as though the moment penalised, that she was very much, looking at/ observing them. Now though, to reclaim from the others, as their closeness's seemed to be prevalent, that which she'd imparted to Judd, and that which they'd kept then as their own. Not the soul of a departed lover, or partner to have been, like the second part of a two-part eternal flame, but the soul of her own stillborn brother, her twin brother. It would cause the breath in her own lungs to almost rise to her throat and her throat somehow tighten to beneath her jawbone at the thought, both then and after. A soul that he'd extracted or she in her innocence had believed he was her love. She neither needed at that point or after their presence to accomplish this. Not now, neither did she require to physically see it achieved, she knew it would be done. It was never the taking of a lover, but the taking of the spirit of a loved one they were abusing, and using, he would find his way back home, they were of no consequence now. The consequences of such an act, even if they could claim to be unaware of it, would have further and far-reaching consequences, especially for them. How many others had they abused in this way was not then now realized by the beholder, it was to be a few hours before this realization would occur, it would also be not them, any of them who would determine their ultimate fate, although how they behaved should help, as doubtful that it could she remained, it too, was neither about forgiveness, and this was never covered as such by previous workings known to her, of scribes, it was now being covered here. Until now, apart from one letter from a hospital and bills, there was nothing that identified her as female, no driving license or passport for example, she didn't even have her own birth certificate to hand, that had somehow got lost somewhere, in relocating in times past. Now though, she was here, and to claim her own. She, Pinto, or 'Pamela' niece of Lady Broadley was to wonder now whether this had been the reasoning behind the constant shelling and bombing by them, - and to him, - simply a playful game they had 'hooked,' him into. On her mind, as the so-called beholder, not any imagery presented by them, or theirs of themselves, that would from now on be yanked away, as though they had discovered and come face-to-face here-on with a crocodile in their very bathwater, none of them would now want what they had abused, and because they had furthered, as though all-around Pinto now was only water, some of it so stagnantly pungent that all it constituted as was a droplet on.

So inadvertently now, as considered would be, from within the pearl a javelin with a spearhead now fixed to the front of it, it would be not only how far to throw it, but possibly at which of them, their youngest or their oldest, the mouthiest or the quietest but most slimy and greedy or that who posed as nothing to do with them, or at the eye of the husband of the eldest of them, or do some research to find out which would be less likely to further, an insurance or lucrative compensation claim, or right between his eyes and then hers and theirs all simultaneously, or why not go for 'the jackpot,' dear lover boy himself. As that crocodile or those, would start at their legs first or an arm and pull them under one by one, there would be no phoenix observed there and no ashes to clean other than that derived from their now infected lungs, now as they then may attempt to draw breath, lungs that not even these types of crocodile would touch. And neither would their smutty mouths or those of theirs be heard, only bubbles, as they eye-poppingly were pulled not so much to the depths, but to just beneath the water, just enough to see their faces and to look at them. She'd been glad to have fed them beforehand, but she did hope that the water would not turn too red, or such images of wonderment would neigh be seen by either of them either. It would be then that the beholders leather-look plastic soled flip flops could be heard scraping on the carpet and then on the plastic tiled boarded wooden floorboards as she so very slowly walked toward the kettle in that so tiny kitchen, it seemed to make somehow a welcome change from the sound of their, her neighbour's wooden flip-flops clanging or crashing upon the stairs outside it had certainly to her seemed, and with every single nauseating step. And to think, the prescription was likely to be increased by mental health services only the following day, I could only think, not a moment too soon, and to think, Pinto had arranged those appointments herself? Was it a telling sign that she was aware of not so much where she was headed, but where, by sheer experience/s, of harm, recorded very officially, done to her by others, she was being yet again pushed to? The doctor, only a day before, had left a message via the telephone stating that she'd call back, it had been for Pinto like walking on eggshells that could handle the beholders weight, but for sure, a party to where not all would be 'invited.' The nicest thing about it was that they had decided that themselves, and for themselves and theirs, from the outset, - and nothing could prevent it, apart from 'the' beholder, and as they or those others would no longer know how to achieve requesting such, only how to believe they could when in fact they no longer would be or were able or permitted to, and none could help them, whoever they considered or believed themselves to be and of whatever possible mimicking whether any prominent personages of past, or future had used any mimickery in the furtherance of 'true' and correct by 'Pinto's' own standard or way of thinking, moral based objective. Or where in other instances and to prevent and offset risk, if slanted or backhandedly abuse in and by attempting to attain even of their own, by them. Not ever, and from that moment on and perpetually forever, 'presently.' In fact, it was a wider belief but known only to a very few, that the only way they could break or restore what had become this, a somewhat woeful tale and scenario would be should Pinto herself, Pinto niece of Lady Broadley, ever 'walk down the aisle' to be married, to a partner, but they had decided that fate too and the beholder, Pinto, then, as though a mere facsimile of what she had once been because of the continual beatings, also then or now just too far away from any notion or desire that any such thing would then or now or ever happen or become a thought. Pinto was now and had become, resigned, to follow, and or, a very and quite personal destiny and that as the waters would eventually purify, was unbeknown to the beholder and obviously to them, her bullies, and abusers, to become apparent. But then there were those awful crocodiles, and more. So- it didn't look as though they ever would now anyway. Neither would dear Pinto even flinch upon seeing their faces and she knew she would, just beneath that water, as would they see hers, as though they were looking up at her, Pinto mouthed to them all, 'don't attempt to sully the water with the or an or your filthy impure tears please,- to do so would be wasting your own breath that you no longer have, -and by your very own design.' It would be only then they'd be blindfolded beneath the water and gagged and with their hands tied behind their backs and non-see-through covers placed upon their heads and loosely tied at their necks. But not their feet, they were not to be denied permittance to tread water, oh no. And their being there? Was never to be noticed, or ever understood or even mentioned, because they could not penetrate the double pearl. None of them could, neither could nor would anyone else, or any entity or body know of its existence, in fact, with them now under water, and unable to now further, Pinto would think then of Copenhagen, though why precisely, only the beholder Pinto, at that precise moment in time, know.

For a moment just a half an hour after, she wondered about the spirit of her brother and thought, he would return anyway despite the treachery and deceit endured, especially now, and because she knew she would not meet with the man she and her neighbours believed she wanted, so much to believe she'd fallen in love with, the beholder Pinto would not lose her head again, not for him and certainly not now, not ever, and never, for them. Then a question did become, and with some cast out to a wider sea, so what were all those uncracked eggshells for? Now of realization and unable to do a thing, 'as though,' cheated or themselves deceived and with crocodiles poised 'watching,' their eyes noticeable just above the water, and their long scaly tails not wanting to move too much to alarm or unsettle but not afraid to either, and with them, those with their hands tied beneath, just beginning to learn, to tread water anyway? What were the eggshells for? Surely, they weren't to become baby crocodile food. Twas the beholder from within that double pearl, holding the capsule and able to walk on the eggshells without cracking them, who'd know that they alone would be hoping and even wishing possibly that it were all so simple or as simple as that, if there was any way at all of their discovering how, what, why or if, or anything with regard to, Their own destiny, chosen by not the bad situations happening or that happened oer the lands of Pasturelands, and not of intolerance on the part of the beholder, or of uncharitable intention, it would be purely because it was not for her to forgive them, she could, and neither would she be tested by them or have faiths or beliefs questioned in such a challenging without just course or objective manner by them or the predicament they 'alone,' were now in. They would know why, if they were even aware now or then, of what was happening, one thing even during the World Wars that they, those referred to, hadn't accounted for, neither would any person they'd now, was, the element of surprise. Was it to become for them like maybe walking, not that they could now, into a bathroom and wondering maybe where an earring had disappeared to, then upon searching for it where you'd sat, realizing then that your phone too had disappeared, or if a guy, maybe a set of keys, then a phone, I doubt it could ever become that simple? From that day forth, and from where they were, neither could they maximise on the fact that many knew what liars they are, or could they that maximise on the fact that they knew and for those reasons they were or and are quite disliked. It also gave reasons why they would have in times past gained fair-weather friends by using terms like 'victims,' or 'underprivileged,' or 'ignored,' because their mentalities were selfish and to abuse, so they were abusing even their allies or those who'd tried to want to like them, under the premise that if they fell, they'd all fall,- in other words, 'don't let us fall,' or else, or because, 'what goes on behind closed doors,' to become the prevalent then 'phrase that pays.' Many would have no idea of what they'd been dealing with, neither would they still, nor would they themselves now. All Pinto could think at that moment, was, 'no more crocodile tears now,' darlings, aww! And 'isn't love just the sweetest thing,' especially when it's not your own, because you God damn done that and burned it out good and proper already. Within days or was it that day, was it paranoia or pain or both, or indecisiveness and a moment of just wanting somehow to not be or feel hassled, was she to attend a medical appointment and a man happened to say loudly, I can do it all again" she didn't think it was anything to do with her and tried to blot out as though to ignore what she'd heard. Instead, she casually glanced around, 'but he looks so very normal and smart, she thought, slightly cheeky, but yes normal,' not wanting to detect an even glimmer of a smile, just in case, her thought then went or was to and of Jesus Christ on a cross, or a cross, but then to think of cross sections of 'a' society etc and that it doesn't mean that as even with 'some' governments presumably, and as some have been known, corruption is never really so far away? Or was it just a something to consider? To think about, anxiety, deliverance, brainfood, desperation, or just a direct conversation where for some there had been little chance, or certainly less opportunity to.

#

One of the things I found perplexing and of interest, was, having or attempting to reach an understanding of birthtimes regarding what would have been Pinto and her twin, although one of them we know was sadly stillborn, was, with all that had been then entrusted presumably to the female of the pair, was or would it have originally been entrusted to the boy, had he survived, and was it meant to have been like this, suggesting possibly that a stillborn birth was totally unexpected then. True, there would have been pre-birth scanning equipment then, the initial pre-birth ultra-sound equipment was said to have 'began to show effective results' a couple of years after, some earlier equipment had focused on foetal cardiac action and where different tissues reacted to different sounds before this period, to help locate abdominal tumours etc, it was concluded at around that time that 'the development of a future baby can be monitored by means of the innovative method ultrasound,' the new then technology had been accepted quite easily and was then being used in clinical obstetrics although the first detection of foetal cardiac action had been reported and documented at near that time, definitely within the decade to follow, thankfully. So, for the twins, maybe it was a battle of survival and a tough time for the parents too, but if the premature birth was unexpected because of complications, it would or may and yes would be unfair to presume regarding then, that the female of the two twins would not have been tricked or fooled somehow, or would possess the strength required not to have taken the bite when that little cherry, and that's basically all it was offered and placed before her? And now, seemingly with hearing what sounds like so many sometimes almost running around, what if anything, do they know, was, or is there more to the story than some might give credit to and where does this in the scheme, or a scheme of things, place circumstances of today, and maybe tomorrow. It was accurate that whilst waiting for corrective / reconstructive surgery, she had many years earlier said, she would wait like anyone else and not accept favouritism should it be presented in any form because of positions held. Maybe her mind had somehow been affected too? And these things were done. As she herself was so premature and so terribly ill, would the other child have survived had the pregnancy gone full term? How might it have affected her? Did she consider this at any time, was it anything she ought to think about or consider? Was it to create within her a solemness, and a kind of latent vengeance almost, but more, 'without,' any will or pre-conceived notion because of all that had happened, a streak or hint of forgiveness, of this she seemed somehow to sometimes behave as though certain, although it strangely was never really thought by her, often it would be, or was the perception or remarks by others, because she didn't? There had been a moment or moments even when she tentatively forgave the guy she'd met, but not those who'd abused, and she believed wholeheartedly that they could do as they always do, because they will not survive it in the fore that they considered they were to become growing and accustomed, that they might consider themselves so good, or astute, however foolishly, to be accustomed , or was it more than even that, that somewhere in her own sub-conscious, she knew instinctively but could not say, because it was deeper sub-conscious thought, all that had happened, she'd have been part of it and felt it, and now by some strange fate or default, she was going to let them do it all again to his spirit? And if she could only base her faith on their bonding although he'd been led astray technically, and maybe unaware. There would have been therefore nothing of her actions, or theirs, that she would be required to 'forgive,' surely. She was doing and behaving in the only way she knew how, and un-harmfully, with no actual malice. So effectively, they were only bringing and causing harm to themselves, - as she'd believed all along. And he didn't need to do a thing about it, or maybe she was hiding something, not the thought that she'd probably been reconstructed with the smallest vagina on the planet, despite how mean she thought originally just after the removal of the bandages it looked then, or that many no doubt, however young, and although still a virgin, they all had a far longer and sustainable start on her, something else. She knew that the spirit of her brother loved her in a 'familiar,' way, and that the closeness was always very strong, so what had they done to whisk it away? Presumably, they'd moved on by now, so that element would not be a consideration at all for them, and because they'd all be happy and doing what they do regardless. Pinto did know though, she had absolutely no intention of arranging a meet to facilitate the return to her of what they'd taken, none whatsoever, and of that she was very certain indeed! But too, equally sure that his spirit, the spirit taken, would return to her, in fact, it was as though it was somehow now, all starting to take shape. So, had they damaged or destroyed, or just played with as though some toy, or abused her own spirit, by tampering with that of her brother who'd obviously been close to her and who'd somehow remained in her mind and physique all her life. Her anger was a quiet anger, her poise, of a fulfilment, her attitude, calm, her sincerity, questionable, her determination, -m of no consequence to anyone but herself, she was a true believer from the very moment she was born, how though? Maybe it was about moving forward now, somehow, but I doubted and wondered because of how her mind could have been certainly becoming, if it wasn't already. She 'seemed' sure and confident sometimes, about some things and situations. Having overheard her on the telephone that day, apart from when she was reading out a document to a doctor, where even she'd noticed and acknowledged then how slow she'd become concentration-wise, was she planning something somehow, was all I could honestly think then and certainly having witnessed myself, some actions of the past, there was every possibility, but none could be so certain, especially me. And whilst on telephone calls to others, she was not putting up with any shoddiness, not from anyone.

The following day she could barely stand up, it was partly exhaustion and because of some other problems she'd had and because again she'd had to trek to the hospital, and before she could do that, she had to get herself ready to do that. Exhausted and influenced by various medications now, all day that day, she was bumping into things and knocking things over as though unable to focus properly. It was scary for her I'm sure, but also Mayday, or the first of May and a Saturday. With the May Day to be had on another day, she wasn't sure which, to her it was, she'd telephoned the hospital twice, and in that condition, there was no telephone being answered from that department, possibly because they didn't answer their telephone calls on Saturdays and so maybe were closed anyway, questioning whether she was being inconsiderate and thankful too that somehow, they were not, and because to her, it was May 1st. But she remembered the doctor saying to her that they would be open and to call by and collect the prescription written by that doctor. On her mind, was that the doctor who'd kindly phoned was on leave that day, their receptionist had told her with a short rather abrupt sounding tone, "Dr Bethesda Courtney is off sick today, on sick leave." Whilst exemplary to Pinto, or Pamela, that the doctor had taken the time to telephone whilst on such leave, the question became 'what was she off work for,' and,' had she forgotten that day would be the first day of May,' even if leading to Mayday itself, there would be no time to think of virgins or ladies dancing gayly around a maypole with flowers in their hair, as without a care in the world, although to her, in her own mind and imagination, however she was feeling, once En-route, it certainly did seem like that with all of the various blooming shrubs in gardens and pink blossoms on trees and quite often new trees too. And smiles, it was so lovely she may have been thinking, but she might not have been, whether some were smiling or not, did she notice that? I don't think she did. As she crossed a main road to the hospital, her open three-quarter length red coat was caught up by a sudden gently but windy breeze, it became and must have looked to others like a red cape rising above behind her, her Paddington style fisherman's hat fastened tightly beneath her chin was also blown right back by the wind exposing all of her face, a man called out, "are you going out of the bottom gate darling," she replied, 'sorry,' as though surprised to be asked to speak, or be spoken to by anyone, he pointed to slightly beyond, where ambulances were, she'd only just started to put her mask on for that reason, a yellow plastic cable was along the ground where work was being done by engineers, she stepped over it and fumbled with her covid face-mask straps, then she noticed that the chap was pointing to some gates that she could now see properly, they were at the end of the road and slightly to the right, she then replied to him saying "no, I'm not." Then she stopped to look at a white pelargonium in bloom in a wooden half-barrel tub, with some other greenery, it reminded her of her grandparents. The hospital doors were only a few feet away and were locked shut. Luckily, she pressed the intercom button and then a person did open their door from inside, how pleased, and thankful she was. She collected her prescription and thanked the person working that day in their reception hall. As she walked away from that hospital department, she did not have sunglasses on, but the sun struck her eyes, just for that moment, it was so intense, the thought the irises of her eyes had turned white, she blinked and thought momentarily of the pink pearl and of how it had seemed to have changed its colour, then she realised it wasn't the pearl at all, it was the silver sphere, it had changed shape, and for the first time, colour too, to look like a pearl. She smiled even more then and was glad that whatever had happened to what sounded like a metal bucket being kicked around, that now was as it was meant to be again, and the knowing that all inside the capsule were safe. It had potential to shed and then resurface with a new outer layer, - certainly, it was a welcomed by Pinto, realization. Yes, for her it was, she collected the medication from the pharmacy and returned to her home as speedily as she was able to. It must have totally whacked her, because no sooner did she get home, she was to almost immediately fall asleep when she sat to rest a moment, until 02.00AM the next day. She dreamed that from within the sphere whilst observing through it, lorries with many lights and much song and dance appeared, so much, a circus had come to town. Pinto then found herself in a room outside of the sphere, with long tables and many who had come with the circus, they were workers for. One of them, a handsome man, sat opposite her, but they were both too shy to speak, there was something very real between them though. Also, there was much choice, where he was concerned. Because of her shyness, she could do nothing about it, she also saw her neighbours sitting at another table. It would be the first time that they would see for themselves what was between the handsome man and Pinto, and realize by their actions what they themselves, not the handsome man and Pinto, but maybe as an illustration somehow, what they had destroyed. As nothing happened between Pinto and that man then, only the realization by them and that seen by her, that they now knew was prevalent. As the circus staff left, she had cleaning to do and carpets to clean. The older of the neighbours said to her, 'I can help,' Pinto looked straight at her and said, 'no thank you, you have done enough.' True, that circus did indeed come to town. The only thing that those neighbours didn't know then, was that even unbeknown to our own virgin, inadvertently, somehow, how I will never know, she had arranged it all herself, all of it! She realised it was and had been in order then that she make moves to begin at some point however recent, or not, to establish between herself and those around her own accommodation, whether and how much they were to be trusted and in which or what or whether in any capacity. Yes, Pinto, however tragic the girl was, had set the whole thing up, because of how she was, and what she had to offer, the most valuable of all the virtues. There was no means or way of her understanding how or why herself, it was instinctive, unaware totally. Just as easy as it was now, then, to believe that none of it mattered, not at all! She thought of them all only, and theirs, seated elsewhere. And of those of good and honest virtue, who would and could be eligible 'to dance around the maypole.' She smiled so much now, knowing they were safe, and that they would be, and presumably for every year thereafter too. 'Now wasn't that just worth the hassle,' she knew, to herself, and only day one, 'oh they could dance around in circles holding hands,' she knew this too, and some so good at it, dear Pinto though, knowing, though as not even an afterthought, or a conscious thought, it would never ever be the same. It would not be possible, even if she neither would know or realize it, they would. As though ingrained upon their souls forever. Pinto, thankful now and more-so, that she did refuse any "help," from them regarding cleaning that carpet, or anything, by them. Was she so not so insecure and afraid, but young because of where she was at, having taken those final steps toward surgery, that she had such a need to put herself through it all, just to know how far others would go, or was she so quick at damage limitation though, whatever was happening that she could know who she could trust was important for her, especially where opportunity presented itself to them. However, or whatever, it would not be long and that day, before she was then thinking of her own house more soon, and of whether to purchase from somewhere a Tradescantia fluminensis albovitatta, or a tradescantia Zebrina plant, a Spiderwort, or a Quicksilver, or a Wandering Jew plant. She was not going to be tolerant of an excuse for, - or of, a very poor actor or a muck-spreader holding a filthy oily rag, or theirs, on that Mayday or any other. Unsure as to whether to be surprised or not, almost revelation-wise personally, I thought 'from where this angel of almost death-defying, unmerciful doll-like character come and where was her next stop, something must happen somewhere, as much in the dark as her though, and for that matter, was there still relevance, that chap, if he would or could then now, whenever he looked at them too, if there was any relevance, would he not see that they could cause him actual harm, could it phase him out to the point where he could no longer tolerate them? If it were like that and whilst attempting to wonder how, if it was and if he now could, so would he know? He would realise they were selfish in a way that maybe he did not like but could never tell them. He could, if he could, only remove himself from them, see them, as funny as it may seem to some, he'd actually see them as males, irrespective of how their bodies were or how they presented, and as even more funny as it might seem to them, and with their tricks, would, could it push his hand and force him back to whoever he sat opposite when the circus came to town, and his own eyes never again seek to wander, but was it too late now? The fact was, for Pinto, or Pamela, and yes niece of the Lady Broadley, it no longer mattered anymore. They'd not be able to hide it from him in the same way that whereas, they'd offered to help to clean, even their attempts at honest deeds would be seen for exactly what they were, in fact, it would be as though looking at garbage. And when he thought of that moment opposite at that table, he'd think only of a harp playing. What any impact of any of this could be more than even their lives were worth to guess or plan or to continue to scheme, but they were none-the -wiser about any of it, and the poor girl Pinto, could it get more stupid, I couldn't tell her, I didn't know myself the answer to that, but she didn't know whether he liked the sound of harps or not?

#

Yes, for a very brief moment, it was as though from a reverse psychology angle, they had used the experience as outsiders, needing to repeatedly cut-in on what was going on, - but the capsule was shut and inside the sphere, safe, and the blinds were drawn down. Myself, as I was wondering about some male and female characteristics or similarities, I couldn't help but wonder, had some seen a wisdom of some kind, or just rephrased some older terminology and instead said 'opposites attract,' in some places and situations sure. Or was it all just a big business? Only an act for some, and not near the best of acts.

Not much else happened that day apart from rest. She ordered a take-away despite having already eaten a meal, because she wanted to "knock herself out," where things at times seemed often unbearable, like many, or everyone, or many, for some of her neighbours, those neighbours, it still didn't matter, she was stressed and unhappy about the day and abut being stuck indoors pretty much all day long again. It wasn't as though she required mischief or to question any possibility of saboteurs, she'd been capable of that herself, where was she heading? Single, with a pocketful of stupid dreams, an odd idea, and a desire to succeed, somehow? Some neighbours she wanted to ignore and not trust, particularly too, as those had actually suggested that they regarded her somehow as 'family,' at one point, something Pinto perceived as yet merely a means of them inviting themselves and obviously with founded reason now, into her life, or into any destiny they chose to invite themselves by the same angled route, to and regarding others as well. They were not relations of hers. Surely by ordering a take-away meal, with the contempt of familiarity, some hadn't even devised a way to munch their way by association into that? She'd had a fillet of fish so was that also to have become to them like loaves and fish all over again?

She remembered some of her so- called imaginary friends and then before her was a jigsaw puzzle, much of it was already set out and completed, apart from one piece of the puzzle, it was an unusual design, but with a design of an insignia that she recognised on the bottom right corner of the puzzle, as like a monogram. She poised, holding in her closed hand the final piece. Earlier as though she had been invaded again by her neighbours, certainly those who had been problematic and deceitfully from the start, Pinto saw many guys standing to her right in a vision, they told Pinto that they trusted her unanimously and not them, and they somehow informed the guy she'd been seeing, that he'd 'lost out.' She wasn't bothered by any of it, for her it was like taking off a big coat, she undid it and stepped from within and left them all behind. It was as though, then, to her, she at last was possibly stepping from what had been, into a destiny, her own destiny, and their attempts to infuse or corrupt or become part of if uninvited, would be now as much of a part of that past as they'd become to her. Dubiously, when a person, a female, said 'give me your hand,' Pinto then walked forward, though as a light source. She soon sat and was then before a large, tall heavily bearded man, who held a crook. He was a man she did not recognise at all but purely as a courtesy she kind of bowed slightly, then considering that it might actually be a representation on another plain of one of her remaining uncles somehow, who she did not get on with so well, but had only respected him because he was of her remaining and surviving blood-line, she'd acknowledged but then said, "I'll not conform to his wishes and I'll neither be or become beholden to him or be in any way denigrated by his countenance or how he maybe would perceive himself at the death of my own father to have become." Then she rose and stepped back and to another country 'presumably,' or that was how it seemed to be, though not condescendingly, far from it. She would never have tolerated that, and her father would have known it too, it would have made him smile and her then quietly because he did. It was then, or just a short while, only a moment before, she was told some had attempted to sabotage, - this she looked as though she doubted, thinking of the chap she'd met, despite it all making sense. Aware that things weren't as they seemed, and the reason she had embroiled such a lavish tapestry – to attempt to understand just whom she could really and however sad, trust. The, or such a tapestry, within the remit and realm of her own settlement and by her own perception although she did not know it then, her own court. It would be some time after, maybe an hour, she would think of her personal nearest and dearest and those actually close to her and to those, she said 'Happy Mayday,' it was then she placed firmly the remaining piece into place within the puzzle, the elements of the design of the puzzle then lit up before her very eyes as though a maze of an elaborate and intricate design and of what resembled almost, fluorescent tubes. Some may have wondered what next, but dear Pinto knew, yes, somehow the girl knew what to do, she pressed it and all you could hear was her voice as she said, 'I am ready now.'

Pinto had found some prescribed scalp medication in her bathroom, she questioned whether it wasn't slightly too 'out of date,' then because it was sealed very tightly anyway, decided, although she knew for that reason she should not, to apply some to her scalp as she'd done the day before too. It was a medication that was meant to be applied twice daily but she'd obviously forgotten first time around because she knew she hadn't and if she had, then it wouldn't be there anyway. She then made for herself a coffee of two types of instant coffee mixed, four spoonsful of coconut milk surprisingly for her, it was some that remained in her refrigerator, and a small amount of semi-skimmed milk, in an oversized mug, it was quite a big mug to be honest, the type you might imagine drinking hot chocolate from. She did have drinking chocolate with the takeaway meal she'd had, and was thankful that they served it, such a rarity indeed it was, to have drinking chocolate for Pinto. She thought she'd try it and thought it was delicious, and as she had not tried theirs before and neither did, she after, not that I was aware of then anyway. The delivery driver remised her of a Marciella Lismore, a friend or acquaintance she had not seen for quite some time. It had been during their meets that each, and every time, Marciella seemed to misplace or lose her phone, it was for Pinto all quite confusing at times. The delivery driver though, a charm, and very courteous, so much that it was so much a pleasure to give a tip, it reminded her of a crisp snowy day, warm gloves and scarves and knitted hats and snowballs and a snowman at Christmas Time. Anyway, she put a sweetener in her coffee, for a first-time making coffee like this, the thought it could quite likely become something she'd willingly serve to any guests she had in future, if of course it may eventually be possible. She soon knocked back the coffee, to the point where she thought about it and decided that in future should she again, it would be a regular cup and one sup spoon of coconut milk only per cup, the coffees, a powdery type and a granule type, just half a teaspoon of the granule type and a quarter of the powdery. An hour seemed then to pass quickly, she switched the television on very briefly, a man on the new was being questioned in an interview, he'd been a prisoner at Guantanamo, she thought how handsome he was, and was happy that he was married. On her mind was matters concerning sex, about having sex with someone and think only of the native country and to grin and bear it, was acceptance of never doing it but thinking the same, the same. Her thoughts seemed jumbled and as result she had to find something else to think about, questioning of herself logic but unable to string it then together as accurately as she might like to. True, a couple of hours before putting that piece in that puzzle, whilst what was happening did, Pinto had been paired up with the guy she'd met, but no more to be abused by any who would do so by such a premise. - And if the 'coupling,' had already occurred, I'd need to see evidence of that soon, or believe that some were merely trying to abuse again, an arrangement that was never going to happen again, or was it? Was it another abuse attempt? It all became too encroaching upon mentality and upon personal being and space. I had said not to them and their continual unwanted 'familiarity,' attempts, it was for me by them, an insult to nature and humanity. Elsewhere, it was a problem they had created for themselves, none of my concern, absolutely none. She could almost hear as though on the tail end of the slightest breeze, 'is maybe how you say in your language darling, the long story, or just too late in the day.' A thought she would not entertain or give credence to, she was glad he was not in need of food. Could I think 'collectively,' but of convents and such places, and monasteries, and before I might hear a further utterance akin to 'best place for you, or something similar, and because he was not hungry. Such places simply because and with reference too, to such a comment being received should it ever, could how I be or am, and what I was going though present as a first step somehow on a journey spiritually, but then would that mean that all before was merely one step? Were those in such places some or many who could understand correctly, their or my circumstances, like his even, not exactly the same, but together although not, would I be like not so much, a missing part of a puzzle, because that could imply that there was or had been a missing part, and atrociously facetious to presume, I felt certain that even if I did not work out another option to what was happening, that from somewhere, maybe those imaginary friends, would clues be received, found or discovered, to what for myself would be a resolve, - and still it was not to matter to those deliberately abusive, it would still be none of their concern, nor any business of theirs. They'd become like cyber criminals but of the mind, and of the pettiest kind, their interruptions and intrusiveness as unwelcomed, as t be humoured without their 'knowledge,' it was also the very reason at that time then, for the creational form- of the capsule and especially at that time during the pandemic, whether some bars now, were allowing drinking inside their premises or not, until it was deemed safe

As Pinto was having a shower, she was thinking about the winds from the four corners of the earth and of where she grew up as a child, when she would cry constantly and complain about seeing faces in walls, this time though, they weren't faces of older people and neither was it a reflection of the fact that she was older now than then, seeing the same wallpaper as then, now they were faces of children, or cherubs, but only faces pushing against the paper, until it stretched over their scared faces, of almost a stony white, like Bossons figures but totally white against the paper, they were saying in an distraught way to her, 'he came, he came and took the coat from the floor where you left it,' it was a sound, their voices, that would fill her with nothing but dismay, they'd not have known what it was, or would they? Dishevelled skin, he slid his arms into it as he pulled it up as though a racing car driver and, in a hurry, as an emotional opportunist might, and left as quickly without saying a word from having been in a flat above, and via the communal door. Pinto asked, "who came," but she knew exactly who it was, and who or what it was not. All she could think was 'thank god the children are safe,' were they afraid or protecting her, because he'd not seen them, she had to say through the walls, to remind herself that there were walls between, but these were no adjacent wall, these were walls from her childhood memories, she knew this because of the wallpaper, this time though, not afraid at all, not because they were children and had noticed the paper immediately, it even had dents where it had been put up in places with a thin layer of polystyrene beneath to then in those days prevent dampness. seeping through and that pattern she'd never forget anyway, and possibly because the faces then were for her just so terrifying and frightening, clear faces, not as though pushing though. A way to describe it could be that its different to look at an expanse or distance through a peephole, where people can walk as though almost entering your viewable, viewing observing space, or as if using a camera lens, compared to if looking through a small round window or portcullis in a capsule or a submarine for example. If you were, she also thought again then of those she'd said happy mayday to, from within the capsule, and the cherub-like faces, those then, then and there, did move away from the wall and were then, however odd, no longer requiring stretching out the wallpaper from behind it.

It had been a strange day, the day before, and even the day before that, Pinto's vagina now with an odd and quite peculiar odour about it she'd occasionally thought, it seemed to smell of mildly stale nicotine somehow, but she is not a smoker? It had been a lingering odour from when her friend Bernadette had called around some days earlier, how very strange she thought. She did recall that the ashtray was still in the kitchen with some cigarette ash in it and how the last time Bernadette had called in, Pinto had disposed of the cigarette butts separately, discreetly in other rubbish of a plastic recyclable kind, it was an empty bleach bottle, to be precise, she just popped them into it. She'd washed but had not douched properly from dilation, so it was soon remedied. She douched a few times and could still smell it near the basin in the bathroom, until she knew she was free of it and cleaner, very possibly she thought, she'd inhaled passively, so the smell would have been in her nostrils anyway, she was slightly confused anyway, poor girl. 'Yes, a lingering smell, and presumably now lodged too, and formerly sealed with the overcoat that presumably had been taken by none other than that racing car driver.' Thinking about how things had moved on in even fifty years and earlier, where smoking had seemed so popular whether fortunately or not, she recalled a conversation between her and a friend of hers, when whilst in their late teens, smoking would have even been a much more frequent conversation topic too, even if just to overhear, and of course there would be also the 'he only wants me for one thing,' jibes, to be heard sometimes too. That she'd totally forgotten about hearing and the horror she used to feel whenever she did, and the thankfulness then, that she was not in that kind of 'happening,' was nothing short of a stark realization to her. Was such a remark as digestible for some as, 'get them in and get them out,' as if mechanically minded, and without consideration, because for both involved, they each in the same or similar circumstances knew anyway.

#

Presently then, it was all about days and nights, and about not being able to do anything and about when can we. Pinto was becoming quite distracted, and it was sending her back into phases of a total inactivity, often just the sound of the communal door, so maybe they, or some, had found a trigger to a loaded gun after all, she woke up the day before, at 21.00hrs, she actually felt as though she could get out of bed, it was also the first day that year where the timed heating was not on, to get her through the colder months, then a while after despite a heatwave, she was to have it back on again as the weather seemed to plummet. Certainly for a few days, but then though her fingers felt as though they had chilblains and the soles of her feet where she'd recently peeled some of the skin off had gone hard, and where she'd become side-tracked, caught up in a trance-like stressed out contemplative, almost scared and unable to care mood. Then at 01.30AM the communal door was to sound again. There were comings and goings at those times then, but which way around was indeterminable, no-one was looking, Pinto did get up and take 200mg of medication should some, if some were attempting to fool her mind, she was reticent to consider or believe for various reasons that it could have been or was paranoia, far from it positively. She made another of those coconut coffees, she'd been dreaming again, about a premises, a business premises, there had been a man there, though he resembled no-one she knew, he was frustrated because he could not get sexually, someone he had become infatuated with, that was to remind her of someone else very much, the guy she'd been seeing, not because she'd ever believed herself to be like that, or even that I'd ever believed him to have been like that, it was as if somehow he'd managed to get inside the guy's head and I was looking at the end result, and then, that guy believing he was him, presumably, because for some strange reason, for me, it did not seem to be exactly normal and therefore it was unacceptable somehow. Then if a woman was seen to walk down some steps, Pinto would be laying on her back, thinking that he was interested in her, though he looked different, Pinto could see his frustrations, she questioned whether it was him or not and doubted her own mentality, he attempted to hide his frustrations, there were blisters on the side of his body, maybe five of them, water blisters, Pinto asked him what they were and he shrugged it off, it was as though something big, with bigger hands maybe than anything normal, even of this realm, had pushed him away. The girl walked across to Pinto, he was in an adjoining room, she, dark haired, but not like other dark haired females Pinto knew of, the girl walked across and seemed to reach across, her fingers touched Pinto's that were reaching up to the ceiling, she pressed her fingers onto the top of Pinto's and as like a circus act, stood on top of her fingers with her feet pointing toward the ceiling, then she moved away. And sat down, the guy then came, he'd realised the girl was watching and said, 'can you stay until Friday,' Pinto then asked, 'what day is it,' he replied almost touching on abruptly, but softly 'Thursday night,' it seemed even more strange to Pinto, particularly as it was Wednesday morning early, the coconut coffee hadn't even been made by that point, it was then she must have woken up. It did make her wonder whether her destiny involves a woman, she could not imagine herself, but she was quite beautiful, it would be at 02.06AM that Pinto remembered where she'd seen that woman before, it would have been twelve or fourteen years earlier, she was a psychiatrist. Somehow, that memory in her subconscious was helping and at such times. Pinto thought how in two weeks from that day, it might be possible to go outside again properly, she should or may be able to. I was saddened to learn that a million people in India had been infected by then and two hundred thousand deaths had occurred and pleased that although it could be tough with lockdowns and how some just cannot hack it, whatever their newfound hobbies in some places may be, that in a place where 1,2 billion people need to eat, and many to fend for themselves, how would they cope with a lockdown and its necessity. My thought brought me then to Ganesha and I did not need to plead or ask, he was happy, so I believed then that everything should and should remain fine, whether I remembered every small detail or not, because of other things to try to remember and do, also I saw a monkey. Pinto was now wondering whether she should start to wear gloves in bed, - and it was after the girl, if it was, stood with her hands on hers and sat down. The guy asked Pinto if she would stay, so she was already suspicious, he was attempting to trick Pinto and, in more ways, than one, whoever that had been or was, and it could not have been that psychologist from years earlier because Pinto had sent to her and her colleagues from within the capsule a Happy Mayday message. Then really did cometh the question, could Pinto imagine herself in a relationship, if that relationship was with another woman, Pinto appreciated the beauty angle of it, but guessed it could depend on many factors, or some, but she could not envisage personally a sexual activity relationship, not at all, and in no way whatsoever to invite that guy to 'help out,' not for all the tea in China she very clearly did think. As much as some seemed to be enjoying her overhearing during those days, whether her reluctance, or not wanting to meet him, was somehow 'driving him to it,' whatever he was up to. Neither did she believe any of it, had he made any moves then at all regarding contacting her, so it had all been lies. - and normal, and more to than typical. Unfortunately, and the longer it was going on for, the more distanced she was becoming from him, maybe his own role was to play, or not to play somewhere a part in it all of this, she thought. Who knows really? It would be as though the planets aligned in Pinto's mind then, in her imagination, as horror struck on his part. He made his bed, that was all she could think, and what was the red dot on Saturn really, she wondered? His bed concerning the deed or deeds. That was not something for Pinto to attempt to somehow wriggle out from, there was no need for her to consider it.

#

After having a shower that day, she remembered calling upon the winds but although she had, then, it was as though thankfully and instinctively, she knew not why. On that day though she would request humbly that they might go gently and not hardly or briskly cold to India, whereby they could deliver a cool breeze that could sustain and help some, if required, in breathing and healing and recovering. On the 22nd of June, she would be still uncertain as to whether it had happened or not, but although news of holding place, to hold up to four million corpses had been seen on the 21st, and despite ambulances outside her home on the day of the 20th and then two paramedic vehicles and another ambulance on the 21st, and overhearing someone saying, 'they are falling down around her, 'she thought of the ambulance and thought quietly to herself 'four million, no.' She was too that there was no case of due negligence and that contingency plans, however the pandemic seemed to be heading, were being met. It did not mean that on the morning of June 22nd, at around 06.35AM, she would not hear a rushing sound like the wind rushing slightly outside, it was slow and quite loud and lasted seven seconds, but she smiled and only thought kindly.

A while after an entry in her diary read, 'I was for some reason thinking, that my handsome Prince who needn't be so handsome really, because I'd know it or feel it if he were, may have moved around everywhere where I live, so maybe he or a wedding band could reflect that it was so.' Pinto even knew what such a ring would look like, and that it might be engraved by Greek jewellers. She then thought about that further and said to only herself, in her own mind, herself being Pinto Neice to Lady Broadley, 'it's them trying to intervene again,' there would be more likelihood of him turning up on a tricycle, bicycle or a three wheeled rickshaw, in fact, she herself was wondering what it might be like to be able to afford one those personally.

#

The capsule had been placed in a pocket in a tight garment, I though wasn't sure whether it was a blouse pocket or a trouser pocket, but it was tight. Those inside the capsule were unaware because it was as though time had even stood still completely as though suspended. - There was a shock, it must have been where the capsule or what it was made of, although now covered by the sphere had cause friction, as though something unprecedented, and unexpected. So suddenly, Pinto then woke up, in a forest, transported in and within a split second of time, everything was black around, and darkness, and I could see what resembled the moon, shining in front of me, beyond some trees, it looked close. I was on all fours, poised like a bulldog, but with the shape more of that of a German Shepherd, hands and feet though were human. My back arched like an animal, I could not tell what my face was like, I started to run slowly and then leaping onto what looked like large round boulders there, totally hairless, I could feel that my spine was totally definitely well arched, my hands and feet felt strange as though blocks somehow, like granite, but it was difficult to describe and because it was dark, I felt as though I was beginning to somehow see, even if I didn't, or even if I did, I could hear though nothing at all. Then men came with capes to their knees open and hats like those of Vikings, and long spears, they were pointing their spears at me, trying to push me, and almost herd me in a direction, but I was bigger than them by then, I could feel my body changing shape and behind my eye, as though I'd been hit on the head and it was cracking but I wasn't knocked out, - and woke up, startled to be there and so instantaneously, I had horns bigger than those on their helmets then, the spears were pushing toward me, but not touching, I looked at my hands expecting to see claws or something similar but my hands and nails were normal. Then prodding very slightly as though to jeer, but not harmfully, what must have been Jesus Christ on a cross and with a crown of thorns, he was being pulled, dragged along as though to discard, I was by then, in huge chains, as far as I could hear them, those in the capsule, I felt the capsule grow now, but inside me, inside myself somehow, it was beginning for that moment to become an underlayer of my own skin, and that the occupants of, could now see through my own eyes, but too, I had to be mindful that they were inside the capsule for a reason, and it was because of the pandemic. So, I placed them to where in a pocket they'd come, - I was a woman, now, yes, I came around from that moment, and the horns were gone, I was no longer in those times of centuries before, a voice came to me and said, "don't tell them that you saw me." If I had to describe how I think, it was whilst climbing on rocks, it would be a totally bald, off white, emaciated panther type of creature. I could think of a panther, especially a black panther, and a leopard, with kindness, though aware that my own face was not the same shape as theirs, and neither would anyone inside the capsule have been affected or aware, apart from the need for compartmentalization regarding the mission at hand? I then came around again in my own room wanting a coffee. All that jumping around on boulders and being prodded had made me quite thirsty. Because of the rather rapid weight-gain since starting the recent prescription, the medication was reduced by maybe seventy percent, and because it was a prescription, she had requested albeit for very real reasons and circumstances known too well by Pinto, however spaced these attacks were or had been in the past, and thankfully they had been recorded, or she would not have reduced the medication so abruptly without seeking consultation, because to do so could have been potentially hazardous and could have in some circumstances given way to other situations and even syndromes with some prescribed medicines then able to take or gain something of a hold. Pinto was thinking of her calculations regarding pills and her accuracy and said to herself, 'if my calculations are correct, I should be waking up or coming around in my room about now,' and sure enough, she did. The weight-gain was only apparent in Pinto's lower abdominal region, such that when on her way back from a shop that day, she found it easier to behave as though she was pregnant, rather than risk horrid comments, jibes, sneers, or rudeness. True indeed, possibly because of the precious cargo, those not so recognised heroes then, were warding away from the possibility, more of the dangers and mindful of confidence, and of what was to become for her, a curiosity. And why take on or presume to have taken on the form somehow of a larger feline, was it not the harm that could befall to those of such persuasion, as to anyone in a darker forest and particularly it seemed, at night? So, the giant that tip-toed around the forest at night ever so quietly and yes, quietly, that you could hear even a mouse scratching its own ear, and then the sound of a huge creaky old metal gate, that obviously needed oiling was heard. The heavy thick chain that had been heard around Pinto's feet, she hauled it up and pulled it into and through some parts of those big gates, she pulled so hard on the chain that her feet whilst on the ground when she was not horizontally pulling, sunk into the soil beneath, well her shoes did anyway, she pulled and tugged and tugged and pulled and with her eyes closed pulled with what must have been every bit of her strength, sure that she would not achieve her objective because of the heaviness of the chain, ,until she heard the chain click, the chain locked links, and then as though it all rusted before her very eyes, like a leaf at the very end of an Autumn-time, that had fallen from a tree, it turned into the tiniest of what could have only really been spider's fingers, if they had them, and then disappeared.

Summer was coming, and with it a hope for a lovely, gorgeous season for everything, everyone, and all, not just a selfish more arrogant few and as the air had cleared in so many places, especially Pasturelands. There was or would be only another ten days or so before everything would or could be kind of back to normal, or as close to as was possible. Some pieces were being moved around on a chessboard; they were not small pieces. Pinto couldn't determine then which, only that they were large and that didn't mean a few fatter than average sows hoping to relocate to feast from their pigsty, into to any Courtyard, expectations were often high there though. Yes. the pieces, more like twisty wooden salt and pepper mills, that big. There was though, no reluctance, so it wasn't such a bad consideration. Of course, Pinto didn't think anything strange of it. It did though mean 'you know who,' yes, an idea was to be had, or was it a game, another game of some form, or other? Was Pinto being over-cautious, was there reason to be. Or, was Pinto feeling, predicting, anticipating now, again, the thoughts of others, or another. She'd hoped not, & that was all she could think about it regarding. She decided to tell herself that she knew not, believing it to be the safer and wiser option of choices that may neither present as too, if, to be considered kind, acceptable.

It would be the type of period at time, whether brief or not, you could think something akin to 'twas the night before Christmas,' in some areas, and maybe in some strange way it could have seemed as though it was, for some, Sure the day although relating to occurrences of a month or six weeks or so earlier, it was actually World Rain Forest Day that day too, how wonderful it could be she did think if during winter months in future, not so many perished, for whatever reason, that all may enjoy that season from wherever in the world they may be. And regarding 'games,' so who or what was the horned character in dreams of hers, and her visions, and why was she meant to see that or ever have been, or be that, or to have been perceived as?

Soon it was daybreak, our own beholder did yawn that day and with outstretched arms as though calling to the waving leaves on the trees, fluttering in a gentle breeze, I will never leave you, whatever phantoms may exist. And whatever drains may be placed upon some lifestyles, your systems shall always I hope, remain intact, secure, and incorruptible. Pinto, oh she was just staring though, she was in a moment of a purest wonderment. She would also think 'I am certain to imagine that you all like honey on your toast, but it's plain dry toast today.' I must say, although even I feel slightly afraid to, that some inside the capsule, were far from pleased at the notion of dry toast for breakfast, especially as it was in the form of a scratchy lick label, far from pleased at all! Although in time suspended, it was the inner-voice, or thought of the beholder I'd overheard then, none of the other capsule occupants, therefore, to have been so displeased at all. Pinto also touched some designs that appeared on the inside window panels in the capsule, and wouldn't you know it, 'as if by magic,' she observed chess being played, and what was being moved and to where. She then transported herself to the precise moment in time, just as she was pulling that huge chain to close those heavy gates. Whilst she was bigger, she'd dropped a hairgrip on the floor trying to pull the chain, at the same time as her shoes were sinking into the ground with such an effort, the hairgrip naturally was bigger too, she stood by those gates and could see inside them, how very dark it all was, she glanced across at the chain and thought to herself 'I know that's one of ours, I know that chain. Maybe she'd had a memory lapse, this was concerning for her, so it was now about remedial action, you see she noticed the links on the chain, they had markings on them, where forged by her own family, she must have arrived just before it disappeared, because the sound of the gate being pulled closed could be heard on the wind, or was it that somehow too, unbeknown to her, nature was helping and she or even that a particular hairgrip, then was to have a special reason to be there too, 'a bird stood perched upon the gate, it looked something similar to an owl, maybe it was she thought, but it was all very dark. She picked up the hairgrip that on her then would have now been the size of an arrow, almost had to climb up onto the chain and with the sole of the front part of her shoe, she pushed and pushed and pushed so much- that she had to hold her breath and grit her teeth, her mouth too just totally clenched. The hairgrip went in between the links of the chain and with what must have been most of her might, she bent some parts of the it around and twisted other parts of it, using her shoed feet and determination alone. The owl-looking bird was facing outward, she could see its eyes opening and closing and its head almost turning, then she clapped her hands slightly and almost silently and whispered so quietly to it that none or nothing apart from that owl-resemblant bird would have heard it at all, she heard its wings flap very slightly as though shaking an old lightweight raincoat, it then flew away, so the gates did disappear. She wondered why she hadn't noticed the bird on the gatepost when she was there, but she was only listening because of the darkness of the forest, listening to the forest, looking too but also delirious, she, the poor slip of a girl had just woken up. And her prescription, reduced, she couldn't think so straight, not so straight then.

Did Pinto know that she had become for a moment then something of an animal, or that she'd had horns for a while, was there, or this a sign that there was something so terrible in her past for her to have recognised those chains as she did? What could it have been? It wasn't as though I could ask, and was it an owl, because it hooted. So, why would she think it was owl-like? It was like peeling an apple at the top and ending up with a long strip of apple peel, that then, should you hold it up, was the top part and the bottom part obvious? Neither did it matter.

Pinto had seen some playing chess, or moving chess pieces on the image of a chessboard that had appeared before her, she then touched on one of the squares without needing to consider which and was immediately transported, she didn't know the location but had recognised the linkage on the chain by the forgers' mark, and only wondered 'why there,' then but as similarly, she had and could think of no reason to question it, no reason at all. She knew that she'd been there, because she could detect her own scent instantly, but seemed as unconcerned just as though there were more important things to deal with. All she thought then, was how she really must invest in a perfume fragrance., certainly of some kind. - out of the farthest corner of her right eye, she could see slightest hint of a glint of a reflected light, of that there was, in the air about the eyes of that perched bird moving around, as it turned its head from right to left, It was a forest of many miles for then, in that second momentarily she thought of the and wanted to think Carmina Burana, but instead thought 'Maria Callas, Casta Diva, Bellini- Norma (Act 1),' then with it quenched by that thought, she thought, it vanished away. Then thinking, 'to save you for that rainier day,' and more, should you encounter more than as a forest, than you already have and so givingly do. It wasn't of course that she was so familiar regarding music, but it was all she could think to do in that brief second.

#

I had been thinking about the relationship she'd commenced a little more than a year earlier, if Pinto was or had been considered a little 'different,' because she'd never been seen with anyone, then even those on doorsteps nearby to where she lived, might have been against the idea of her meeting anyone, or him meeting her, preferring him to be with someone 'more normal,' so the odds then were already being stacked again, against her, similarly to the perceived odds of her surviving as a female when she was born, stacked against in respect to her happiness, anything forming there? And if he'd himself have considered it then as something 'casual,' was he using her because she was not 'normal,' believing he could just enjoy himself with no attachment, was he building around her, or what if he'd been attempting to drain her completely throughout. Ok it might be June 22nd before all the pieces to that puzzle fitted, or all along he was looking for someone considered more 'normal.' So, where she'd believed she was being tested by it all, if something had happened in her past such as she'd offered to God a vow of silence in some things, what if she'd been such a young child then, what if that had been part of something that she didn't or hadn't realised and with regard to the complete circumstances surrounding her birth, and what would happen after or subsequently, that she would not have even then been aware of. Or, did he realise, did he see it all, if he'd known or realized, just a little too much of a mountain for him to climb. So, if she was, as strange as it seemed, destined somehow to never actually marry. Her meeting him when she did, wasn't him sewing his oats, was it her having her first only and final fling. He'd contacted her on 22nd June, although she did not show that she had seen he had. So was t him being tested and she didn't realize it, and not her. So, her believing she somehow was destined to be how she was and knowing his own background and how he had been since was fantasy? But what if she genuinely couldn't for other non-health reasons, have vaginal sex, and whether she physically would be able to or not, just because of her birth circumstances, and the time as then or now was or is, or was it something many had been through? I doubted that to be perfectly honest, knowing the background, I really do. It was time though, as it was with her, to continue to deal with the here and now, so my thoughts on attempting to question reliably further, were possibly ending. Her decision, about vaginal penetrative sex nothing to do with him at all. Or what they had, or what the girl thought she believed they had. She was right when she'd said to him before, "how you are is as integral to you, as how I am is integral to me, and how I am." So potentially he was being tested and not by her, and she apparently didn't know it anyway so what was the point, if any. Was it a demonstration of the woman Pinto is, and always has been, I wondered? Oh, indeed I did wonder! What if, and as on June 23rd, she thought and remembered making that vow as a so young child unbeknown to anyone, and if she'd tried so many times whilst at junior school to never speak again, what must she have been going through? Was on the 23rd of June, she to think of not only how sad it all could have been or was to have ever been like that then, but whether or not the guy she'd met might prefer it if she'd never opened her mouth at all to begin with, and yes, just to get on with it, what was worse, she could not bring herself to consider, whether together or apart though, she did think, 'ok if that's how you want it baby, be my guest,' but it was only a thought. That by her doing this at such a young age and not asked to by anyone or, or prompted, might have constituted to having kept her safe after all these years she thought was the most beautiful of things she could think of. She was so humbled by it all, and only briefly wondered why, was it, could it have been that the right person for her, one day may come, was it him? It was and would be then a circumstance and situation she could, and because of her inexperience, as sad as it very possibly could seem, tell. What if she never did, and if he was not the right person for her? And what if then, recently he was now with someone 'normal,' but what if, she gave up somehow on the idea because nothing seemed to be happening and impossibilities regarding a vow of silence with school, she decided to offer herself to other forces, and what if when she'd met that guy, she in her mind before her surgery, had agreed to 'offer herself to him,' as some kind of sexual human sacrifice, would it now matter whether it was him or not, especially if he was with someone else now, should it matter and could it be the first person who might happen to offer to provide that, and non-judgementally on her part, irrespective of circumstance, like some kind of free-for all jamboree, as it surely all would amount to the same? Was she wanting really someone to rescue her from such a destiny or fate, and what if those darker forces, then, had sent a man to collect, not that it had been offered, and not that she realised everything about herself then? Would those ghoulish faces, some of them, or any of them now be say, that may have terrified her so much in the walls as a child, pushing themselves through so that their scary faces she could actually see, and that made or caused her as a very young child in that bedroom to get on her knees with a curtain open and her palms pressed together praying to God for help, her parents of course they loved her. But they would just say "don't be silly," when she told them and they's smile at each other and tuck her up in bed. Then she would hear that bedroom door know as it, the bedroom door closed. Then alone again and they would appear. What if one of those ghouls possibly from then although then they were male looking, were to now say in a very rude and daring, totally obnoxious and inquisitive way, 'jamboree, who'd wanna rescue er, who'd wanna rescue that old thing, let him 'ave 'er, let him devour her and watch her really, squirm, knowing'? Now would not that be a treat if Pinto knew, but then, some were prevalent at domestic and neighbourly abuse, even during a pandemic, whatever stage in recovery everyone was supposedly or at, and dear Pinto, she knew gatecrashers, and yes, they were again, trying to gain access to a party where they were not welcome. So, he was now with a person considered 'normal,' and happy for him was Pinto. It had been questioned that warmer weather in Pasturelands was not easily visible or felt in recent days, therefore she decided to remain happy for him, for others who did not appreciate cold and because there was presumably a greater covid risk should the weather return to colder climbs, other than some mountain tops, beyond Ingagook territories of older times and in other places where it was meant. Her feelings though, now, she understood, she could never in future tell him. Whether she would have thought to tell him in other ways, was debatable though, whether she'd have mentioned to him in- person, had he not been so distracted, or otherwise engaged, was to remain a thought only Pinto herself would know. Twas part of a depth to and of her love. Neither could she let him in-person know about that either, or anyone else, in case he then abused it, or someone who may have wanted him might overhear, and could- and could cause possible problems unknown to him in their own furtherance. Was Pinto wise for her years I wondered, or playing it cool especially should the weather begin to sizzle again, or maybe she knew him not so much better yet, but was happy that she did and that he was happy, somehow however he chose to behave, or misbehave? Maybe she thought she knew him better than he knew himself, that possibility there was something only I'd knowingly considered, and not because she was sometimes secretive, maybe because she was changing, now as though by-the-day, so to the best of my knowledge, that had not been a thought recently of hers and if it was or had been, you'd have not known it. She'd received messages from him, swearwords, because she sent him a message saying, 'I hope you're ok,' and then after apologised saying 'oops, sorry, I forgot it was Wednesday.' She'd sent him a photo of herself then, and his response was she thought 'amazing,' but was it because in the photo maybe she resembled someone else he was seeing, or someone he was already now visiting, and staying with. Did it matter to Pinto now? Was that they thought it did or may, of any relevance to them, did Pinto care? I doubt it, somehow, I really do, like a cat playing with a piece of string, Pinto's was a feline he'd never forget if ever trapped in a lift with. Pinto was prioritising far differently now, and if I may say so myself, even slightly more transparently than ever before, but never obviously and not like that for reasons of shrewdness, none that were obvious to me, she was moving from being as a teenager might be because of her surgery, and to commence as a woman, I knew this because I saw tears well up in her eyes as she thought, that would be something that the chap she had met would never have had the pleasure to see, even if she smiled about that, you would see her eyes glaze over as though tearful, but it was not tears of a sadness. Prioritising though, too because charters, of a description or kind had been signed off. What I was attempting to portray regarding Pinto, was that my impression and hers, regarding that chap, was that she would never have been good enough for him, by his thinking and that of others, and it was not a confidence issue, irrespective of what she did or however she tried. Where her core beliefs were strong, if his were not, hadn't been or were different to hers, could that matter? Pinto had questioned everything. Would it have changed the situation at all, if there was, or could that have very much formed a part of her own integral structure, even if it was only that she had to be as sure as she could be, or she could be demonising or out-ruling even though not deliberately, maybe someone of her own belief structure, or risk hurting someone very much who would care? Her own late father, her memory of, or her parents generally and grandparents? Or the set of structures themselves. But if by her not being 'normal,' in that she wasn't as 'indecent,' as some he might like to visit, and often, as to the levels of how things can develop, she consoled herself often, with how relationships can change, although it would not as often be a thought that acted in her favour. Was that she could not be as 'easy,' a barrier, did it make her come across as frigid, unrelaxed, or cold, or was it just that he enjoyed the non-committal lifestyle, but weren't some of those he was visiting regularly, especially if staying over, achieving that? They played a clever game borne of experience, yes for sure. It didn't upset Pinto, she could smile and now, certainly on 23rd of June, even without a glimmer so very sadly for them, of a trace of a headache. She did think when or if wasting a thought on them, my cat if I had, wouldn't bark, or make the sound a mule might make, and I didn't need to train it. Or was he keeping his options too, much to their dismay and discontent, discouragement, and anger, open at all times? o, it was neither he nor Pinto really losing out, or both? They were bogged down with principles then. It was for Pinto like that, but she had said she'd 'know it should she meet the right one.' Similarly, with him. Did the fact then, irrespective of whether changes were to have actually been implemented to the end date, that there would only be another ten days or so remaining whereby she was still in social distancing under covid regulations in lockdown as he was too 'supposedly,' did that have any effect, if he was to return to what had been his job prior to furlough and she could start to go to places again? If of course, he hadn't indeed been persuaded to change his job. She was not and had not been of a mind to be concerned enough to ask. Optimistic and enthusiastic about what could happen, certainly within the weeks or if need be, months ahead. And did it involve him, not horribly or resentfully.

At that moment, a loud bang was heard coming from above her flat, as though a wooden clog had been dropped on the floor deliberately, then plop plop plop plop plop, tik tik tik tik tik, and then more plops, a staircase suddenly appeared outside the capsule. It looked as though it had come from somewhere high above and nothing to do with or connected or associated to the property Pinto was in, it came from somewhere high, way above through any clouds and way up far in the sky, or any glitter dust where diamond rain had hit and bounced reflectively from an asteroid, that was for sure! Then, whatever else it was, stood outside the capsule. At first Pinto thought it was a chess piece, a large chess piece, but it wasn't. It didn't move, it was a dark wood-looking tall oblong structure, object, or thing, of around five feet in height. But from where those in the capsule were, it looked enormous, and solid like a totem pole, but quite plain, so not really a totem pole at all, a strange totem pole, they, those in the capsule watched, and waited, they waited until way past fun tea- time and still nothing happened. Nothing happened at all, it just stood there towering away above them all. What if it were to topple over Pinto wondered, all of us would surely be no more. Beholder said, 'there is nothing we can do about it now, apart from wait and watch and maybe wait some more, even though it does block some of our view completely.' Maybe we should look at it she said that it is as though you had gone to the loo and forgotten to take your underwear down and it's the last pair you have clean,' with that, there was nothing anyone would be able to say, even if they could, if of course they could hear it at all, but they could not. It was then as though one of the occupants of the capsule could be heard laughing so much, the sound though, was coming from the very structure outside? Was it a large microphone of a kind? The fact was, that although it had properties of becoming a microphone, only in those very unusual circumstances, it was something quite unusual. The beholder and only because there were things about her- I did not know, didn't know what it was either but said nothing. She wasn't lying or misleading, she just could not give any, not the slightest or remotest indication, or say why, but there were some safety elements that although some may have been afraid slightly, she must believe with all her heart and all she was, that it would all be fine, with and despite all that had happened, she had to trust. On her mind and strangely was the thought that she had imagined before that Dum Dum birds were born in nests in trees, why she was thinking about it now, she found confusing, but then thought that really it could never be like that because of how very clumsy they were, their parents would be exhausted and if only from continually attempting to pick them up again. It would be a week or so though, before we, 'all of us,' would all realise what was happening. How bad was Pinto for saying nothing and keeping us all on tenterhooks and quite terrified, but she genuinely was stumped. So, she didn't really know at all what was happening, although she maintained a composure as though she did, and there were some other surprises too, and whether she liked it or not, also for her.

The following day, and as not much seemed to be happening with the wait regarding the lockdown procedures in place, and where the capsule was, whilst still it seemed, I certainly was puzzled, and wondered whether others were, because I did not know whether they knew or not, as to what the surprisingly "rather plain looking," very tall wood-like structure was. The beholder, or as they or we were in a place where time was still, so shall I give her a name, 'Pinto,' yes, I'll name her Pinto I'd thought then, or was it before? Would anyone really have noticed anyway? She was observed looking at it, just staring, totally focused and with no distraction, at it. She then said, "it can't just sit there like a huge lump of nothingness, or can it"? Who am I to suggest that it should and cannot, and as it seems to have positioned itself quite clearly, but it is blocking the view, having become the viewpoint? Why she did not think to relocate the capsule, I did not know, maybe she was afraid but unable and possibly because of experiences whether past or much more recent, to show it. Then from somewhere above way out of actual view, streaks of what resembled yellow paint swirled all the way down suddenly all around it? Pinto could see the top of it, or that edge of that side of it, but only if she lay on the floor of the capsule on her back and push so far that she was then unable to move any further, no-one then was allowed, to even consider wanting to leave the capsule, not that any of them could. Any doors, entrances or windows were locked down, secured, and bolted, no matter what was happening outside and however loud and whatever voices or sounds may or could at any point for then be heard. It would be like your mother staying at your grandparents' house for a few days and then whilst there, speaking to you on the telephone saying, "we all have to be in bed by eight-thirty every night." Nothing, sound-wise of any form, or any objects whether inanimate or not were permitted to enter the capsule, and it was all set on a secret back-dated timer, so there would be no skulduggery of any kind, by those who might seek to attempt whatever confusion some might attempt to believe they could achieve and by whatever or any means. The yellow streaks like a red flavoured rippling you might see in some ice cream cascaded down in swirl patterns and some even like helicopter wings.

'Premiere ascension du Lady Scott Chatelaine.'

Those tiniest of the brightest yellow helicopter wings that were a contrast to the slightly deeper yellow continually trickling ripples would then, the moment they touched the ground, as though the most delicate of watery mist icicles, would simply disappear before our eyes, we were looking at our reflections on the windows to the capsule too, but all were also quite focused. Pinto could hear piano keys almost, uncertain what to believe sometimes then, as the icicles touched the ground and felt quite cruel that presumable others could not, because their heads were motionless and she knew that no sound of interference could be heard by any of them or us, from within. Pinto whilst not wanting to seem a bore, did think though it was all a peculiar display. She stood up and leaned across totally, with her eyes almost pressed on the window or as though from her clutch bag she'd pulled some binoculars, or opera glasses, to better see just that little bit closer, and cautiously, what was happening. She lifted her right hand as though holding glasses and said, 'it's moving, it's doing something, something is happening,' as though none of the other occupants would be, or were aware, then as quiet as it was, apart from Pinto speaking, and her imagining tinkling of piano keys, if it was imagined, it started to quibble. Like a person who had sat down and was quite uncomfortable and then attempted to re-position themselves in a seat, or even on a bus wearing a large hat with some brightly coloured red, orange, and green feathers in it. Very slightly it shook from the base, then just as suddenly as any of the movement that had happened did, it just stopped. Nothing happened, even the trickling stopped in its place and the remaining helicopter icicle wings dispersed. They must have then waited thirty seconds or so, until small red polka dots started to become released from the top of the structure. At least that was how it looked, these were like small red peas and they moved quite slowly, once they touched the ground they bounced, oh, there were quite a few of those, thousands in fact, but although they travelled slowly there were far too many for anyone to count, after they'd bounced, they too just vanished once they again hit the ground. Then as though getting out of a very wet swimsuit the whole thing started to shake. And that was all it did. Then moments after, a white cloud formed around its base as if it were a rocket ship about to take off, there wasn't a lot of cloud or what resembled cloud, then that too, simply disappeared either into thin air or even into the ground beneath, that was so quick it was difficult to know exactly. In fact, it wasn't easy to tell what was happening at all, it was cloud-like, it certainly though didn't float upward like some clouds sometimes have or did, sometimes had, or do, and that was very certain! Then the brown very wood–looking object jumped off the ground, only a few feet, and only as high as the cloud that had formed at its base, it turned left and landed in the exact same spot as it had been before, but if it had been before facing North, it was now facing East, then nothing, nothing at all. Pinto was aware that it made no further sound either whilst doing it, and there was no explanation, none whatsoever. Surely there was something to happen she thought, there had to be something, but no, there was not. That day though, greater distances were placed between the capsule and anything else, Pinto herself didn't even realise that had happened, or that even if fearfully, yes fearfully, she had somehow also been quite tantalised by more-so what had not happened. She did wonder though, as she stared out of that window at it, she did wonder, and all she could think then was, 'I don't care what it is, or who, or what it may think it is, if it thinks, the sneaks, if it relates to in any way, or if they are, should they attempt, they are not going to fool me.'

She forgotten that she had made a garlic, apple, chopped tomato, sundried tomato, oregano, red lentil with the slightest dashes of salt and some ground chilli, not bigger that the size of a slice of haricot bean scratchy lick sticker that shot out of a tray at the bottom of a screen once she'd touched the ingredient imagery she wanted to use, the others on board would remain unaffected, none the wiser, that it had even been back then very early breakfast time at all, as though they were still snoring or just asleep in the land of loveliness and big cuddle times. Pinto named that scratchy lick 'Pear-skinned smaller Braeburn with texture of Russett.' She only licked it once but thought to herself 'lip-smacking and very yummy yummy tasty.'

Although the capsule was still in a shirt pocket, as if it didn't and to neither be obvious or to matter to anyone at all, in some places such, if poor behaviour could have been frowned upon and considered possibly as quite rude indeed considering some of the occupants, the capsule was quite invisible to a normal naked eye and where it had been placed was well out of harms reach or way by anyone. Suspended in air only one centimetre above the ground, and motionless. If anything, even a three-eyed grampilooper were to go over it whilst rolling across the ground to find a blue lawn to flatten, because that was what they did. The capsule would neither feel it, or be damaged by it, or even moved by it, if it did, neither could the capsule, from where it was it seemed, be affected by winds or breezes, hot or cold. Unfortunately, though, there was a three-eyed grampilooper that would now have a very slight dent in it, so somewhere there would too, soon be a blue lawn with very small tufts, but they were very fast at repairing themselves so it thankfully wouldn't be a tuft bluer lawn for too long. Cylindrical and a little like a chocolate Swiss roll at each end, the grampilooper, certainly the three eyed kind, at both ends of their cylindrical shape, had a nose, a long nose, yes, a nose at each end and three eyes. Their eyes close once on a blue lawn, they are blue to them anyway, they puff out invisible glitter-dust, the dust forces their ends to open because there is often so much of it, almost as though spluttering out, it's not easy for them poor things, then they, their noses, decide whose turn it is, sometimes for days they'll argue before they decide, , as often where the lawn smells the same at either side, they cannot decide properly, or as easily as they might like to, then once their decision is made, eventually, and after they again confer to make sure the decision is correct, the nose of the side whose turn it is digs itself slightly at the lawn and then sends a message back saying how nice it is and then once dug in, the cylinder rolls around and forms a perfectly accurate and neat circle, these circles are used at then a later time, or an earlier time, by the hairy characters, Pinto referred to them in her imagination as the Bracken Huddlers who have a very special thing that they do involving fur shaking and prisms, when its right for them to do it, and it obviously had been a right time then, or almost, and because a grampilooper had rolled over the capsule in the first place, although the resumption of their unique tasks would not be realised, if at all, until around about midnight or just before, to be as precise as it would be possible, possibly on the 27th of July and would that coincide with other things somehow scheduled, and how? If at all? If for example Pinto was herself unaware, or was she?

Still able to rescue messages during this arduous process and with then, only a week to go, although that week was eventually then suspended for another three, Pint received a text from the guy she'd met the year before, requesting that he could be permitted to come to visit her the following day early. - He had also told her he was back at his job now. The suggested time seemed a little early for Pinto, and because she had somehow believed that such may not happen for at least another week yet, but in a romanticism way and totally, she put safely the capsule to one-side and ensuring absolute safety in that, being sure to, and doubly sure, and then agreed. She then had to pace fast through the land of Black Snow, it wasn't a nice place and awash with dangers for Pinto, especially noise, from crying, yes crying, usually a dragon, and thankfully, not because it's brothers or sisters had been removed or slain. It was because with the black snow there, and the rain, and the rain there sometimes, and often it's like black pearls, yes, and those black pearls make dragons cry, and especially, certainly the dragons in Black Snow Land. The reason is not exactly known, though some believe it's because those dragons don't have eyelashes like some others do, neither would it have been known then, that where a dragon had cried so much and started sneezing wheezing and coughing too, that some spit landed on a purfy-mush, it looks like a stone and a mushroom too but it is neither, it was where Pinto rested her head a while just to have a brief moment of rest, she hadn't even noticed it on her hairgrip, why should she? But it turned out to be not such a difficult task that day at all, there were the usual floating and triangles, all quite silver coloured, balloon-like type of creations to get past, falling or floating down from somewhere and in a perfectly straight line, they'd touch the ground, then back up they'd go, each of those had a different coloured quite fluffy pompom on top of them. Pinto didn't sleep that night, all night she waited and waited. No message came through and he didn't turn up anyway, the blessed girl was hurting beyond hurt by this and at this point of time, it was extremely upsetting for her, and whereas she'd usually have cried, this time she could not. Her own tears would not now fall, they, if it was or were they, between them somehow had even caused changes there, the radio then, playing softly in the background, was playing a Tchaikovsky piano concerto, this seemed to almost mirror her inability to cry, and the surprise that she couldn't when usually she would have, and probably only because she would have before. It was a good sign, as was the fact that the Covid restrictions had been lowered too. She quietly and sadly, if truth be known, returned through the mire and didn't notice the balloons this time, although they were there, nothing had changed, she returned alone back to the place where the capsule was, and was happy in a way, - maybe not so happy, even if only because of that dragon crying so much, an because it was how he planned to commence his return to work with her, as something of a joy and happy it seemed then to want to include her like that, but alas, it was simply not to be. And she'd have lost her virginity had he come too, she thought then, and even if at that what would have only amounted to a very quick hour, even if as an excuse by him, amidst a morning rush, to Pinto, it would have constituted as 'that special moment,' special enough anyway, unfortunately, or fortunately, and even if not for Pinto, that was an experience and circumstance that others, or someone else had utilised she thought, although to surmise that she thought it would be a very real and quite as generous understatement? So, was it special enough a moment, would that not depend not so much on others, but on the application by Pinto herself? Even if it would not be until around June 25th that she'd consider things quite like that? But then, hey, it wasn't as though Pinto hadn't learned, not that she'd been obviously taught it, not in a then perceived conventional sense, about time and motion, as a very young child.

Dragons from Black Snow Land don't like black pearl rain because they get laughed at by the clumsy Dum Dum bird when they attempt a landing in slush, not only do they loathe being laughed at, and to frustrate them more, they cannot breathe fire at the Dum Dum bird because of their use, - and not only that, but because the great great grandmother of the King and Queen always loved them so.

Where the man, the beholder 'Pinto,' had met a month or so earlier who then after was greeted outside by one of the neighbours, and together they then did soiree the remainder of that day away together, it was just because he did not show, not to be any different to as it had been then, except the same neighbour who had met him then, although arrangements had been made between them, overheard a whisper on the wind, and left the evening before to this time intercept him, and distract him, and then to finish off, with cakes and jellies at another of the neighbours friends' somewhat makeshift hovel after, but he liked roughing it, as he called it, so it added to the fun, and they liked it that way anyway, so there would thankfully never be any real urgency to change that. Like denying a glorious mud-bath to an elephant, it was something no-one in their right minds would want to ever really consider. They were meant to follow the route 1967, but instead, the beholder, 'Pinto,' had got to the road signs beforehand, just in and within a split second and had caused them in their car, to have their destination changed, instead they took the route 1958 where in their, or her, open top convertible car, alter direction, they not only were met with an unusually they remarked upon, longer than normal drive, but also with a dumpster truck that had, because when or as they had gone through the fictitious or changed route that of route 1958, unbeknownst to them, they, and their car, had also taken on the image of a manure holding point? Neither were they ever to realise from then on, and certainly that neighbour, that she was to smell as to and of then after, all of too, her family, like manure, and especially to him, and would others they all, in the furtherance of what their agendas had been, or should they be of similar objectives or motivated by. Neither could or would it matter how much perfume or scent they applied on any of themselves, whatever they wore or whatever clothing they had or even if or when they bathed, even if not in sweat, even if of, 'the moment.'

So, however they bathed, or in what, the main thing was that it would never ever be or now become the riches they craved so dearly – neither and could anyone tell them. It would be an odour so foul, that the only explanation, could be, whether diagnosed or not, it would too, the odour, remain for them and others should Pinto choose, and because some obviously enjoyed that 'chosen' feeling, 'untreatable.' A question that remained, was would Pinto, could Pinto? Pinto did think that they should never consider it as an embrace of any kind, or hold it for the same reasons, she hoped that should their reputations if they had any, become soiled, that they'd never be forgotten kindly. It wasn't that anyone would forget such a smell anyway, but whether Pinto was thinking like that I could not ascertain. She did say think however that she hoped they would not smell like any gardener she'd ever had the pleasure to meet, only in the worst way possibly, and that was sadder maybe as such an odour might be quite feint, but just enough she thought, enough yes to warn others, or alert them to surprises in store, especially upon any to interactional involvement, and yes, why not, she thought, between them and anyone else, should they come to within two metres of anyone else.

Yes, their convertible car had reached the dead end at the old Cobblers Farm, or Older Cobbles, or similar, the road signs all looked slightly different in how their wording appeared in that part of Pasturelands, so none were ever totally sure, oh many attempts were made to tidy up, but some just changed the signs all back again when no-one was looking. By that wall, too, could be seen only hands, trying to reach from beneath what could only be described as something huge dark and slightly grassy and very moist and steamy, and it wasn't even a cold day there, in fact the heat was searing hot. With their car parked nose against a tall wall, and on each side thick heavy dark wooden sleepers, similar to those used on railway tracks but bigger and heavier, maybe five high and on either side of their car, just enough space to create that perfect spot, that quite perfect parking space, for them, and yes, too there was even spaces alongside equidistant, room for cars and their occupants just like them. Pinto looked on and thought 'yes, you reach as high as you can for those stars.' All of this was alongside some long glasshouses, they certainly had a carful on their way back, and thinking it was route 1967 too, and not realizing, they hadn't noticed the difference at all, as though quite blinkered in fact. Another thing about that trip, the more frequently that'd decided to take it, the more fragrant they'd become, so, Pinto was giving an amazing opportunity really, and Pinto herself hadn't even noticed her own kindness excelling. She was thoughtfully thankful that they'd be remembered, even if by only their life choices and personal standard. Of, course we all knew that preferred would be a nice perfume or scent, even if natural. It didn't mean she didn't like the smell of manure, she loved it, especially for roses, but not to personally sleep on, or with.

Pinto had overheard that they had been staying at a huge mansion, and had visualised them sitting by a pool, or a young lad, the man she'd been seeing was elsewhere presumably swimming, as there was much splashing about, the lad seemed to be alone, smiling, and happy, and just watching, unaffected by it. The day after was horrified though, as if her hair had gone curly and blonde during the night suddenly as she now knew which of her neighbours had been removing the flowers and snapping the prize blooms from and in her window boxes, -and why. Pinto hadn't recognised the lad, there was no reason why she should, or would, it was obvious he did, or they did. He was the son of the person he'd been staying with in recent times, and who he had been taking to school sometimes some months earlier. Or, a child belonging to another attendee, or one of those involved with Pinto's neighbours' children's club during lockdown. It had enabled some group meetings to take place. The guess was that although there was a pale blue background, the pool was not associated to a mansion as such, it could just as easily have been a blue painted backdrop or painted wall in an area that housed a pool and even with a large wire fence around it on the outside. Very possibly, Pinto thought. They'd acquired a property to use, or friends had loaned it to them, or they were guests, invited and staying there. Amazing, she thought to herself again, quite amazing!

Pinto the Virgin had never considered herself a road builder, but she too wondered about carving roads now, or had she all along been aware, and of the damage some it seemed were intent it seemed, on causing or somehow protecting her, whether she approved or not? If that wasn't all to contend with, suddenly from the wood- looking object begun to resound, "why can we smell horse poo everywhere," yes, the fragrance had too permeated the capsule's air-ducts too, somehow, just what was happening? It was true, there was a vague odour it seemed now, everywhere, Pinto became rather embarrassed and hoped or believed that her blushing would not have been noticeable, or was thankful that it was not, although to be honest, it would be more like deciding to leave your flat with untidy-Ish hair, and realising that some neighbours in a flat above and one of them being a handsome chap, and his partner, they look a lovely couple, Pinto always thinks that, anyway, imagine if she'd decided to take a quick jaunt up a couple of flights of stairs in the building where she lives, only to bump into that chap on a landing above and then embarrassedly walk down saying nothing, wondering if the neighbour had thought she was mad, and then standing in front of her front door to put her flip flops back on as he walked past, both Pinto and he in total silence, where usually they would say hello, as though he, and with a quite bemused look, wondering what was going on? Well, it was that kind of embarrassing, and Pinto in a lace frilled dressing gown too, in the afternoon on a Saturday. Naturally, she'd initially believed as though not isolated, and then realised. Could it have been that it jumped back a generation or two, or three, and then re-surfaced through her having met the boy she'd met and his subsequently having met the others? It seemed to all be becoming something of a puzzle, a puzzle that apart from anything else would need to be resolved, hopefully it, the fragrant air shall pass, she thought. Then the wood-like structure seemed to speak again, "I like horses," it said, it sounded just like a person who was pinching their nostrils tightly together, "but this is all rather a little too much." Yes, it was, or had become again something similar to a loud microphone or sound conveyance device or a speaker, and possibly even for the capsule occupants, all Pinto thought was how a German dictator generations before had used 2.6 million horses , but here no animals were harmed, even if this had been realised on 26th June, but on that day, many would have been busy watching a football match, the Pasturelands team were for the first time in a while, certainly where pitches had many spectators, were playing a game, Pinto would never have known that if she hadn't overheard it whilst at a cobblers the very same day, the soles of her red faux suede shoes had split right across both on the evening when she had been drinking and was brought home by the police van. So, "no animals had been harmed" in this process. Pinto thought how it all, really must be A1 or top notch for efficiency, only moments before she'd sent a message to the fellow saying, "we aren't going to get anywhere if you don't come to see me," it obviously had been as though he was showing no effort at all, it would be difficult only to let go of all that had happened between then since almost eighteen months. His phone had been switched off for three hours, she was already feeling somehow with an odd inkling, that their fate, or their fates were inevitable.

She started to believe of herself that it was not her intellect that he possibly did not want, but without being discrediting to herself or without confidence, she did feel that what he was accustomed to or had been now by way of experiences or choice was far more than she could ever be and that in, or concerning those factors she personally somehow lacked, this she did understand and without question. Pinto had, regarding the 'fragrance' issue, and appreciation to horsepower, also decided that it was akin to analytically having say, a thousand-dollar credit limit on a credit card and reaching the six hundred dollar spend mark at last and with regard to paying back more promptly that you may or could otherwise have, to the point where your available credit at least was more than that owed at last, of her own situation in the first two weeks of May, hers had stuck half-way for months, it was tough. and things after had not significantly improved, but she was becoming way more attentive than she ever thought she could before, and far more cautious. Then at precisely three hours after, bearing in mind that just before his phone switched off, she sent him a text, this time it said, "if it's my punishment somehow that I have to be available to meet you whenever you want, then it is, whether you or anyone refers to me as the virgin, or not." Yes, she'd been feeling guilty, or guilt ridden for thinking that they meant more than was necessary, or that in some way it meant she was somehow different to anyone else, whether her circumstance had any uniqueness or not, didn't everyone's she thought? She also wondered how, if others were perceiving her as this, and even if she was disguised, and sometimes heavily, whether it might have prevented him and caused a barrier between them, so maybe it was about horses more, she again thought, or certainly about getting off higher ones. At 17.11PM a response to her phone came, it read, "I'm trying to meet you soon."! Her response then was, "ok, when it's possible, say if you can," yes, a short swift reply. Then he replied immediately, "I'm not sure yet, maybe tomorrow." She thought instantaneously about all that had taken place recently concerning him, and all that had happened concerning herself, and the capsule and its contents and of how in times past he'd seemed, whether deliberate or not, to be able to extract a power source, she also knew that "tomorrow," was Wednesday and that he'd just ad a busy weekend, and where whether again inadvertently of not, a main contributor of an energy source, if it were appropriate to consider that, had been none other than herself. She fully imagined that he'd suggest coming early the next day, very early indeed, but having already struck, was there need to? Firstly, she confirmed to herself that it was safe, and especially with the capsule and contents to consider, nothing was going to invade there, it would be then, that she felt something on her shoulder, she stood perfectly still, rather like one of those dreams that she had only once where a person was massaging her back and she actually started to think she could like it too much as the person somehow wedged his foot or feet in between her legs from behind with his hands firm on her person, but this time, and however gay a day to some it could seem, it pulled itself up onto Pintos' shoulders, she could see its eyes but was afraid to look directly, it had long rabbit or donkey-like but very pointed ears, and whiskers, those were twitching almost as though it was somehow amused, the eyes of whatever it was were moving from left to right and right to left and back again, then up and down and down and up and then again back again, as though looking for something, but quite mysteriously, or wanting to give or create that impression, that was for sure, what it actually was, was as indeterminable then, but Pinto knew it was doing things, something, to dispel or alter kindly, in a kind way Charles Bonnet Syndrome, or maybe it was a test, but not a gamble or deal stuck, or that could have been, rather a sign of a kind, whether it would be possible then or not, few and certainly Pinto would never then know, or even if she would then have seen a sign at all, if it was? But it was nice of whatever it was to be just so very kind she thought. Pinto at that moment then, recalled some deeds and an amulet that she'd been given in handed in times past, quite a time before, certain somehow though, that all of this was nothing to do with, or connected with any of that, the deeds displayed were nothing of property she thought, but of actions, and to display possibilities, so her reaction now was or seemed for her under the circumstances now, quite justified, and the amulet? Nothing but a master key to many rooms, it would certainly have been nothing then for sure, of anything that at that moment in time could be used constructively, but did Pinto quietly just place it, as only a reminder, if for herself somehow, and how, if relevant at all, it was certainly not ever a key that would crack open the combination here and neither would the presenter have been aware then that there might be a safe of certain somewhat 'untrivial' in reality, to Pinto kinds, to be cracked, not ever would he, or 'they'? All this had done was to put further security by Pinto, upon that unknown of by he and others, and those known to him and of or by. The faces of some from Pasturelands who would only then begin to realize, that whilst they were out enjoying fun together, with new conquests would be seen. The horror upon or with and in the look upon their faces as they realised they would never be able to turn back to attempt to intervene – or t intrude, or to see what they'd missed and out on, or to gain any leverage either would never now be from outside gained, even if they believed somehow then, that what they believed they had, had been nothing somehow in some circumstances, to what they believed they had lost, as confusing as sometimes it was even for dear Pinto, and could never now gain, neither could they be touch or become part of anything on that bridge, however they might try, but by the time they'd returned to Pasturelands because of their playing together, the distance between those on the bridge and those particular persons at Pasturelands would be able realistically and honestly, not for a while anyway, truthfully, not under any circumstances be gained or regained, It could make them very ill indeed, as they would realize more, but there would presumably again be nothing they could really do, nothing at all! She also thought of air assaults and anti- assault missiles, and of covering ground quickly, and preventing recapturing of locations that before may have almost rendered void, and not necessarily of anyone's doing, 'knowingly,' although who really knew what influences could attempt to wheedle their way through the annals of time somehow, and what form might they take and what influences might they use in the furtherance of what then could have become for some a very personal objective, or even a mission and even of sacrifice. This did not please Pinto at all, especially if part of some stupid blackmail attempt or emotional trickery gameplay, and this would be certainly realised as in considered, or the latter part of, by Pinto, on 19th July. Also, all that would be remembered by them, whether this was considered then or on the 19th was another matter, but all that would be remembered by them, Pinto thought, as they were or had become predatory, and mimicking constantly by word and then deed, and of the somewhat fragility of the gentlest trickle of water they'd heard before, and seen going under that bridge, they'd never actually again, because they'd never be invited to, not by Pinto. And with each hour, and every minute and every act of theirs, even if attempting in a group to gain in distance, it would be the reverse. How could they try to recover, if they even could, it might be that they'd try to give that impression, or in the meantime, hook in as many others as they could, to try to entangle others again emotionally, making it more difficult for accuracy of absolute decisiveness and action, should such become or necessary, could Pinto be that harsh? Did she need to if those in the capsule were safe? Could or would she, if she needed to, to keep them safe? Would she? And how? If warranted. What if they attempted to give the impression that none of it mattered, would the truth be that they'd realise that there was nothing they could do now anyway. Just what had they blown, if they'd blown anything, Pinto wondered, oh she wondered, she wondered so terribly and in the early hours of the 20th way after, that she thought how she had just about had it up to here,' on the 20th of July that day, and the possibility that they were sacrificing anything, made her shudder, 'as if, 'coldly.

But his last messages there, back then though, were at 17.57PM, and at 18.05PM, and it was to be her concluding moment, thinking of everything and or how she wanted him so much. She replied too at 18.05PM, with 'simply not possible for tomorrow, sorry.' She then lay down and thought of what she'd said, and why. Would it, her action, in the grand scale of things, unbeknown to him, who was never now said no to, certainly by women, that time to make every amendment to safeguard implemental furtherance of another, or of the wider objective, that of recovery and sustenance. To her, Pinto, it felt as though she was giving her life, because deep down within her very soul, she knew she wanted him so very much, she could though say nothing more. Nothing, she lay in complete silence. She just lay in total quiet, until she dozed off and then woke up again four hours after. She stood up and stared across at the wood-looking object it now looked as though a white coloured gas or smoke was exuding from holes up its sides, or was she imagining it, having thought as she'd done only hours before, it made her feel sad, not though that it was happening, or seemed to be, she was not afraid, and there were things she could do. Whether to or not, was to matter. She hadn't noticed the small holes on its sides when it faced the other way, it wasn't possible, or facing them now. It lifted itself without a sound from the ground very slowly, then turned again, ninety degrees and then just as before, re-positioned itself in the exact same spot as before, now one hundred and eighty degrees turned, from how it originally was. So, she was now looking at the back of it. It didn't look any different than the other side, and the strange smoke by then had stopped. It then just stood there, doing nothing, motionless. Oh, she wondered what it was, she really did, but most of all, would he understand that she does odd things or has reasons to sometimes, and that her own reasons are valid too. Or did nothing of it matter anyway to him? Another thing she'd thought that day or had been wondering about was how in the past few, or maybe a month, every night he was tucked up in bed early, no going on phones at all, not even during the night now, and before, the opposite had been habits long-standing, also that he would not even go on the phone until past 09.30AM daily, unless he was arranging a meet, and that it had also been a month now since that happened, he was being a very good boy for something, or someone, or was being extremely careful, to be at home, every single night certainly after 20.00hrs, and uncontactable. Between 17.57PM and 20.00hrs, there would never, no matter who he knew, apart from Pinto, be enough time, nor the wear-with- all, available in such a short space of time, to make up that much lost ground, definitely not. She also though it was frightening to be thinking in such a way regarding or concerning a person she loved. But, consoled herself with the fact that how he was, or his background as was hers, was merely a series of catalysts of other things, then to happen to facilitate changes, or furtherance, and it was not always in the best interests of mankind, despite thoughts concerning, if anyone even did, or neglect or ignorance, or selfishness, greed, appetite, living, situations, or anything, no-one would have realised, maybe a few, or guessed some elements, but what could they do, especially if they were or had become like dogs playing with a squirrel, but barking then up quite the wrong tree. She then thought of nice things, like red poppies and of white cliffs and of blue birds, as though it, was somehow a reminder again particularly as so many were and are, fortunate to have survived Covid-19. Including, for Pinto she liked still to think, however it looked or however some might want to suggest or imply, her own who was for her, a quite special man. At 22.57 a message came through, all it said was "x."

Some twenty minutes after, could be heard very really, the sound of many aircraft propellers, as though possibly maybe hurricanes or spitfires were taking off, or flying nearby or almost overhead, not that she was familiar with plane types, but it was not a sound to in any way be fearful of, on the contrary. Pinto couldn't believe it at first, and had to really strain her ears, yes, she thought she was having aural hallucinations. Somehow, it was though quite real? But such planes rarely flew these days, only on very special occasions, and in recent decades it hadn't been heard of that it would be at night, probably she thought, a nicer sign somehow, hopefully anyway. How did we get into this? Pinto was or had briefly started to want to become more protective of her chest area, so she then put a thin sweater on.

#

Pinto had been thinking about the Cobbles as some of the signposts had called, or Cobbles Farm, or the grange and farm there, she knew that place well because they would venture there as children, it seemed a strange place for routes or a route to finish, but too, she remembered and knew what was known as route 953; and because she remembered the signs on the wall saying, "Route 967 ends here," There were off and side-roads, En route, but if you didn't know them too well. On the other side of the wall, they'd started on 967 and veered by accident onto 958 – But we knew it was no accident, on the other side of the wall was route road 952, it ran off to the right and was not visible from the other side of the wall at all. A totally pained wall on the 952 side, sometimes it might be easy to wonder who'd bother to do all that, to paint it, along the whole length of wall, but some did. She imagined that she'd found a coin on the ground and popped it into her pocket, then back at the capsule, she'd wanted to think before finding that coin, that she hoped the driver of that convertible car might be more careful next time, to think about how or what might happen next. And if then, at 22.57, he'd sent a message, however vague, it was because he could, maybe he was sensing his freedom now.

Despite being back in, or part of the capsule integrity, it seemed possibly as it was May 12th, that some interference was achievable from external sources. It would be 16.00hrs that Pinto then arranged from within the capsule that an invisible cave was formed around it, as a further security measure, because there were then before restrictions were attemptively to then be relaxed. It had been a difficult night and a night when it appeared to be darker somehow, when it was not, fear had caught up briefly with Pinto. She had stopped taking the prescribed medicine now, that had been prescribed by the local medical practice, at her own request, - it was the effect of reverting to normal, or the thought of insecurities. - she had visualised some of those she knew and had telephoned the medical practice to speak to the Doctor whose name was on the prescription, but they were not working that day. She thought the person seemed quite short and very rude, but also knew well, that some like to give that impression. It was though she thought, the kind of abruptness that makes your back kind of stand up on its own with annoyance and your chest stick out so, as you breathe with an awkward quirk-some also awareness should doubt as to professionalism or quibbles regarding standards be allowed to form, so then, whilst it was a concern, the thought of it soon passed. The next day she was put though on the telephone to the doctor, where she mentioned that she had stopped taking the medication and stated reasons why. The Doctor was very thorough and about to attend a meeting anyway, - after questioning the reasoning it was eventually agreed that although Pinto would need to be she'd need to be 'talked-through,' another medication of anti-depressants would be prescribed, Pinto having explained that she thought she'd been on a lull. The Doctor agreed to telephone a couple of hours after, and Pinto said, 'enjoy your appointment, Doctor. 'Pinto was asked, what about your aggressors? She replied, 'it's ok, I imagined them when I saw them today, as though in a play, and what role would I cast them kindly as.' She had indeed, she imagined one of them as The Prince of Pasturelands, and said, 'Oh, dear Prince Despoter has a new camel, as they were getting into a car, - they drove off. The person who'd hear it or for whom such a remark was concerning, had been the only one not inside their car at that time, the door did slam closed so hard but not before they paced and huffed near the car, very angry and upset about something, obvious too, that their scraggly hair seemed to look even more scraggly that day, not that it was real hair, it resembled stringy straw and was similarly coloured too and as Pinto observed, you could almost smell them, almost, Pinto sprayed some air purifier as it almost came into and through the windows, such was the degree of their anger and their chatting outside. As they sped off, Pinto thought, 'oh how lovely, they weren't to find Prince Despoter though, in fact the likelihood that they ever would again was becoming vaguer by the second, with every slam of any door by them in fact, and every horrid unfair act by them, or theirs, even if they considered it funny, I only made things worse, and it was very possibly as irreversible as their behaviour. That person, an elder relation of the Hargrosse's, Pintos' horridest neighbours, their hat with the very large flower on top of it, bounced across the beam of the car door as she'd got into it, before the door closed and all you could hear was "sweets or lamb, I must have sweets or lamb." Why, or how, in a car baffled Pinto, a boiled sweet if they were anticipating a long journey and felt nauseas, she could understand that, but lamb? She did wonder, tenderised with mint, or maybe with some honey and ground white pepper, or ground black pepper but not too much, but honestly, she had no idea and did not want to guess and because she'd never eaten lamb, not that she wanted to recall then, that day, at that moment.

Pinto then recognised that the ruder voice of that hospital receptionist was still almost as though playing repetitively on her mind, but was a couple of new camels, though they did spit, you could see it, as they said things loudly that bore no relevance connectively to what the conversation had been, that they seemed to want anyone who'd listen and were intent to force anyone who did not want to, to overhear. The language was the same as most others, but the dialect different, Pinto was not interested in hearing what they were doing or about anyone they believed they knew who Pinto also knew. So thankful indeed now that their car had driven off. As too, the voice that receptionist teetered with continued to say, "that doctor prescribes whatever she asks for," as though she'd been listening in on the conversation, of course, that was not possible, because the doctor had telephoned Pinto back from the office telephone number after the call had been put through by that receptionist. Then an hour after, their car re-arrived, and those inside got out, the stemmed yellow flower again hitting the top of the car again and almost waving about as if to say 'hi everyone, we're back, 'as they got out of the car, Pinto heard them say, "it's much better to feel included rather than as though you do not exist." It was obvious that this had been something of an oversight on Pinto's mind, and that these slight but real changes were not all quite so negative at all. It was or could have been yet another slight murmuring of a start of what was to become the three days that followed, and as many believed, the final day of relaxing of restrictions. Pinto could not get the sight of that flower and those fluffy dice moving about in the front window of that car off her mind, but the doctor kindly did telephone again and after much discussion, as much as Pinto would have preferred to commence on a higher dose of medication, and because of the time it takes for the anti-depressants to react, the doctor's decision was that Pinto commence on the lower dosage.

#

Some could ask, what had prompted Pintos' decision about activities concerning the capsule, it was, or is indeed, a long story, but we might have to recall that Pinto herself had been a very prominent image on websites globally until she met the person she was to meet. Pinto wasn't a gambler and was analytical, so many things had to be weighed up, including the actions of the chap or why, could there have been possibly an over-riding element that had not been picked up on, and what could be done so as not to arouse suspicion, if there was any slight possibility at all, - and how far could, however horrific, some situations had become too, for those situations then to be applied as a smoke screen for other matter or situations to raise their heads or surface, or just do as they were, or could have been intended. And with each action or cross-section, other possible reactions or circumstances. Even then, it could still have been possible, for security reasons potentially, to access or consider what might have been going on in the foreground and background too, as for the centre-stage, who really knows apart from Pinto, would different people find or discover different narratives and just what those be. How complex was it all, or was it for dear Pinto, just another very normal day?

#

Pinto would be faced with a dilemma upon getting out of bed, the night before, unable to move and in pain just to get to her own pillow, and noises of people moving around, like three ants running along a bath and up a wooden doorframe and the other down the side of the bath and then disappearing as though none of them had ever really been there before at all, or had only been noticed once a quite unusual light maybe, and because of what dear Pinto was, had been switched on. But maybe it was just a normal regular lightbulb anyway, she, Pinto, thought of them and smiled. maybe. But she, far too exhausted really, from that Wednesday and Thursday, that had now been and gone. There was, when she checked her phone having woken up at exactly midnight, it said 00.00 on her phones' clock, so it must have been, no indication that the guy she'd met had checked his phone, as monotonous as it often was becoming then, she had wanted to think 'check-out,' rather than checkmate, but was unable to, as crass or ludicrous as it seemed, and with his phone still switched off. She dozed off again until 01.0AM and then noticed however obsessively it could seem, that the messages at his end had been read. In her last message then it had said, 'another day, lining them up for you, and another day with nothing for me, soon all of this will end, as my own and the time of freedom for many soon begins. Three days or so from now and this lockdown., a prison-cell for me since more than fifteen months, hopefully with each day now draws to a close.'

She was now as though having been presented to the highest court in the land, now to hear, "they caused you so much pain and yet you showed them kindness," to which she could neither smile, nor respond. Instead, she did think however, that if they knew much more closely of her being a virgin of such a kind, luckily somehow, even if by odd happenings and unluckily because there were times when she wanted, especially after 27th June, to just get someone around, anyone, and just do it quietly for the sake of getting it, that deed, if it were to be considered as such, out of the way and with no fuss. It would achieve nothing if they knew she thought, presuming they did not, and not to imply either-way, it would only vindicate a present angle on things, and I would be nothing more to them than a pawn she though, - and a helpless one at that, simply playing and paying into their hideous and unscrupulous endeavour and personal deceit of me, and with arrogance. Then if I were not a virgin anymore, this would tell them not that I cannot, because I was forced or cajoled into it, rather like if you heard a person on a phone saying, "I'm not a virgin, I am natural," and yes, or that by my own actions maybe, I myself decided not to just lie back and take it from them repeatedly time and time again, not from them anymore, she thought, not for another single moment. For this, anyone could think of sovereignty, and country or certainly a citizenship Pinto thought to herself. Unperturbed by it all and staring thoughtfully across a pale grey Formica-topped table at five books, a vase of a few smaller pink, reddish and white carnations and a white ceramic unplugged lamp with its cream-coloured shade, and with daylight appearing, and her seeing what were her wet clothes from washing, hung on wooden hangers, now resemblant certainly of stiff cardboard where they'd dried, and the pungent aroma coming from her loins, what was that she thought, well she hadn't washed for a few days she then remembered, tragic Pinto, how sad she'd become then, spraying room spray onto her clothes, most days she could and would though change her underwear and her nightdress or clothes generally, and all, even if she did still manage to squeeze out a very slight smile, sometimes. She decided to do nothing, it is now, what day is it she wondered? It was a Friday. The time was 05,40AM and all that could be heard was a bird outside, no other sounds, a bird that had said good morning to the world only fifteen minutes before. At least her tearful eyes had now dried, not necessarily feeling older but staider and more resolute that ever before, and with a different kind of determination today somehow. - though for what, it would just be too early to say. She now could hear the bird gently cooing, but it was not so near to where she sat. Regarding her thoughts on relinquishing herself personally of her virgin-ship, if it could be described in that way, or ever should, she alone considered, what would I do if he were here now. As much as she'd love to have his company, and to be with him and to feel that he was physically there with her. Even if laying on a couch or asleep, that she was how she still was, was not a problem now for her at all. He wasn't here or in the same actual space, but she thought, she hoped he was still fine. As then she heard a very young bird chirping as though in a nest in the rafters, it instead of calming her, would cut, until she compartmentalized, even though not for more than a month after, through her like a knife. She then remembered how days earlier, a man could be heard outside saying, 'if she leaves, the birds will go too.' She overheard the same thing being said again the day after, then in the distance she heard what could only be described as a policeman's' metal pea-whistle, from Victorian times, one solitary, as though maybe three streets away, if she was in a street. The fact was, that they had questioned it, and not of herself, presuming that they or those persons or that man, referred to Pinto, this demonstrated a tenacity and choice option to her, to express such a concern, that there would be such a care, - this, she thought, should save future interests, however in her own thoughts, should they- at point in time, seem altered. She recalled the bird-lady of Arransby-Hortley, with her own form of flower that adorned her floppy large hat, and her almost floor-length brown woollen double-breasted coat that was always buttoned up even on a baking hot day, and yes, she thought in kindness, how she hoped she was well, and hopefully, as a mark of respect and appreciation too, and yes, of course Pinto smiled, and of course, somehow, the bird-lady of Arransby-Hortley, although now giving out not white broken-off pieces of bread to the birds, still did smile very slightly back. Then she heard another voice, like that some might wonder, of such as akin to a dear old friend as maybe being called dear Eliza herself, "and give them geraniums a real damn good soak, they'll thank you for it," she said. There was not much more she could think to say at that point then or just after. Within a short space of time, she would be considering her own comment regarding being or feeling "staid," that in some circumstances or situations was what it was all about? Not always feeling obliged to return to the exact same place, could that also have been why some had difficulty sticking to the regulations regarding Covid-19, she knew that her mind was wandering slightly, to have been it seemed to her briefly then, 'thinking quite so charitably.' It wasn't so much about the imprisonment but more about restrictions regarding other freedoms, as if it were a high boredom threshold, or something like that. So, in some, could the restrictions that everyone was expected to endure then, yes, actually yield other results in other ways, even though an indirect consequence of. But where does that place then, those that refused. Should some be glad that they had formed somehow, credible excuses or reasons, despite Pintos' thoughts earlier during the outbreak, and her attempts to come to terms with things that then, she certainly did not understand, as though she herself because of how and what and when, was almost being punished, although she did know it was not the case at all. Her forgetfulness compacted by the abuses, somehow though, and as much and as often on all-fours, pleading just to be able to see a way forward. She hoped that within days then, good could come of it, or some good somewhere. As for her love-life, she'd placed an imitation engagement ring on another finger, just to see what it looked like and just to know it was not the same. Again, she was attempting to build or create from somewhere within herself, a personal sense of a kind of stability, that for her she rarely would realise, so if she didn't, who So if it was now all presumably or allegedly 'bravado, 'all I could wonder was what on earth was she now planning? I really couldn't tell and even thought more about what may have become her childhood, desperate or whimsical offer to or suggestion or promise somehow, despite circumstances prohibiting such, for her, seemingly alone then, and possibly, very likely, with myself being aware of how those circumstances had been then for her, unable to really mention any of it, even to those who really did care and she them, her vow of silence and how that should eventually, or could develop and into what and how and why? And especially as it was now very much me that just could not tell. I had absolutely no idea at all, as to what she could or may be considering or planning. She did though at that precise moment, stand up and walk into her kitchen, she wanted to make for herself some porridge with water and a dash of lime cordial, she accidentally knocked the sweeteners over and they fell in their packaging onto the floor, she couldn't pick them up and just then ignored it as though she didn't even notice. She looked at the mirror that hung above her kitchen sink that had belonged to her father and smiled when she saw what a mess her hair was, usually she might have thought, 'if I don't laugh, I'll cry,' but not this time, she thought of her father and laughed inside, that laugh became a very slight smile. 'And I have not had my porridge yet, 'she thought to herself, 'but it will be delicious, very.' Then she thought, 'but first I really must deal with this now, immediately,' it's disgusting! She walked back into her room and picked up a box of panty-liners, there were some remaining in a box that she'd purchased since leaving hospital, she then dowsed some 'intimate' skin care slightly perfumed product along the whole length of it, but not as to soak it, then she shoved it into her knickers and pressed gently and thought 'oh that's much better,' now for that porridge and a nice coffee, and I wonder will there be any mail today? There the panty-liner remained until she could get to have a shower some considerably few hours after.

Was whether anything was being planned by her, to prove as nothing more than a presumption on my part, and had that presumption, or was there more to that than had been realised, had she, did it matter? Was it ever to matter? Certainly, on 28th June, she went to visit, to view a new flat. On that day though, not the 28th, she remembered that it was her friend Mounir's birthday, so soon those of other friends and too, that of her brother-in-law and her friend Jean's close friend Florence Breeny, on the very same day as his. Her thoughts strayed briefly to things that for her presumably are often considered a dream and achieving or reading those dreams. It was to remind her and make her think certainly about how to a person, such as the guy she'd met more than a year before, how must or how could she have looked to him then, and how normal and so very plain was she now? Was it that it was not as natural, in that it was make-up and wigs, or was it that she really although very unaware of it, then lacked confidence- even in them? Or had things for him, and by June 28th for her too, moved on so far, yes for him, that now or then and subsequently, after that, to have become something unattainable anyway, for her to even consider attempting to reach if she wanted to try. And or, had other factors formed, a wider gap between them both, then and now. -It wasn't that he'd given up, but that his sights were always elsewhere anyway then. - And how could Pinto respond to that now, or in two days' time, or three. What if she was unable to think even about how to deal with it now, as though there was for her now, nothing to deal with? Would she arrange to meet him just before she moved, for one hour, and when he realised, she was not like the others, then after really dealing with his need, screwing his brain to the wall basically and without a hint of a smile and then just moving away the next day and telling him nothing. She imagined he would smile at that, but she would not do that, and he would have known that and as well, that it meant nothing, it would mean nothing, nothing at all. If he was back at what was once before his normal job anyway, if, or during that week. She tried to believe him, and she did, but also, she knew as did he, that work was and is, work and that the right position workwise, is like gold-dust, that much she did know and whilst knowing her friend Jean. But how far did work overlap now, or encroach or had it become so enjoyable, and at what point does manipulation of fact become abuse, and are there consequences for that? As in consequences for bad and treats and progress without fear and with greater accomplishment and behind you, as though all the way, whether 'unspoken' somehow, or not. And what if work had become so enjoyable and if it was from bad origins, of such manipulations of fact? It wasn't that opportunities were not available then, but some liked to fill other 'gaps in the marketplace,' but then abuse those they learned from potentially, in that process? Fortunately, Pinto was a big girl, oh and did her daddy know that when she was born and very possibly her mother did too. If he was to resume his former employment that she hoped he would, and because it would have made a fool of her when they'd first met, where yes, she'd thought 'that man, he really needs a break for a while.' It would have been within the week that ensued anyway and no, she didn't like being made a fool of, and yes, definitely a big big girl, a big big girl, but first she had some things to do, and yes, she thought, "work indeed, is definitely work, and I always enjoyed my job, always, and you and your cronies, I hope shall not forget it, but I know you, and does it matter." Then her mouth turned up at the sides and her eyes opened wider, and she stared as though to say, 'get real you idiots, then she pulled lower lip inside her mouth and slightly touched it beneath her upper incisor teeth, then after she released that, her top lip she very slightly bit between her upper and lower incisors. Then she took a deep breath and thought, stay as you are, if you decide you want to, your choice is, and your choices are your own. Quietly she had hoped that even if for her, he'd have returned to his normal job, but she wasn't holding her breath, on it, inquisitively, that was for sure!

The large brown wood-looking object, nothing more for a while was happening there, it remained motionless, but this did not mean that nothing would. Something quite poignant for Pinto was to happen, and no, she never would have guessed or had any idea. Like moving into a new home and discovering in spring that bulbs had been planted in a garden or near a pathway, hundreds of them, or maybe just a few. Some can imagine creatures such as The Wiley-Eyed Stickle-Fincke, that Pinto knows, and the Dum Dum bird, and some ignore it or dismiss it. Some too, have taken then for granted for so long, that they would not know them now if they had opportunity to see them, that they did, but for those reasons, no, they wouldn't. Some would think it all is crazy and stupid anyway, Pinto could not have mentioned any of it to the guy she'd met, he would willingly and not only for that reason that he thought it was silly, have seen her wheeled away to a lunatic asylum and yes, oh she could imagine him laughing and especially remembering how her hair looked when she looked in the mirror whilst getting porridge. Even she wasn't always certain then as where, what or even whether they may have even been ghosts she thought at one time then, but they seemed to like her and it made her feel humbled and it made her want to cry, sometimes and even then, her tears would well up, or was it a month or so after when that was to happen, when she thought that soon she would need to finish her packing. Then she wept.

But, such clumsy ghosts, she then asked herself, the fact was, a probe from a World had landed on a planet in the future, oh it sent lovely photos back and film of nothing, just sand and what looked like dust and rocks, a report claimed that they found no signs of water there, so there would not be, or was no life there. None! On that planet though, they had stores, not like supermarkets and shops, but depositories, on other planetary systems. They didn't need, the inhabitants of that planet, to have because they were kind, like how in some countries, like Pasturelands for example, you could but a jar of pears that were grown in Argentina and packaged in Taiwan, and although Pasturelands grew pears too and quite delicious ones at that. They were very advanced, as too, were their inhabitants then. They didn't need to even have visible water, they liked the rocks and dust more, they didn't want their planet to look the same, or even slightly the same as other planets, and because they were slightly experimental, or some were, they were 'expected,' to be. In fact, even water on their planet, because they were so very advanced, unravaged by wars, arguments and disputes, they did know what those were, it didn't resemble water that you might feel wonderment at when you look at it or feel it on your face, neither did water there have the same consistency, not the exact same consistency, theirs was filtered and filtered at the depositories on other planet systems and they didn't even, because of how those planets were constructed, require chemicals or did, for those reasons, it even have the same consistency as water recognised anywhere else. But it was water, and it did the same thing that water on other worlds would do. Anyway, the probe, a beautiful looking ting indeed and it was not even noisy, and when it landed it didn't even land with dust clouds, just four foot looking stems, the problem was, whilst the astronauts were laughing and earing eating each a rock cake, it, the probe, as the stem-like legs became smaller beneath it and the body of the probe landed or settled, it landed smack on the house of the King and Queen of that planet and totally flattened it. Their landing even though calm and monumentous for the day, flattened their house so much that it became almost gone, and it was breakfast-time there, what a way to start anyone's day. Although flattened, such was their structure, that it still survived, just flatter at the time. It accessed data from beneath the probe, without anyone on the probe or involved, being aware, and then, after the probe left, and even though they were images of astronauts as it was controlled from elsewhere, the inhabitants of the planet, set out then, to locate the place of origin of the probe. Just as a homing pigeon would find its way back home, they set out on their voyage of exploration too, or was it? And what form might that take, especially if everything about their planet was indifferent anyway, or was that it was not the same, all that somehow made it the same for those controlling the probe? Not of course that I know how homing pigeons manage to get back to their homes, after being sent out to deliver secret messages, but then maybe that was something of a secret that I did not feel a need to know the answer to, I was sure though that their babies, chicks would recognise the scent or voice, even if squawking, of their own parents. It just wanted to reciprocate in such kindness, hence their own voyage after of exploration, that was all. None of the inhabitants of that planet were harmed, they and the house of their King and Queen just strung back to their original shapes after, and condition. Off they did go, and as hot on the trail as they could have ever been, back in time, to the planet where you, and Pinto live. They were hit whilst travelling, or following, by an asteroid, that then sent them or their ship, hurtling spinning around and around like a straight type of boomerang, through the galaxies, until it was sucked into a black hole and then with a huge burping sound, they were spat out of the other side, only to be caught up in the hunters and gatherers net of constellations, where it was sifted and sifted and thrown around like a Frisbee or a dogs rubber play-bone for what seemed like an age, certainly a long, long time, between them, until it was deemed as perfectly harmless, just presumably as those involved with the probe, might and did say there was no life or would not be without water. It was suitable to be allowed to pass. Pinto had been one of the first to see them, only because of how she is, they'd have been perceived as having presented naturally as scared or too shy to have been seen otherwise, although they did not know what fear or shyness was, it was how they were. They would though have been somehow or looked as though they were too shy or scared to show themselves because they would not understand why they could not be seen anyway. So, they would have looked as though they were hiding when they were not. So why and what was the oblong, wood-like object? None had any idea still. That day though it started to shake again, not a lot, a little, certainly not as much as before and again, it left the ground and turned again ninety degrees and landed in the exact same spot as before. On all three sides so far then it was all perfectly normal? Nothing unusual at all, all sides of it the same as the other. No predictions had been suggested at any time that such would ever occur, so any impact could neither be accurately guessed. Some might well and would ask, 'oh well, if Pinto had come up with the idea regarding 'the capsule,' and why then, and now, and yes with and because of all that was happening on the planet then. It, the wood-like object, their ship, had got stuck inside a black hole, for a while, like trying to stick a whole chocolate bar in your mouth sideways, not that anyone would, it was wedged for ages and ages, in fact, those on board could have thought they'd be stuck there forever, if they knew what forever was. They didn't even think 'oh no, whatever now, all they wanted to do was to reciprocate a kindness. It was a good thing then that their water supply was different from everyone else's, presuming 'everyone else,' used the same kind of water, but it was not about becoming confused, and so was what they ate, not that anything on Pasturelands then would have been capable of it. Little did Pinto or I know that whilst it was 'plonked,' in front of and by the side of the capsule, that it was eating, in fact, it was eating a lot, far more than normal. Something was happening, 'something' certainly was. It was the reason why it would lift itself a little, it couldn't de-stabilise air or weather temperature negatively, it was harmless and its need to release excess gas, was because it could not change shape, possibly because of being stuck in that black hole, there was a rection to that, as it would have attempted to secure, even if it did not realise and even if because of the black hole itself as a reaction to a reaction, neither though, could it burp. It didn't have a mouth, it had eyes, of a kind, but those were not visible on our planet, but it was 'observed' quietly and harmlessly and in a friendly way, and because they knew no different, from theirs.

So, they hadn't even realised that the probe had flattened the house of their King and Queen, or that it had made into squash all of their food supply, or even that it had made all of their staff too, flat like a huge pancake, just as the wooden-oblong shaped object had adapted itself, whether as a reaction to the black hole or not, they too after returning to their natural state, increased what would have been their level of security reaction, as they did not know what security was, naturally, their existence was reactionary and only about co-habitation and kind, but they were not like people, or animals. Neither did they need a vaccine, or if you didn't like them, or want them personally, all you'd have to do, if you ever were in a position to see them, say so to them, because of their existence and how they lived, they would and could never bother you anyway, and certainly again for the same reason, if they by, if you did see them, in and by your own perception of, by accident did. So why now? Surely not just to reciprocate a visit and say hello back? Pinto and maybe because it was now Saturday, seemed not to be bothered, she thought it was all, the oblong thing, now quite boring, or she was just looking forward to Monday when things were said to have been returning to a sense of normality, she was quite hungry for normal food though. Scratchy lick stickers were nice, but she wanted to taste again a real orange or a real pear, or a grapefruit, or a real banana and breakfast cereal. And no, she didn't mind whether it was without milk or porridge cooked with water, such was life inside the capsule.

The day passed quickly and smoothly without glitches, somehow because of whatever it was, having lifted itself up three times during that short period to adjust itself, it could not adjust, as it was not accustomed to the structure of soil, or Earth, or it was but didn't know it? Evening came and Pinto was becoming worried, the earth around the object was starting to slightly rise, something was causing it, and just in front of it, was it starting to alter position again and what exciting spin would whatever it was, put on it this time she wondered? From within the capsule, it looked as though it was starting to lean forward, Pinto found it difficult to move, the towering structure, slowly but quickly really, because there was no time to react, as much as usually it would have been easy to move the capsule somewhere else, could not, there were intermittent flashes from and around outside the capsule but no sound and everything started changing as though from night to day and back again, like someone playing around stupidly with a light-switch. Although nothing to do with the capsule, Pinto, and presumable others, because at that moment she forgot, clouds moved quickly and trees shed their leaves and then all re-grew them and then did the very same again, and then reverted to the tiniest of saplings, and all whilst night became day, like the flashing of a camera. Then she thought and thankfully that none of the occupants of the capsule would have seen that, because for some it could have been upsetting. Then in only just those moments, the oblong object had moved again, it leaned forward as though it was toppling over somehow and looking at them, then suddenly and very quickly it just dropped. -And then it stopped, to within one centimetre it seemed, of the capsule itself. Everything around had become smaller, it just stood and stayed there as though resting on them, but not touching, had it rested on them completely, they would have been totally crushed, 'presumably,' anyway? Then after a few moments it just stood back up again and jumped and completely spun around as though overjoyed, back to what would have been its original landing position. What looked like smoke started to billow from beneath it, then it shook and shook some more, and what looked like long curtains came from the top of it and draped completely around it, but it wasn't fabric, it was like larva from a volcano, and it looked like what some would suggest was water, t draped the whole length of it and as everything around was now smaller, it looked as though six feet above the ground that watery substance suddenly stopped too. Below where the watery substance ended, the wood-like structure then began to change, now to something not as smooth appearing structurally, but to something knotted, and with a more strand-like, grainy-looking consistency or appearance. Then nothing, nothing at all. It just stayed in that position and did nothing. Whilst staring at it as though waiting, poised, eager and wondering, what Pinto was really wanting, was some fruit flavoured water, so she went for a peach and nectarine scratchy lick label, then she sat by the window just quietly licking and watching, as though there was really nothing else, she could do, not one other single option.

#

There always were two very different sides to Pintos' as she'd believed it, 'boyfriend,' although the last time they'd met that must have been seven weeks earlier he did, look very different to how she'd remembered him, even compared to any time they'd met before. Since then, all she'd heard was 'I met the most beautiful man,' from a number of those he knew or who seemed to know him, and some Pinto knew he knew, his 'acquaintances,' and some even shared the same house as each-other, they, some lived lives similar presumably to how some sisters might live, but although in a property where sisters did or had lived or stayed together, those were not real sisters. Although, sharing and doing whatever to keep him there? They knew they could not stop him from doing some things, like travelling around, but the more they could attract, the better chance they had of putting something 'entertaining,' before him. Sometimes he'd be naughty and test even them and stay out, with them, those he visited, for longer than an hour, or then, one and a half hours each time. The side she'd seen of him just a few times, and that they had not, was very ugly and troll-like, ugly as in horridly ugly, as much as she hated to admit it even to herself, and she really did. For Pinto it had been horrific to recognise this before and something she chose at that time, to obliterate from her mind, because of her thought of him and because as a younger woman, she had hoped to meet a man perceived as an ugly man because she thought no-one else would want him, and to her he would not be ugly because she would love him, to her, he'd have never been ugly, not ever. She knew little of who she was then or that one day, although for many years she only remembered thinking that back then, because she since felt so personally ashamed to have though it, or anything like it back then. So yes, naturally they would never see that now. So, you see, he was the very 'man of her dreams,' the man she'd always in the wildest when she did, of what had become her distant memories, waited for, so quietly, and then eventually settling into a situation where she had accepted that she would remain single, until they met. She did meet a man back then, he wasn't what you'd call conventionally attractive, and she wondered, he was a philatelist, she didn't know what that was then but was thankful to look it up, nothing happened between them in a relationship sense, although they did remain as nice friends and even had a few mutual friends back then, for a few years. This was different, extremely. It wasn't desperation, and on 30th June, she was determined that it would remain so, especially when she, without his knowledge, accepted a new apartment. It, the apartment was an empty shell, so it would be a while before works were completed, quite a while. On July 1st, thinking of everything, and of how she herself was quite different now to how she had been back then, she recalled again how in recent weeks, some had said they were going to "give her (Pinto) hell,' Pinto smiled and again said "thank you." It could be argued that where there were so many look-a-likes around, and of both Pinto and the guy she'd met, that somehow whatever happened, a ticket somewhere had been purchased to keep them both 'on the bus,' what direction it of theirs both might travel, might and may not ever again be the same, it was still early days but regarding house-moves and relocating, not too much time remained. Some would say as a means of interfering with Pintos' mind, "he's working hard to buy for you a wedding ring." It was a lovely thought but was that wedding ring being paid for elsewhere as they both somehow enjoyed the pain, struggles and difficulty and hardship, as struggling through the swamp that was Covid-19, even if it was often and sometimes the seen and recognised hardship then of others more and pressures associated with that. Would such a wedding ring only be noticeable to Pinto because of who she was, would she tell him about it, or just think kindly of him, and now that would be enough, again.

In recent days, Pinto had received a message from that chap saying that he was in hospital. She thought that it was just him trying to explain his absence away, or maybe someone else was putting him up to it, that did seem even then as concerned as she was, and sadly, that she would have to consider things that way at all, 'on the backburners, sizzling away like fried onions in a frying pan. She was really upset thinking that he may have caught a disease, but also having to be mindful of and how complications could potentially arise if scruples were frazzled, and to think of his well-being within such a process and of course others and their various backgrounds and situations and consider any possible plausible impact regarding. That other may have indeed put him up to it, to 'extract,' from her further though abusively presented a somewhat potentially dangerous situation and with that she had to decide that irrespective of whether they had or not and irrespective of their covid-19 circumstances that were unknown to Pinto, it was a difficult call for her, there is no doubt about that, and considering they would not have been aware of how or what she was doing around or concerning covid-19 and that their reasons could be as much to do with Covid-19 as they could their own personalities, greed, jealousies, or a combination of all of those factors, even if only to further their own exploits, without thoughtful consideration. Thoughtful that her own emotional resources then had seemed to have been 'weaning,' because of stresses placed, as though her mind being emotionally stretched, to see how much pressure could be applied before she would snap, had her countermeasures and actions before, been sufficient, had she already anticipated all of these moves from the outset, and yes, because for her quite possibly, much of it, she had seen before, so therefore, it would only be the sadness that she was having to endure it again, unbeknownst to them who would believe they were just hurting her, that fortunately she would have to deal with. It was a far worse hurt, especially for dear Pinto. Far worse. Whereas for them and unbeknownst to those who wanted to consider themselves as her captors somehow, the pressures they were placing upon her, for some of them would have constituted what for them with their own agendas, have been a quite fine wine indeed. Would they have known though that the sediment of what had been, was and had been sufficient some months before, and she knew, it, to keep them occupied for quite some time as she made her own arrangements and coursed her own strategy without them being aware of any of it. By the July 2nd, Pinto was packed and ready to relocate and again unbeknown to any of them. She'd told the chap that she had visited and viewed some flats and that she had more to visit, and she did. Pinto loved architecture so for her it was like a mini holiday anyway, those happier wonderful hours, just away from it all, but wasn't that maybe what her friend had been doing too anyway? Pinto was just waiting for work to be completed. Or were they extracting just a very fine juice, to make a nice wine, or to attempt to mimic or clone if to introduce it somehow to some of the look-a likes who'd then pass it on too? How amazing Pinto thought, truly. All she thought during those days was "your kindness and kindnesses shall very much be rewarded; of that I am quite certain." He was taking then, but putting nothing back, he either didn't care or trusted her, or was just abusing, it would sadden Pinto obviously, and that some thought it was very funny, she would stare and think as though whispering softly and almost with a detectable hint of a revenge somewhere, 'that does saddens me terribly, just so terribly,' but I couldn't tell for certain, or even whether she had really packed at all, or whether it was all an illusion tactic, as she focused on the capsule and safety of. Was he under some pre-emptive illusion too that when Pinto relocates, that he would somehow move in with her, all so conveniently, that they'd be together at last? Or would it be just to do all the same again that he had done and for whom now, exactly for whom? She'd implied that there may be some future regarding, he was biding time, would all that had happened though actually drive that final wedge between them and with them both having a bus ticket of a time, was that how it was to pan out? No-one knew. Unfortunately, in a vision, she was to see him run away from a place so quickly, as though into the night like something with a new territory to explore, she knew him so well, and he ran so quickly as though under cover of night, though the troll, as so not to be recognised by her, but of course, she knew. Oh, Pinto knew! Pinto remembered when uniformed soldiers from generations ago had visited her, although then she hadn't fully understood why, she hadn't at all understood why, and a chateau, and an expanse of a beautiful woodland forest there and of what happened there. She thought of the woodland forests here and decided to restore peace and tranquillity to her own, she hoped that only that in her doing so, sending one of the two versions of Judd, that chap, in a rocket ship, to the stars forever, that they loved him as much as she had. She knew too, that there would be much 'stomping,' around, and that the 'beautiful' man would never return.

She imagined him in a rocket ship, and yes, staring through a solitary glass panel, and in her vision, she waved as it took off, she was holding a handkerchief and started to smile again, with now the troll having been restored to and returned to its original glory, in a forest, and 'he,' would never be seen or return again. - And like the North star, would remain a guiding light, in the sky, or as part of the gas around, that other could see more clearly and if they choose to, follow. If they dare. She hoped though that such stars would continue to shine so clearly that there would not be confusions. She heard him knocking at her only once from within that ship, that wooden ship, you see, his own ship had broken when it crashed to earth years earlier. It had been a life-changing opportunity that he abused, - as did those mirroring him, they abused Pinto. To prevent him navigating or attempting to, Pinto then also relieved him of his stolen mirror. Also, she would make certain of it, she thought of those officers back then, and said to them; 'May you now rest in peace eternal. 'That her abusers would say things like, 'stupid girl, we were setting him up to marry you,' had no impact anymore, they would have known that Pintos love, love that she had was a purest love, and yes, they could always find imitations and persons younger for him, and he'd enjoy them as much, but they could never be the same, and not because of age, irrespective of their own personal circumstances, they could offer more, but none would ever be the same, their circumstances could never be the same at all. It was not possible. Before the rocket left, she looked at him and smiled and said, 'yes, it's party-time baby, and I've been expecting you! And 'do bang all night as though it were your last.' She wondered why he was moving and almost running away in the vision from the property, when she watched him from that angle, she didn't realise until that moment that he was the troll, she'd seen the other side of him before and when they first met, in a photo, but didn't think of it? She refused to believe it and thought only that she wanted to make him look less unhappy and terribly horribly exhausted and devoid of genuineness. Now concealed inside the rocket ship, she could hear those he had got to know, trying desperately to work it out, but all of this had been put into action some time before by Pinto. It too was soon to become irreversible, unless certain conditions known to Pinto and concealed, were met. So yes, those thoughts, now as confined as he now was?

#

Pinto remembered the Silver Birch Forest and thought of how confused she may have been then, to have thought she'd seen a Wiley-Eyed Stickle-Fincke, it wasn't at all, it was indeed a Chimook, and she'd had to imagine it was a Wiley-Eyed Stickle-

Fincke instead, and not say, she'd gone along with it, like a game then, now though they would tease, though not deliberately, just because of how they were, the troll, he'd chase them and never catch them, because if he did, he'd surely gobble them up. Pinto was glad and thankful to have seen the Chimook and, on that day, too, in the Silver Birch Forest, and that the reason she'd seen a Chimook at all there that day would be realised. Neither too, would he, her friend, be able on the rocket as it took off, to eat cake anymore, unless the scratchy lick type, and then just leave the bits he did not or no longer wanted or liked, or that he could not use. Not that he, from where he had originated could eat cake that would be known to many anyway. As some he knew were obese, was he to help them, or was that now all too late too, they could always remember, Pinto thought, just as Pinto herself would not ever forget. Now certain that those with whom he'd become acquainted, her neighbours and often those some of them knew or had arranged to invite, or would, they would now be as distant relatives, and even to the point of quite unrelated, to him. They though would remain his food source, 'intellectually,' for generations to come. But they'd never be able to get just as close to him, reach him, or play with him again, - juts as Pinto had been, - and their own love would keep his little star twinkling in the sky, or the gases there, as they are, forever, whatever the cost to them alone personally. If ever they wanted a release from that, they could always beg on their knees, to Pinto, who alone would decide, or unless one day Pinto herself decided to release them from it. - Pinto had always known how to be very kind and helpful too. It was sad that they hadn't then realised, or that it might be too late once they ever did, or could, and that it was all actually ever an irreversible real consequence or possibility. Something they could never interfere to, or with, or interfere with or change, if they ever attempted anything along those lines, it would seal a fate further beyond even a change of mind by Pinto and could or would only make things for themselves far worse than they ever could imagine, whilst and should they eventually be able to, without their steps and actions considered as contentious. It would remain foolish of them to attempt, and they could only accept responsibility for that occurrence and not blame anyone else. And as the soft sound in the kitchen or the refrigerator in most kitchen, if you listen to it very carefully, with no other sound about and if the light in the room you are in, you switch that off, could demonstrate, and too with some other electrical appliances.

As the rocket ship took off, a soft wave of the coolest fresh air came across the entire Kingdom of Pasturelands, Pinto knew that if he now, in his original form were to ever contact her again, 'Pinto,' or anyone, he would never sound as he did before, as he had become, and neither could anyone else hear or see it, or be party to any conversations between them, if of course Pinto herself wanted to respond, she could, and if any though, he'd become 'acquainted,' to, or theirs ever tried, they would only push the rocket ship farther away, and should they attempt a reverse psychology by ignoring or should they naturally move on, whatever of those choices they chose, would determine among other factors their fate and the fates of theirs, and some of the outcomes quite 'unpleasant,' so they had best decide and choose very wisely. And should their choices be blatantly selfish and vindictive, they would push the rocket ship so far away that at their cost, it would wither away or vaporise. Of course, if that was stage two, of Pinto's offensive strategy, even stage one, and stages three, four and five had not even started yet and no-one other than Pinto would know what those were. Or they'd be so consumed to have realised.

Then she wondered, how do larger snails and slugs balance near holes of shot out leaves of Hosters, after they'd been ravaged by a deluge of hailstones, we were all soon to find out. Neither would it or he ever be a star to which they could conveniently anymore latch onto, because they would never be able to properly see, certainly with their 'beadier,' uncaring selfish ungrateful eyes, the star or gases around which star he was part of or near to, because if they were to search by staring up at the sky, they would always see only many others mimicking it. Officers who'd communicated with Pinto subsequently said only, 'Thank you,'- we are no longer now no longer be concerned and shall no longer investigate matters in the future. Pinto then responded to them courteously in their own language, and just said, 'thank you.'

Before the rocket ship did take off, in the sky there was movement, the clouds seem to be forming shapes of their own, the ship looked as though it was charging its batteries and looked rather shaky, rather like Pinto trying to imagine something was but wasn't really, but the clouds had formed letters, or numbers V.IV.MMIV, or that was what it looked like then, and it said Paris, and the 'r,' looked somehow brighter, not many would understand whether there was any relevance, and whether Pinto decided to look into it, was neither here nor there, maybe it was a secret message of the most top secret kind, who knows really, but 'in Pasturelands,' a secret message with so many nosey's interfering in others businesses and affairs, Pinto thought? It was just how they said thank you, 'we'll never know,' and that it could speak after all, she thought. But why Paris? It had all seemed very strange indeed.

Where the wood-like structure had formed a skirt of something that could have been water, and neither he was crying now, nor she, beneath that, the lower part of the structure, had started to separate, in amazement, they if they could all see it really, because technically they couldn't, only the nice parts, or parts of interest, it was similar to selective hearing but more viewing, almost as if by a royal appointment, although she did hope somewhat cheekily, that they weren't mimicking, if it seemed that way, it would be only a thought and not ever intended as or to have been deliberate. Where beneath the skirt-like part had started to become grainy, the grains started themselves to separate, then they, each of them, each grain strand, broke away until what looked like the lolly stick centre, - only remained beneath the skirt-like watery substance. They were Wiley-Eyed Stickle-Finckes, and each of them had their unique roles to fulfil. Vapour from what had been the bursting bubbles would then cause each of them to hold in their hands a rhododendron flower, it was like raspberry, and strawberry and cherry cordial all rolled into one ocean of colour. So, if a probe had originally landed on their planet, and they'd become like a pancake or a pizza or something like that for a while but then managed to recuperate, regaining their original status, and if they were being now watched or controlled from another planet, their own, what would they do with as much of the badness that they could eat, as their rocket ship had absorbed whilst it was extremely hungry and eating. But then, could a question then become, who organised for a probe to be sent to that planet in the first instance and why? So now all in Pasturelands could live happily ever after Pinto thought? As if it could ever be so easy really.

The Wiley-Eyed Stickle-Finckes could see what the tail fumes from their rocket ship was presumably, but no-one or nothing else could, they could smell those fumes too, but again, nothing else could, and they were totally harmless, but they, or their tongue-like noses, much preferred what was for them by far the most yummy and the very stickiest aroma of their rhododendrons, - of which they were immensely grateful, humbled and so very proud. The trail seen by them of their ship leaving, looked as though it went on forever, until as whilst self-processing, it disappeared like a vacuum. Of course, before the ship left, what resembled water, the skirt, seemed to dry up, It had eaten by consuming all the badness that it possibly could to allow the releasing not only of the Stickle-Finckes, but Dum Dum Birds too, where the Stickle-Fincke had moved away from the base of the ship whilst it stood, there must have been forty thousand of them, before the water-skirt dried, it started to move, it was making bubbles, as the bubbles dropped away, as they dropped away, they changed colour to pink, and burst, like very small fireworks, although of course they weren't, because there was no sound to them or flashes, only entertaining lights, they were baby Dum Dum Birds, all pink, pink and fluffy, they looked just like blossoms. It was at that moment that all of the Wiley-Eyed Stickle-Finckes, an army of them, raised their rhododendrons maybe because all of what looked like a watery skirt was now dried and stuck to the side of the rocket ship, that now was much smaller and never identifiable as female, and it would be dangerous to attempt, if not from their planet or origin, because the consequential penalty for doing so, and there was and is, was and is and always would be just too awful to ever consider considering. The rocket ship that then was smaller, than before, but still taller than the capsule, did then just take off so very quickly at that moment, until yes, it vanished. The baby Dum Dum Birds became drawn together in what had been the slight tail wind and it was that which could be seen although not the reason, unless quite analytical, it was that that had spelled of cloud, V.IV.MMIV Paris. So dear Judd, no longer consigned to a metal bin, and his new captor having been scrutinised by the gods from a heavenly place, or certainly the constellations, some of them, - themselves, could they too although a probe initiated the sending, have been sent by her own ancestors somehow, even if now themselves on another plain? So, if they had returned home, if analytically speaking, was Judd and she from the same place? Was that what she knew, and he was afraid to admit, would that, their behavioural traits have been merely traits of their own origins, if they had been, as though a difference between male and female of their species, or more, and like others, what they had become? Although regarding some, Pinto would probably say; 'what have they become'? And by Pintos' actions now, was she behaving as coldly, and no different now? Did that matter, or had things reached a point where she felt there was no other option, or were we really seeing Pinto, to have arranged for him to be caught and shipped away permanently, or would she find it as almost hilarious somehow, as she knew he would? She had already imagined that day that she'd see him bounce from the planet where the rocket ship was headed, on a bright orange smiley-rabbit-shaped space-hopper back to Earth, all she could think then, was 'not this time matey, not this time, no.' And it wouldn't matter a fig whether she did or not, to neither him, or Pinto, or who he was using, or how. Pinto knew this, did it matter whether he knew or that he knew that she was aware that it did not matter to him, or did she know that it could. How careful could she be really and considerate and far even to those whose morals were not so objectionable to her, but that her inexperience, Pintos was becoming to Pinto more realised, and the hurt associated to it, it was not associated to her own choices, so decisions she made regarding, she could not imagine solace, she neither would want to deliberately hurt presently, and of not so much potential consequences of which she was unafraid anyway because for Pinto it would be damage limitation and self-defence and possibly against a virus that not all definitive were known then and withing her professional remit as she perceived it, 'to act- or respond accordingly,' and this she would do!

#

As for that man Pinto had been seeing, or was, her, - what she'd thought was her boyfriend, maybe if we were to consider that she had been harsh in her thoughts, to have sent him away in a rocket ship to another planet far away, maybe he had really simply returned to work, to his normal job, and such was the high esteem she had for he that or who had been her hero and he was working very hard, to get things ready for the following week when so much would change if the restrictions would be relaxed, they hadn't been , an extension period was added, although that soon would pass, then a time when people would be free again , certainly in this country or these islands. Of course, Pinto was worried for those in other places too, many were working so very hard as we all know. With what was to happen, how could Pinto really, and on the evening before the Monday when changes were due to take effect, in fact, just as 23.59PM happened. The capsule would rise up and to a point where to a point where from within you would barely see but you still could, the petals glimmering in the light of Rhododendron held by Wiley-Eyed Stickle-Fincke, then as if by magic of the very purest kind, it would all, and those who had become the capsule occupants returned, not that they had actually ever left, or any part of them really, to their homes and families as though nothing at all had happened. However, on the night before, at 04.00AM there was a knock at the door, how that could be achieved as they were then still in the capsule, was a miracle, but it was her boyfriend. He told her that he loved her very much, and that he never wanted to be apart from her again. Obviously, she was quite overwhelmed, and happier then, than a happiness could ever be, more than anyone in the whole world could ever possibly imagine. And wouldn't you know it, before possibly and maybe again, it could be written, that everybody lived happily ever after, not content with being cast back to the heavens for the rest of eternity, he stood in front of Pinto. An angel then did draw itself up from beneath Pinto's feet, so very tall. Her boyfriend tried to consume the light by bathing himself in it, exactly as he had always done before, Pinto stood back very slightly as though she would or might fall, though she did not realise at all, to some, because of how she had been or was, and it was never ever anyone's fault regarding her own circumstances, and certainly not her own, and why she never knew, she had become to some like the pot at the end of the rainbow, that he could dip into whenever he felt like doing so, for himself at his own whim, but give her nothing, he'd refused to even contact her, he just bathed whenever he wanted, because then she just gave and he knew who she was, and since shrouded in cloud and mystery then, within the confusion that he had placed around her as he, not like any band she knew, played on. She knew though as he placed Pinto into what looked like the exact same ship, as that he'd been put into, and then put her onto water in it with only her face this time visible, through the glass-like panel, she was motionless. His intent was to push her out to sea. But as his own actions would propel the rocket he was already in; these acts constituted his own removal. But then, as though they knew, even if by his actions, they knew, the pair of them, Pinto and he, she may have well been dressed in a pure white gown with a small hand-held bouquet, as he attempted, prior to, and whilst doing, - to pull in various reigns again, - they dropped to the ground so obviously too, when those officers from back then, actually did now appear to and from immediately behind him, stepping from the very light of the angel,- he'd foolishly and cleverly he'd presumed, and thought he'd attempted to absorb, she wasn't even aware of it before then. that somehow it was a protection she had. He stared at Pinto as those officers took a firm hold of him, he knew, there was now nothing he could do, absolutely nothing at all. They, unbeknown to even her, this time were waiting for him. Obviously, she, even in her motionless state, thought how sad it was, she couldn't even look at him, she just stared forward. She could almost hear him saying 'you bitch,' but she just stared, as though wanting to smile but unable to. As sad as it was, she was thinking how nice it would be to eat some low calorie, gluten free, sugar-free biscuits, at only twenty-seven calories each, she was too happy to be concerned. She smiled and thought kindly of him, and thought too, 'I wonder if they do these biscuits with jam,' then she thought, no, let's leave it exactly as it is. Then and whilst still in a rocket ship floating on water, she thought, 'how nice it is to see my wardrobe again, especially after being inside that capsule for what seemed like so long.'

The Angel was of a pure light, of that she was sure, as sure as trees have roots, - she quietly assured herself, it seemed to push what looked like the others had become acquainted to, who or what he'd attempted to rein in, by pulling them all together before him, on honey styled thick rope, and to it also held what resembled and made of the same light, a large gun- like bow and arrow, or a long gun with an arrow on it, to keep 'the troll,' away, but he'd somehow bypassed it then, it was then and that at that time that had attempted to bathe himself in the light and assume the identity of that too, maybe it wasn't what could become ever considered 'a normal troll,' at all, maybe it wasn't a troll in the sense that Pintos recollection of could have been confused, maybe whatever that troll, as now, was once a nice or even a bad troll, not that it would have been deliberately harmful, until that had itself become absorbed by 'something,' something far greedier than a greediest of giants maybe, and something horrible, consuming, or maybe whatever had consumed it, if that were the case, it just made a slight mistake somehow, it was difficult one for Pinto to work out exactly, but she knew that whatever it was, trolls would never be that clever or manipulative, and even if slightly clever, she hadn't considered any of them to want to 'absorb,' to become something else, they would never ever want to do that, maybe it was slightly unwell, she wondered. Surely trolls couldn't have become affected by Covid-19 too? If so, then it would be about correct thoughtful application, however it panned out regarding the troll. It was at that moment then from behind and around him, that Pinto watched, as the officers restrained and took him away, maybe they were doctors of a kind, whatever, she knew they were being kind and not unkind, or she would have very definitely have spoken out or done something about it herself, and hence her remaining silent then and saying nothing regarding, and their leaving was thankfully, just as peaceful.

Regarding the light-angel, from its right hand stretched out, - what looked like a long sock that concealed within it a small bouncy ball, but all of the same light, it threw it outward, and it stretched more until it softly hit the very top part of Pintos' head, it was intended to wake her up, - this it did. It was then as though an outer casing, formed by him and those he'd become acquainted to, that surrounded her own body and that she herself had been unaware of, dropped to the ground, to reveal her, between Pintos eyes she felt a slight pain, but she knew she was now free, somehow, how, we might never fully understand. He had, to Pinto, because of such bathing and attempting to assume identities, already changed again from the troll and again back into the image of how he looked 'to her, in her mind' now, although still actually in the rocket ship. Although he'd placed her in an identical craft and now on water, would do nothing, she couldn't, he worked as quickly as she to some had been or become renowned for, but certainly for the troll element, little would he know, as would Pinto, that surprises were in store. He had maybe become such a hateful and hurtful troll, his messages and whilst many in isolation, and especially Pinto, would cut straight into the pot where he would extract whatever he needed to, or interfere, it had become as though extending an open invite, that others he had become acquainted to were already doing anyway, so he would have been now only furthering their objectives, not even necessarily his own. They even had devised a way that to a troll, such as that troll was, to manipulate him, and to cause him to by the same method to manipulate Pinto and to attempt to eat her, but not for himself. The reason he, then hated Pinto was and because he didn't understand that he was being manipulated, had got to a point where he now believed he hated her. He was a prisoner in a most horrible set up, cruel and vindictive and all intended to extract, especially from Pinto whether indirectly or not. The hate he believed he felt toward her, that had been manipulated too, because he did not understand, he just hated what he was being expected by his captors, to do. Thankfully, not, the captors, that unwell and very bullied troll was now with, they had given up on trying to make him better long ago or to cure his weaknesses regarding his thought processes. It was all though, the very finite reason, why Pinto really did love him, more than he might ever realise, or some might ever care, or even ever consider, because of how they were, or had become, give any hint of any consideration to.

Although he'd placed her on water, and yes in an identical rocket, she just lay in that craft, motionless and knowing the officers had taken the troll away with them. Soon the craft did drift to sea and with Pinto in it, still motionless, as though totally paralysed by what had happened, it was as though to everything bout at those moments that she would die without him, even as though she was dying, it could even be heard in rustling of leaves of now distant trees, whispers, "she'll die without him," and as a crow or a blackbird upset or caring might squawk, " she's dying a terrible death anyway," and they did squawk so much at those exact moments too. Pinto could hear them still, the sound travelled on the wind to her, oh she heard it, still unable to move, but smiling so much inside as though so much smiling could force her to suddenly break from the sense of feeling so paralysed, but move, -she did not, lying still she remained, for a while, just staring up through the glass panel, there were clouds floating by but she could not acknowledge their presence, or that the sky was blue, she just stared, as though dressed in a long white dress and holding with both hands, a small posy of flowers, she had some in her hair too, those could be seen around her forehead, just small flowers, so small, that to some could seem quite and totally of no significance at all. The Sea then opened, and in a moment, she in her casket or rocket ship, was pulled to down to the bottom of those watery depths. She saw the ocean close on top of her and knew what was happening but could not register it all, or just could do nothing about it, all she could focus on was her own heart, she hoped it would not stop beating, but was aware too that it could have, then at the bottom of the ocean she, or the casket, stopped. At that moment she thought to herself, 'I really don't know what some people must think I am, do they think I'll or I should have disappeared in a puff of smoke or something?' Then, the bottom of the ocean floor, where she rested and was not afraid, thinking she'd been put there for privacy. The pressure from where the ocean then released her was so much, that she, or the casket could be seen for miles around, as she was shot out from the water and up into the sky, she was actually spat out because the wind heard the sea burp and say with a lovely deep gurgling voice, 'thank you that was nice,' Pinto might have said 'charming,' if she'd heard that, but alas she did not. The rocket ship, or casket as it may have seemed, went so high, so high that it could not really go any further, then it stopped. The rocket she was in then so very slowly turned around, when it did, there immediately in front of her, only inches away from the rocket she was in, was him, in his, facing hers. There, with their hands at their own sides, they just stared at each other through the window panel of each rocket, they though would never be aware that this action or placing might soon form an alignment, an alignment between that which was above them, whether visible or not, to those who might understand, and too below. That they were there at all though, was that to be of any consequence, to what, or to both, or others, or just because somehow, in this space for these moments, these pieces of some greater puzzle, yes, - and unbeknown to either of them, were as they were. Pinto looked at him as though they were both wearing huge hazmat suits, she mouthed the words to him quietly and afraid slightly, 'hello,' neither knew exactly what to do or even how to think properly, or whether to smile or not, Pinto then mouthed the words "what now," and raised her eyebrows very slowly. Neither were to say or mouth another word to each-other, and what else was there for them to do, it wasn't as though they could style bedrooms or plant a tree? On 7th of July, even Pinto's house-move had been delayed by two more weeks, there they both remained in their memories, the images of each of them remained as seeing each other through those panels, they mouthed the words to each other, 'the things people do.' Both in a way at either ends of a very wide, difficult, and treacherous spectrum, and yes, so near to each other, but they could not touch each other. News reports some two weeks after, started to indicate that those types he'd 'gone with,' had started to realise quite large bald patches on the backs of their heads, Pinto smiled as she remembered and thought of, and about him and at him. Her thought was, 'thank God I am anti-gun, she knew that the commencement of what was her stage three offensive had begun, so how would they deal with stages one, four and five she wondered. There were no thoughts between he and Pinto of Covid-19 should or would they have done things differently, the circumstances prevented and prohibited. They did all they could, of that there was no doubt, and they both knew it! Their glances to each-other remained as and of a quiet-peaceful knowing, and alluring to each-other only, contentment, a freedom and too a unity, a togetherness to be shared with no-one else, not ever.

As much as from where they were now though, Pinto could think of and did imagine stingray fish, that might swim in waters where those he'd been with might have and still would swim, and all too much, she knew that too, he could think of screaming girls running through woodlands, as easy as tying up his own shoelace, so without even blinking it seemed at mot times, they just stared at each-other and smiled. Their work now complete, he then stared at her and mouthed to her "where now," her reply to him was, 'with you.' Believing he would be happy with that, where she imagined them running in fields together, into and he, and yes holding hands if they wanted to, she thought she heard him say, 'I'm trapped.' She misinterpreted it, and thought he felt trapped by Pinto herself, she immediately and unhesitant said to him, 'no, you're not, you're free.' Then his rocket ship started to spin around hers, but he could neither get out of his rocket ship as get inside hers, how long would it spin for and did it matter, would it fizzle out anyway, would he run out of gas, would he think it was her fault that she did not share the same view of Covid-19 as she and her experiences had taught her, was she being over-cautions or just doing her job, whether his he believed had ended now anyway, had she been simply doing her job all along, it wasn't even because she was a virgin at all, albeit an unusual virgin, or ever a virgin at all, that that he now would spin as though around her, 'where to now,' was all she, the poor girl could think, where to indeed, and indeed it was!

It would not be long, in space-time, before dust particles formed what looked to Pinto like sparkly fairy-'like,' characters, dancing around his rocket, somehow, he dismissed them, but one of them with her hair up and short dress of tiny sparkling mirrors, pirouetted and of course, like knuckles to a grindstone, he followed, it was as though then he left Pinto's rocket and disappeared. Only moments after though, he returned, not in his rocket anymore, but flying like a fairy, and said to Pinto, I only went to get a hammer and chisel. He danced and pranced about excitedly and broke open the lock on the craft Pinto was in, where she believed she would remain for all of eternity and was and had become resigned by then to that. Quietly then she was just held there, not by him, but in suspense, suspended, alone and unafraid, he unlocked the craft she was in, though it was so frightening for her, trembling as she had done much in recent times when she felt alone, although she did not understand why exactly, rather like when she was motionless inside the casket on water, although not obviously to any onlooker that there were trembling issues at all, and at that moment then, there had not been. She was trembling because she had no idea and did not know how to respond being near him now, it terrified her, as did the thought of being with a man, and many would jibe and say things like, 'only the strongest survive,' and 'open the door,' and 'men like something they can grab hold of,' for Pinto this was all new to her, despite her years as many seemed to enjoy reminding her and despite her quite individual circumstances and the situation, and her 'experience,' and experience that told her, to continue as she had been, and yes, for him and hers, and theirs and for the sake somehow of good, whether some developed bald patches or not, and some more no doubt would or could, she wondered, although she hoped they would not become as obviously stressed or so very 'concerned,' by that. She was afraid that he would compare her and dismiss her with preference for others. When she was released, she spun around him so fast and yes, of a light that caused him not to be able to turn or look quickly enough, or copy, such was only 'her' Pinto's knowledge and experience, her spinning around so fast created a very small hole in the atmosphere, she saw it and the hole then as immediately repaired itself as soon as she moved, with nothing harmed. He dropped like a lead weight through the hole, as small as it was, and she smiled so much, would he disintegrate before hitting a planet, she asked herself? Knowing that within a second in time, he would, Pinto flew to him and stopped him in mid-air, she then placed him into a capsule and sealed it, then Pinto put the capsule inside a pocket concealed upon herself, then she looked at the universe and saw holes everywhere, holes in the atmosphere itself, she asked herself, 'what now,' as she glanced at them, then at the thought that she could drop like a lead weight too, she flew away. First though, as she stared at Earth, she had an angel of light who had a bow and arrow and what looked like a ball in a sock, to thank, for waking her up.

As Pinto flew away, - another good thing was, that although her home move had been rescheduled after, so that hadn't happened yet, by the time she'd eventually move, those neighbours would be happier anyway because they'd be under the impression that good things happened because she had moved away, then though there was on 8th July, some weeks after, a thought that maybe they had paid her boyfriend, or so called, to build a relationship with her, just to facilitate her eventual moving from the property because of what after she would be forced to endure. It no longer would matter then to Pinto, she was even purchasing wallpaper for her new home, her actual home to-be, certainly by then. In fact, Pinto was, on the 8th of July, quite excited. So, it would all actually make no difference to them, her neighbours at all, and thankfully she thought, as high as they believed they'd fly on that little balloon for as long as it was air-worthy, or still could, that their own plummeting back to Earth would be wholly commensurate with all of, and other factors, and stages, any known or unknown, un-played and if ready to be played out yet, to unfold, involving or concerning therefore, how they themselves, had chosen or been somehow destined to live, dwell or reside. And with courtesies the likes of which they knew of, but sadly not their disciplines, likes and disciplines that somehow, if Pinto had been correct in her assumption, they had thought they knew how to deliver, particularly as they certainly had seemed to have been so pre-occupied, rather carelessly, vindictively and quite cruelly, in and at serving up such 'deliverances,' certainly until what would then be recently? Pinto consoled herself peacefully and quietly as the sound of one blackbird could be heard squawking outside today. The music of hunger shall for them alone take on a new meaning, not because they feasted and ignored, but because Pinto had never, by those standards if to have been considered as such, ever eaten - and certainly yet. And yes, she thought regarding them, that whatever they had said to her, that they meant it. 'I really hope you did,' she, to herself thought. Then the moment for Pinto was, irrespective of him now, 'what shall I do with all those so little holes now captured from the universe? They 'gave me hell,' Pinto quietly said to herself, she could only now or then think how grateful she was, I truly am and shall remain, she thought. And if I may say so, with a now almost richer depth to her female vocal tone, 'to think that they never even considered what unprecedented meant, they didn't care.' 'Oh, my dearest goodness of all,' was all she would then think. The sound of music of hunger, if it were ever that, and not just known recognised selfishness and unadulterated greed, were their tunes, mirrors of each other, a manifestation in some circumstances, a progression, or an all too convenient combination, that of an enticement, if not innocently, then why? Unprecedented as far as Pinto was concerned would remain unprecedented, - and with that, some, would have no idea of what could happen, and yes, because they hadn't and did not care.

Pinto briefly imagined lots of girls on earth now or soon to have larger than average newly forming bald patches on the backs of their heads, unrelated to alopecia. And, for those who had suffered with similar and been good, that their conditions instead too, would become somehow healed and thought of baguettes, Magdalena cakes and cherries, strawberries, apples, lychee and pears, and how often some had said "she needs a good man behind her," or she needed then, 'cest la vie,' she thought, cest la vie, and tata, t.t.f.n until next time, if ever there is.

It would be some two weeks after, Pinto would return, she found herself in of all places, Paris, having arrived there alone, towering or looking over beautiful Paris itself, she rested, sitting on, as though a rein of a kind, an invisible collar on a gargoyle, the collar made from one strand of the very finest silk thread in all the whole world, to Pinto it looked pink, but it might not have been, it had been placed there long long ago, the thread, but no-one ever knew, because it was invisible, apart from Pinto somehow, or how could she have landed on it? She was at Notre Dame, why Paris and for what reason she wondered? Did there have to be a reason, she also wondered, as she looked around, and as, she said hello to 'Fritz,' who knows why she called it that, but she did, she just said, 'hello Fritz, you're looking well.' She was getting her bearings and so was thankful for the opportunity to rest for that short while, whatever the situation, it was a warm day with a very light breeze, the fact was, she just wanted to catch the end of the fluffy pink blossoms of Paris for that year, and that, especially from where she was resting, with Fritz, certainly and only just did.

As for her 'supposed,' boyfriend, she pulled out the capsule from her concealed pocket and saw it grow, she then attached it to two small cannisters that then appeared on her back, in between her wings, so he would not lose out, and could see what she was doing then, always, then, as though a zip appeared in the air itself, she unzipped it and stepped inside it, with him attached inside that capsule to her, it then closed as though it never existed at all. It was as though all of Pintos arrows were now used up somehow, or with new destinies and resolve and she had no idea, but the name 'Pinto,' would be recorded forever of course, as it when translated by the Ingagook peoples, the ancestors and those that followed, and who were and who had been, meant, 'not grey or black, but white cloud.'

Then as though a yellow plastic duck was being held down beneath bathwater somewhere, another zip appeared, it opened by her side, and yes a yellow plastic duck appeared, she stared at it and said, 'oh come on, I just can't cope with this anymore,' she laughed, kind of and was by now sweating, she was blowing and breathing deeply as though to try to calm down, her earrings were swaying from side-to-side as she nodded and said then, 'Thank you, but just don't, look, I really don't care anymore, do have a good day now.' She hoped privately for a wedding ring of course, but she also knew it was not so important at all. She thought to herself, to have been left with a plastic duck and having survived had to be a testament to some somewhere, even f not only quite pleasing to her smiling ancestors. Maybe it was an indicator that she was to travel to York, but no, it would then be as though, having been somehow cast down in a beam of light, she'd then stepped off a rainbow disc, and then could hear beeping car horns, so she knew what planet then, she glanced across to her left and saw her television and her table and was, in her clothes, drenched through with sweat, her nose was slightly dribbly too, but she was ok, unaware of what day it was though, but relieved somehow and ok, she was not bothered by it. She found her reading glasses, they had been close to where she must have laid, how long for? She didn't know, her tummy was hurting, and she was afraid to make noise of any kind at all. Pinto stared across at her table with her glasses on and saw the prescription she'd been given and that four pills of the new strip had been used, so after giving it some thought, she recognised that she had doubled the initial prescription intended for the first week, and these were not anti-psychotic medicines, it made her personally happier to know this. What would this day bring, still afraid, but not, more as though just not wanting to be involved with some, or they played on the swings and cheese-cutter just a little too rough for her, and on the roundabout just a little too fast and for her it was new. That much she did think or remember, and of the damage they'd caused, - and why.

Not wanting to look at her phone, Pinto thought she heard someone say, "she should have been beheaded," surely not because she was summing-up, and rationally? Regarding that remark, she then thought to herself of its origination point, 'it's still early days yet, thank you, goodbye now,' and 'no man requires a coal scuttle should they visit me, and not because coal is no longer used, and neither shall they.' Neither would she consider supplying to them, chimney sweeps' brushes. Let them fry in their own fats she thought to herself. A change in career was to become a consideration for Pinto, though some of her friends might have wondered about whether there was a looney bin somewhere and not a big metal bin, and with her own name on it, then she glanced at her phone. A news report came through, unaware of names then, or who, or registering them, it said "choirs in Pastureland were still suspended and choir practice because it was deemed covid-19 unsafe. The report also said that Soprano,' Doris Sulley, was very upset by the news that had just been released by the Council.' As unaware as she was then and deliriously, she just thought how it was nothing to do with, and so ignored it, 'I must try to have a shower soon, she thought. But first a coffee? No, she said, 'oh, dilly-dallying,

I just don't know.' She then wondered, as the news item was still on her mind, whether they had planned to sing, On the good ship lollipop, or, Rock around the Clock,' I just do not care anymore, and as though the poor girl had indeed been pulled through a hedge backwards, get me out of here, she thought, please don't make me beg, not now. Then with a smile on her face and a slower paced and joyful heart and fond memories, and thoughts of what might have been, or become, if she'd met the right person, she thought. Had she though, or hadn't she really, but if she wouldn't now ever know it, because of all that had happened, was it to be that he'd, or whoever it could, or may, - or was to be, may have and would, have done whatever, to be with her, and her alone, irrespective of circumstance, nothing would have stopped or prevented him, had she been the one for him, but it was Tuesday. Pinto went to her bathroom and washed, as she stared at the mirror, she thought for the very first time ever that she could ever recall, 'wow, you look nice,' she pulled in her lower lip and licked it slightly, and thought, 'there is something now I must do.' There had been a message from him asking if she would meet him, three, as were there three question marks and an exclamation mark after the first question, - the second question or comment, was 'can we meet on Tuesday early, then that afternoon, another message at 15.05, said, 'no Wednesday. Pinto's response was short and sweet, she said to him, 'no but you can come really early if you like, on the Thursday morning, I guess not, - it's ok if you can't, I'll see what I can do,' that was ow she left it. Then she set out to do what she'd wanted to do, she went to The Silver Birch Forest, it was daytime, and to the wibbly wobbly stream, there was some rustling in bushes, and she knew there was Wiley-Eyed Stickle-Finckes giggling, she could feel them, not how you or anyone else might giggle at all, but how they do. With the gathering at that time of what had been of the two clans, those of her Father, and his, those of her Mother were to join them after, this was not necessarily why sounds of thunder could be heard, although none were exactly sure about that and certainly not Pinto's Father, despite remarks and observations, they placed upon her a veil, that covered her face and head all the way around, there was no doubt it was beautiful, however plain it may have been and so soft. The thunder that was heard, blocks of thunder, it was quite strange, then it petered to not much at all, but it was sufficient to register across the front of Pinto's brain, veil or not, and undo any horridness that had been planted there by unkind, it would not be until the following day that she realised that the spirit of her lost twin brother, had because of the forcefulness of her clan, now been returned to her. He now had been restored to part of the mentality even though a small part, by those unkind and greedy and selfish who had caused damage. It was possible to be a Queen of one land and a Princess of another, as well as her twin brother, had he survived would have been an heir and would have taken precedence that despite her concerns was just and so, over her, although it was never determined which of the twins was born first, certainly not yet anyway. Pinto smiled, and said, it really doesn't matter, it really doesn't matter at all. Their gathering then, did, as it was too, to herald a future of hopeful quest and healthy fortune. - And the two missing stones now since had been replaced.

She stood there and smiled and saw some deer staring at her, they were quite happy, and she left them to it. Her thought then was, 'I hope you this time remain, as one day, I may cross the wibbly wobbly river myself. Pinto although she'd never been across there, knew what was there and that for everyone it was safe, everyone apart from Pinto herself that was. For Pinto, a very dark and very awkward place, to say the least, oh yes, on a dark night, you'd even hear the owl hooting in a tree so high up, but travel through there alone and you, even if you were Pinto, might be asking for trouble of a kind, certainly that part of the forest.

She'd have a dream on the 10th of July and woke up as a tiny girl in what was her bedroom of years ago, where the faces were in the wallpaper, she realised only then whose faces they were, and soon she was to move to a new flat with metal bars at the windows? He had accessed that part of her memory, and to see what and how she grew up, to discover whether the was a small girl and how she looked, the facsimile image of him holding such was how he, or Pinto had allowed him somehow to see what she was like then, a very confident pretty girl who wouldn't play with other children. Somehow, she knew now that he had found his virgin, he intended she believed to keep her exactly that way, what she couldn't work out then was why? It would be as though the voices of cherubs were saying to her, although hesitantly, despairingly too, "don't go," don't go where she wondered?

#

So, the two clans that had earlier met, nothing to do at all with those horrid neighbours, hat with a colourful flower on it or not, who'd after and then be pushed further back, their behaviour considered as nothing short of the feeling a dog might feel if it had picked up a flea on its tail, as though the flea was attempting to suck blood out and as result the tail hairs were somehow reacting, or maybe if such a pooch really had tapeworm and had toileted and there were small moving small tapeworms still attached to the outside of its anus, wriggling about, the discomfort not necessarily recognised by the dog, only a slight distress might be observed with the dogs uneasiness maybe observed. There actions had removed any possibility, however they might attempt to fool Pinto, of their having any credible involvement regarding facilitation or anything regarding the clans, only in so much as they may have been aware that something was happening, but their own motives displayed themselves whilst other work was being achieved without their invitation, whether accepted offered or not, either way, in fact, had they had a slightest of involvement, no meeting would have ever occurred at all, however brief it may have been, or actually was. At the time of the gathering of those clans, an intermediary character also appeared, similar in appearance to a court jester, maybe it was something of a sign, or that an attempt had been made to emulate or copy yet again, as if to attempt to fill the shoes of someone else, with your own energy or belief in such possibilities irrespective of affect, a kind of trespass or liberty-taking, if without permission, and possibly dangerous too. Or was that what so much was about, challenging vulnerable or vulnerabilities, or taking what you believed you were owed, greed, jealousy, realisation of possibilities, abuse? Or was it to 'let the victim know, or ward them of dangers because you were so immensely clever to have achieved personally,' amazing and amazingly convenient too? Or - was it charitable, and on whose part but you weren't a client of a registered charity run by that person? Are you? If not, isn't that abuse or should we say, "pushing boundaries, 'gently stretching,' and what if it were on a cliff edge, was it helping each other through bad times? Yes, then the court jester, dressed in a black and gold horned outfit, towered in front of them, almost as an almost perfect copy of how Pinto had visualised herself some months earlier, and did that develop, it saw Pinto chained by her left wrist- to her bed, to them, she, Pinto was like a devil but all white, and with horns and hooves and her own breasts very naked, unable to move. The character said to her family who were standing to her right, "you have looked after her well," she was still a virgin. Yes, and of a very unusual 'unfortunately,' some could think, kind. To her boyfriend, or the man she believed she loved or could, she was his ideal, or perfect match, like two parts of a cut in two, as though halved apple, to some, or like a socket that found its plug to others, and yes maybe dear Pinto, connected to what though? Or just in a bag with other loose electrical odds and sods, bits and pieces, a junk pile for some, a treasure trove for others, if you needed them, or part of. And what if their, or a destiny for them, had been that should they become 'joined,' that they would only ever generate good for everyone by such a joining? Wouldn't that have made most men run for the hills, that's how Pinto would have thought anyway, had she known, had she been experienced enough in 'those,' matters. It would be partly though, the, or a reason why she might have experience in other matters, so yes, she was still a virgin, and yes, they very much had looked after her, whether they knew it or not, the fact was they were only doing what parents do, who was to know what may happen? That jester? Soon after, within a day or so, Pinto returned the image of that character quite reciprocally, to, or as the decoration to the top of a lacquered wooden pencil case.

But yes, holding the paper, the facsimile, he was to make a final attempt, to become a final stand, a stake, however Pinto wanted to or chose to consider it, if she would. Yes, it was July 10th, her late Fathers birthday, a sound horrifying was heard by Pinto at around 16.00hrs, she had just woken up having deliberately eaten food to knock herself out rather than tolerate abuses that day or risk of them, she was three pounds below her target weight then anyway, having starved herself for much of the week, and weekends were the worst times for her, and often Wednesdays, the sound was as though a lid had been removed from a cup or a vessel that had held within it a ghost, the sound, a gasp and almost a scream as though reaching for air then, was so horrific for Pamela to hear, yes, her boyfriend, to put it loosely she would think, was making another attempt, he had even managed to get her somehow to believe, by linking to the spirit of her departed brother, that 'they,' him and her, not her brother, had been together since Pintos childhood, maybe she had wondered that at some point as though they had been some kind of soul-mates and 'intended,' to be together, but she was twenty one percent sceptical these days, and no longer nine years old, or even eighteen now, whether he saw her then as a nine-year- old, for the first time, or not, she remembered how a boy made her push his bike all the way up a steep hill when she was that age, then he took her beneath a tree and told her to remove her clothes, Pinto was terrified of him, and she did this, he was older and had wanted to look at her naked. She stood there beneath that big old Oak Tree at the top of a hill, but out of sight from anyone, all that could be heard would have been the sound of older trains, the types that had luggage racks above the seats and separate carriages passing just twenty metres away. That she would on the 11th feel like that again and realise how her body was not like it was then, she was thankful, more than thankful, grateful, and that he never touched her, as attractive as he was, as neither did her boyfriend. She had been laying in her bed on the 11th and was just unable to move thinking about these times, afraid to move even her hand, but she did, she touched her breasts that she did not have then, but more to check that they were still there, and so afraid that they might not be, then she checked her nether-region, and that was all intact too and as it was meant to be, she kind of sighed with relief but was too scared to actually do it totally, a disbelief of where she was at, where she found herself now, was something she could not fathom, how could she ever want to meet anyone, a partner, with such overwhelming joyous feelings now inside her, and it was nothing to do with a partner, and yes, things were difficult, and everyone was still in lockdown and it had been the birthday of her departed Father. She had believed that having resumed from her pre puberty times, as though somehow going back to an earlier place post-operatively, by default, - not deliberately, of by personal choice, or persuasion by anyone, she was somehow moving forward from where she had left off all those years before, there was more though, her mind would be wrung again and she would be pushed back even further, to the point where just after birth, or maybe a year after, when she was just a baby girl, she remembered how thin her fingers were and even imagined nice fingernails, although probably impossible at that age. Then she had to move forward again, but this time without her boyfriend's interference emotionally, infecting or diluting her essence, or replacing it emotionally and deceptively as there was nothing happening between them, with his 'maleness,' and for what, or whom, or for what reason. She would think of a swimming pool ok, and of possibilities he may be 'foolish to attempt with her, but if he did, he would take his own life in his hands, this Pinto knew. He'd again in her thoughts, managed to place himself, she was aware that there was something not necessarily right, it would be something he had not banked on then, and neither, it seemed, did he know what that was. Like trying to tamper with a discovered arc of the covenant, he would not know what it was, she would though have been aware of the risks regarding its safety, and those were so real. He would tamper with its corners and try to twiddle with it, but he didn't know what it was, so how could he, he tried to break it from within her, but that was not possible, just to see what it was. He would never have been aware of so many factors, it was then, at that moment, that he again had taken, or so he thought, in a trickery or test, the hands of, by connecting to, what was her memory of, or part of the memory of the spirit of her twin brother. She heard her father's voice then say to him and as clear as day itself, he said, "she'll dance rings around you and leave you standing, you have no idea." Pinto then glanced across her right shoulder at her so-called boyfriend, her stare like the coldest ice imaginable, it was then she told him, 'Those are not my brothers' hands you are holding, that is not my brother you hold, that is a facsimile, not even or certainly a mirror or reflected image, of your own image, now be careful of those holes,' she said to him. He then, she believed, stared one last time straight at her, with nothing in his hands, holding nothing. Pinto stared, still across her right shoulder and just smiled at, to him. Pinto had also realised that as much as any woman, to him would be a virgin, but because of how she had been 'reconstructed,' too, was any male to her. And that they would be precisely and exactly that- for her.

Whilst standing by the wibbly wobbly river that day, before she walked away, she thought how they, whoever they were, and kindly, must now allow her to get on with her own future, and because she feared not, what may happen, if without him. Would it bring a smile on the 11th of July, and would such a notion be ill-placed, should she listen to those cherubs? That they would remain safe was to her, far more important. She then thought about parts of the remote background of hers she could remember or knew of, and wondered whether it was the meeting of the clans or not, they hadn't been? Could they have been so long ago, as families, or torn apart, separated, as likened to a family separated at a birth, or soon after? A decision by a very wise King or Queen or Chief and his wife maybe, I was now more accepting of possibilities and that unusual things and circumstances do occur, and besides, regarding those clans, Pinto trusted that the floppiest of flowers that might have adorned that hat and if it had been like that really, a gathering of, had it been quite like that, then those most horridest of neighbours would have surely been wronging a family generally by their actions, she thought. So, the fact that it didn't happen like that really, that at least made it less incestuous for dear Pinto and him. Pinto though, did she ever find her Prince really, and would he be a prince if she did, did it matter anyway? Could it matter? Who knows? Pinto wrote on a piece of paper, and I feel I must say 'Pinto,' continually presently, because under the situations as is at this time, should I say, 'she,' some will latch onto it, you see there is a reason, and it very much is for your safety too. I may not like all the time Pinto's experience/s, but for now, I must go along with it, 'for my own sins,' should there be any. Anyway, she wrote on a piece of paper, 'as for any thoughts on such things as cruelly beheading, and without even wearing nice perfume to do it, or nice shoes, and maybe to find a person with unhappy looking feet and the most horrid of toenails that could be found on the whole planet, so that those would be the last thing such or any culprits would remember, I do not condone violence, all too much a way too familiar view, but if there is any to be done, and I hope there shall not be, just tie them up in groups of three, and just line them up for me.' There'll be no 'special' treatment there! Pinto then took a deep breath and the air cannisters across her back were replaced by not arrows, but with a sword, and in her hand a rose. The walking headless body of a person wearing a long floor-length V-neck dress that draped across a carpet of red, did stand behind her. A large dress cape rested upon those shoulders, and a voice was heard, a female sounding voice, "I'm pleased that those stones were returned, but you shouldn't have bothered." Pinto stared at the headless figure and still had the plastic duck on her mind from before, she thought to herself, 'nice colour if decorating a chair, but otherwise, I prefer something less loose and less flowing for daily wear. But violence shall no doubt beget, he said to herself, even if not with some level of cruelty. They will learn eventually, as many do, and may have, or did, - or have, at least that much is hoped, and they can twinkle to show it, and all powered by a gas from one account, amazing. And now since I have been replaced, obviously, she thought, He did read her response at 09.30AM and did not reply. Obviously, Pinto or what Pinto offered, was not enough for him to change his Wednesday thing, or to leave early on the Thursday, to get to her flat, as she had anticipated anyway, now vilified and vindicated, he lived less than an hour away, and had access to a car and transport, he could have easily slipped away even if for an hour, had she meant a single thing to him, so now, it would be his actions, that would vindicate the rest of and not the resting of her own action plan, stages one-to five, and with the ball obviously now rolling, and too, her it seemed.

One of those he had become acquainted with, or by, the person who months before had said to others certainly, that they were doing everything they could to get Pinto and he back together, at least that was the intimation, confidence tricksters, when in-fact they had all along meant another of their own. None of them would have seen the image that had been taken of herself and sent to him by Pinto, it would be an image that would say more to him, and them if they did. But any images were only copied by them anyway, so it all seemed pointless. They had seen it though, and now it was just too late anyway. She had received some bad news that her new flat was further delayed, or works to, for yet another month, it was then, at that time, although weeks ahead, now July 12th, it was very disappointing news for Pinto, and again, it knocked her out with the shock of it and she slept from 16.30hrs until after midnight and after mentioning her health situation to them again and the possibility of complications. This information though they had records of. Back then though, Pinto saw an image of the neighbour pinned to the ground, Pinto stood over them and said, 'I'll have you strapped to the ground myself by the time I'm through with other matters, and I'll have stinging ants eat your flesh and whilst I can cope with such boredom, just in that initial moment, be sure that they will consume your flesh until nothing of you remains. And when there is no flesh remaining on that carcass, I'll just know that this was done in the sole hope that it may place some kindness of a beat in your most shameful abusive heart, and because I know it never can.

And when all that remains of you has dried in the heat, I will burn it and have yours eat the remainder of it." Then whilst all this was happening, Pinto said, "from now they cannot hear each-other, able to see them though as though they were now in separate compartments, knowing fortunately, - that they could not do a thing. As for him, it was as though he was now in confinement, and not because he'd become engaged to any of them, quite dis-engaged, as in never, he would be to Pinto as though she was staring at him through the window of and whilst in and from too, a similar hazmat suit, on a hospital bed. The glass-like panel, although it was air-conditioned or oxygenated, from within, now becoming almost dampened by a condensation of a kind that would form and ultimately prevent her from seeing him at all. That was how she believed it was, as that ship left on that day, oh it was all a confusing time, but mindfulness and keeping abreast of things, Pinto believed was what the whole Covid-19 thing somehow was all about, and if you or some were, then others would be too, was there time though and would the vaccines, surpass all expectations anyway, of course Pinto was hopeful. Such a hopeful girl and caring, she was in many ways. Who could ever really doubt her? No more to be affected by the sounds of doors closing shut, the troll had then been all that then was to leave, if on an earthly plain. - The beautiful man they believed they saw, the deceitful thief, the trickster and liar, and greedy ignorant selfish thing he'd become then, his arrogance, and their selfish deeds, now and soon to be forever gone, unless he was in hospital, and Pinto as per their possible, if true, arrangement, called to visit, or as odd as it seems, and as peculiar, or quirky, however quirky it could present or however 'old-fashioned,' unless 'he' physically kissed 'Pinto,' herself, in-person.- And we all know who Pinto is, or should Pinto, the niece of The Lady Broadley herself, turn up at such a hospital without a mask and removed him from his concealment, and kissed him herself. - Such was her own unique love- and because of who she alone, not had become, was it all wrong for some to believe it was or could be so impossible to achieve it, because of who she alone had always been. Or was it just because it was not them? But none of this was Pinto's fault, none of it.

Unlike when what seemed such a time now, before a long time before, as though whilst at a so quaint chateau, and nowhere near Pasturelands, as midnight happened and as a door there was heard quietly closing, it would not be the, or a power of a darkness that, or of the wood, that would enable a safety for him this time, from then on, or now, he would be caught and engulfed by fire wherever he went in the night, a fire that would become so intense that he would have no option but to turn back, because it would destroy him forever, he would be burned alive, by a similar darkness, no more could he mimic that which he safely conveniently for him, hid within, as though in that forest back then, the forest that surrounded that very chateau, though this time, now alone, he would neither be able should he continue,- Or distance, or mimic, or become. He would clamber between twisting writhing arms of trees as though they were being caught in his hair, then one of them would grab him by his hair, - it pulled him to an upright position, Pinto approached him then, he could see her, in his worst nightmare, he could see her, though not because he hated her, that was the saddest part. It was he, now unable to move, and yes, just as her move had been delayed, she was a fast learner was Pinto, and still, despite her actual years, so very young, because she had been able to pick up from where she had left off as a child after her recent surgery. She stared at him, the look in his eyes was fearful, and no, he could do nothing at all. What did Pinto do there? Nothing, the forest dropped him to the ground and like a sad, the saddest of the most pathetic of forms recognised by Pinto, he scuppered away. Then, would have been only time for him to smell her, if he was of a mind to, - it would be a unique fragrance that only Pinto's forever partner would know or notice, and never whatever perfume would he find it anywhere else, no matter how quickly he would move, or to wherever. Would he have really seen that in the photo she had sent him though, was that it? It was, very much, but could you really. Or did that not matter if you could copy what you saw only, was that why some were so eager to keep them apart? Whether fortunately or not, just as when they'd, he and Pinto had first met, there were problems, as though they'd simply met at the wrong time? That was what she believed. His present actions though were synonymously funny, in that rocket ship, although he had no idea, and too, that it would leave sooner than Pinto would secure other accommodation, from where it would have been safe, she wondered, to meet him. So, by whoever, again the die had been cast, she would not see his face again, or theirs. And whenever she looked at the sky after, she would smile, 'now which star is he,' she would ask, wonderful she then thought to herself, of him, 'you're a star now,' your wish came true.

Pinto had been thinking about another aunt of hers, a maternal aunt who was the older Sister to her mother, she never understood the rift between the aunt and her mother, until around this time, but more-so, on 14th July when she woke up very early and noticed that she was changing. Changes were occurring within her mind and soul. You see, Pinto had always been told by her mother that her aunt had been bereft of a child, a girl, at birthing, and Pinto's aunt, 'Rosie,' had been told that had the child survived, that the child would have been quite unique because of her appearance, even then. So, the spirits were fairies she wondered, she always knew it was a girl and a boy. As she changed, she saw them both, still children, together, holding each other as though in a huge hug and as happy as any child could ever in their wildest dreams ever want to be. They danced off together and Pinto, she didn't smile, but she was happy too, more than many would or could have understood, she hoped too that the rift, if it really was at all, to be very honest, of many generations was now resolved. And she was extremely thankful, more than anyone could ever understand, comprehend, or consider.

Where she had been almost cut off or locked away since her pre- junior first school years, in a way, her opinions now, so many years after, would be like looking at the world and many of the happenings for the first time since then, afresh, as though removed from all society all these years and as her own person started to evolve, since her corrective surgery, certainly after for her, the initial six months, she was having to see the adult world as that which resembled an adult, but for her, still through the eyes of the child she still was, although at this time she had moved on and head quietly even celebrated an eighteenth birthday alone and secretly, then had to slow things down because all of those years seemed to move way too fat in her mind, from pre-puberty to eighteen in a matter of months, armed though with experience and a knowledge that her years in the work sector had allowed her, although not many, would have been aware of all of the facts, that she could not have a 'normal,' relationship for example, some would and could suggest otherwise, but it was how she felt, regarding her personal issues, that now were corrected. So, for her, and even though no longer in mind, pre-puberty, and accepting that she had to move forward from that, if only because of the age she was, still of knights and castles and dragons and Wiley-Eyed Stickle-Finckes and others though, and of forests woodlands and friendlier trolls, she knew herself because of how she was, the troll had not really been such a bad troll, not that one, the term 'troll,' had been bandied about in many ways in recent years, and some from some places other than Pasturelands would have not been aware or have considered themselves to be grown up, and so or had been considered as by others and assumed powers and identities, of what was basically something, in this case possibly,- quite innocent. Of course, when she looked at her father's rosary, although he never spoke of these matters or so very rarely ever, she really did wonder how far some had pushed boundaries in a hope that by some other than themselves, they might one day be better understood, if it was like that at all?

That troll, Pinto believed, when she pictured him, was not such a bad troll really, he wasn't dangerous in that he would wait beneath bridges waiting for people to cross and imply a hefty levy or terrify, men too, and demand that a toll be paid. That troll, Pinto thought, was misunderstood, and maybe too, he'd slipped one night whilst trying to tip-toe across the stones in bare feet, a froglet jumped onto a stone and it scared him so much that it made him scream but so quietly as though whispering, with his hands up high in the air and then on his mouth and covering his eyes after, peeking through his big huge fingers to see if the tiniest of tiny froglets was still there, so afraid he was, maybe that he might fall onto it, he lost his balance completely and his big clumsy foot got trapped in between two of the stones, it was why he might be afraid of a small froglet at all, that was to become more the reason she would suggest that he was not a harmful troll really, not at first. So, it was only the badness and misconception that had been taken away really by the officers that day, or was it, you see, that troll actually loved butterflies and flowers, he'd make anything scream that he believed could harm them and was afraid because some did or had. He even made Pinto scream though, but only because she was inexperienced, she was thankful that with the help of her family, the two missing stones, that were like jewels to her, when she thought of planets, even those such as Saturn, had been returned, so no harm was done. Neither though she hoped, would anyone have realised it, that he liked flowers and butterflies too, and neither did he realise that they hadn't realised. She, however, was on the way to market then, and wondered what did or does any of this have to do with the price of a loveliest of eggs anyway, for anyone who liked and appreciated eggs, and strangely, not that those officers had ways of making him talk, or did they? And if they had, just who were they, in a friendly capacity, to dear darling Pinto?

So yes, that particular troll had just got then his big foot caught and wedged in between two of the stones, and where he tugged and tugged and pulled and pulled, and boy did he pull, he was sweating so much, even though it was night-time, he pulled so much that it dislodged those stones, and they'd then sank to the bottom of that deep river, the problem was, the deeper they sank, the more invisible they'd become, but often with everyone and the forest dwellers often just getting on with the normal problems of life then, and those that would or could be caused by such unprecedented occurrences, it wasn't as though the animals could do anything about it? And if they tried, who would care for them whilst they used their energies and time to attempt it, even a Wiley-Eyed Stickle-Fincke can't imagine licking the nectar from a rhododendron flower, if it is so pre-occupied wondering what way the wind might blow that day. It had to trust somehow, even that it was doing the right thing just by doing what it does best, even if that was sniffing nectar, and many people loved smelling flowers anyway, so they would understand and as for those that did not, they didn't know about them, or that some people liked smelling flowers, but if they liked smelling rhododendron nectar, it meant that rhododendrons would have a place, and others might be spared having to give attention to, if it was needed somehow. And we weren't even thinking then of mermaid hair, some did, but you'd rarely hear about those, or them mentioning it, Pinto thought that was slightly strange, and not just because Pinto happens to be a female.

Yes, the missing vanished stones, certainly had paved the way for a gathering, of those, - of those - of the restorative clans-folk. The troll's wife, all of her hair fell out, maybe that had set a course, and would explain, maybe, why some women were then developing such large bald patches on the backs of their heads, he would not stop crying, because he saw the stones vanish and did not understand, not only because the trolls Wifes' servants, her maids, travelled through that same forest almost every day, they scrubbed and scrubbed all day long for crumbs thrown on the floor by her, and didn't even realise she was there because she was so clever, she wanted them to believe he was the man and the only head of their house, and they his maids, and now, if they made it to there at all, for those who by then weren't staying over secretly on some days, even out of the view of his spouse, such was their trickery to him, the thought of seeing their bald patches every single day whilst they were scrubbing made him weep even more, he wept so much, even his eyes were starting to look beady, and where so many tears fell from them, this would cause those maids to have to mop and scrub even more? They had turned him into a naughty troll for sure because he was too generous of thought, and he hadn't even realised, to him it was all just a game. After they'd gathered their crumbs, from the floor, often they would disappear back to their own dwellings, it was on such a night where they had enjoyed their fill of crumbs, so much that the floors did not get cleaned and his wife cried and lost more hair and scratched at her scalp and what was left of her hair, that he had gone across the bridge to find out why they had not come, or when they would return. Apparently. The maid and house cleaners would lie and lie and lie throughout the kingdom, to cover their tracks and as often to each other, and because it too was, they, he would cross the bridge often to visit, if at night, to play with both inside and with them, then, - 'until' the stones went missing, outside the forest. Their lies though would cause so much intense pain, that whether the stones had vanished or not, they almost destroyed forever the Kingdom of Pasturelands and because of getting on with their busy lives, it was as though they themselves, and theirs, and all of theirs, had even forgotten it ever existed at all. They knew the fruit trees flourished and that there were always crumbs to find and other food to find and to sell now for a good price, even if their husbands, of those who still could, would ask. But often they would be working the fields anyway, keeping, fixing, and watching the wheelbarrows in motion. And all as Pasturelands was crumbling beneath their very feet and as though by their hands? And for what, surely not because they felt as though they did not exist to many- or some anyway?

A sign was scribed and placed by the river, after Pinto walked away, it said: *"Ye would think careful to cross here, should thee break up on two stones, then cover thy track. And listen too, good foe, - or friend, and as though crawl quiet round naked bend, then with truest real goods in thy sack, should she find out, you'll not make for thee, - the best good back."*

Pinto though, her mind was already on other things but I did wonder if she were asked about the sign, what could her reaction to it be, she might say possibly, would it be like saying to others "you deserve someone who phones you back quickly," But no doubt she would be more concerned for a dog barking in a field somewhere, if it sounded desperate but she was thinking by hen though how when she'd been dusting in her makeshift pantry some weeks before, and reorganizing, that she'd accidentally then left a jar of lovely strawberry conserve on the top shelf, she was inadvertently thankful too, that it hadn't, unlike the yelping dog, or was it a fox, or a hyena on a very windy day, where it's wanton cry may have become slightly distorted, been pranged yet.

Regarding the problems potentially caused throughout Pasturelands that almost caused a breakdown, all the lies and mistruths, deceptions and covering up – would any realise what serious harm they could have brought upon themselves? Or had some just not actually cared at all, only for themselves, On 17th July, Pinto would have to ask herself what if when restrictions are lifted, all go about their daily lives as normal, and what if should a terrible thing occur, suddenly, without warning things go wrong to all, catastrophically, despite all of the efforts regarding the many 'various' vaccines. For Pinto a question she felt was being asked of her, if she had use of a mechanism whereby, she could and albeit at risk of harming many too, as that mechanism was or would be unknown to her, only the effects of it, a blinding light so intense that a virus could never survive it, but would everything else? Would she at the very last moment when or if all was lost to the virus potentially use it? She thought about it very carefully for all ten seconds, and then thought in response, no, my trust is sufficient, it would not be necessary at any cost and of this I am much more certain.

So, it hadn't been that the troll had been sneaking out, to play outside the forest, or whoever with, that had been the problem, but the deceit to cover it all up? The deceit or a deceit that would hurt the most sensitive of souls, Pinto's, so very deeply, certainly initially. And because she'd not have seen it then? So, now the troll was returned to the forest, in a dream she walked back there through an opening and wondered, but all was perfectly green and wonderfully normal, and quiet and as a woodland should be, she could almost feel him there but too it was only that she knew he had been there at some point, whether he would return properly again in-body, was another matter. It all smelt so fresh and the grass beneath or near her feet that she noticed, and because of its cleanliness, was lush. She could after, imagine bluebells there very easily, but not in that season. And the inscription placed or laid near the crossing, Pinto by then was now back at home and had trekked to the local shop.

As she walked out of the shop, she saw a man there on the ground with what looked like bags of clothing, plastic carrier bags, each of them, three, with their handles tied together at their tops. She went to an ATM there and withdrew one note that she needed, then as she walked near that chap, she stopped and walked back and withdrew another note of the same value, as she was about to walk past him, she bent down slightly and gave it to him discreetly. He said to her, "Thank you, may god bless you." When she got home, she was very puzzled because he looked somehow familiar to her, not that he looked up at all, so she never saw his face. His voice of a similar background to many or some of those in her hometown, and certainly of her on father. Then in a dream some hours after, he came to her. It was all very strange, as though she could do nothing, or as though it was normal and she couldn't anyway, normal for either him or her somewhere along the line, he took her aside and placed her behind a large curtain and put a crown on her head, then he said just to her, Pinto, in their own accent and so quietly that you would hear a pin drop even on a carpeted floor, "The Queen of my heart forever." Obviously, Pinto was slightly afraid by this, and an hour after, she got dressed again and she went back there to that shop and the place where he was sat. Pinto wanted to ask him only if there was anything he needed, - but when she got there, he was gone. The bags were still there, so she walked around a little to see if he was local somewhere, but no, he had gone somewhere else. She walked across to the bags and without wanting to pry at all, she noticed they were all now open and untied, she noticed that one of them had her favourite foods in it, and another full of mini sausage rolls. She looked up and a smile so wide did appear across her whole face that it could have been seen from the stars in the sky themselves, not that she'd have realised that, that smile remained, however silently, as she walked back to her home, her knowing, that somewhere he was out there.

#

Regarding the lies, they'd simply kept adding more on and lavishing in the power as it caused so much hurt and distraught declines and climbs, and pain. Then, - as though she snapped it all, the deceitfulness, into small pieces, at that moment back then, of the discovery of their behaviour, and of how they had gloated about it, and of the suffering and of the suffering caused and that it did not, none of that had mattered to them, who'd have only languished. It was at that precise and exact moment, that the inscription was laid and that the missing stones returned to the river. They floated up from the very depths, yes, they floated up, as heavy as they were my friend, would I lie to you, would I lie to her, would I dare? Of course, those heaviest of stones, they were really the smallest of pebbles, in what was really, the dinkiest, dinky, of the tiniest of the narrowest of tiny streams, so tiny that if you did not know the forest, you might not ever see it at all, it hadn't been as though little Pinto didn't have personal things to think of too. Had there been a situation where the pre-pubertescent Pinto, oh no. She knew something even then was wrong, - that she might have cried so much and cause a block in her mind, to force it out for the decades that would follow, and then somewhere during those times, as though her own life then had been placed, unbeknown to her, on hold, and then as though totally somehow frozen in time itself, until the day that the changes occurred, or were made possible for her personally, had those or any decided then, instead of letting her piece or somehow darn together, or pick up where she had left off, and if it were Pinto's sub-conscious, that had told her this, - for her to have been as she was, - had some taken that youth from her? It wasn't the boy she had met, did they see that in him, or just join in with the fun, as though keeping him on ice for a later date for themselves, so by fretting, allowing the abuse to continue too?

She'd been chatting to her friend Bernadette, who'd recently started at a new job with a local Jam factory, she'd brought her two jars of what looked to be delicious damson jam, the labels had come off. She said to Bernadette that she couldn't wait 'to get her smackers on that.' Pinto thought to herself then, and regarding those abusers, those thoughts to give an idea of timescales, had been back on the 26th of May, I hope they are all very happy, I really do. Because she meant it, she felt the many tears shed, returning in that moment to her own eyes as likened to a torrent, then though, only then realising so much more, to replenish, and assist her in the recovery and furtherance of actual destinies. So, they'd been cashing cheques but using Pintos' money, amazing? I guess it's fortunate then, that Pinto would never realize that. Was it like being sure somehow, that if you or anyone should accidentally bump into someone else, and say pardon, or excuse me, or apologise, that abusers couldn't consider that too as an opportunity, a free ride by hearing it? Or was it to be considered charitable but somehow to attempt to not to become discouraged, downhearted or emotionally damaged or traumatised, to what could potentially have before become the or a point where some such lovelies, might see or hear an escape route by hearing such, and without even the need to venture to a church, should they be so inclined, or was it really just about forgiveness, should that be forgetfulness that may compound the issue further and then become a manipulatable structure within itself that some unscrupulous could use. Maybe then, as much as some could say not everyone reads books was a judgemental statement, would it ever by such actions present a case too where they would not need to anyway, because as a book was being written, then, before, it was already out there, so wasn't that the need and necessity and right to privacy 'by all,' being presented. Jumping on a bus without buying a ticket is normal everywhere? The terms 'abide with me,' and 'turn the other cheek,' and 'all is fair in love,' and 'love conquers all,' were fine in principle, but surely not when intellectual theft, or such cruelty and unkindness, - was based upon a lie itself in the first instance, or intended to deceive or manipulate initially, however disguised it could be or ever however truthfully become. So where did the inscription come from, the inscription by the bridge. It had been copied from the underside of one of the pebbles that when, or as it did rise from the depths, it rose to the surface upturned and thus upside down, or maybe that was rumour, like as though a kid might nap just for a little while maybe? As if Pinto would never have realised. That any of them might think somehow that they only had months to live must be the most ludicrous thing of all. That anyone could presume to think they were good enough to affect my thinking or consideration, that I may derive any form of even a mild satisfaction that they, any of them may squirm, even slightly. How conceited they must be, in fact, she thought, positively more very extremely anally retentive. That would strangely make Pinto giggle quite a lot, and she was thankful even more then, that the air in her room was so clear. Why dear Pinto might think those peculiar thought, maybe we'll never know, but in honesty, she would, in a reality then, be angry or upset that she needed to consider that as a more plausible option? Or to justify her thoughts or actions to anyone, and certainly not to herself. But if then I am to imply that there was cause, - then too surely I can reserve the right to suggest, in kindness, that if they indeed are "anally retentive," or possibly, again kindly she thought, of a 'roughage deficient disposition,' or is that constipated she wondered, 'oh I don't really know she thought to herself, then she dismissed as disgusting all of them, that thought and them,- from her mind and any thoughtfulness of any just consideration. Then of course, her thoughts went on to thinking of lovely green and mildly brown shades of acorns still in their cups, and regarding him, she thought to herself, he can try dancing his way around, and as I no longer care whether, or where. Would she ever lie to him though, or was she still being just so very true, as none could ever be, - as they would never be her, not even now by his estimation, but whether he knew it, - or would ever, or not, to him?

Another way of looking at it all of course, could be to suggest that if Susan Strumpett should have, or maybe was owed or deserving of an ode, that if where some could say, 'they keep stealing her man,' that if he could be 'stolen,' in that capacity, he was never really hers in the first instance anyway, and she neither his. So, Susan Strumpett was now free and just as, if she had of course, gone out and drank alcohol on that day, and during the course of that evening was halted in her very tracks, where her skirt, still requiring to be taken-in again around the waist because of her continued weight loss during Covid-19, didn't slip accidentally down to her knees, oh she was indeed 'stopped,' then, and legs totally swiftly moving apart to attempt to catch it before she would be forced, to then slowly squat down on the spot as though in some so delicate curtsey, then collect it in both hands, and blushing, like picking up a halo that had fallen to her feet, and if that wasn't enough, she collapsed again on the way home presumably because the skirt had fallen down again. She remembered and would be haunted kindly by that image or recollection as she was carried in what for her must have been more a nightmare, facing downward at the ground, arms and legs splayed, her then scraggly hair, lank and fallen down across her ears and both sides of her face, as she was picked up by the police, and very dignifiedly too, she would after somewhat 'personally' embarrassedly recall, - then to remember being put face down, -feeling and very probably looking like a corpse, quietly into the back of a police van by those officers, yes, she remembered feeling like a corpse that night, nightmare or not, and then crawling out of that van on all4s near her home, and being woken up the following day in the communal hallway, Pinto then in just underwear and shoes, woken up by one of her handsomest neighbours, and yes, she would be even on the 22nd of July, glad that he as do the others enjoy what look like healthy and good relationships, woken up by him staring at her saying only, and kindly, with no agendas other than to help, "is there anything I can do for you," to which she giggled and smiled at him and said, 'no, it's fine thank you.' Now, maybe that was the reason for that dream she then thought.

So yes, dear Susan Strumpett would be remembered by her from that day on, though by others, - very possibly not, by with the sound of that policeman's whistle and any Judges' mallet and any witnessing of a cell door closing and being unlocked with kindness and a thought of gratitude and in kindness, without a hindrance of reservations. Or simply as a reminder to all, that if, - for whatever reason, however peculiar or strange, you should ever be asked to drink alcohol, be careful indeed. Had I been from Britain, certainly remembering too, a Rover, the Panda, and the Humber for some reason as well, that was for sure, dear Grosse' Britannien she would think, dear Grosse' Britannien. And of course, thank you to that kindest neighbour and too, to dear Ruby Heussemann Schindler.

And regarding the looks upon their faces back then, those looks of horror on the faces of those other such 'for convenience,' neighbourly types, even if they'd realized then and thought how they'd somehow skipped past and evaded or just got on, by the time the 21st of July had come, and now passed. Would Pinto be happy regarding the decisions she took, would any of them then, have more to think about than they ever considered back then that they might? How professional was Pinto really? How in tune were her personal ethics and morals? Would those that survived live happily ever after? Not of course, that some, whoever they were, could rightly interfere, and certainly not wrongly, or correctly now, without complications for themselves, interfere. Only time my dear friends would tell, only time would tell, where dear 'Pinto', despite, how 'some,' might bat a ball still into their own camp, whilst reaping joyously and without fear among and scavenging the flesh of the fruits of labours of the foes of their closest, would without pity, now considerably, - only ever hope and as not as though the poor girl could wish.

As none of us knew what may or may not have happened back then, what if it was not a man sent to 'collect,' and collect what, but Pinto herself to collect, whatever it was she was intended to, if it or she was. Would she know? Stop hissing, how do I know?! Maybe a sign of how vulnerable as a female a somewhat 'scuppered' darling, dear Pinto was to become, as surely such a rescue, should neither require, nor demand a sexual act to fulfil it. She may as well have just had her wrists tied behind her back, been dragged through the town and if she hadn't given herself to him, been thrown to him. Some would think like that, and some, whether affected or warped, that she deserved to, and she would know this. Did she, somehow had she? Very probably not. She'd have probably said 'dream on,' or if there could ever possibly be, and especially in Pasturelands, far worse.

Pinto, or Pamela, checked her phone, there was a message, not from him though, the message from her lovely dear friend Jean, she'd been hospitalised. Pamela telephoned her and Jean aid that she'd tried a new chocolate bar, and mentioned that she rarely had chocolate but she'd been excited to try some, 'and darling,' she said, 'I dyed my hair, I will never use this colour again,' she exclaimed, 'it came out like an emotional firework displays, and a roller coaster and roundabouts all at the same time. I was so shocked that I fell over and where I'd picked up before a large terracotta planter, I dropped it as I fell and it smashed into many pieces, and the batteries in my remote control are finished darling,' she said. So, it means I can't watch television and although I only listen to the radio on it, it's now stuck on radio loud all through the day and all night too, it kept me awake all night last night, and so many wires on me in the hospital,' she said. Before she switched the phone call off, Jean said, you were in my dream darling,' she said, 'as clear as day.' She then asked Pamela, 'are you okay'? Pamela explained that she was just on her way to work and said, 'what will you do about the planter and shall I call round after, at say five- thirty this evening and should I pick up some batteries for you maybe, if you like,' Jean said, 'oh yes please, that would be quite fine, I'll use it to line the bottom of flower pots.' Then Pamela said, 'ok see you at 5.30pm.'

After they disconnected the phone-call, Jean laid down on her sofa, she saw a large shadow form, although not of bad, of a wonderment, that had itself cast over so much that had been. She could only think that it must be wonderment, because it changed shape to and from what looked like a long cloud, into then a whale or dolphin-like creature, mixed somehow with a duck-billed platypus too, then she saw it dive into the sea, to the ocean floor, where it developed what resembled very much what looked like some twelve large feet rather like human feet, but shaped then like a very large centipede, it as though charging hurriedly and uncaringly, but excitedly, ran across the ocean floor, its feet looked quite heavy, it was not small, a very large clam shell opened, was this the moment where an alignment would occur, and what could it, all considered be. As though it was quite tired maybe and yawning, the clam-shell opened widely and the twelve footed creature became a silver sphere, it was you see, a sea-dragon, the silver sphere then changed to a beautiful pearl, which then in turn landed inside the clamshell, and just as it had all been, the largest of a larger clamshell did close quite firmly onto it.

Chapter Two

The Eye of Terracot

'Little get'

Pamela woke up very quickly and suddenly, she was quite scared although it had been nothing out of the ordinary for her certainly for almost ten months. She'd dreamed that the man she had been seeing was standing immediately in front of her, she herself at that moment seated in front of an old small half-extended oval shaped oak drop-leaf table, he was stood to the right of that table and was putting what looked like legal documents and a property deed. along with what appeared to be a metal amulet of around two inches in diameter onto the table. Obviously, it was another of her dreams still, because there seemed to be a very large snake writhing about and around his shoulders and neck, certainly that she could see. She sat back slightly, it was indeed a big snake, with a diameter at its thickest part of maybe seven or eight inches and probably some five feet in length, she didn't understand why it was there, but it didn't look as though he was happy about it, her impression was that he was more concerned about the few smaller snakes that had their fangs in both of his forearms. Those were maybe one foot long and possibly one inch in diameter each, Pamela didn't count those, there were a few and they were still quite obviously alive too. He said to her, almost like he'd been dragged away from his place of work to get there and was wanting to get back in a hurry, "I can't put any more on the table, if I take off,' meaning presumably that if he attempted to change any part of how he was, because he said, "if I stop doing what I been doing," the snakes would bite into him more. She hadn't asked him for anything. He looked scared but not terrified, exhausted but not as though he was unsure as to what was happening to him, and that he was there at all, particularly as contact between them had then ceased. He talked around the table and the snakes disappeared. He'd walked around the table on the other side to where Pamela was sitting, so to her it looked as if, as he walked to the left side of the table, he was then though walking into the room and so, was directly in front of her and facing her, now though, she saw that he really did look totally exhausted, shattered. He said to her, 'I'm sorry ok, my hands were tied. She knew his lies like the back of her own hand, she stared straight at him upon hearing that, and said, 'I shan't ask, is that the best you can do, good, then she said I know you enjoyed it, 'with that he fell, full-frontal flat to the ground in front of her feet. Smoke of some kind seemed to emanate from his body as he hit the floor, like dust flying up. He was totally dead.

Pamela was in shock slightly but soon perked up and went to the kitchen to make some coffee for herself, he'd tried to trick her again. That he could attempt to sneak his way to such depravity was no surprise at all. Not to her, and not from him, you'd think, 'butter wouldn't melt. 'Pamela felt a sparkle in her eyes simultaneously at that moment, something she certainly didn't anticipate at all, as though, sure, she'd seen it on quirky films but never imagined it would really happen and definitely and certainly not to her, the irises of her eyes, she felt them turn red. There would be no more of him. Plus, she thought she'd already dealt with matters, as in his games, that very day anyway.

Then, in the dream too, just before she woke up and before she made coffee for herself, two men had appeared too. She knew one of them, the other was almost identical to him. Both, big strong men, as in big built, not that she considered size as in muscular mass stronger than a thinner person, but both were big, and she knew one of them already, he was huge, build-wise, there was very little difference between then at all. She said to them, it was a trick and a lie, can you throw him down there for me please. She pointed to two doors, they opened them, she said, "just throw him down there." Then she thanked them, and they left. The reason she could not believe him wasn't because she could not forgive mistakes, oh no. It was all very much based on fact, it was only at the point where he said those exact words, that his "hands were tied," that she knew irrevocably, lies. Pamela had wanted him so much during the initial lockdown, need was fed possibly by disarray, it was and became all so vicious. By my action, she said, it was never that I did not have faith, amidst before and during the crisis, it was only that I did and continue to. That it is not permanent is an endorsement of that very fact.

Things had slowed down between Pamela and Judd, the man she'd met, there was no doubting that, their affections had withered so much that she compared it to the pace of a snail, even she fondly remembered the fable of the tortoise and the hare and was determined not to allow the circumstances to become too bothersome for her. They were still talking, they certainly hadn't argued, but they were not commenting to or of each other at all now? Then a day came when she decided to post a profile photo of herself online, that space for while had remained empty, and yes, she'd not wanted to upset him then, so no longer had a photo in it making her visible to others, just a shade of pink was associated to it. He contacted in his usual way, exactly as he had before although she didn't want to lead him on, because she thought it was unfair. The pandemic situation then was still on, and she'd not met him since four and a half months now, she'd not actually met any guys. It was risky to meet him, she believed she had enough purity of conviction and faith in herself and of her personal depth of feeling toward him but still she said no to him.

The next day......he contacted her at just past 07.00AM and asked again if she would meet with him, maybe there was some careful gameplay in even that approach, she thought, but still she said no, she was too afraid. Later that day, hours after, he contacted her again and said he was nearby. This startled her, it was a lazy Sunday there and she was actually still in her nightdress and hadn't even showered yet, it was around 18.02PM. Having a sense that he'd possibly visited someone else instead, she was more hurt and disbelievingly angered than upset. Her eyes opened very widely like she'd just been squirted in the face with a water pistol unexpectedly, she didn't even notice the numb feeling on her tongue until she thought of it again a few days after, as she licked her lips and her mouth opened, with eyes wide by now and her mouth still open as if to ask 'what'? She also got the feeling however stupidly it could seem because it was how ridiculous it had all become, that the meet he had there was not exactly meeting of his expectations? Possibly because of limitations regarding lockdowns, or maybe something else. Certainly, something had upset him, he'd not been satisfied at all, because if he had, he'd have not been contacting Pamela or anyone then, not immediately after and from the train station where the person lived. Maybe it was because he'd had a week off work on holiday and was utilising every last remaining second of that break as if it was his last. Again though, she said no to him. She sent some paragraphs of a document she'd sent to a clinician that day regarding her feelings toward him and the importance of the surgery and how integral it actually all was. Realising presumably that even she, couldn't with her typing speeds have typed all of that up so quickly, he seemed to chirp up considerably. Thinking that she could have a shower quickly and agree to meet him, she asked him how long he would be there, thinking that she could shower very quickly even though not too far away. He told her, "You're too busy, I already left there." Pamela replied, 'so whilst you were at Chaltentnar Main Station, I was typing documents to a clinician, attempting desperately to get things moving regarding my surgery.' He told her, "Well you don't expect me to be 'bagging' for a reply, I don't waste time." He meant begging of course, was it possibly an indication of feelings for her, or he was being so extremely arrogant, either way, she smiled. She had no choice in it.

Stirrings were very much afoot with Pamela, it wasn't any intensity of heat in the weather, now though she had a far clearer idea even than before of how things were, she thought. She'd told him somehow to reassure him but was so scared to, in case it drove him away, ultimately although sexually how she felt about him and for the very same reasons, if truth be known? He said he missed being with her similarly. She said to him cautiously, wanting so much but so very afraid, because she knew he could kill her because of her health situation, as she was very much in an 'at risk' group, let's try to meet this week. He didn't know she was in an at-risk group, or she was certain he'd have said no himself. She smiled and said, as he asked and secretly yearning, 'when,' "whenever you want to." His reaction was quick, and he said how about tomorrow either before work, or after? She asked him, how early, he replied "7AM". He was taking longer to reply to messages by this time, only a minute, but she felt that something else was happening too, someone else he was attentive to possibly, it was normal, 'or had become so,' whether deliberate or not, she didn't want to wonder why or who, her thoughts naturally them became only to secure their meet as best as possible and should anyone else be trying too. It took what she thought was a while for him to reply in answer to her question to him, 'will you send a message early tomorrow,' meaning when he was about to leave his place, so she'd know he was actually up, out of bed and still actually coming. Sixteen minutes in fact had elapsed before he replied. She also noticed that replies were coming through from him, but now with no indication that he was online, this had become another occasional first occurrence for her. A little over a week before, she had deleted her media account and removed photos that would have been on his part of their pages. It might have possibly upset him slightly, she later wondered whether his saying he'd been on holiday all week was because he didn't bother to attempt to contact her? As she pulled her shoulders in, as if giving herself some kind of reassuring hug, she felt with the movements of her eyelids, the very extreme tips of her eyelashes, yes, it was as if she 'apart' from noticing in some photos, had discovered that she had eyelashes, and how any notion that he would have thought like that, was so sweet anyway, and that he might say something like it?

A message came the following day at 06.00AM sharp, she'd been up most of the night and did doze off for a couple of hours, but then was totally relieved to wake up at 04.00AM. She'd waxed her legs, not that they need doing often and even put some make-up on at 05.30AM, coffee was to a minimum, it was as though it was a rush, but it wasn't really. She was apprehensive and panicking slightly and anxious wondering what might happen, how their meeting each other again would be.

As the journey time from where he lived was forty-five minutes, she was slightly surprised when he said to her that they could spend time together until only 08.00AM, he also said that he might arrive slightly earlier. An unusual thing this time, was that he repeatedly said to her 'make sure you are ready'? Now it formed for her the opinion that he really was not into or had become accustomed to some cautiousness because of the pandemic maybe, or that he wanted not to waste a second or to make up somehow for the time they had lost, so he wasn't coming round to have his feet rubbed or take the weight off them. It then was to be some forty minutes after, he sent a message and all it said was, "I'm on the train now."

This made her think that he had only just boarded a train, so if it was already 06.45AM and a forty-five-minute journey from his home, how much time would they have remaining to spend together. Bemused, she presumed that he maybe stayed the night before somewhere near or closer to where she lived, and so, she said to him, where are you now on the train? He replied that he'd just passed Findl Market, Pamela checked and sure enough, it was very near to where the day before he told her he'd been to, but she hadn't realised exactly how near until the day after they met, only one stop on a train, so maybe he had been there before to that location she thought, but had realised that one station was nearer and the other further away so guessed that Pamela would not bother to check? She wondered, had he gone back there, to whoever he'd visited, immediately after their own conversation the evening before?

As their meet was to happen within fifteen minutes or so, she was horrified, and upset by this, and now a little angry with him. She paced about slightly, then went to the bathroom and changed the colour of her lipstick from a quite vibrant dusky pink shade to a very red shade and gelled her platinum-coloured hair quite tightly down. Before, when they'd met, she always wore a wig so her own hair would not have been noticeable. She also slipped into a very slinky skin-tight, flesh coloured short thinly strapped silk dress, it was so body hugging it looked like liquid silk and too, she'd managed to go from a dress size eighteen in those earlier months, now to a size twelve-fourteen. She had no bra on, and her nipples protruded, the dress fitted well. The black stockings came off and her black patent leather shoes, they were replaced with a more skin toned business looking pair of heels. She meant business, but were her thoughts to be crushed? Yes, of course they were, the very next day when she realised the extent of what had happened. She took the stud earrings off, they were replaced by thick one-inch circumference hoop earrings with emerald cut imitation diamond studs in them, but none of it seemed to matter now.

As if the prospect of possibilities wasn't enough for her, he then texted and asked her address? Surprised again, quite stunned, she cautiously, still typed her address detail to him, although now more apprehensive than ever, she didn't say which flat number, only which doorbell to press. She'd wanted to use some un-fragrant language tones and ask him to leave their meet for another time, but she actually felt more drawn into it because of the anger and her personally now wanting to 'enquire.' It was as if meeting him was no longer important to her, not on his terms, or for the reasons she, in-part believed he was visiting, she was hurting. And she did still miss him deeply, she just had problems accepting that to herself.

Just a few minutes after, from a window in her room, she saw him walking along the street, and was pleased too that he had a mask on. He rang the doorbell four times like it was an emergency, maybe because he wouldn't have heard it from outside, Pamela went to respond on the intercom, as she did so, she put her phone in a drawer quickly and walked into the hallway and buzzed him in.

The light in the communal hallway comes on automatically when any of the doors open, so as she opened the door of her flat, she could see Judd clearly and with the amount of light shining in from the hallway, he'd see her even if the light in her own small hallway was not on. He didn't say anything, it was all very quiet, he just quietly walked in behind her. Once in the room he said, "hi." She said hello back to him, she was still intrigued and muffed beyond belief that the little scallywag had tried to trick her, their hellos were all standard stuff. He removed his coat as if he was attending a dentist, then he removed his mask quickly and said, "I can't deal with this anymore." He had looked from the hallway as if he hadn't seen her quite like this before, but she too had become aware of the many choice options he'd had within the past few months, she was fully aware of that, because of experiences she'd endured with him, she had learnt now, where he was concerned, not 'expect' anything. The fact that she was still awaiting a medical procedure that had been postponed in March because of the pandemic, was also a hinderance, it affected her confidence. I don't know that he understood how much exactly, he didn't need to give it a thought, he didn't need to change it, he knew there were many other options elsewhere, it also meant unfortunately for dear Pamela, that however she'd dressed that day, it wouldn't have made any difference at all? From her point of view, how he was, she believed then, was as integral to her as her surgery was, and to them both, at least that was what she wanted to believe.

In many respects that day, what happened within that hour, were firsts and potentially lasts for dear Pamela, but as he stood across the other side of the room, out of the corner of her eye, he was removing his clothes. She didn't want to look up but was aware that he was staring at her whilst doing it, she was sitting on the very edge of the side of her dinky white single bed. At the point where he was just proudly standing in his underpants and white very short sports socks, she obviously was still angry though, she was seething, she was livid, that he might have come to visit her, after four and a half months, from somewhere nearby who she'd have considered to be nothing short of an utter sleazebag. They'd already hugged and it to her seemed real, she remembered very quickly how she'd missed him, her doubts caused the reaction to him from her end, to be not as she'd have wanted or preferred. He walked across to her, by this time only in his white socks very proudly indeed. He stood directly in front of her, and his hands reached for her breasts, he seemed to really like them a lot, it was as though before he hadn't even noticed them, he'd only vaguely touched one of them once. In fact, apart from that moment then and what happened during that 'hour,' no-one had ever touched them?

She then stood up and put her left arm around his shoulder and then her right arm until they touched, he was pressed extremely firmly against her, they couldn't kiss because of the restrictions, but said to him quietly, "did you go back to Chaltentnar Train Station after we chatted yesterday evening"? He responded, pulling back slightly with, "what do you mean"? You texted and said you were on the train today and then in the next text, that you were at Findl Market, did you travel here from Chaltentnar, or from your own home, she didn't want to say to him 'it was simple' for fear of totally embarrassing herself and him. He looked not so much afraid, but as if he didn't understand at all, she therefore couldn't determine whether he was an out and out liar or not, or plainly stupid. She said to him that it was okay, he said he'd visited a friend there yesterday and that was why he texted from there. Knowing there was no point in pursuing the conversation again, because similar conversations had happened before, and possibly because of her surgery, she let it go. Instead, she lifted his right arm and to within centimetres of his skin, like an animal might smell prey before eating it, she decided within seconds what she could detect and whether she could continue their meet. There were faint traces of a strong body odour that were his and a lighter fragrance that could have been a stale deodorant. Then she cleaned him using anti-bacterial lotion and finished it off by applying a deep penetrating moisturiser. It was quite obvious that he hadn't washed at all, but then she thought that as it was only 06.00AM, he could easily have in fact just woken up, thrown some clothes on, grabbled a bag and then came straight to her with excitement which would have given him ten minutes to get to the train station, followed by what would have been his normal forty-five-minute journey to her. Were her doubts ill-founded or deserved, with all that they'd been through, or that Pamela believed she had, for sure, if there was any flicker of anything left between them, something, the moment she'd dreaded since months before, it would require some careful re-building, but had he totally treated her as though she was of no consequence at all? It would become as it had been for her, after their meet, moments where every or anything she said or thought was like a double-edged sword, a double entendre, how much could she handle, was a constant thought in her mind, the swords at least were clashing now, yes crossed swords and sharpening, as Pamela became somehow however stupidly, still in shock and for various reasons, determined that they should.

Whilst they were together, she did sit on top of him, on his lap and put his mouth on her nipple, she'd wanted that to happen for a long time and especially when they last met, she actually reminded him of it, telling him that the image he left in her mind that day, although it had helped her through the months somehow, was not at all the image she saw today. He didn't understand the comment, as though it was irrelevant, there was no doubt that he was affected by it and because for him certainly, there was no relevance. He'd looked really hardened now, by something more than the pandemic situation, he seemed quite unsure as if just doing the motions, so much that she didn't know what to, or what not to do. She got up and went and put her glamourous wig on, he seemed to like that a lot and became less defensive, he soon then perked back up again and became quite his usual self. During the earlier days when he'd turn up then after working long hours and exhausted, that was how he'd looked during that hour, certainly to her. Had damage been done that was irreparable now, during those horrible months whilst he was furloughed from his work, and how exactly?

#

08.00AM soon came, he got up and walked across to the other side of the room and was some three meters away from Pamela, he looked at some pictures although very discreetly and at he obviously noticed the cups and saucers and the teapot, then from out of his bag, he pulled one anti-bacterial wash cloth from a packet of them, he washed himself almost with an intensity, then with others from the same packet reached for in his hand held bag, he dried or wiped himself off, almost un-noticeably and even though he was standing next to a table, he raised his right arm slightly and casually just dropped them onto the floor. If she'd not been so angry still, dear Pamela might have laughed or smirked, finding his rudeness almost laughable, but she did not. He then said with a deep and very concise accent, "I will have a shower when he got to work" and, "better to get to work not late." Did Pamela though smile just as discreetly at him then, and very much as unassumingly, as if to say, 'it's too late now.'

In what had become her selectively, or somewhat questioning, observant, although reasoning 'she hoped,' curiously suspicious mind, she wondered more about how he'd got meets down to an hour-long, not only whether there actually had been more to it than she realised at first, but during their conversation the evening before, had he, because of the sixteen-minute delay in responding, managed to arrange to meet another in between any available time between meeting her and then actually getting to work? There was none of the usual after-meet pleasant chat at all, not even on the phone immediately after he left, that was unusual. He'd just stared straight into her face as he left, not sheepishly in any way as he'd have done months earlier and said, "good to see you." Pamela, after he left, sent a message to him saying she hoped he enjoyed meeting again, maybe he didn't text because maybe he'd had issues boarding a train or something, which would have been strange, especially at that time of day and locally, it was 08.23AM, his response was immediate as though finely tuned, and at 08.23AM as though he'd anticipated it. The train station was one minute from where Pamela lived. She had an idea that something was going on, or was it just her mind, was it really? Her imagination? It was very difficult to appreciate what they too, unfortunately, had been through? Also, at 08.23AM, he asked and said in two separate messages, "How was," and, "yes I did"! The next day when recollecting, her own thought, when she became very aware whilst and during, that he'd gone on another of his excursions that very afternoon, though this time with thirty minutes travelling each way and a fifty minute stop off, so he'd that day even further reduced?

Aware that she should be feeling 'used' or abused, somehow because of what they'd been through, she actually didn't. Possibly because of her first surgery postponement. She did manage to send another message to him, just to say, 'if you come here again, you can have a shower here next time if you want.' That was sent at 08.38AM

With the journey from her home to his place or work being thirty minutes, there was no response, he was focused. At 09.02AM she texted and said, "And I'm sorry, I should have said you could shower here, I was still surprised I guess." Yet again, she was feeling strangely at his mercy somehow, in despair, cowering on the floor almost. She finished that message by saying to him as though grovelling, that it could have been because she was uncertain as to how he wanted to do, 'his things.' Possibly, this meaning of course that he had assumed or believed he had, in spite of his demeanour, a level of control. She decided, even with the knowledge of his latest excursion, again to bide her time. She wasn't actually as bothered really. He wasn't aware that she knew, or maybe he was aware, and was playing her out, or teasing, who knows? She really felt totally and unquestionably and unreservedly that he was definitely 'playing the field,' tough, more than should have been under any 'normal' circumstances acceptable to have tolerated. Was there such a thing as 'normal circumstances,' in how he was, was Pamela expected to just toe the line and say nothing? That aggravated Pamela because it made her feel like a total 'bint.' How much did she know though, and of what, if to presume effectively? For sure, it was becoming her understanding that if her mind was feeling constantly like it was being screwed up by actions or inactions of another, or others, or her wanting to trust although seemingly and unrequited, it was certainly preventing her from wanting to meet anyone else. But surely that was more of a crazier thought, oh Pamela knew this! And that possibly he thought that too, or certainly presumed.

At 09.32AM he read the last message she'd sent to him at 09.02AM. As stupid as it sounds, it would be easy to think of it all as an exaggeration, but as his last and only responses were at 08.23AM, where he'd been the day before their meet was only five minutes away in a car and twelve minutes on the train, they were so frequent, Pamela would not have been surprised to find out that he'd hopped back to there and arrived at 08.23AM. His message then read, "I have problems with my back in morning, I do some exercises to help." If the meet there the day earlier for some unknown reason was 'unsuccessful,' did he use someone local and 'convenient; like Pamela, simply 'to discover a way to overcome problems he encountered?' In response to his message Pamela simply said, 'ok darling.' Was it akin to receiving photos from someone like him that say, 'let's try do this if we get together,' it was one of his tricks on the evening before their last meet, she couldn't understand why he was sending photos of others and making joking remarks about what if etc, or we should? Then only the day 'after' their meet, did she remember all the times he'd ask her for photos of her, he even asked her to do a video two months earlier, but she blatantly refused. The thought that he'd been cajoling others into 'doing the same as' or looking for someone like her photos, became a very sickening possibility. She knew that there had to be a reason that he was so insistent on visiting, maybe it was just because he knew somehow that she'd lost interest, did he have other plans, surely, for Judd to have created a situation where Pamela had somehow begun to have become somewhat reliant on him, it often seemed as though he liked the edge of feeling more, that she was dependent, was he paying her back for having deleted her media account two weeks earlier. He had a convenient excuse lined up too, to remove from her at least a fifty percent slice of any intellectual gain she inadvertently by his knowing his standard of work may have gained, he told her that he'd been on holiday for a week, and to let her think or believe that by her actions she had actually missed out on opportunities to meet him. And otherwise, also that could cause some to wonder what he had done during that time? Yes, it was all very clever, or so Judd thought. It rather perversely had said to Pamela only that he was actually too busy to notice, and what better way that to have Pamela believe that it was her who'd been caught out, or was even 'no longer required?' Did he realise that it somehow was 'crunch-time' and that there was no way that she would try to either attempt to, or to make up, or to put up with any of it, not this time around? It didn't seem to Pamela as though it was for him 'fin,' it was as if he had a quite personal agenda, but she just couldn't work it out, she even presumed that it could be a pure vindictiveness, or even jealousy that somehow forced his arm. She wanted to say to him, 'sorry darling, I don't mean to or want to 'put a cat among the pigeons,' but it's too late now anyway.' Pamela had not been to mixed sex parties ever; it was not her fault. Maybe it had said more about Pamela's personality, that she had bought just a few, a couple, two cups and two saucers online, suggestively from the country from where Judd had claimed to have originated.

#

Aware that some would quite easily have just got on with the odour she noticed about him, considering it 'manly,' and as she herself when they first met, did like his bodily scent. She hadn't regretted washing him, they were after all, still she thought then, supposedly in the final throes of the pandemic situation. Pamela remained content in the knowledge, and as she was experienced indeed, also quite aware that cells of the virus had been discovered in faeces by scientists. She was glad to have cleaned him up, hopefully setting a precedent, where others would not have even cared, or more selfishly even actually given it a second thought?

Was that to be the last day hey would ever meet? Was there another wider agenda at play? Would either or both or neither survive? Did it matter to them? On what was certainly then, the last day they met, yes, that he started work at 09.00AM having stayed until 08.00AM was to her 'off the scale of reasonable possibilities.' Had Pamela underestimated how he had developed himself whilst in furlough, had he planned two other meets for that morning, with half an hour as it would be on the same train route to get to his place of work armed with his body-wash after, particularly as he'd messaged at 09.32AM. True, he could then have showered at any time during the day, as long as he looked reasonable. As Pamela had already messaged and said to him, "ok darling," she decided it was best to just let him get off to work. She did send one final message as it wasn't quite 10.00AM, it said that she thought and hoped that next time they could enjoy themselves a bit more. A reply came at 13.30PM, that being one of his usual times for checking responses and making 'personal' arrangements, she knew this well having been a recipient. His reply said, "I believe you" in response to his "was good" question, and "Yes I will." in response to the other. Pamela responded with, 'yes ok.'

At 15.00hrs she dozed off having created a space in her apartment where he could relax if he came there again. Where there had been two armchairs in use, and a sofa upright and covered, she switched them around so that the sofa could be used instead. Whilst asleep too, she must have been thinking of him subconsciously, as if her mind had been somehow invaded with all her own attempts to understand and adjust to where she or her emotions or feelings were at. In her dream, she visualised not only herself standing there confidently as when she'd met him on that day in the silk dress, but also a dark- haired person in a dark suit too. He was in the dream as well, the other person, she seemed to shout to but not at him and quite loudly, "you're totally shagged." It was enough to wake Pamela up only moments after as it vaguely did resonate within her own intellect.

Pamela wondered, was it a person he worked with who was about to start the next shift with him where he worked, the person was quite smartly dressed. Pamela then visualised Judd going to lay down as if at the end of a tiring shift- and not going for casual encounters. So surprised was she, that she felt she observed these particular images, that it all seemed quite disturbing for her? It was just like when he'd turn up before looking exhausted from work but this time, again it was like looking at a video screen in a dream for Pamela. It had happened like this, the visions Pamela had, many times before, and certainly in recent months regarding Judd, but before on different subject matters, visions of Judd before, had not been of him in that context? She again then thought of how he'd been on holiday somewhere away in the first lockdown for a week, or so he claimed, in which case, she again questioned, why had he looked so rough? She was observant though and noticed that with an almost renewed vigour, he didn't look so tired when he left her flat? Had she become to him simply as an account of a kind, that he could access when he alone thought it was then fine to? It was something the jury was still out on.

#

Pamela's background although reasonably happy, but quite strict, then again what kid maybe would not think it could have been strict, but she knew there was really nothing about it she would have changed, was of a background whereby on her father's side it was a large family, ten children in fact, four girls and six boys. He father drank alcohol quite regularly, but it was how some of his family had become, they lived almost four hundred metres away from a huge forest then, and were often told when youngsters, not to venture into the forest, especially at night. Some though did, sometimes playing games or some would not realise that at sometimes of the year when nights drew in at an earlier time, that it would get dark before they got out of the forest. When she was growing up, her father who was often angry she certainly thought, had not realised that there might ever have been reasons for this, the seemingly strict upbringing. Her Father was never exactly close to her, although he when drunk would sometimes speak, he would warn her about one of his brothers and swear about him and remark how he used to harm some of his brothers and sisters in a violent way with sticks, at least that was how he remembered it when he himself was a child, it would send him sometimes crazy with anger, to the point where to release himself from that anger he would throw something at a wall or even punch a hole through a door panel, such was his upset, he would even punch a wall to demonstrate that he would not have been afraid and that he never had been. He was one of the very youngest of them and learned to fight at a very young age. On Saturday nights, sometimes there would be gatherings at the family home, often many would come, there would be music and dancing and drinking and much laughter, and sometimes arguments too if things got a little too out of hand, though they were rare, the amount of alcohol that would be drank seemed like so much. Pamela's mother was not an alcohol drinker then to such a degree at all, and would have one lighter type of drink, not the stronger alcoholic items that some would just love so much it seemed. It was as though it sometimes had almost been some plan by them all, to warn of perils that alcohol consumption can bring with it, or even to set an example. But also, there was the getting together and chatting and sometimes others would come who were also family members, usually it consisted of maybe eight couples or less. Pamela would sometimes sit at the top of the stairs in the hallway with two of her younger brothers, her sisters were very small and young, other brothers had not been born at that time. After a while, Pamela would be sat on one of the lower stairs or halfway down, and it seemed as though they would then be allowed to enter that space after a time. On one particular night, there was a real shindig happening, a record player was playing songs, Pamela had been allowed to choose those, some of Pamelas cousins were there and the uncle that her father had spoken of, he wasn't drinking quite so much as the others, but they were all laughing and joking, that uncle was sitting on a low footstool. He was in full view of the others, his brothers, and sisters where he was, but Pamela for one split second when everyone else was partying noticed something. Pamela's mother did not know the conversation between her and her father when he was drunk, so would not have necessarily have cause to be watching as Pamela had, she saw him glance at her cousin and one of her sisters, it was only for a split second and some would have even thought of it as normal, maybe it was, but Pamela stared at him he didn't notice, Pamela was maybe twelve years old or even thirteen, maybe even less, but the cousin of Her's he looked at was younger, and was younger than Pamela too, as were all of the cousins who were there then. Call it inspiration or intuition, but because of what Pamela had been told of him, she was fearful though of nothing she could understand. The cousin was maybe three years younger than Pamela. Although there were no sticks to beat anyone with, Pamela didn't like the look he just for that moment gave or that she saw. Pamela looked at him and maybe just because she was the oldest of them all, she immediately thought, 'leave them alone, do not attempt to go anywhere near them,' he looked away. She noticed him look at one of them again, not even noticing whether anyone else was watching, it all happened so quickly, Pamela feared immediately, she didn't even think that had he tried to harm, not that he'd have had opportunity to because he would have been killed, there was no doubt about that. She didn't understand. She stared at him and thought at him, 'you take me instead of them. Leave them alone.' Pamela was on the other side of the room and it was very doubtful that he'd have noticed her anyway, even though it was not the largest room, maybe four metres square, just enough to get a television and a radio and a white with black diamond shapes on it, plastic covered three-piece-suite and coffee table in, he just smiled and looked away. There was also the matter that it would only be at that time when Pamela saw her cousin getting undressed because the girls stayed in one room and the boys in another, that Pamela noticed she was not like her cousin exactly, she would remember them almost laughing about it, but none of them knew why. Pamela never saw that uncle again, or heard of him although within some years, possibly maybe fifteen, he died anyway, so had that cousin of hers and her cousin's younger sister.

Details of conversations Pamela had with her father, were confirmed by an aunt of Pamela's shortly before shortly before her aunt passed away, she actually said that her brother had raped her. All Pamela could do was stare that the wooden cross that hung on the wall behind her aunt. Pamela asked her father about it, and he told her that he'd been bad to them all and that he was told this as one of the youngest. Pamela doubted that he'd have ever attempted to abuse her father, she really believed that it would not have been possible. It appears too, without wanting to go on about it, that what had happened to Pamela's aunt by him, was not an isolated incident. Pamela was left feeling quite cold and shuddery just to think of it. Her aunt was very distressed, and Pamela looked at her then and wanted to cry too, she was crying inside though. Just as she'd always questioned their alcohol consumption, that was way too excessive, in that it did not seem normal, she always seemed to have an understanding too. When she looked at her aunt intoxicated and in tears that day, wired up to breathing apparatus at her home and asking her husband to get for her a packet of cigarettes from her coat pocket in the hallway. Pamela noticed how long the cigarette was, she smoked it almost without stopping in front of Pamela, Pamela was speechless anyway, she smiled and thought, although she felt unable to comment in amazement. She said to her aunt and not in an aggressive way either, because it was an aunt, and because she knew that the health situation of her aunt would under no circumstances, even with walking sticks and with her wired up and more, not mean that her aunt would not be feared, "you are totally crazy you are," but in her mind, Pamela knew she'd smoked that cigarette deliberately in and front of her, and she smoked it hard, as she did it, on Pamela's mind because she understood her anger, and the real unexplainable hurt, causing Pamela to feel as though the hurt was running through her own veins, she might not have fully understood then but she certainly felt something. or certainly believed she did, she told her aunt 'Don't worry!' That was less than two weeks before that aunt died. There was only one paternal aunt and one uncle from that generation remaining.

#

Judd's background, he lived near Gusafaedstaedt, his father and he did not get along as Judd himself became slightly older, until one day he was forced to leave, or it was made very difficult for him to return and to eat unless he could help by paying, yes, his mother disapproved but his father did not. He did odd jobs where he could, that was what he told his father, and no-one really knew what those jobs were, but his father new the area where he had been seen with others, it was not an easy place to get along. His father thought he was just learning, so did nothing and said nothing. One day, he was sitting, he was a young lad, a man approached him, he was of age by then anyway, but the man was a religious man, now and then he would just give him money, it was as though he saw the sadness and difficulty, he was not from that country and went there on holidays and had done for sabbatical, where he was paid to take leave for work or study. On this occasion he met Judd during his three weeks stay, it was an unusual long holiday, but he had worked without a break for a long time too. Judd told him he had bills to pay and said that he needed a specific amount of money. The man who was a reverend, Reverend Streuwikk did not carry this amount of money around with him, and actually did not have this amount of money available to just give, instead he advised him of what to do, and how to discuss the options, that he thought Judd could not understand. Judd was determined though and although he looked startled, he was given some money to buy food and items, but there was nothing more the reverend could do. He had been to this village maybe four times and had seen it as a place where trouble could brew and genuinely wanted nothing more than to try to help. When he returned to his own town though, he was to be frightened by something he never expected to see, he was twenty-five years older than Judd, and in his own town, he was part of a Lesbian and Gay Community, although especially for some of a particular faith, and he was involved with various religious studies groups, and in one of those groups had even become more directly involved in their management. He had helped too, to organise the church one of Pamela's friends, 'Jean' had been to, though not the Matlin Church Hall. Although the Reverend since died, he was not regarded as a man who had been recognised as Gay by students, indeed an article had suggested that he spoke out of more a responsibility towards others, rather than self-protection. He had a dream and hoped that all was well because he had no means of contacting those he helped or met, not where Judd was from, in the dream he saw an image of Judd although Judd was staring at him through a mirror, it was quite confusing for him because he wasn't sure whether it was the mirror in his own bathroom, or a mirror of Judd's, although he had not obviously ben to Judds accommodation, it had a thin wooden frame and was not a large mirror. In the dream the mirror smashed and a shard of glass slashed Judd's throat in front of his very eyes, then Judds face changed to something so very angry, something he neither expected to see, or could contemplate. It was a look of hurt he thought, and certainly too, of anger, of an anger he had never witnessed. It would be only weeks after that a magazine then 'outed' him as being Gay. He was told by the school that he was not to have any further engagements with 'such groups.' It was after that he became involved in helping to set up the church Pamela's friend knew of.

So, Pamela and Judd both had backgrounds of a kind, each as steadfast as the other and each with a clarity, were they aware? Did Judd ask for money under the premise that he wanted to pay a bill, when really, he wanted to move up a level, or to set himself up in accommodation of his own maybe, was it to buy a car, "to help him find more work"? No-one really knew, or would ever know about that, not now, yes Reverend Streuwikk, died but of natural causes. Could Pamela have recognised his ambition if it was that?

#

When they'd met in the January, for an odd reason, she was as apprehensive as hopeful that a second meet between them would happen and really happy that it did. To her, it seemed more important than the first meet and the third or even their fourth. Because of his antics, should she have been glad of the distance between their meets, or had those few meets in reasonably quick succession actually been too much for a more sensitive person, had he broken her naivety, and would that be where the damage then did lye. She was aware that he had started to meet someone else too, on Wednesdays, he denied it, well, not as such, he'd seemed to think it was important to say to Pamela that he was not meeting others, and would never knowingly it seemed, give indication, but Pamela knew. Was their own meet the day earlier, enough to encourage him that there might be something worth hanging on for or trying for. In which case, would their own next meet as a second time, constitute as their second meet, was it any more important or relevant than their meet recently. Or was the person he met in their second week on the Wednesday, the second meet if there was any importance to that? Pamela was in need of a surgery; it had made things difficult for her and for him. Was the person Judd was meeting female, male? She could not guess. There was no means of Pamela knowing this at all. So, just as she'd been forced to, she had no option available unless he decided to make changes to his Wednesday arrangement or any part of that, to do anything with regard to it, or to influence in any way, it would be futile even attempt to. She'd contacted him the night before. It was 17.30hrs, another of his usual media checking-in times, depending on which shift he was on, So, as he'd checked-in, he was indeed on a 10.00AM -18.00hrs shift after all. Pamela said to him then, or asked, that certainly as then, only three people were now aware of her details on that particular app, which would have been a shock to him, that she'd changed it and become less available seeming, and because she'd been thinking of various occurrences and wanted to be sure, she asked him if he would scroll down and be sure to remove her address details from that page. Also, when they were together, her phone made a sound where someone was texting or trying to contact, she was aware that he'd noticed and also aware that it was earlier than 08.00 when it did sound. Yes, when in the dream she heard a resonating, it seemed sufficient excuse for her to act swiftly. He promptly gave a thumb–up sign via his device as if he was aware of something? Sometime before, she'd mentioned to him in a text conversation that it had been possible for another person to gain access to some apps if they could get access to QR code of the phone they wanted to tap or link to. And that this could be achieved if for example, a person was so tired, 'meaning trashed,' and asked by the person who wanted to locate the code, or their associate or friend, and encouraged or then told to go and lay down to rest, leaving their phone behind in a bag maybe. Or if the person happened to be using the shower at the time and the person who wanted to peek, had access to the phone, she also advised him of just how very quickly some are at achieving just that. It was alarming for Pamela, as dear Pamela was becoming aware of how devious and shrewd some could be.

Pamela had realised that her chaotic mind, where she was trying to improve things, he'd had a taster of, but much had changed since. Would the changes now be enough? Had he now moved on just a little too far? Was she reading into and worrying and thinking and wondering and trying to rationalise her very hopes? There seemed still so much that she didn't know, but this day was Wednesday, not the same Wednesday as then but the following Wednesday from the last. Had her feelings become deeper because of, or had Pamela herself basically started realising that there was more to it all, and that some could potentially be quite vindictive, it was new for Pamela, oh my, had she had a run-in?

In the afternoon of the day before, Pamela received a telephone call. Recognising the phone number, she responded, it was the hospital. She was really happy to have been advised by the hospital, that her preliminary appointment regarding her surgery was now scheduled for the following month. Aware too, and sadly normally, that Judd was in the throes of embarking on another of his excursions, because she'd seen the online moments, the exact same patterns as before. She sent a message to him because she thought he might be interested to hear it. Not that it would stop him, there had been times before when she knew and she even pinpointed it to the moment when he'd be walking into the home of the person he was visiting, and he'd just block her telephone number for two hours, then he'd be apologetic although without apologising, as if in shame, he'd just go completely quiet, totally silent. He'd done the deed, he'd say his words of thanks in messages lasting a few seconds with whoever he met, then he'd disappear and rest again. This time similarly he so courteously responded to Pamela's remark regarding her surgery with "Waw, I'm glad for you." It didn't stop him though, that was it for messages or texts to her, he was off like a ferret down a rabbit hole, she knew how he worked. No longer a clock-watcher, oh no, she knew precisely, exactly what time to check online, each time, daily. This time, it looked slightly different in that it looked like either two train journeys possibly, or a twenty-minute journey, but then a further twenty minutes as he located the place, the way back was often five or ten minutes less, but she knew all this. Some of the times anyway. He always either responded to comments made online or sent them immediately after leaving wherever it was, he visited, then she knew that if the journey time was thirty minutes to get there, that sure enough, thirty minutes after, he'd be online again briefly before resting it off again. More usually than often, but not always, sometimes other things happened too.

This time though, it was fairly normal, though he'd obviously managed to get it done in fifty minutes instead of an hour, must have been good, or not so? Who knew, only him? It was evening, he'd often say something in a message that was more reflective of what he'd been up to during the meet or was planning regarding future meets with them, whether he intended to or not, it was his honest approach to the matter at hand. After the waw I'm glad for you message, another message was sent at 15.28PM. He utilised any excitement factors regarding Pamela's news with his next conquest, as if to maintain a high, it was basically just a free currency for him. So that was when he went online anyway, often at that time. Then it would be one pattern or another, but decipherable, you could even detect the ongoing excitement at certain moments, like he was a child in a sweet shop, or wanting to give a younger impression, excited to be able to just do t and possibly he thought unaware to others. Ther would be a reason for that too, particularly as he told some of them, he was married, although he would make them feel that there was no one else but them for him, almost as though snaring them somehow in a strange premise. It was to do with the speed of log-on's and offs etc and lapses. She'd seen it all before with him, but before with her. Anyway, on this day, he'd gone and done and was now back. It was the Tuesday, yes yesterday. A lone message came at 21.29PM, she was surprised because usually he wouldn't chat, but more recently he had been sending odd irregular messages, seemingly to look interested. It just said, "Cool." It seemed to her indignant and pathetic. But he presumably didn't always know how aware Pamela was. That wasn't the last of it, talk about getting a mud or cream pie in the face. She decided at 22.36PM to very carefully attempt to confront him. Bearing in mind today of course, yes, it's still Wednesday. But nothing is going to shake his normal Wednesday plan, she could have texted as much as she'd wanted. He was unlikely to message at all, and particularly now that he's back at work too after being furloughed, not a response until the next day anyway, if at all. Before, whilst furloughed, whilst the Wednesdays started out as one night away, they became two nights, then until more recently even four days during furlough, or back on the Friday night, followed by another quick excursion in evening, it's a lot to explain. Once furloughed, the travelling time from his home to Pamela had changed to forty-five minutes each way. He learned to operate within a much tighter radius and kept her dangling and now, since meeting him, totally alone and totally isolated throughout the whole pandemic. Before, Pamela had adverts in various websites, she never met any of them, just a photo of her, but was like a sex counsellor/advisor free of charge in her spare time. She advised on std's and sexual health. He though, had tricked her, not lured, and managed to get her to meet him.

At 22.56PM and 22.57PM Pamela sent two messages. They asked and said, Will there ever be a day when you might want one person only? Or is that a difficult question. And then, 'I know it's a silly question, too silly.'

At 22.58PM he responded with, "I have a wife, yes!" Pamela was stunned, she felt as if the blood drained from her body, she cried and whilst in tears visualised two very long lines of maybe thirty to fifty scantily dressed women facing each other, they seemed to move out of the way for her as she walked through them all, hoping to find him and his wife, at the bottom of the line laying down or something, but she stood there and looked around, there was nothing. She then must have been knocked out by it or something because she didn't wake again until just before 03.49AM.

It had been and still was her first relationship or attempt at. Her first encounter with a man. At 03.49AM she sent him a message simply saying, "I'm pleased for you." Then after 08.00AM she sent another couple of messages saying that she noticed that he didn't remember where she lived or even that she'd dropped from a size eighteen dress size down to a size twelve to fourteen. Then she sent the same photo of man with a person dressed in female shoes that he sent her on the morning the last time they met and said to him, and you say to me, "let's do it like this." Wow! She then typed that she wasn't bothered anymore and reminded him that she wasn't personally like neither of them in the photo he sent to her and said, 'oh my goodness,' as apart from footwear they were naked. She attached a somewhat provocative photo of her own buttocks but with her bending right over wearing black skimpy underwear with a black fishnet dress and the straps of a very thin black thong and said, "me, of course I'll enjoy." She said that for personal reasons because she'd heard that from him whilst she was in lockdown alone, but he knew how to twist her mind, he knew way too easily how to, so easily that it was almost natural for him now, as though he'd cloned himself or taken from those, by deceit and the giving therefore, by those he was meeting so regularly, that it would just grow and grow. Certainly potentially.

Also, she apologised that the photo she sent was not a gif as the two previous ones had been from him, she actually wondered where such were located online and still after a search could not for a while locate them, it was as though her mind would then not function properly, this to her meant that others were either sending them to him or he was asking them for them, just as he had of her. It wouldn't be long before she found easy ways to making gifs so quite possibly, he'd slipped up there and was just trying to cover himself, yet again. Pamela didn't let on; she just went along with it. She then said how sorry she was if she 'hadn't seemed nice' when he came to her days before. She said how happy she was to see him and again and that she really didn't know what to do or say that day. After all, she had been incarcerated without even a greeting card in the post from him. She said again "I really didn't." meaning meet anyone, she knew she hadn't, so did he. She was pleading with him, and more aware again that it was Wednesday, he was stripping her mind of her emotion, reducing her to a wreck, and this was his plan, Pamela didn't realize it then. It was his plan. He wanted to feel that desperation, to be aware of what to aim for with the night ahead. And now dear Pamela had also been hit with his own news, that he was claiming now to be married, she even wondered, was he trying to tell her he was 'bisessual' (bisexual) as she would pronounce it, or something similar, but she knew what bisexual was, what was Pamela to eventually discover, how would Pamela's own experience although un-noticed by Judd, or any of them presumably, become utilisable, and by whom, or what? The marriage thing though, this was something she'd heard before but not from him directly to Pamela. Pamela had set up a fake account and he'd told a person on that fake account she'd set up to catch him out, that he was married. He even wanted unprotected sex with her. Pamela very nearly sent him to a made-up address but instead deleted the account but retained the notes and photos of himself he'd sent.

She then told him how she'd explained about him to a friend of hers recently and that her friend had advised her to steer well clear. It had caused a row between Pamela and her friend Bernadette, because she refused to believe that he was not so nice. Again, apologising to him, saying how sorry she was if in any way she'd upset him when they met, and that the reason was because she really believed throughout the isolation that they would never meet again. It was actually the last thing he needed to hear, he wasn't bothered, just as he'd said to her before, "I don't need to bother," so had her mind become impacted by it all. Or that was how she led him to believe. Pamela did not like behaving like this to him, there were times when she hated herself and felt as though she was lying to him, but also, she was aware and that in itself, not only was she hurting herself to put up with it, but resolute too. She then went on to further explain that when the phone made a sound when he visited her that it was a health worker and that she could prove it to him if required by allowing him to examine her phone.

She said, "as I said to you four and a half months ago, if you want to check the apps or messages on my phone you can, it's ok, it's not a problem really." Then she retyped, 'it's not a problem.'

Then she said, "Even before four and a half months ago, yes- they were only quickies then, because you were busier than now. There was nothing in it. Much happened to you in sex since, because so much free time you had. I felt this more than you could ever know. It was the most difficult months. It was horrible. It's not happening again. I'll find a real man. It's ok darling. You have no idea." Then she typed underneath, in case he thought it might somehow question his gender and partly because she doubted his marriage claim and presumed that it might be more to do with whom he'd been associating by the looks of the photos he'd sent to her in recent days, "instead of a boy. xx Yes enjoy!"

"You had your fun and spread your wings a bit more. It was good, however strange that somehow an opportunity for you to do all this came. I used to be upset when you were so overworked. It did upset me. I'm glad you had time to explore. But you explored me out of the picture in the process. It's normal. Enjoy!"

She then typed that she had things to do anyway and explained how no-one is ever going to fancy her with the photo she now has on her profile, it had changed then to an unattractive looking image, Pamela imagined him smiling at that. She then reminded him that at least he knows who she is. Then the very last of the set of five messages said, "and besides, it's Wednesday. xxx." All those messages were typed between 03.49AM, then re-commencing at 08.22AM, until 12.32PM. There was indication that he had seen all of them whilst online but had not replied. He last checked in at just past 15.00hrs, but even she knew not to involve herself at all because of what day it was. The messages therefore a plea from the heart, another opportunity that she knew he would laugh at and ignore. He hadn't before changed, and she knew he would not budge now. The kid found the cookie jar in the sweetshop this time, the same scenario all over again. Not though, she well guesses, because he was married. Two final messages from her that remained unread even at 16.33PM meaning he was well and truly on his way to his Wednesday shenanigans because he hadn't been on since 12.30PM remained unread. They simply said, "Are you looking forward to Saturday," and ended with, xx. She asked that because had he read it, he'd have been perplexed by it and it would have strayed his train of thought for the rest of the day. Because Pamela, he, when he turned up recently with a safety face mask on, when he then removed it and stared at her and said "I can't handle this anymore" saying only that, with reference only to the mask? Presumably yes, she thought, glad too for the experience she'd gained with her background in the course of her own work and to those who introduced her to it. Also, as important, were the stories and tales of her own then clients, and of those heard of from her friend Jean, such as Stan Fyffe and Florence Breeny, she was thankful that she remembered them all, whoever, now though somehow, as though she knew each and every one of them herself personally. Then, as so much of those days seemed to be concerning business affairs of some kind or other, when she thought carefully about even events in recent days and how they tied in with happenings over the past months, she started to wonder whether somehow, or certainly with the situation regarding Judd, supposedly A Hotel Manager, just how much revenue do all of these businesses bring to economies and about maintaining levels and ensuring to do your utmost to be certain where possible to keep the best staff, as if to rally up the crowds that these businesses needed, she even asked of herself, 'bizarre or bazaar'?

What did Judd see in Pamela, to have said to her either, "good to see you, or nice to see you"? Instead of the same usual "I'll see you again," words he always said as he left, whenever he'd visited before? Was it that they couldn't hug like before the pandemic? Had her washing him, offended him? After all, he did carry in his bag his own cleaning fluids and wet wipes, would it be like before, or was it that the pandemic, had finally forced them apart? So many questions that she could not find answers to there and then. Did he sense or source something, did he basically slaughter her and move on, just because he could, or was he himself to think of what had happened? Had he changed that much too because of it all and with whatever he'd been doing during all of those months, was there now enough between them remaining, even with its problems regarding her surgery, enough? During that hour, it was the first time Pamela had ever been totally naked with anyone before, since leaving school in spite of her issues that then Pamela and Judd 'somehow' certainly they were, between themselves, able to overlook. This was also a concern because niggling at her was, the thought that possibly, although she doubted it, maybe he was actually saying that he couldn't cope with that aspect. She doubted that afterward because she remembered his movements and actions. Her seemingly vain almost idiotic and quite intolerably almost, quite pathetic slither of some totally insane hope still remained, that what they had or shared, for him somehow had still been sufficient? She would never know whether he went straight to work after, or not. Was he inspired enough? She painfully though wondered too, was she herself now? The jury was indeed out on that too.

#

Having slept for a few hours, it was funny but often had been the case when the thing with the nipping in and out of each-other's lives somehow by way of logins and outs, certainly with some situations, but Pamela had previously only ever experienced these extremes in certain situations. AT 19.06PM that same evening, she happened to just briefly check that particular media account and it was as if he'd been poised waiting. As if annoyed angry and waiting since, the 17.28PM hit where she reminded him of how he spent his Saturday's and obvious the comparison or he'd not separate them would he, then within that split second, he vanished offline. She ignored it as stupidity, it was after all no different to how she'd experienced similar before and certainly during the past eight months with Judd. She texted a message and said I hope you're ok, to see if he'd come on-line, then because he hadn't messaged all day although she saw he was, or that his account was active throughout the day, said "it seems as if you are avoiding me." and left it at that. An hour after a message appeared, it said "I was busy at work"!!! Suddenly through her mind, she remembered the occasions when he'd turn up and be speaking on the telephone and he'd say that, almost word for word, except obviously he'd be saying to someone that he was at work. It was disconcerting for Pamela at those times and left her feeling uneasy, she presumed with past experience dealing with scammers from overseas for example, that sometimes these things happen deliberately in conversations to put you off your guard. She didn't want to believe that of Judd and still didn't, not in that same way. It didn't mean something hadn't been going on, or that there weren't others he might often meet. That for Pamela seemed the most acceptable option. Was she though now becoming like one of those desperados herself? Was that part of a conscious effort in itself? Was it how Judd survives? At 21.30PM she sent a message saying that she remembered hearing him saying similar elsewhere when he visited her. She then realised that yes, the furloughing had ended, and things were exactly now as they had been prior to. Maybe the Wednesday thing had actually fizzled out too. It was obvious he was online whilst she typed that message and intermittently as if he'd just got back from an excursion and was doing all the lovely to meet you chit-chat now again, yes at 21.46PM his intermittent bursts like he wanted to get to bed but was being polite to whoever he'd visited were still happening. Pamela at that time was typing to him, "I had eight months of this, when the letter comes confirming my medical appointment, I'll send a copy of it to you," she typed to him, just to let him know that if he'd been having a bad time with it too, as crazy as it seemed, and even more-so if he's married presumably? At least he'd know that matters are in-hand again. Unfortunately, though the time between 21.46PM when his last two second burst of flavour went to that recipient, and 22.21PM went quickly, he'd obviously got back to where he was staying, home or his workplace if he was on an early shift, another mission accomplished there. And no, neither of the messages from Pamela had had been read.

Pamela was really beginning to feel as though she wanted to 'put the boot firmly on the other foot,' or so to speak, she'd had enough. It was time to re-think because among other things, although quite accustomed to it now, it hurt being the recipient to his.

'Robots ice-skating'

And if he manages to get around to see all the newcomers first? Yes, those who post ads seeking casual encounters or dates, after all it was on or from similar sites Judd had contacted Pamela. By getting around to see any newcomer first, it would if his technique is proven eliminate competition, it was one multi-faceted game for sure, and yes it was all wonderfully free Would there eventually be a cost associated with it, or would it remain as it was, did it matter, how bad would it be allowed to become? It also meant that it's an available group he can set up on his very own and all then totally accessible via a media app. There is a story about such, where Pamela discovered that she wasn't alone when she removed her details from the media site and basically became like a part of some imitation of a harem. What he hadn't banked on was Pamela's experience with Jon whom she worked with before and his Egyptian background. He often babbled on and she never quite understood why, maybe he was arming her for something, she never realised it. He'd often remark on her shoes how nice they were, or her, in a complementary fashion only, but until now, she never realised quite as much and felt quite as thankful for that experience. He'd told her so much. All she kept thinking to herself at that moment was 'he thinks he's so very clever.' It was also at that precise moment, she worked out how he was doing something, if he had a chat going with a meet, he was now muting notifications in the profile app settings from others individually who might 'interfere' or cause a distraction that could be the difference of him landing his next acquisition or not, he would have known that in those circumstances, a fraction of a second could have got a potential meet to go with someone else if using the same app, or if inexperienced as many of them, she had absolutely no doubt indeed were. How clever was that? By muting notifications, he would not have received notifications that messages were coming through, so yes, no doubt at all, she was very right, and he was indeed quite "busy at work," mmmmmm yes, very busy! If his game had been just to offload whatever crap of him, he had, it had to be inexperienced or innocent types, oblivious to what they'd be left to deal with, or strong enough by ignorance. Then many just left as potential carriers of what?

So, he can basically play with any of them at a whim, whenever he wants. Pamela had also remembered noticing that when he called round, he stood at the end of the room whilst getting dressed and was looking greatly with interest at how her room was organised and split into partitions with furniture. She remembered thinking to herself after 'oh my god, what have I done to have invited him to her home.'

As for the visits he was making, she was never unaware that whilst too, from her work in sexual advice, there were those who 'do the rounds' and those who very much don't mind receiving them too. She even wondered how she might be if she wasn't waiting for a pesky surgery. Above all, it seemed to be about various circles, acceptability's, and about involvement.

There was also the strong point, that if married, he also needed the banter and those in that group who may have been jealous, or even how he possibly thought at least, dear Pamela had become, he could have no real idea apart from guessing either alone or maybe even with a friend of his, of how she actually was, what it could unleash, and what Pamela herself might witness or how. But apart from that, how else would he manage to keep up the pace with his dearly doted on, and much-loved, 'wife,' without it?

Another tact with his so-called marriage, if his wife was constantly accusing him of going with other women, would he be lying to her if he didn't meet women but went with men instead? And if he's going to be constantly accused and get the exact same grief when he was doing nothing, if innocent, why not just do it anyway? The balances would surely be the same?

So, he's linking up too with those experienced and getting photos of them from them. Then contacting younger newbies and sending them photos of albeit attractive looking experienced people. Then they think he's doing them a huge favour, so want to repay him so far or are grateful or feel beholden somehow, because they are young enough to be fooled or to enjoy it, or don't say at a low confidence ebb? Low self-esteem? So, are grateful too? Volume-wise as in quantities. Vulnerable, challenging, even a challenge for Judd as each time he might have younger, busier, competition. But does it really all need to all end there Pamela so quietly asked herself. Obviously not for Judd. She got up and made for herself a coffee having just had some home- made vegetable soup for tea that evening.

For the past hour or so she'd noticed he was online again, ignoring her two earlier messages, if notifications had been switched off, he would have thought she'd gone, or he was just way too focused elsewhere. She wanted to see how he'd respond eventually but she wasn't in any way bothered. She heard the click on the electric kettle, the tv was on in the background, but she couldn't hear it. The sound of another train could be heard just passing in the background, Pamela, now, desperate to go to the loo, her legs were squeezing together as if she was about to burst. She was hoping it would not be uncomfortable to use the loo this time, it was another reason she'd initially closed her media account a couple of weeks before, to get away from Judd, because she felt that his playing about and particularly with her awaiting surgery, it was impacting on her internally in not such a positive way, sometimes having to actually stand up in the bath and pee even, because she couldn't do it normally, it was here she was imagining him with others and she still hadn't yet ever been with anyone. It was so bad that sometimes she would lie in bed with the duvet at her face and in a coital position tightly and just sob into it so no-one would hear her. These were moments, he would probably never understand and a hurt he'd thankfully possibly never himself become a recipient to Pamela of. If he actually knew that some are possibly more sensitive, or thinking they are actually 'in love,' stupidly, that they could be affected in this way, where did that place him for ignoring it and carrying on? But they hadn't said they were in a relationship together, and he'd just earlier that day, or was it the day before said he was married. She noticed he logged off, her messages still unread, at exactly 23.11PM. It was now 23.26PM. She returned from the bathroom, it hadn't been particularly great, she knew she had an uncomfortable night ahead and that it wasn't going to be easy and that she'd probably be up and down to the loo all night long and yes, eventually having to stand in the bath. She stared at her coffee and checked her phone. Realising he was by now probably just tucked up into bed, she decided, no, it doesn't have to end there. Was it important how he responded when he did? She knew that he would know that she saw him online during those hours and that he didn't notice her messages. She wasn't so bothered, inquisitive as to how far he might push it, yes, and how and under what circumstances, yes. She was very much looking forward to her surgery. She'd sent to him a photo earlier, it was quite sufficient by her own standard, in that she was clothed.

She checked the phone and noticed that at 19.58PM when the messages she'd sent stopped showing that they'd been read. At the same time as he'd sent the message saying, "I was just busy at work." She was now fuming inside though, it was affecting her, if he knew, it was cruel, had it been in any way designed for cause and effect, it was definitely crueller, and a hotel manager, or should Pamela have considered that it might get like that, sure she wanted to see how it would pan out, but it was not planned by her, or part of a personal plan or structure, it was how she was, she didn't actually realise any of what was going on at all, and now, or then, again experiencing pressure difficulties in her nether regions. Maybe he was busy?

#

The following day, things seemed quite normal for Pamela, the postal worker had got a plastic wrapped package stuck inside the letterbox and both her and he were tugging trying to pull it one way or the other in order to let other mail in. Then she sat and enjoyed such a lovely orange and peach fragrant tea, not a bad day, dreary looking at first but the sun seemed to be shining nicely now. She'd been thinking about power games and various possible struggles that had in years past involved the person she knew as Jon, he constantly seemed to come up in her thoughts. Jon had been a person who for quite some time was under her charge of care, although they did manage to carve out a kind of friendship too, she remembered him contacting her a few times after she was no longer so directly involved with the company she worked at before and decided that among other things, a little visit might not be such a bad thing.

On her phone she noticed that at 07.50AM darling Judd had checked and read the messages she'd sent the evening before, he'd also turned the notifications on again, on the app they used, she wasn't bothered or concerned and decided not to even dare think about it, or the possibility of coincidental patterns. She hadn't slept particularly well and couldn't help but accept blame for what had happened, having sent the photo of herself which she'd sent to him that day, in spite of the fact that although the photo was clean, albeit of her clothed posterior. Had it sent him over the top? Knowing that he couldn't come and practice his romantic swings and gestures on her because of her scheduled surgery, had he instead again sought something similar elsewhere? She had seen two sides of him, so when she referred to him as a boy, she now wondered, could even that have put a spring back in his step too? Should she have said, 'older boy' in the same way that since she was twenty-five years of age, some, because she was a workaholic, or certainly in a pressured job, was less interested in meets, or the complexities of a commitment and challenges some relationships she'd seen, did and do sometimes enjoy. She now questioned again, of the moment when he removed that health safety mask and of what he said about "he couldn't do this anymore," was he referring to that pace of existence, or solely the mask? But why then, if she ever posted a more made- up image of herself, although she would not have realised it at the time, did he seem to want so often to come? When he was getting dressed to leave, she was standing just in her heels with hair totally dishevelled and smudged lipstick, her mascara and eyeshadow on her left eye was smudged too. In fact, when after- she saw it, it looked a real mess, she shocked herself, the dress, and panties she'd had on were on the floor. She picked up the dress and then reached for a vivid orange knee length zip-up flared skirt that was draped over the back of a white painted wooden seat, the curtains were drawn closed and she questioned to herself whether he'd have noticed the illuminous green flashes of fabric sewn along the waistband to conceal where she'd altered the skirt to fit her new waist measurement, but she doubted that he could because of the subdued lighting. She then stepped into the skirt and pulled it up to her waist, her back was facing him, the zip could be heard as she zipped it up even though the television, covered by a thin piece of cloth was playing classical music. She turned then to walk toward him, they seemed to almost ignore each other as if it was all some terrible guilt-ridden secret, but it was just nerves. She still didn't know what to do, she believed she loved him so very much, so yes, she'd have definitely been blushing, and genuinely so, purely, and only because, of so desperately wanting him. She reached across to the wardrobe door, to where there were some clothes hanging on the door and was embarrassed as she wrestled with a blouse that had become stuck in between metal-wire clothes hangers, hangers sticking, or such disarray was something that never usually happened, it made it all seem very clumsy, if she could have fallen over too, it would have clinched it. The very thin fabric, cap-sleeved ruffle front pale pink blouse, she then pulled it over her head straightened herself up, then after, as he made his way toward the door of her room, with his back to her, she attempted to very quickly tidy her hair? It was at that moment, when he'd have seen for the first time a couple of handbags on hooks behind the door, maybe he tied the ensemble together, because he certainly turned around very quickly and stared straight at her, eyes to eyes, their faces were maybe no more than twenty inches apart. It had been at 'that' moment, then, he'd said, "nice to see you." But why did he appear to look so sternly, she since wondered, and whether he might have been saying, 'not exactly the prettiest picture you might see on any wall or in any website darling.'

She could understand the notion that even in casual sex, some might go into meet others and, 'take what you need' from it. But by mentioning to him that her dress size had gone from a size eighteen to a twelve –fourteen, what she now was worried about, because of how he may be, she thought, or had possibly discovered, had she given him now his very own size comparison chart, possibly to manipulate in his further 'acquisitions,' and even wondered again, was he always such a lone-wolf though, did he actually have an accomplice, and to what end? Did he want Pamela, or was it all really, just to get his end- away? Maybe it was a confidence let-down, but even she knew that there were many choices he could have utilised, Pamela's surgery and postponement of, further exacerbated that and added to frustration rather than something that could have been more relaxed and less strained, what was he up to she wondered, she believed it had caused some real sticky situations to handle and endure for them both. Much had become difficult for her to determine. Despite what she knew or had seen, or believed she'd seen, for her and yes, maybe also for him too, the swings and roundabouts and unbeknown to certainly Pamela, considerably more, were very much indeed yet, and still to be properly played out?

#

Pamela telephoned the phone number she had in her address book for Jon who'd been a former client but they kind of got on anyway, there was an automated voicemail message, she left a message and asked if that phone number was still his telephone number and left her number, apologised for any inconvenience, and invited a text response. A couple of hours after a call came through, it was Jon, or at least she thought it was, he sounded like Jon but there was something not quite the same as she recalled, he seemed chirpier and more himself, didn't say much at all though. He often seemed pre-occupied; she asked if she could pay him a visit. He was very thrilled about it, he said he still lived at the same place as before and they agreed that she could call to visit him on the Saturday afternoon.

When she arrived, she wasn't so surprised as amazed that Jon opened the door to 'her' flat and was now 'Jean.' Nothing was said about it at all, why should anything be said? Her hair was now totally greyed out but longer and scraggly and she was wearing a loose blue gown made of cotton and wearing a big necklace, she had painted red nails, they looked manicured too, or certainly well cared for. Jean asked if I wanted coffee or tea, I said 'tea please.' She said to remove my coat if I wanted to and said to make myself comfortable, so I sat on the sofa that was now on the other side of the room. Not too much had changed with Jean's home since I was last there, not much at all. Because I wasn't sure how the land was with her now, we'd not had direct contact in a while, I didn't ask questions, because I knew that in times past, he then, or she, had wanted to move on. Jean soon came in with tea and some sandwiches, they were pre-made sandwiches, because I could hear the clingwrap being removed from then, she placed them on a coffee table, then she went to the kitchen and fetched some paper napkins. She didn't sit next to me, I thought vigilant still of distancing measures, but even as Jon, he was I recalled, always like that anyway, always. It was uncanny, all the things we'd been asked to do amidst the early months of the scare, were how he always was? She was smiling, it was an unusual smile that I attributed potentially to her having changed. We had separate side-plates as per, and she poured tea, and asked if I wanted milk, then said to help myself if I'd started using sugar and that there were sweeteners in the kitchen if I wanted those instead. I wanted neither but was thankful.

I asked what she'd been up to, she went to take a drink from her own cup of tea and took one mouthful, then she said, "enjoy your Lewis darling while it's hot," I asked what she meant, she said, "oh you haven't changed have you." She said not to worry and that she often gets words mixed up. So, I said, ok. She said she'd been writing about some past times and remarked that she couldn't say too much about it just at this moment but would certainly love to very soon. I said, ok, there's no hurry Jean is there? Then she said, "Oh, and eight months ago I wrote a book, 'Nom Penny,' she then asked if I'd read it? I said 'no, unfortunately not, but I've been rather busy anyway and besides, I'm not actually such a good reader of books. Then she said, so you actually think I have ever read a book myself? "Initially I felt quite ashamed of myself, to have written a book and for that very sole reason," she said. Pamela asked Jean, why use a Nom de plume, I didn't think it was simply because she was and always had been not so much a nutcase, but just full of surprises, and too again, it was nice to meet again.

Jean didn't respond straight away. It had seemed odd though that she would write a book and then not want to give indication of by whom such presumably had originated, then Jean said, "it's a book that has a generative approach, not intended to be harmful and I would hope, not destructive by design, generative," she said.

I said, 'oh thanks for that,' I couldn't help but notice a vague look about Jean though, she'd only seen it on a few occasions, none of which became or were the happiest of circumstances. Jean then said, "you know they slaughtered them all don't you, all of them slaughtered"? I said 'pardon, slaughtered who'? She said, "don't worry darling I'll show you very soon. She then said, "almost all of them, but they ended up coming unstuck." I was beginning to become intrigued, also slightly alarmed. Jean often wandered thought-wise though, and vocalised it, but certainly not ever before about this subject matter?

I didn't stay too long, not that I was totally uncomfortable, only forty minutes, but asked if it would be alright to visit again the following week, Jean responded saying, "oh yes, that would be very fine dear." She then said, that if I liked, she could tell me about the Ingagooks and the Ingigooks. You know, the strangest thing about you Jean, I told her, I could never be sure of exactly what you are going to come out with next, I was happily surprised that she seems to have mastered or encapsulated and retained what were some earlier personal traits marvellously and that not everything changed, not that I would have minded anyway.

I put my coat on and we touched elbows, then I left, before that, I told her that if there were any problems to text.

Before, at around the time when I visited Jean who was Jon, from now on I shall refer to her as Jean only, because there would be no point otherwise. Jean associated with many and was always very professional. Some of those she was acquainted to and with more closely were what you might term or deem as 'visionaries.' Some, if not all of them also had links with what you'd regard as conventional churches. As for my own background, I never really mentioned it to any of them, not that they did not want to know, I simply never told them, you see, when

Jean mentioned the Ingagooks and the Ingigooks, was he was reading me? It was a long story and yes, some bad things happened, as sometimes unfortunately the do. Look at Covid-19. Itt involved a ship and basically a charitable disposition, not a person enduring sadness on that occasion who felt it necessary to become a stowaway. And then a stable family, well as stable as it could have been in 1665. And before then even, stories passed down through the ages, until one day a member of my own family asked if I would purchase a book. I said, "of course," the only question for me personally after, and it really quizzed me, was how could that family member possibly have known of the existence of such a book? It was before the times of internet even. Just as why did I used to visualise of places I have never on or in this realm ever visited, I shall attempt to recall and explain to you. For example, you can look at pyramids or photos of them, but can you imagine a sand filled maybe even mountainous in parts valley, with pyramid where-by their tops actually glow with not so much a gold light but similar to the colour of a dullish lightbulb, but there was no doubt, those Pamela saw, oh they were glowing and quite brightly.

And who was Nanne Fitch? Well, she was burnt at the stake in 1646, she was survived only by one daughter of almost twenty, who found her when she returned from a long trip to find mushrooms, had she been in the woods not too far she thought, from where they lived, that was a kind of croft, she survived. And where did the Ingigooks live? I shall try and fill you in on developments or the lack of, elsewhere too.

#

For three months of the year, they hacked away deep wells in the ice way back then. They didn't know what snow was, only that it happened at certain times, not long before the big snow came, the ingagooks would stop coming to play. The big white clouds then covered their homes in the rocks which themselves were always covered in ice or snow and everywhere, so deep that they could not go out at all and if they did, they had to try to cut their way through somehow, this was why the deep wells were inside their homes and also so close to their homes, it was there where they kept their fish stocks and meats so they would survive over and through what was, had they still been around, wintertime, a time when even the distant forest was white.

Sometimes, if and when they'd find animals that had died, they used their fur to then cover themselves with, also there were other animals that they ate, often birds, but only at some times of the year. Millions of them would fly over and some would drop, they were still alive, but they thought it was fine to eat them, but only after those birds had, 'gone to sleep' could they do it. They were always so grateful, the blood would still be warm, they believed that somehow it helped them to keep warm by eating it as soon as they could.

The Ingagook, similar to woolly mammoth, but was not so top-heavy that it could not stand up, but it was taller than them when it did, and they were big. It had tusks, but they went out to the side, sideways tusks, so when standing, from behind, they looked like horns. Living near the frozen lakes and sometimes on ice, they shared those locations with the Ingagook which by nature was naturally fearsome. Baby Ingagooks had hair like fur, it was believed that adult ingagooks, mainly the female ones, would blow air into their fur, especially when they were born, so if they ever fell through holes in the ice, they would know how to float until they could be pulled out. Fortunately, too though, they could swim. Their tusks were used to help break the ice if ever they became trapped, but they really didn't like water, maybe because if they were a certain age, they would sink to the bottom and disappear forever. They did not die, they simply stayed there.

The Ingagooks had been revered, as more than animals, dogs would bark at them and it frightened them, but they would sometimes force themselves to growl back at them only because of the noise, and things would restore to a normality, there were scratched out images of them on skins they wore, scratched with bones. If baby ingagooks ever did sink, because they never died, they would always have company.

Ingigooks, not the ingagooks though, were much smaller with smaller snouts and ran fast even on the ice, sometimes they would be caught, only to let them go again because they believed it helped them to learn about things and grow. In some other places though, they would be eaten, beyond the mountain. It was widely thought that they were eaten there because some believed that they would taste better than any food in their whole world.

The only thing that seemed to be able to kill them, they believed, was life, so yes, they were nervous, but they also were usually happy because they would habitually not want to generate negativity.

That was until one day, a young man known as Juk,' he had long hair and he made for himself a long spear, it was longer than anyone else's spear, some wondered why he would need it but he had plans to go to the far land, the forest near the far away spoken mountain, he wouldn't have known that inhabitants of that region used nets that they'd carefully strung together, also they had clubs with shells and others, sharp wooden pieces embedded into them, some even pushed sharp animal teeth into their clubs and their spears, his spear may have looked big or impressive to some, but stupid to many others, but you could not argue with him, not ever. Some were fearful of him for that reason and some even wondered what may become of him, was he to become as so fearful, it was a normal practice to just let him be and watch but not too attentively, and in case he caused difficulties. His upper front teeth were unusual, not that they hadn't been seen before like that, some had wider gaps in between their two front upper incisor teeth, but he had just one slightly larger tooth in the middle. It was not a problem for any of them, but it was to become how he himself would be recognised later on. He'd reached an age where he became so angry, maybe because of his tooth, he looked different to the others somehow, but it would have been only his imagination, he would feel his one middle central tooth and look at others who had two, whether there was a gap between them or not, it affected him. Maybe it gave him a sense of needing to prove himself somehow, maybe that was why he made such a large spear, to try to impress, though it seemed to make many just find it not so funny but strange and pointless. Some thought maybe it was because he was young and that he would change, but he did not. He couldn't. And just as he'd gone so far to the edge of their wide enclosure area and stared at the mountain, they all knew that one day he would go there. He'd stand looking that way and hitting the ground with the base of the spear as though to show his strength, but it was not to be. Yes, as young as he may have been, one day he did leave, he was alone, a while after when he did not return, they just carried on. Some hoped but it also was a lesson to them all, not to wander away. Until one day yet again some, a group decided to. It would take them two months on foot to get to the mountain, so five or six weeks to reach the forest. They had not seen Juk before, they did not know him, but they soon returned after nine weeks, having seen on a spike a skull with only one tooth, as though staring at them to warn them away. The elder knew, when they pointed to one tooth, that it was Juk and that he did not survive. They were not a scared people, they were timid and had a quiet existence, they had great respect for the mountain and the forest that they knew of, for some, now they had a far greater respect for the forest. Sure, there were exaggerations by suggestion, to prevent others and young from wandering too far in case they got lost in the cold, or should they become injured or ill or fall into water that could suddenly appear beneath them.

#

That night, after again checking the phone in the evening and noting that Judd's phone was switched off between 15.38PM and 17.25PM though guessing from the time he replied to my two messages sent at 15.37PM and 15.38PM, he'd been online because he hadn't been on all day, Pamela wanted to see whether the Wednesday thing he'd had on since they first met was still actually on, because he would usually stay overnight there, she wondered if he hadn't gone across to there after his meet the night before and if today was a day off for him? In which case he would not have checked online at 15.30PM, but he was already online at 15.25PM until 15.28PM, she somehow knew he was off again, but didn't anticipate his reaction to her messages, or should she have? The first earlier message sent minutes after at 15.27PM was to check how long he'd be offline this time for, by checking the time he went back online after and read it. It said, "Thinking of you, it's nice." The second message sent at 18.04PM when Pamela noticed his phone had been switched off at 16.37 said, "I'm going to plead with them tomorrow to ask that they my surgery will be done quicker, so that more nicer choices are open to me, and much more soon. It's such a hurdle for me, I must." She also realised yet again, that everything she was saying to him, he was potentially manipulating, he could use much of this with others, although in a sexual context. That realisation again for Pamela was quite horrifying and grotesquely disturbing. He was obviously totally selfish and inconsiderate, she had realised before of her actual 'post-operative' recovery, when it did eventually happen, particularly as the operation was a five-hour surgery. Or was he, she'd told him that before though, he then stayed out for three whole days. Checking in online, she was very soon to realise why and how and gain some insight then, into his personal mode of operation. Anyway, his response came at 18.12PM, on my mind, because of the time, was an overture of Pyotr Ilyich Tchaikovsky, his reply, complete with smileys and winks, yes, he'd been out, "Yeah, after your surgery, you'll will have a lot of choices, smirk, wink, wink, wink). It kind of finished Pamela off, she had to go and lay down. She then texted to a medical professional she'd been in contact with had started and typed some distressed moments, as a point of record and reference, to be kept. She chuckled to herself, as unhappy as she was, and thinking about her friend Jean's book, that there were so many records texted to his phone, that it was a book in itself, it encompassed too, all, the entirety of her science-based work and details too, of all the posted links to the various media platforms, throughout the whole covid-19 situation. Judd never ever knew of any of this. Pamela worked throughout and too during those months in total isolation. It was one of those situations where she thought, 'if I had resources enough to get all of it onto paper, it's all filed, but who'd really want to read all that boring stuff.' Especially trying to get out of the Covid-19 situation, not deeper into it. It might one day be a record that could help some, but she felt more thankful to those in the various medical and scientific fields, those on the front line. She saw then and would see the anxiety on their faces, she knew exactly what they were going through. And for her, some of the almost farcical parallels that some could draw, or seem to, and that she was then to investigate logically and file a report on, should any of it in such situation, be of any actual more discernibly noticed relevance.

#

She fell into a deep sleep and dreamed of snakes and serpents. Usually, she would have been afraid of snakes, but they liked her. She also saw people who knew that, from what looked like another country by their attire, dancing over but somehow for or even because of her, as though Cleopatra herself had arrived again in Rome. But what were the snakes? Snakes of all sorts being put near and on her, she had an almost regal appearance around her and although quite unafraid and unaware, some of them were huge things, and she didn't budge, she just handled them and so vaguely smiled. It was different from how she had been in the dream where there were two rows of ladies or women, then she had what looked like a headdress but similar to those that you might envisage on a deity, that was and because she had been crying, presumably, she certainly thought that then, it was the only way she could reason it all to herself, 'why' they allowed her to pass through them how they did. Or maybe they just knew her anger, but obviously they could not have, or she didn't think about it properly, or she would have said, 'why did, oh please do tell me, why did some of them smile then'?

In the dream, everything around her had turned into what looked like one big snake, everything, nothing could be seen by her, apart from a writhing entity, then she noticed that it shed its skin, out of it a girl appeared, pretty much semi-naked, she was on all fours, as if spewed out. At the same time, she must have then woken up, as she remembered then, being and knowingly feeling, very much after, within the safety of trees, as like inside a Bradley within a wood or even a forest of some kind she thought, or even near a small meadow with trees around, or a clearing, but certainly safe.

A defence mechanism instigated by Pamela, some time ago with regard to reaching certain levels or possible danger points in such dreams had caused her to wake up almost instantly. She imagined too, at that moment, that she'd called to Judd because she was somehow telling herself in thought, 'you really have absolutely no idea about me although you think you do.' Then from outside her home she thought she heard a child, what sounded very much like a boy cry out "no, don't leave me." Then Pamela calmed down and reassured herself, it had been like this every week, I must maintain calm, she thought. 'You know he is like that, accept it, say nothing to him directly about it or this about any of this, as much as it hurts you personally,' Pamela thought to herself. I realised then at that moment that the girl spewed out, was possibly somehow Pamela, I certainly felt like she was herself again, yes, she had herself back somehow, her own hands and nails, it was as though she could feel from the very depths of herself somehow, what she believed she somehow was or maybe had become? At 04.19AM Pamela was sitting up in a white cotton lace-trimmed V-neck nightdress, she glanced down at her smooth legs, she must have smiled but then for some strange reason, almost disbelievingly.

And then she thought again, he has no idea, no idea at all. Thankful and glad that she'd said nothing to him directly. Or had she? You see, there were always those imponderable potential dilemmas, always. Did it mean that he had met someone else for example, but she'd been through that with him many times before too? Also, the spewed or shed character, as much as she believed it was her, because they seemed to join, Pamela had seen a character like that before in dreams since meeting Judd, he was having sex with a dark-haired character like that, but not the same. Was she seeing who he'd been with that day, she wondered? Or was it a kind of metamorphosis on Pamela's own individual part, so had the serpent shed its skin and simply grown? She did see in the dream skin drop to reveal. Or, had the character survived and been regurgitated? Certainly, there were feelings that something was happening, some other elements of the dream gave cause to Pamela to consider greater accuracy. Pamela then smiled and thought to herself, oh well, maybe it was only a dream after all?

#

Fortunately, Pamela had always had dreams and visions anyway, and as much as she was and had to attempt to keep things 'in perspective,' for herself, where possible on a more scientific level, some situations were and had been thrown up for her to 'emotionally' or otherwise find a way somehow to deal with, certainly then, particularly as help wasn't often available and if it was, who would she really tell without looking scared, or totally loopy altogether. She even had to imagine how would she react if a person told her that they'd gone through these things, and apart from Jean, spoken of Ingigooks and Ingagooks, like that was to have been the only outlandish situations she would be confronted with? Did Pamela deal with them like a pro though? She'd for a while even imagined that the covid-19 situation could have been that "what would you do if there was a pandemic," situation? It wouldn't be as though anyone involved globally could have told the public at-large, because the full-scale effort required could not have been implemented successful, and there presumably would have been arrests made, although we know that whilst there were, or are some who could have come up with such a master or final solution, or plan, it wasn't as though they were devoid of great thinkers? The likelihood because of ethics was extremely slim and it would have been illegal, and they'd have known that too, so the notion kind of discounted itself, or blew itself out somehow. Pamela had not so much wondered about all that but had been scared and afraid of the possibility that there could have been something more frightening that Covid-19 and to be honest, it had bothered her a lot. What, for example if there had been somewhere an officer's mess, and thinking laterally, what if the uniforms of those in that mess, were indeterminable, as in, Pamela couldn't distinguish where they were from, only that they were not from where she lived, but she could see and understand them. What if then, something happened that she could not understand. Imagine a very large property, a very old property, the type you might see in Bavaria or Germany or possibly France, a large chateau perhaps, maybe the type that could even have been used as a medical institute or even a hospital for a while at one point, of maybe four storeys, surrounded by what must have been dense and quite tall trees, to the point where you could not see beyond them even if looking from atop floor window, all you'd see was the tops of trees. The soldiers, all uniformed, didn't look as though they were planning to fight, nothing like that, or anything like that at all, it was all very calm, they felt safe and they looked as though they were confident, to the point that whatever they were doing, and yes, some even had helmets on, they were winning something, what exactly was not understood, that they looked happy and contented, seemed to say more, they had absolutely no reason to think that anything other than what was their easier usual routine there, was actually likely to change. Then something entered those premises, something that none of them could see, something from the forest maybe, but it might not have been, maybe it had been simply disturbed, whatever it was, a force, not a spirit. It was big, it moved around quickly, destructively, was indiscriminate, even a far wider than average full four tier filing cabinet moved on its own through the air and down into the stairwell where and on top of officers as they attempted to scramble, shocked, not knowing what was happening, it was looking for something and didn't seem to be able to understand or consider that people were anything, even whether they were alive or dead, only if they posed a threat, then they were crushed, it just threw them all over the place, they were fully grown men. There would be mythological comparisons in other situations, such as the medusa, Pamela recognised this, though that, even mythologically now seemed somehow very tame by comparison, this was not something you could readily dismiss, just like though, the earlier days of Covid-19, no-one knew what, or how, standard issue weapons would be of no use, those confident officers just had to let it do whatever it wanted to do, there wasn't even any point in trying to run, they, those, didn't have time to even question whether they could, or whether even the forest could have been a hiding place for them, if they'd got out of the building at all. Then it seemed to find what it was looking for. So, what did it do? Destroy it, when not deliberately, because it didn't understand, it didn't know what people were, so people around it, as it moved about were just being destroyed anyway just by the sheer destruction caused as it searched, unless they were, as suggested, in any way a threat, then it just took them out without giving a second thought. It picked a soldier up into the air, of course the soldier was on the defensive too, so he thought he was about to die, as so many had just then, there was no other thought other than that, by and because that seemed like an invisible invasion, they simply just did not know what was happening. A little like Covid-19 I guess, an invisible killer yes, but not quite. All it did, using an invisible hand, was to put something wet, possibly it's saliva, or something similar in consistency, on the front of the soldier's hair, the soldier it picked up. Then, it dropped him to the ground, and as quick as it came, it left through an open upstairs window of the room those were in. The soldiers then non-condescendingly became like, or Pamela certainly saw them all, not in a sexist way, as looking female, stripped, as they all tried to clean up, wondering what had happened. The soldier not knowing why he'd been marked in this way was desperate to try to wash off what had been put on his hair in case it identified him personally should whatever it was return or made it easier for him to be located by it. Some were then seen standing by a sink, frantic almost, something like an old large Belfast sink, he was frantic too and saying to the others, how do we remove it from my hair if we can't see it and we don't know what it was or is. They didn't know whether to use water or detergent for example, they just did not know. They believed it was going to return and that this was the reason whatever it was, had been smeared on the soldier's hair. It was as though it owned the place, or something like that, such was its force, or it had an overwhelming control. They believed momentarily that it had, just because of its speed, gone beyond the forest then. Then from those upstairs windows, some called that the forest was ablaze, starting from the far distance and moving closer to the chateau, the chateau was far enough away not to be burnt. It was at that moment, Pamela, sitting in her nightie and flip-flops, and who'd finished her cup of earl grey tea, could hear what sounded very much like an owl outside, the sound it made gave her some comfort and thankfully for quite a while as she had been quite scared by it all. So, the whole forest was burning, had someone set it ablaze to stop it in its tracks? What would the point of setting light to it, to stop it in its tracks have been, if it had already gone, she thought? What had been smeared on that person's hair, it was also like thickened urine or a thinned snail slime in consistency, though invisible to the soldiers. Did it wash out, did it affect how some might parent, had the fire been started to prevent further harm? Had covid-19 happened somehow to prevent Judd from returning to her, she even however stupidly, wondered. She remembered what a person at a hospital had said to her regarding her surgery and surgeries obviously, "we're making the place as safe as possible, so you'll be safer from risk of covid-19," Had that, or could it have taken on a new or greater relevance now, was it meant to, she wouldn't realise anyway, even if it was meant to. Whatever it was in that chateau, only Pamela could see it, it seemed to speak directly after the forest was seen all ablaze, it said to Pamela, "it's the end of the line." This made her question all kinds of things, including fires around in parts of the world, and obviously, even fires in the Amazon that seemed to be all over the news prior to Covid-19. She started to ask herself, was it some kind of revenge, she even asked if it was distant ancestors somehow giving or presenting with warnings of possibilities, like a fool, she even questioned whether, because somehow the voice was or was heard as, or became, similar to Judds, that it might have been not so much about Judd, but of who she might end up with after her surgery, or more strangely and pathetically, even if she remained single. Then it started raining outside, it was all she could then hear, like drips on a metal dustbin, and sweet wrappers being scrunched in the palm of a hand all at the same time, and now and then you'd hear the sound of the odd droplet hitting the base of an upturned plastic bucket.

She seemed quite certain that for some strange reason that she was unaware of, the soldiers looked German, although she really couldn't be certain about that at all and therefore presumed it was a part of her sub-conscious and her imagination that provoked the thought, rather that intuition, she did know though that somehow, something had to intervene. Would such, or any intervention, ever to be truthfully realised, and would it be as expected, but also, it made sense to her, however oddly, of something she heard only days before where a voice seemed to say to her, "I'll set fire to the trees." Something had affected Pamela, had Judd or those who he knew even by association to, or by jealousy, deliberately set out to create a desire in Pamela, to get even on the girl who never seemed to want to meet anyone, because she had personal reasons and never wanted anything but the real deal and not selfishly, but because she felt she would be cheating them unless she could offer that. Or was a person who if the circumstances were right 'partly,' just wanted to see if dear Pamela would drop her golden principles as quickly as she could, they thought, because some others would, drop their knickers simply settling for a naked swim after dark. It was difficult to know exactly, because she never was able to, because of her need for surgery, so why the same seemed to be always beating the very same drum year on and year off, she noticed, could neither be questioned nor faltered. Enough that if she'd said to him that she wanted him, or gave indication eventually, it had provided a convenient and very live and direct access route for him or them, if it were so, had some game, sick pathetic game set a die of its own by way of a cruel, if it were the case, 'experienced,' deception been cast? Even if by default. But dear Pamela didn't know. And just as those soldiers even though they'd looked as though they were involved in something war-like if only by their attire and their occupation scale at that place, didn't know what was happening to them, presumably, neither could those who might have then 'chosen' to 'take Pamela on.' But remember, she would have no idea, putty in their hands effectively. If Pamela didn't realize, they never would either? How were they likely to? So, it seemed as though they weren't, or hadn't even been bothered by Covid-19, by how it affected so many. So did Pamela know then that she was going to end up in a situation that s with her now, we'd not had direct contact in a while, I didn't ask questions, because I knew that in times past, he then, or she, had wanted to move on. Jean soon came in with tea and some sandwiches, they were pre-made sandwiches, because I could hear the clingwrap being removed from then, she placed them on a coffee table, then she went to the kitchen and fetched some paper napkins. She didn't sit next to me, I thought vigilant still of distancing measures, but even as Jon, he was I recalled, always like that anyway, always. It was uncanny, all the things we'd been asked to do amidst the early months of the scare, were how he always was? She was smiling, it was an unusual smile that I attributed potentially to her having changed. We had separate side-plates as per, and she poured tea, and asked if I wanted milk, then said to help myself if I'd started using sugar and that there were sweeteners in the kitchen if I wanted those instead. I wanted neither but was thankful.

I asked what she'd been up to, she went to take a drink from her own cup of tea and took one mouthful, then she said, "enjoy your Lewis darling while it's hot," I asked what she meant, she said, "oh you haven't changed have you." She said not to worry and that she often gets words mixed up. So, I said, ok. She said she'd been writing about some past times and remarked that she couldn't say too much about it just at this moment but would certainly love to very soon. I said, ok, there's no hurry Jean is there? Then she said, "Oh, and eight months ago I wrote a book, 'Nom Penny,' she then asked if I'd read it? I said 'no, unfortunately not, but I've been rather busy anyway and besides, I'm not actually such a good reader of books. Then she said, so you actually think I have ever read a book myself? "Initially I felt quite ashamed of myself, to have written a book and for that very sole reason," she said. Pamela asked Jean, why use a Nom de plume, I didn't think it was simply because she was and always had been not so much a nutcase, but just full of surprises, and too again, it was nice to meet again.

Jean didn't respond straight away. It had seemed odd though that she would write a book and then not want to give indication of by whom such presumably had originated, then Jean said, "it's a book that has a generative approach, not intended to be harmful and I would hope, not destructive by design, generative," she said.

I said, 'oh thanks for that,' I couldn't help but notice a vague look about Jean though, she'd only seen it on a few occasions, none of which became or were the happiest of circumstances. Jean then said, "you know they slaughtered them all don't you, all of them slaughtered"? I said 'pardon, slaughtered who'? She said, "don't worry darling I'll show you very soon. She then said, "almost all of them, but they ended up coming unstuck." I was beginning to become intrigued, also slightly alarmed. Jean often wandered thought-wise though, and vocalised it, but certainly not ever before about this subject matter?

I didn't stay too long, not that I was totally uncomfortable, only forty minutes, but asked if it would be alright to visit again the following week, Jean responded saying, "oh yes, that would be very fine dear." She then said, that if I liked, she could tell me about the Ingagooks and the Ingigooks. You know, the strangest thing about you Jean, I told her, I could never be sure of exactly what you are going to come out with next, I was happily surprised that she seems to have mastered or encapsulated and retained what were some earlier personal traits marvellously and that not everything changed, not that I would have minded anyway.

I put my coat on and we touched elbows, then I left, before that, I told her that if there were any problems to text.

Before, at around the time when I visited Jean who was Jon, from now on I shall refer to her as Jean only, because there would be no point otherwise. Jean associated with many and was always very professional. Some of those she was acquainted to and with more closely were what you might term or deem as 'visionaries.' Some, if not all of them also had links with what you'd regard as conventional churches. As for my own background, I never really mentioned it to any of them, not that they did not want to know, I simply never told them, you see, when Jean mentioned the Ingagooks and the Ingigooks, was he was reading me? It was a long story and yes, some bad things happened, as sometimes unfortunately the do. Look at.Covid-19. Itt involved a ship and basically a charitable disposition, not a person enduring sadness on that occasion who felt it necessary to become a stowaway. And then a stable family, well as stable as it could have been in 1665. And before then even, stories passed down through the ages, until one day a member of my own family asked if I would purchase a book. I said, "of course," the only question for me personally after, and it really quizzed me, was how could that family member possibly have known of the existence of such a book? It was before the times of internet even. Just as why did I used to visualise of places I have never on or in this realm ever visited, I shall attempt to recall and explain to you. For example, you can look at pyramids or photos of them, but can you imagine a sand filled maybe even mountainous in parts valley, with pyramid where-by their tops actually glow with not so much a gold light but similar to the colour of a dullish lightbulb, but there was no doubt, those Pamela saw, oh they were glowing and quite brightly.

And who was Nanne Fitch? Well, she was burnt at the stake in 1646, she was survived only by one daughter of almost twenty, who found her when she returned from a long trip to find mushrooms, had she been in the woods not too far she thought, from where they lived, that was a kind of croft, she survived. And where did the Ingigooks live? I shall try and fill you in on developments or the lack of, elsewhere too.

#

For three months of the year, they hacked away deep wells in the ice way back then. They didn't know what snow was, only that it happened at certain times, not long before the big snow came, the ingagooks would stop coming to play. The big white clouds then covered their homes in the rocks which themselves were always covered in ice or snow and everywhere, so deep that they could not go out at all and if they did, they had to try to cut their way through somehow, this was why the deep wells were inside their homes and also so close to their homes, it was there where they kept their fish stocks and meats so they would survive over and through what was, had they still been around, wintertime, a time when even the distant forest was white.

Sometimes, if and when they'd find animals that had died, they used their fur to then cover themselves with, also there were other animals that they ate, often birds, but only at some times of the year. Millions of them would fly over and some would drop, they were still alive, but they thought it was fine to eat them, but only after those birds had, 'gone to sleep' could they do it. They were always so grateful, the blood would still be warm, they believed that somehow it helped them to keep warm by eating it as soon as they could.

The Ingagook, similar to woolly mammoth, but was not so top-heavy that it could not stand up, but it was taller than them when it did, and they were big. It had tusks, but they went out to the side, sideways tusks, so when standing, from behind, they looked like horns. Living near the frozen lakes and sometimes on ice, they shared those locations with the Ingagook which by nature was naturally fearsome. Baby Ingagooks had hair like fur, it was believed that adult ingagooks, mainly the female ones, would blow air into their fur, especially when they were born, so if they ever fell through holes in the ice, they would know how to float until they could be pulled out. Fortunately, too though, they could swim. Their tusks were used to help break the ice if ever they became trapped, but they really didn't like water, maybe because if they were a certain age, they would sink to the bottom and disappear forever. They did not die, they simply stayed there.

The Ingagooks had been revered, as more than animals, dogs would bark at them and it frightened them, but they would sometimes force themselves to growl back at them only because of the noise, and things would restore to a normality, there were scratched out images of them on skins they wore, scratched with bones. If baby ingagooks ever did sink, because they never died, they would always have company.

Ingigooks, not the ingagooks though, were much smaller with smaller snouts and ran fast even on the ice, sometimes they would be caught, only to let them go again because they believed it helped them to learn about things and grow. In some other places though, they would be eaten, beyond the mountain. It was widely thought that they were eaten there because some believed that they would taste better than any food in their whole world.

The only thing that seemed to be able to kill them, they believed, was life, so yes, they were nervous, but they also were usually happy because they would habitually not want to generate negativity.

That was until one day, a young man known as Juk, he had long hair and he made for himself a long spear, it was longer than anyone else's spear, some wondered why he would need it but he had plans to go to the far land, the forest near the far away spoken mountain, he wouldn't have known that inhabitants of that region used nets that they'd carefully strung together, also they had clubs with shells and others, sharp wooden pieces embedded into them, some even pushed sharp animal teeth into their clubs and their spears, his spear may have looked big or impressive to some, but stupid to many others, but you could not argue with him, not ever. Some were fearful of him for that reason and some even wondered what may become of him, was he to become as so fearful, it was a normal practice to just let him be and watch but not too attentively, and in case he caused difficulties. His upper front teeth were unusual, not that they hadn't been seen before like that, some had wider gaps in between their two front upper incisor teeth, but he had just one slightly larger tooth in the middle. It was not a problem for any of them, but it was to become how he himself would be recognised later on. He'd reached an age where he became so angry, maybe because of his tooth, he looked different to the others somehow, but it would have been only his imagination, he would feel his one middle central tooth and look at others who had two, whether there was a gap between them or not, it affected him. Maybe it gave him a sense of needing to prove himself somehow, maybe that was why he made such a large spear, to try to impress, though it seemed to make many just find it not so funny but strange and pointless. Some thought maybe it was because he was young and that he would change, but he did not. He couldn't. And just as he'd gone so far to the edge of their wide enclosure area and stared at the mountain, they all knew that one day he would go there. He'd stand looking that way and hitting the ground with the base of the spear as though to show his strength, but it was not to be. Yes, as young as he may have been, one day he did leave, he was alone, a while after when he did not return, they just carried on. Some hoped but it also was a lesson to them all, not to wander away. Until one day yet again some, a group decided to. It would take them two months on foot to get to the mountain, so five or six weeks to reach the forest. They had not seen Juk before, they did not know him, but they soon returned after nine weeks, having seen on a spike a skull with only one tooth, as though staring at them to warn them away. The elder knew, when they pointed to one tooth, that it was Juk and that he did not survive. They were not a scared people, they were timid and had a quiet existence, they had great respect for the mountain and the forest that they knew of, for some, now they had a far greater respect for the forest. Sure, there were exaggerations by suggestion, to prevent others and young from wandering too far in case they got lost in the cold, or should they become injured or ill or fall into water that could suddenly appear beneath them.

#

That night, after again checking the phone in the evening and noting that Judd's phone was switched off between 15.38PM and 17.25PM though guessing from the time he replied to my two messages sent at 15.37PM and 15.38PM, he'd been online because he hadn't been on all day, Pamela wanted to see whether the Wednesday thing he'd had on since they first met was still actually on, because he would usually stay overnight there, she wondered if he hadn't gone across to there after his meet the night before and if today was a day off for him? In which case he would not have checked online at 15.30PM, but he was already online at 15.25PM until 15.28PM, she somehow knew he was off again, but didn't anticipate his reaction to her messages, or should she have? The first earlier message sent minutes after at 15.27PM was to check how long he'd be offline this time for, by checking the time he went back online after and read it. It said, "Thinking of you, it's nice." The second message sent at 18.04PM when Pamela noticed his phone had been switched off at 16.37 said, "I'm going to plead with them tomorrow to ask that they my surgery will be done quicker, so that more nicer choices are open to me, and much more soon. It's such a hurdle for me, I must." She also realised yet again, that everything she was saying to him, he was potentially manipulating, he could use much of this with others, although in a sexual context. That realisation again for Pamela was quite horrifying and grotesquely disturbing. He was obviously totally selfish and inconsiderate, she had realised before of her actual 'post-operative' recovery, when it did eventually happen, particularly as the operation was a five-hour surgery. Or was he, she'd told him that before though, he then stayed out for three whole days. Checking in online, she was very soon to realise why and how and gain some insight then, into his personal mode of operation. Anyway, his response came at 18.12PM, on my mind, because of the time, was an overture of Pyotr Ilyich Tchaikovsky, his reply, complete with smileys and winks, yes, he'd been out, "Yeah, after your surgery, you'll will have a lot of choices, smirk, wink, wink, wink). It kind of finished Pamela off, she had to go and lay down. She then texted to a medical professional she'd been in contact with had started and typed some distressed moments, as a point of record and reference, to be kept. She chuckled to herself, as unhappy as she was, and thinking about her friend Jean's book, that there were so many records texted to his phone, that it was a book in itself, it encompassed too, all, the entirety of her science-based work and details too, of all the posted links to the various media platforms, throughout the whole covid-19 situation. Judd never ever knew of any of this. Pamela worked throughout and too during those months in total isolation. It was one of those situations where she thought, 'if I had resources enough to get all of it onto paper, it's all filed, but who'd really want to read all that boring stuff.' Especially trying to get out of the Covid-19 situation, not deeper into it. It might one day be a record that could help some, but she felt more thankful to those in the various medical and scientific fields, those on the front line. She saw then and would see the anxiety on their faces, she knew exactly what they were going through. And for her, some of the almost farcical parallels that some could draw, or seem to, and that she was then to investigate logically and file a report on, should any of it in such situation, be of any actual more discernibly noticed relevance.

#

She fell into a deep sleep and dreamed of snakes and serpents. Usually, she would have been afraid of snakes, but they liked her. She also saw people who knew that, from what looked like another country by their attire, dancing over but somehow for or even because of her, as though Cleopatra herself had arrived again in Rome. But what were the snakes? Snakes of all sorts being put near and on her, she had an almost regal appearance around her and although quite unafraid and unaware, some of them were huge things, and she didn't budge, she just handled them and so vaguely smiled. It was different from how she had been in the dream where there were two rows of ladies or women, then she had what looked like a headdress but similar to those that you might envisage on a deity, that was and because she had been crying, presumably, she certainly thought that then, it was the only way she could reason it all to herself, 'why' they allowed her to pass through them how they did. Or maybe they just knew her anger, but obviously they could not have, or she didn't think about it properly, or she would have said, 'why did, oh please do tell me, why did some of them smile then'?

In the dream, everything around her had turned into what looked like one big snake, everything, nothing could be seen by her, apart from a writhing entity, then she noticed that it shed its skin, out of it a girl appeared, pretty much semi-naked, she was on all fours, as if spewed out. At the same time, she must have then woken up, as she remembered then, being and knowingly feeling, very much after, within the safety of trees, as like inside a Bradley within a wood or even a forest of some kind she thought, or even near a small meadow with trees around, or a clearing, but certainly safe.

A defence mechanism instigated by Pamela, some time ago with regard to reaching certain levels or possible danger points in such dreams had caused her to wake up almost instantly. She imagined too, at that moment, that she'd called to Judd because she was somehow telling herself in thought, 'you really have absolutely no idea about me although you think you do.' Then from outside her home she thought she heard a child, what sounded very much like a boy cry out "no, don't leave me." Then Pamela calmed down and reassured herself, it had been like this every week, I must maintain calm, she thought. 'You know he is like that, accept it, say nothing to him directly about it or this about any of this, as much as it hurts you personally,' Pamela thought to herself. I realised then at that moment that the girl spewed out, was possibly somehow Pamela, I certainly felt like she was herself again, yes, she had herself back somehow, her own hands and nails, it was as though she could feel from the very depths of herself somehow, what she believed she somehow was or maybe had become? At 04.19AM Pamela was sitting up in a white cotton lace-trimmed V-neck nightdress, she glanced down at her smooth legs, she must have smiled but then for some strange reason, almost disbelievingly. And then she thought again, he has no idea, no idea at all. Thankful and glad that she'd said nothing to him directly. Or had she? You see, there were always those imponderable potential dilemmas, always. Did it mean that he had met someone else for example, but she'd been through that with him many times before too? Also, the spewed or shed character, as much as she believed it was her, because they seemed to join, Pamela had seen a character like that before in dreams since meeting Judd, he was having sex with a dark-haired character like that, but not the same. Was she seeing who he'd been with that day, she wondered? Or was it a kind of metamorphosis on Pamela's own individual part, so had the serpent shed its skin and simply grown? She did see in the dream skin drop to reveal. Or, had the character survived and been regurgitated? Certainly, there were feelings that something was happening, some other elements of the dream gave cause to Pamela to consider greater accuracy. Pamela then smiled and thought to herself, oh well, maybe it was only a dream after all?

#

Fortunately, Pamela had always had dreams and visions anyway, and as much as she was and had to attempt to keep things 'in perspective,' for herself, where possible on a more scientific level, some situations were and had been thrown up for her to 'emotionally' or otherwise find a way somehow to deal with, certainly then, particularly as help wasn't often available and if it was, who would she really tell without looking scared, or totally loopy altogether. She even had to imagine how would she react if a person told her that they'd gone through these things, and apart from Jean, spoken of Ingigooks and Ingagooks, like that was to have been the only outlandish situations she would be confronted with? Did Pamela deal with them like a pro though? She'd for a while even imagined that the covid-19 situation could have been that "what would you do if there was a pandemic," situation? It wouldn't be as though anyone involved globally could have told the public at-large, because the full-scale effort required could not have been implemented successful, and there presumably would have been arrests made, although we know that whilst there were, or are some who could have come up with such a master or final solution, or plan, it wasn't as though they were devoid of great thinkers? The likelihood because of ethics was extremely slim and it would have been illegal, and they'd have known that too, so the notion kind of discounted itself, or blew itself out somehow. Pamela had not so much wondered about all that but had been scared and afraid of the possibility that there could have been something more frightening that Covid-19 and to be honest, it had bothered her a lot. What, for example if there had been somewhere an officer's mess, and thinking laterally, what if the uniforms of those in that mess, were indeterminable, as in, Pamela couldn't distinguish where they were from, only that they were not from where she lived, but she could see and understand them. What if then, something happened that she could not understand. Imagine a very large property, a very old property, the type you might see in Bavaria or Germany or possibly France, a large chateau perhaps, maybe the type that could even have been used as a medical institute or even a hospital for a while at one point, of maybe four storeys, surrounded by what must have been dense and quite tall trees, to the point where you could not see beyond them even if looking from atop floor window, all you'd see was the tops of trees. The soldiers, all uniformed, didn't look as though they were planning to fight, nothing like that, or anything like that at all, it was all very calm, they felt safe and they looked as though they were confident, to the point that whatever they were doing, and yes, some even had helmets on, they were winning something, what exactly was not understood, that they looked happy and contented, seemed to say more, they had absolutely no reason to think that anything other than what was their easier usual routine there, was actually likely to change. Then something entered those premises, something that none of them could see, something from the forest maybe, but it might not have been, maybe it had been simply disturbed, whatever it was, a force, not a spirit. It was big, it moved around quickly, destructively, was indiscriminate, even a far wider than average full four tier filing cabinet moved on its own through the air and down into the stairwell where and on top of officers as they attempted to scramble, shocked, not knowing what was happening, it was looking for something and didn't seem to be able to understand or consider that people were anything, even whether they were alive or dead, only if they posed a threat, then they were crushed, it just threw them all over the place, they were fully grown men. There would be mythological comparisons in other situations, such as the medusa, Pamela recognised this, though that, even mythologically now seemed somehow very tame by comparison, this was not something you could readily dismiss, just like though, the earlier days of Covid-19, no-one knew what, or how, standard issue weapons would be of no use, those confident officers just had to let it do whatever it wanted to do, there wasn't even any point in trying to run, they, those, didn't have time to even question whether they could, or whether even the forest could have been a hiding place for them, if they'd got out of the building at all. Then it seemed to find what it was looking for. So, what did it do? Destroy it, when not deliberately, because it didn't understand, it didn't know what people were, so people around it, as it moved about were just being destroyed anyway just by the sheer destruction caused as it searched, unless they were, as suggested, in any way a threat, then it just took them out without giving a second thought. It picked a soldier up into the air, of course the soldier was on the defensive too, so he thought he was about to die, as so many had just then, there was no other thought other than that, by and because that seemed like an invisible invasion, they simply just did not know what was happening. A little like Covid-19 I guess, an invisible killer yes, but not quite. All it did, using an invisible hand, was to put something wet, possibly it's saliva, or something similar in consistency, on the front of the soldier's hair, the soldier it picked up. Then, it dropped him to the ground, and as quick as it came, it left through an open upstairs window of the room those were in. The soldiers then non-condescendingly became like, or Pamela certainly saw them all, not in a sexist way, as looking female, stripped, as they all tried to clean up, wondering what had happened. The soldier not knowing why he'd been marked in this way was desperate to try to wash off what had been put on his hair in case it identified him personally should whatever it was return or made it easier for him to be located by it. Some were then seen standing by a sink, frantic almost, something like an old large Belfast sink, he was frantic too and saying to the others, how do we remove it from my hair if we can't see it and we don't know what it was or is. They didn't know whether to use water or detergent for example, they just did not know. They believed it was going to return and that this was the reason whatever it was, had been smeared on the soldier's hair. It was as though it owned the place, or something like that, such was its force, or it had an overwhelming control. They believed momentarily that it had, just because of its speed, gone beyond the forest then. Then from those upstairs windows, some called that the forest was ablaze, starting from the far distance and moving closer to the chateau, the chateau was far enough away not to be burnt. It was at that moment, Pamela, sitting in her nightie and flip-flops, and who'd finished her cup of earl grey tea, could hear what sounded very much like an owl outside, the sound it made gave her some comfort and thankfully for quite a while as she had been quite scared by it all. So, the whole forest was burning, had someone set it ablaze to stop it in its tracks? What would the point of setting light to it, to stop it in its tracks have been, if it had already gone, she thought? What had been smeared on that person's hair, it was also like thickened urine or a thinned snail slime in consistency, though invisible to the soldiers. Did it wash out, did it affect how some might parent, had the fire been started to prevent further harm? Had covid-19 happened somehow to prevent Judd from returning to her, she even however stupidly, wondered. She remembered what a person at a hospital had said to her regarding her surgery and surgeries obviously, "we're making the place as safe as possible, so you'll be safer from risk of covid-19," Had that, or could it have taken on a new or greater relevance now, was it meant to, she wouldn't realise anyway, even if it was meant to. Whatever it was in that chateau, only Pamela could see it, it seemed to speak directly after the forest was seen all ablaze, it said to Pamela, "it's the end of the line." This made her question all kinds of things, including fires around in parts of the world, and obviously, even fires in the Amazon that seemed to be all over the news prior to Covid-19. She started to ask herself, was it some kind of revenge, she even asked if it was distant ancestors somehow giving or presenting with warnings of possibilities, like a fool, she even questioned whether, because somehow the voice was or was heard as, or became, similar to Judds, that it might have been not so much about Judd, but of who she might end up with after her surgery, or more strangely and pathetically, even if she remained single. Then it started raining outside, it was all she could then hear, like drips on a metal dustbin, and sweet wrappers being scrunched in the palm of a hand all at the same time, and now and then you'd hear the sound of the odd droplet hitting the base of an upturned plastic bucket.

She seemed quite certain that for some strange reason that she was unaware of, the soldiers looked German, although she really couldn't be certain about that at all and therefore presumed it was a part of her sub-conscious and her imagination that provoked the thought, rather that intuition, she did know though that somehow, something had to intervene. Would such, or any intervention, ever to be truthfully realised, and would it be as expected, but also, it made sense to her, however oddly, of something she heard only days before where a voice seemed to say to her, "I'll set fire to the trees." Something had affected Pamela, had Judd or those who he knew even by association to, or by jealousy, deliberately set out to create a desire in Pamela, to get even on the girl who never seemed to want to meet anyone, because she had personal reasons and never wanted anything but the real deal and not selfishly, but because she felt she would be cheating them unless she could offer that. Or was a person who if the circumstances were right 'partly,' just wanted to see if dear Pamela would drop her golden principles as quickly as she could, they thought, because some others would, drop their knickers simply settling for a naked swim after dark. It was difficult to know exactly, because she never was able to, because of her need for surgery, so why the same seemed to be always beating the very same drum year on and year off, she noticed, could neither be questioned nor faltered. Enough that if she'd said to him that she wanted him, or gave indication eventually, it had provided a convenient and very live and direct access route for him or them, if it were so, had some game, sick pathetic game set a die of its own by way of a cruel, if it were the case, 'experienced,' deception been cast? Even if by default. But dear Pamela didn't know. And just as those soldiers even though they'd looked as though they were involved in something war-like if only by their attire and their occupation scale at that place, didn't know what was happening to them, presumably, neither could those who might have then 'chosen' to 'take Pamela on.' But remember, she would have no idea, putty in their hands effectively. If Pamela didn't realize, they never would either? How were they likely to? So, it seemed as though they weren't, or hadn't even been bothered by Covid-19, by how it affected so many. So did Pamela know then that she was going to end up in a situation that every last one of them would endure and feel, and for the actual innocents, and not those directly associated. No, she didn't, she never would. Whoever it was, if it was deliberate, they hurt Pamela a lot, so much, and laughed about it, still almost a year after. Yes, it was now Autumn, October the twelfth and the time, precisely one-minute past midnight. Access to them from that moment on, now denied. Would her own tactics prove to be something to be 'desired?' The day before, Pamela posed for a photo by a tree, the leaves had indeed turned the most beautifully colour of a burnished gold.

#

Jean had a friend known as Lucy, but they had not caught up in quite a while, Jon had arranged to meet Lucy and her partner Bernadette much earlier in the year. They'd arranged to meet fairly near to where Pamela lived, Lucy had a slight eye stammer, Jean had suggested ways of handling it and they were recommended ways told to her by another friend she knew who'd had a verbal stammer, it therefore had become between them more of a wink now, such was the depth of their friendship. Jean noticed that something had 'kicked off,' in the restaurant, but wasn't sure exactly what it could be.

When she came back, Lucy's eye was almost uncontrollable, but you couldn't say anything, because you couldn't determine whether she was winking anyway, because he always did, it was disconcerting, but you just ignored it, though it wasn't always so easy to, not that night.

Pamela had been walking past a few churches that day and smiled politely and courteously, possibly as in years gone by some gentlemen possibly might have tipped their hats, she too, was also undergoing some other attempts at personal lifestyle changes and there was something very much on her mind. She'd recalled a conversation between herself and Jean, where reference was made to Lucy, who'd become a long term friend from years earlier and where someone else known to Jean, had been or was a warden at a local church, in the conversation with Jean, Pamela recalled, that another friend of Jean's, Florence Breeny had mentioned to Jean, whilst attending a service that it was compared to that of, "a golden oldies club, "Jean mentioned that she'd known of a few attendees at that church and that it was nice that a friend of a friend, had been visited by a friend of a friend even, Jean, intrigued, had then enquired of the 'friend of a friend' explanation-wise, and said, "do tell me more," at that moment, they were enjoying vegetarian sausagettes, home-made, similar to sausage rolls but not quite. Interestingly, Jon who was then in the process of changing his name to Jean, had experienced another similar odd situation, though for Jean then, it had taken some ten months to work it all out.

First, exhaustive checks had to be made and even then, the shrewdness of it all made it difficult to consider pointing a finger if any of them wanted to, but nonetheless, facts were facts. And more recently, thanks to Clara, Jean herself had made a conscious decision within only weeks, not to visit the Carrot and Rabbit Hole eatery again, yes thanks to none other than the church warden Miss. Clara Gringold. Had some puzzle pieces began somehow to form for Jean, even to new climbs somehow, it would be impossible, even inconceivable to know then whether they could have maybe been part of any wider puzzle, but it had been how some aspects of daily existences, had been or then became. For some strange reason on Jeans mind, were pigs in blankets, a dish made of sausages with bacon wrapped around them, but more to the point, the bacon just fell off them. Had the bacon dropped off Jean wondered, or was she bringing it home?

Lucy Green, that close friend of Jean's for almost thirty years, now lives twenty to miles away from the church hall where Florence had attended the funeral with Jean, but some thirty-one years earlier she'd actually lived location-wise near, only streets away in fact, from that same church hall, Jean was totally surprised to learn this, from where Jean now lived, but some thirty years earlier. Only a few months had passed since Lucy visited Jean and they met at the carrot and rabbit hole, and yes Lucy's partner Bernadette Smithers went along too.

On that evening, they's been invited by Jean to that venue, 'The Carrot and Rabbit Hole,' it was there that Clara Gringold seemed to appear, as if she'd been hiding behind a pebble somewhere on a muddy path, Jean actually regarded Clara as something of a slimeball character-wise anyway, and although reluctant to introduce Clara who'd rather forcefully interrupted the trio, felt obliged to, but in the knowledge that her friendship with Lucy was strong, and in the hope that Lucy would see through any elements of something not quite as it should be, Jean was interested personally to see what Lucy's reaction would be, so was not worried. Earlier, Clara had been chatting to two people outside the Carrot and Rabbit Hole, she invited Lucy to come to meet them, it all seemed to Jean somewhat impolite and impertinent, if not rather odd, though for Jean, she was not surprised neither would she be totally surprised by it, and certainly not show it, if she was.

Jean, at that point and because of Lucy's rather flamboyant hand gestures noticed, especially in the light of a quite glimmeringly lit place, how her diamond rings were really quite dazzling, also observed in Clara, manners that could only really have been described surely in those circumstances considerately, as sycophantic. Jean and Bernadette chatted, then after five minutes or so, Lucy walked back in. Jean didn't know how to react, Lucy stood immediately in front of Jean and just stared, her face looked pale and as if shocked, it was almost as though she'd seen a ghost or something like that. Jean even wondered, 'oh what has Clara been saying about me,' and even the eye stammer had stopped, but Jean didn't notice that, not that there was anything in Jean's opinion, Clara could say reliably, such was Jean's expression to Lucy. Jean did think then that Lucy in her summing-up of Clara Gringold was way too charitable and as result was shocked, when Lucy said, "she's a hustler," but Jean certainly wasn't surprised to hear the particular term being applied quite audaciously. Clara had also recognised Lucy, from thirty years earlier when Lucy had been involved in some photographic work as topless model? It was strange too really, that Lucy met Bernadette some three years after and had always referred to her as; 'The Tops.' Jean was only to return to The Carrot and Rabbit Hole one more time after, Clara was seated smugly when she arrived, Jean knew then that as much as she thought the place was nice, that she would very probably not want to associate herself with it again, when leaving that night, just as about to walk out of the door, a friend, the friend Jean had gone here to see in the first place was walking in, they briefly chatted for just a moment and went elsewhere to finish their more private, though not personal, conversation elsewhere. It would then be a few weeks after, that Jean would realise whose interest, the decision by her, not to return to that place because of not trusting Clara, was in, of course, none other than Clara Gringold's. Was a cover about to be blown? Not to do with the venue, certainly not. And that Clara might have become involved with a church as a volunteer and was helping with any form of 'a game' certainly there, seemed even more deplorable. Then, thinking of the day when Lucy said she was a hustler, had she changed from those days really, or was she 'working a ticket.' The thought on Jean's mind for that moment was, and to what degree? Sanctioned by mental health? And an oblivious church. Jean had somehow imagined or considered, or decided then, that with every drink consumed by Clara and every deed whether seemingly good or bad, that a problem, because of Clara's mental health issues, could only deteriorate, and no-one else any the wiser. Thinking of many things and mainly the neat snugness of it all, or how it seemed, certainly gave way to her, to the cliché,' 'snug as a bug in a rug,' and meaning. Jean envisaged Clara standing above or in front of the church's cardboard cut-out nativity scene, with its cotton balls sheep and a lighted match, then Clara licking the whole length of a kebab skewer. In that vision Jean, to some still known also as Jon, stared at Clara, and said, 'it aint (isn't) no fire of Rome darling, and you eat way too many kebabs as nice as they may be, as it is.'

As, oddly, as it was to some a peculiar subject-matter, though not to Jean, Jean had been thinking of how those dead, must be honoured and cherished, and respected as you would for the living. Maybe because she was considering somehow as to Jean it seemed a dilemma of a kind, whether with Clara's somewhat unique mental health issue, and because she'd not known of such before, whether it would, or could actually ever be possible for Clara to honour those who had died concisely, and not the opposite, and whether by default, such or possible anxieties if un-noticed and unrecognised at those places, whether it might actually even help some along, almost as though rather than trying to stop a person jumping off a cliff, or if in a wheelchair that had moved too quickly, rather stop it and pull it back, whether it was possible that Clara might actually inadvertently, by default of her issues, actually give it a very gentle shove. It was only a minor detail, but a concern. And what if not aware of it, and so the inclination then, by natural default and whilst all along just sitting snuggly and waving the church incense around at weekends or when required to, as then possibly, a convenient smokescreen or backdrop. Jean decided to think of it as nothing more than a top button on a cloak with a monogram known as interest and was somehow certain, that cloak did not actually belong to Clara Gringold. Another thing on Jean's mind, was, since that funeral service where Florence attended with her, what was the relationship even thirty years ago, between the person who had died, and Clara, and just as with the smug look in the Carrot and Rabbit Hole, when that day Jean decided to return to there, had Jean witnessed or realised another situation, or gained an understanding too of what may have been going on. Dumfounded now, and more concerned mainly for the safety of others, even if there was really no need to be, it would be Jean who would deliberately decide to keep away. It was not a decision based on fear, but in order to better think things through and how best to tackle it to try to bring about a well-intended, or good resolve privately although possibly with better implications.

Jean was aware too, that an organisation she knew of, a Wexxen Street Care Group supported financially a group that Clara attended, though some of the reasoning now seemed possibly tenuous.

And of course, three months before the meet between Jean, Lucy and Bernadette, Jean had just completed a total search, top to bottom, of her apartment, lifting rugs, looking behind cupboard and searching any pockets, for a ring she'd had for a couple of years. It wasn't a real diamond, but Clara didn't know that, neither did Clara's friend. There had been no other visitors to Jean's flat since, apart from a very close friend and his partner and even that had been within the past month, all of this happened within the six months, so just before Pamela met Judd. Clara, who sometimes called around after church, suddenly and just as mysteriously had ceased visiting. Sussed, or dissed? Or were they possibly 'casing the joint,' anyway, Jean thought? And with what, as a pretty backdrop, but were they caught out? Had they realised that Jean would realise. Personally, I doubt that very much, because they'd have not imagined that under usual circumstances, she received no other visitors. And of course, so very wrong to point the finger of accusing. But it's fine, 'smug, snug,' she told herself.

And of the person who died, he'd been a Minister at the same church that Clara volunteered at. Jean remembered sadly that only months before his death, even though a few years earlier, Jean having noticed that his name was on a prayer list, actually asked Clara very directly to convey a message professionally and expressed concern. Clara didn't at any point mention that he had actually been a Minister performing services at the same church for a few years before his death. Clara had said nothing at all about that, not once, ever and it seemed strange to Jean. Had Jean been aware of it at all, she'd have gone along to the church. The sad hope for Jean, was that whilst he was a humble man, that his end-of-life care was totally professional, although there was probably not much point in doubting there, as despite his circumstances, he must have arranged all those details himself personally. Some might say, 'experience, borne out of a wealth of experience,' and maybe fortunately, that was what astute Florence had meant too, by, 'the golden oldies club.'

One thing it had done, was, Jean firmly believed, to be able to separate herself somehow, from what was or had been Covid 19. It was the difference of a choice and to be able to determine at least how to begin to attain a space from where to then attempt to move forward. Was it something directed at anyone in particular, Pamela for example, because during those long months, apart from those who could within their professional remit support, and close family, she'd felt so much hate, and was able to draw comparisons with situations years earlier, so logically, it could not have been Covid-19 causing that? Had what Pamela saw, been spewed out just for Pamela, for her to see where Judd had been, or to hurt, or did no-one apart from Pamela know, but those who might attempt to batter and then infiltrate could watch prior to, and hope then to invade her personal thinking space when they saw how she dealt with things? That was not a concern for a few. Not at all though, Pamela had guessed that it might possibly have had something to do with his usual Wednesday thing anyway. But if that person had been recently blown out too, there surely could be a lot of hate from there, she thought. Knowing very well though, that the, or any such hate, because Pamela would not be responsible for that loss at all, would be therefore quite mis-placed? At least she did think that. Or was she directly responsible for it? Oops, too late now! And especially if it were, if all we're led to believe about some serpents, was all 'merely' or simply, a test of trust? Had the character that seemed to emerge from discarded skin, wanted to first become consumed by the serpent, because Pamela could imagine that character with a dagger, now standing above it. Or had it become for her, about rejuvenation? Talk about 'trying to teach an old dog new tricks,' she thought, of course, she'd wondered about that some time before, a while earlier in fact. The main thing was, whilst sitting on the loo one day, she thought of those Judd was meeting, and she felt herself swallowing, although it was more a gulp? It was then, Pamela thought, and pleasingly too, how it would not be Pamela who would be consumed, she thought to herself then, 'it won't be I who is 'consumed' by it all, however to some, it may very well indeed present?

Certainly, one of the things he did say to Pamela, just before meeting her recently was surprising. He said to her, "I hope you can cope with all of this." She thought that maybe he had simply got some words mixed up, because she could not work out what he meant and besides, there wasn't actually much time before he was due to arrive when visiting her then for that hour. The experiences during the past eight months had given her something of an insight she hoped, into what he possibly meant. For Pamela though, it was more a case of, 'oh my goodness, what will I go through now with his confidence tricking technique.' Often, Pamela, just as she had in the most recent days, had been laid up and experiencing difficulties anyway. She'd realised today, that it was not just when she posted a new photo of herself, he would want to come to see her. Because he could get someone else not in need of surgery, she was never allowed to forget that. He worked in a hotel as a manager. He'd be accustomed to rotas and staff titles and their responsibilities right along to the cleaners who emptied the bins. Was he visiting prostitutes who inevitably always looked as he liked, and could afford to get breast implants etc and 'treat him so good,' because of how he then left them feeling with his carefully constructed emotional cocktail blend, usually of now, innocents, those who crave excitement, desperados and just those who would anyway, or did they believe he was all innocent Judd, working in his mundane job and needing a break? Exactly, as he mentioned the issues with his back, passing it all along to the experienced person in that field who'd simply, "handle it" and empty the bins for him after, rather like address labelling from home, and each one of them, because of the trickery of it all, believing it was their lucky day. To the emotional hilt every time, and yes, of course not wanting to eat into their revenue/earning potential, aware that certainly for them where clients were concerned, 'that time is very much of importance, therefore a currency of its own too presumably. So, when he felt that basically, his 'personal and quite undeniably selfish enjoyment,' by what he was able to leave them with, 'or without,' was threatened, he'd then visit dear Pamela? And now, he'd even got that down to just one hour and not now even monthly, when he desperately needed to, because she had distanced sufficiently from him, for her to have needed to post a new photo of herself, so his plot, his game, seemed to him maybe to have started to become ineffective. Otherwise, those he visited would charge him as a client, wouldn't they? The phrase, take from it what you will, was beginning to at last, now make sense for dear Pamela. But had he attempted to mimic her somehow, using a mirroring technique, then to make her obsolete by wearing her down after, as he took what he gleaned, on to others who could offer that much more to him for his perceived stash? Was any of that, what he meant by 'married.' Oh, my goodness, she thought. But if he'd managed to get her to remove her own personal advertisements six month earlier, had he not accomplished that, it made the way totally clear for him to expand, he and his cronies, could after and throughout it all become privy not only to photos of herself that she'd sent him, but her very own patheticism by how she responded to him, had become then a currency too, in even something as trivial as messages from her to him, at what she'd so foolishly 'allowed' herself to become. She certainly opened the door ok, but rather, was it to become a scenario whereby, as some would say, you may not win the battle, but you could win the war, was she really so inexperienced, or just enough to let him believe she was? Was it ever to matter to him or them how Pamla might respond, it mattered obviously as much as their easy acceptance of the hurt she'd endured had?'

Yes, getting someone else to do the jobs he didn't want to do, had become very much a norm for Judd. Whilst there may be an element of truth in that, what if he was unaware though of how it was impacting on her, what if it was about chemistry and each time if he went with someone else who he could have intercourse with, it caused some kind of a reaction? If inadvertently it impacted then he would not be to blame, Pamela squirmed and thought to herself, not because she was jealous, only hurt at how she had perceptively become, then there was the thought that had someone else contacted her, a younger person for example, not that she would entertain it, a person without his experience for example, who then might her interaction, having met Judd a few times, impact on them and how? Would it mean for example that such impacts could even potentially unwittingly breed hatred toward certain groups she wondered? Was his statement that he couldn't deal with it anymore because they could not yet do intercourse because of her surgical need. She had said to him after their second month that she thought they had simply met at the wrong time, that was when her surgery was to be completed by the July, but in the March of that year, it was postponed. She was desperately unhappy, and she decided then that whilst she had waited all her life for surgery, work too priority in many of those years over personal life, she wasn't then interested in meeting anyone, she always just found it easier to believe privately that she was the ugliest woman on earth, she couldn't even discuss it with anyone. After the surgery was postponed indefinitely, she decided that she could not sit by and expect him to wait, she was pleased that they remained in contact and that sometimes they met, despite then very real frustrations. It was all considerably more embarrassing, or painful than simply passing close to each other and wanting, whilst reaching across to a wardrobe to grab a blouse.

During all the months they'd known each other, she wasn't thinking that he'd have slept his way around the whole city and beyond by the time they eventually got together, if they ever were to. There were times because of it, when she even started to doubt her choice that he was right for her at all, and if he would be able to, or could want to change from 'a busier lifestyle,' should they ever get it on fully, and whether all, for those reasons and more, whether it all wasn't some even more peculiar divine intervention? She'd been thinking during the night about moving forward alone as she'd always been, just working and certainly as she'd grown accustomed prior to her having met him. There seemed much to consider, but really, who really knows? Certainly, until they ever had the chance to fulfil that part of any destiny of hers, his, or maybe theirs?

#

It was now Saturday afternoon, she sent him two photos of herself dressed in a skin- tight body stocking, one rear view and another frontal, it was obviously crotchless although worn slightly at an angle so that the photo remained clean. She sent it, just because it was Judd, she wanted to send the photo too, no-one else. She didn't put a mark across to hide her nipples, aware of course that women's nipples could not legally be overtly visible, although only if the photos were used publicly. She got up and walked across the room and switched her television on to listen to some music. It was 01.55AM now, there was a helicopter flying around probably very close just above where she lived, she could hear it, she liked that? But recently again became quite bored of checking whether he was online or not, but as he'd read her message from the evening before at just before 06.00AM that day, she wanted to find out what time he left work? She checked at 01.30PM, He wasn't online, he hadn't been all day which was unusual if back at work. She presumed that it must have either been a good day, or days, the day before, certainly something had happened this week, or and possibly because, he was getting through quicker to get away earlier or on-time, or that there was no need to make arrangements, at certain times as his arrangement had already been made, hence the notifications regarding receipt of her messages either turned off to focus on his newest addition, if, or had she become 'of a lesser priority' this week, again. There had been many similar occurrences over the months, she knew it and she believed that he somehow knew she did, either that, or as she'd thought on many times before, it did not matter to him at all, not one iota, what she thought about it anyway, as though she had become or never actually was anything to him.

He was online at 13.05PM for just a second or two, so she sent the photos at 13.11PM. His phone had been switched off. This was quite unusual, it rarely happened. It must have either been something very special he'd left work for, or he was travelling on a bike. It was only then, in that second, she then wondered about the distance trackers on some websites where you can tell how close, or not another site-users phone is to your own location, because she wondered if maybe he was meeting someone who lived closer to where Pamela lived, very close indeed. Thinking that he wouldn't, or hoping that he wouldn't do that, Pamela chose to believe that he would not have been putting such measures in place because of her, in some ways, for that reason and thinking of others he'd met too, maybe, there was someone else he was thoughtful of, and possibly because of how many he had on the go, he was hiding from someone else too. He would have been unaware that she had observed it, but she believed she recognised certainly signs of a kind, she felt it, poor Pamela's whole body was to feel it, her very soul. Did she really deserve that?

She had the phone on to see when the next check in would happen, it was a two second log in twenty-five minutes after, so he was telling whoever he visited he'd arrived. At 14.07PM she sent another message, the referred to his comment the day earlier and posted after her photos, "nice of you to say by the way, xxx". His phone then was back on, but he was not online. It would be one hour and fifteen minutes after that he went online again, it was a thirty second chat he was having, to say thanks etc presumably. Her photos still hadn't been viewed by him. She'd surprised even herself with how she looked in those photos. At 15.14PM, knowing he would be making his way from where he was to his work or his home after (possibly), she sent a message, it just said "x." His phone sure enough was again off.

At 15.25PM a message came from him saying "Lovely pics!!!" Not only later that day was that remark to horrify her. She thought about videos etc and thought of youngsters and their eagerness and his entrapment techniques and the rape by thirty persons in another country and who clients, as sickening as it seems or sounds, could potentially be for such activities, some who would not be even noticed if they disappeared and it wasn't as though any of them really had time to research it as she had, unbeknown to Judd. She also sent a message to him, a brief hello, and recalled then too, very much, his excitement when she set up a fake account to try to work him out, it was an account that looked like it was of a person considerably younger, Pamela had a friend who sometimes contacted her from a website to chat, unbeknown to Judd, it had only a thousand members but Pamela asked if she could use some of her personal photos for an hour or two, she agreed without reservation because she trusted Pamela. The photo he sent of himself to that fake profile was nothing like any of those few he'd sent to her, and he deleted it after sending it within twenty seconds, when Pamela asked for it again, he ignored her question totally and moved on very swiftly and controllingly and evasively too, as though wanting the person to believe he had other calls coming in too, he probably did, but his eagerness was way too real, Pamela knew it like looking at a favourite ice cream, to 'do you have a boyfriend,' and told her he was married although she was now his ex, and that he 'hadn't seen her anyway since a few months.' He was like a bee around a honeypot, and although Pamela sent photos of her friend with four different ex partners all taken within two or three months and boy did, she looks slinky and game, but younger than twenty-five, because the site was over 18 only. In the fake account Pamela said about unprotected sex etc, he asked leading questions, but then said that he only ever did sex without a condom anyway. So, were now talking about those potentially considerably younger too, her though as stupidly as it was, was, what else might he have her doing, and for whom and more to the point, for what?

#

'Smiling serpent, trifling man'

They may not have been speaking or commenting to each other before their own last meet together, but had something else been at play, to what context and would Judd recognise that things no longer would be the same. Maybe he'd wanted it that way, she had no choice but to say nothing more to him, unless he contacted her. She did though wrack her brain for a situation where before his phone had been switched off like that, those same circumstances. It was exactly the same as before, in their earlier days, when she knew he was up to something and he'd ignore you, as if you did not exist, then after the deed, he'd feel guilty as hell and totally disappear for the remainder of the day, until 'you'd' calmed down. So now, since her dream about the serpent, he was already training someone else! He could simply tell them too, as he had with her back then, that the phone had been switched off in the office at his workplace because he was busy, and just like as she couldn't then, there was nothing at all they could say or do about it. Yes, it certainly was another 'gulp' moment, and not only then for dearest Pamela.

Feeling that she could hear or imagine, a person with a female sounding voice angry and screaming that someone somewhere may be on his or their game, Pamela ignored it. Then walked into her kitchen. She hadn't seen any flies in her flat in six years, not one, she'd seen spiders, the type with very long thin legs, to two and a quarter inches or more but she tended to just either leave them if in a pace where they'd cause no issue and would not be visible should anyone call round, or she'd put them outside carefully. The fly though was big, it was making sounds and twitching its wings a lot on the door of a kitchen wall unit. She put some water in the kettle and switched it on, then found a large empty coffee jar. Her first attempt to get it to stay so she could catch it in the jar safely failed, it flew around her and promptly landed on a mirror that was part of her late father's estate. He'd asked her if she wanted it whilst he was alive, but she wouldn't take from him, she smiled and said," no you keep it." She could remember that moment even more now, as if he was still alive and with her, it made her feel slightly tearful, and she was happy that he might know it. The fly however, she put the jar over it carefully, then a plastic flat lid to cover the top of the jar. Consciously trying to remember to leave door latches on, she went from her room into the large hallway of the property, it was built in 1888. She opened the front door, it was a nice cool morning and now 03.25AM, although there were some lights showing from rooms in properties opposite and the Dickensian style streetlights were on, they could well have been original, she never checked, but certainly liked them. She removed the plastic and let the fly out of the jar, it must have moved quickly because she didn't see it fly away. She then held the jar up to the glare, cast by the light in the outside porch, the fly's wings were obviously quite fine. She turned and walked back in, then as quietly as possible, closed the street door behind her. As she walked to the door of her own place, a phrase came to her thoughts, that phrase being about "wanting to be a fly on a wall at that place." She smiled and thought, 'oh my goodness, there's a damn good thought, now let's go and get that coffee and maybe a nice apple." She was to realise, eventually, that as shrewd as some could be, so would those who knew them, potentially also be, be it taught, picked up of copied habits, natural or learned, and as often as it always seemed, too often unproveable.

#

Pamela at 04.26AM had been contacted by a person who she also likes a lot who lives in Dubai, there had been him contacting now and then and a man from Paris. She liked them because she found them to be so handsome. But too, some Princes she had also found to be very handsome, but they were only kind gestural thoughts of well-wishing and to hopefully evoke a genuine calm in kindness without intrusion or bad feeling. None of them anyway, could she meet, not only from a financial perspective because she could not afford to visit them, or another she'd spoken to in Chile, or another in Nigeria or another in Brussels. They had only ever contacted and chatted in texts or messages. But it had all stopped when Pamela met Judd. Supposedly it all seemed fine, and she'd believed it was by her own choice because she thought she had met what she believed to be her first ever boyfriend.

When she believed without doubt, that he was straying, because he and her could not 'get together,' in ways that would be natural and have and give a far greater importance to them both, it was simple, as soon as they caught a look at each other, they wanted to make love? She adored him from the very second that he walked into her room. The reasons they met and their closeness formed over some time were of no importance to her, this for Pamela, was more than any of those thoughts could ever generate, and the fact that she, because she'd been so busy in the first month, hadn't even noticed that he'd been trying to contact her since a month earlier, had that aroused his competitive edge and had that given way to his treatment to her subsequently, so he wouldn't have been bothered that they could not do sex, it was that she didn't notice that he'd been attempting to contact her, it would have screwed him up, especially if he was not accustomed to that, so Pamela, totally unbeknown to Pamela, she was already out to meet a man, before they'd met, who sought a revenge on her, and she didn't, or wouldn't ever realise it. It was only after their first break up, or possibly the second when she was aware about his Wednesday meets that she found his few regular emails sent over a few months before they did meet. She though was thankful, that he'd been persistent, it was in her eyes, the saving grace, but she was new to relationships of this type. Now disappointed by how things panned out, though yet again, she had to just let him do it and because of her surgery situation and because she didn't know any different, she had to only believe and accept in that, that this was how some men were. Now she thought, why should he have remained consistent, when she was a little older than him, not much, and inexperienced with meeting men, though very experienced in other ways, that he may be trying to learn from her the intricacies of how to approach inexperienced, was for Pamela not to remain merely an afterthought. This was her experience, to notice these things, she was always as careful as she possibly could be in all that she said to him, but he learned quickly, this was demonstrated often extremely callously toward her, to the point then, that it caused her sincerely to question where he was going, who he was meeting and how often and from where or what circumstances, and what situations or influences. Could his seemingly newer experiences be causing his almost callous neglectful and cruel bitchiness, there was no other explanation for it. There had been times before he was furloughed for those four and a half months, when she wondered if he was jealous of her somehow. Had she misinterpreted a loathsome revengeful hate. Neither of them drank alcohol. Something certainly was influencing him though, was it really that they couldn't bond as he could with others, or simply that he could with them, or some of them, or that they mainly were one-offs? Had he been playing a game from the start, 'ulterior,' or personal motives though, was she seeing the real him through maybe a thinning veneer. Or were his choice options becoming that much wider that he could exude such harsh and a cold confidence, or was it just anger, and in the same way that she was forced to hold him at arms-length too, he had no choice but to be cruel to her in response, because he was very much in pain and also suffering as result. It was one thing to be held off for a month by a person who had media profiles, it was another to then be told then that his perception of her home-made cherry cake was locked away when they did meet. And to think, she'd asked him if he wanted some quiche thinking he might have been peckish after travelling forty-five minutes when they first met. Could it for his ego, have been a double blow possibly and sent him over the edge? But again, Pamela didn't know any of this? Certainly, quite recently when he said, "yeah" almost sarcastically, regarding her operation, this showed a part of him that she could now and had to learn to further ignore, or was it all part of his anger somehow, hurt, and bruised confidence, but she didn't know? It no longer tore her to shreds now, as she wondered or guessed regarding his whereabouts and hobbies. To be able to do that regarding those and other mood swings displayed, she'd become aware a considerable time before, that even the privilege to be able to think that way, she could not ever display the remotest evidence of to him. She knew it had affected them both but didn't even ever think that it all might have sent him totally around the twist, she was too busy wondering why and not thinking of his ego, but only of the hurdle presented to them both, that none, and no-one ever, could be blamed for, a hurdle then impacted by Covid-19, presumably? Was he somehow emotionally or even mentally challenged? Pamela had mentioned to him in texts that she was waiting to undergo a surgery, maybe he thought she was trying to fob him off. Could he have been influenced and then poked fun of, by some who wanted to control him, and could he then have decided that he still wanted to have his cake anyway, to teach them, or that person a lesson, was that how they liked him, so Pamela was always just another pawn. Would Pamela realise in time and had either of them, or any of them bitten just slightly too deeply that it could not be washed away a bacterial wipe, did Pamela not have an ego of a kind too? Or did that not matter, if not, why the need to even attempt to very foolishly 'mirror'? And especially in such a pathetic way and for such ludicrously idiotic reasons. Especially with Pamela, they would not have cared had she not survived, none of them, Pamela did eventually realise that much.

#

An interpretation of Pamela's with regard to, had been, that if when they had met, they still got on anyway, yes, they had to improvise, maybe she was just too sweet and kind, but if they still skipped through, what else might that experience had driven him to, and into who's 'arms? Was she to be thankful if he was meeting certain types, some he might want to know more, and some would want to know him more? Were the Wednesday meets now off since certainly the past two Wednesdays, or had the gameplay changed slightly, had it become not so much about why, but how? Where were the gains, the takings, what were they, did he know really, or not? Like butter wouldn't melt. Of course, another thing about visiting so many, you could establish possibility for potential growth in various ways, including circumstances and structure of the persons home visited and size of? What for though? And could it ever become of any relevance at all, as to whether he liked dear Pamela's figure or not? Was it just sufficient to have seen it for a while? When she sent the two photos to him the day before, the thought that went through her mind then was, "here's the real girl that you left on the floor for dead." Her eyes now almost piercing, as though Pamela had become now, the epitome of Satan himself, something she could never even usually say, lest of all ever think. Maybe a question therefore, with her having met with Jean the day before, should be, why now could she think like that?

Just to see whether it would be the same as a day earlier if he checked messages at 06.48AM, she sent a message at 06.30AM, only to say thanks for the comment about her photos, that was all that she typed to him, "Thanks." His phone was switched off. It used to be sometimes switched off on Saturdays in their earliest days when they first met, but rarely, he just wouldn't reply to messages, so you grew accustomed to not sending them. Maybe he was out, or the Wednesday thing had moved to a Saturday. Or maybe he was with his so-called wife, or one of those others he'd been visiting? It was no longer as desperate or tedious as it could have been, she was getting to grips with it all and planting some seeds of her own. Whatever, he obviously either wanted to not have messages coming through or heard, because of reasons known to him. Or he wasn't up yet. She rarely typed messages so early. The thing was, for her, it had reached a point where it no longer mattered, would he have realised if his message sent at 15.25PM the day before after he'd just returned from an excursion, saying "lovely pics" had not been responded to for the rest of the day and whole evening, until the next day? Such was the effect of how she'd been played with emotionally over months, she deliberately avoided now even going on-line at all herself, apart from three times within an hour after 15.25, he then as normal, went offline at the very moment she went online. Had he burnt his candle at both ends 'again' and was wanting to claw somehow for the coming weekend. She'd seen it all before and all far too many times since having met him. Phone off on Saturday was not like simply not responding to messages though. She was even afraid to think something as silly as 'he'd have to work harder than that,' for fear of what it would mean and the distress it would cause her. Were there dynamics associated to lots of women waiting on an app for a phone to go on, and could that be manipulated? And what if he only required unbeknown to all of them, only certain ones to be waiting, at his very beckon call. The only problem with that of course, could be, what happens if now, today, if or when he finally logs in, there is nothing there? Pamela could stop herself from giggling. She knew she was very naughty, the problem was, he hadn't bargained on it yet, because they never yet had the chance to properly discover it. He'd kissed her neck, she loved it. She'd felt him just standing close to her, and they weren't even doing anything. But she'd never kissed him yet. She wanted to so very much, but it was not then to be. The thought that he was kissing others, and because they couldn't get that close themselves, yes, they were behaving like animals and how some others might naturally, with their forced 'compromise.' How would they ever kiss when by default, their meets had been reduced, because they couldn't do what was natural 'for them, as a couple,' irrespective of how others chose to, or did behave, to nothing more than a personally perceived, a shame filled, dirty hideous excuse.

It was though one week since he'd contacted her again although in the evening just after 17.30PM, and tomorrow would be a week up, since the following day then, when he went to visit a person close to where she lived and had switched his phone off, and Pamela had presumed it was not such a good meeting for him then. At that moment she heard a train making a sound, it was like a whistle or a horn, like an old steam train type of horn, but it was very probably electromagnetically produced, yes it was as sweet to hear as disconcerting, but she knew that she must not be alarmed by the fact that it would be a week since and knowing how he liked his routines. She was though alarmed and distressed at the real possibility emerging, that where she, Pamela, was emotionally forced to improvise sexually, and not only forced, because of reasons of personal religious temperament, that it had merely shown him, as with other matters or issues, or excited him sufficiently, how he might like to, or could successfully eventually, then tackle a situation elsewhere, had it not been such an advantageous meet sexually that day. Pamela then felt reassured then to know without question that he would not be contacting her at all this weekend for that very reason, as he'd have been on his way to becoming quite content. Or would he dare, as a break from there for a couple of hours, attempt it? Believing Pamela was totally stupid. Was the balance therefore, if she was correct, in how well Pamela had sexually improvised, as sad as it was for her personally. Saturdays though, apart from last Saturday oddly, were usually the one day, unless the Wednesday thing was on, with Saturday going into Sunday afternoon, where he very rarely went on-line during those times and if he did, on Saturdays, it would be almost as if he had to do it sneakily, like his every move with his phone, and because of where he 'then' was, was being carefully watched or monitored and not by Pamela who was watching it all. And how quickly, like a rat that had escaped from underground captivity via a drainpipe, he was back in the-land-of-the-living in the early evening of 'every' Sunday. Pamela stared at her pelargoniums and quietly thought, what if, apart from all of this and more, he had kids. Horrified at the potential ramifications of what she believed she'd experienced or felt she knew, who'd believe her?

Pamela then sent a text to the health worker she often texted to, it read: "The worst thing about being desperate, especially also as having done so much additional work charitably, since maybe twenty-five years now, is not being able to speak about it amidst tears. Good day"!

#

Pamela had thought about chemistries again and wondered whether hypothetically, if a person were to engage sexually, with, for example, a person who might have a disability- or a person who for whatever reason was unable to engage in a way that might not be exactly as 'normal' for the other person, would, or could it push them, if it was just casual sex, or until a compromise could be found, into seeking what felt better for them and met their needs more aptly after, like a kind of 'once bitten twice shy' type of situation, as if to say, I won't put myself into compromising situations as a person who could be vulnerable because of reasons not their own fault, with a person who might not think twice to consider it. On the receiving end of that, she felt hurt initially and still sometimes does. She also wondered whether in some circumstances and with some individuals, if they met a person who was younger than themselves, would it inspire them to meet someone of similar age after, or someone older, and the reverse of that. Surely it was about consensualism and whether the experience was indeed memorable and how. But if then that person was deliberately, for whatever reason manipulating what they'd learned, to create scenarios whereby there yes would be a long queue of women waiting, because the space was already taken up by something else, even if another group. And whereupon their seeming to wait, but not actually ever accomplishing and not knowing why, might create an almost intellectual entity of its own, even if basically a placebo, but worthwhile enough for who could access it. Or would they be planning other things, or had they already?

There had been times when Judd had been totally incommunicado, there would be no messages either way, Pamela knew at those times, just as she felt then, it was another of those occasions where he was totally intertwined with someone else, so had 'her jibe,' during the week where she'd said to him, "are you looking forward to Saturday," simply armed him again too, he'd even managed to manipulate that. Since a month after their meet, she had to be wary about anything she said to him, this surely is another real example of how devious he, or some, or someone she knows he's acquainted with, is. Or was it about purse strings? In which case, he could be with anyone. Oh, she'd spent so many nights, even having visions of who those might well be. It horrified her, unable to offer the basics, and making way with every move for others who could pay, or afford because they did not require surgeries, to move in? Pamela could imagine him easily saying, and how he is with her, his activities of course being of no consequence to her, 'if you are going to send photo like that and then disappear all day and for the rest of the night, then I can take my phone off all day tomorrow, and let's see how you like that you bitch.' Or, if he even needed to at all, he could have realised, especially where Pamela is concerned, even from afar, 'or not so far,' that she knew exactly where he might be right now. Just like the last time it happened, times before, not like the excursions even, though there were occasions where they became more frequent meets for him. And yes, if she was right, he will need to work on this one in some ways. It was basically another piece of cake, or simply 'a piece of cake,' anyway, though? Pamela knows only too well, what a very 'sweet' tooth Judd potentially has.

His phone remained switched off or unavailable until 14.30hrs, though he didn't read messages at all or log in online. Pamela checked throughout much of the day at all of the usual times he'd usually log in, he didn't, not even once. There were mixed messages she was detecting, she walked across to one of her Victorian, glass fronted oak Barristers stacking bookcases, and slid the heavy glass door across, inside it were various object d'art, she cupboard comprises of three cupboards, two of which are possibly eleven inches tall, and they are all approximately thirty-three inches long and maybe ten inches deep. The top cupboard is double the height of the lower two but has a shelf through the middle of it and all three are fronted by heavy glass sliding doors. The glass feels heavy and sounds like a guillotine might have, as it opens or is being closed.

She'd never used it before, but she carefully pulled out a crystal ball and the plinth it rested upon, it had been gifted to her years earlier by a friend. She was mindful of what Judd had seen when he last came, that being, "nice to see you," and determined now that he would only ever see his life-long desire unfolding in Pamela whenever he thought of their meets or saw anything about her in any photo or image on her own profile. He'd to her before that he believed her, he'd never said differently of her. It wasn't that she wanted him, it was that she did not like being bullied, or bullies generally, they would become dictators of their personal fate. However, if he, Judd wanted Pamela, and if for true reasons, of course she would not refuse his advances. It was though most certainly, where he was concerned just like trying to find a needle in a haystack. She knew that really, she was totally aware, but she would not turn him away, not yet anyway. She did believe that there was not much left of him now, of how she knew him, for her to turn him away anyway, it had become as obvious as it could have become that there was nothing there from the start, but Pamela was stupid and besotted and she had ideas of her own too. Pamela placed both her hands upon the crystal ball and thought carefully about the mixed messages she'd heard, where some had too, been like a female voice, although she knew she could never be totally certain and because some she'd found do tend to mimic when desperate, or if with greed-based quite personal agendas, the voice she'd hear said something like "I've got him here now, you aren't going to pull that back this time." Pamela was to very soon learn that whilst there might be those thinking like that, to leave them be, because that would be their only focus. And he might be enslaved, and whilst that, or such persons could think determinedly to do well, he could also be making out to be dead too, because he had no other choice but to follow a path he sometimes, whether he believed he enjoyed it or not, that he sometimes felt obliged to be on, because of those same rather limited choice options, or experience. Depending upon the ages and experiences of those he associated with, that could be a complex situation which she believed she understood. It was never though Pamela's intention to interfere, only to relieve. It was now 01.38AM of the Sunday, he hadn't been online throughout the whole of the day before.

#

It had been extremely windy outside for the day before, Pamela had gone to the shops wearing an orange peach flowy knee length dress, it was as if the wind itself somehow loved it, she though, well, it made her smile a little, bringing her slightly away from the torment suffered. On her way back, just before she reached her home, the postal worker was delivering mail, he said, "Good Morning, a bit windy today isn't it." She was happy to see him and said good morning to him too. Some of the shrubs were losing their flowers but smaller new blooms were forming too, she stopped and carefully pulled one of them down to compare fragrance to how it had been a month before, it was subtle but still quite lovely.

She'd put the crystal ball back into the cupboard but didn't pull the glass door closed all the way. She was also determined that any mixed messages she did not like, she could hear still and yes there would be a response, but that any response would serve a correct purpose and keep the sender or message originator very immensely pre-occupied. There was no point in checking online to see whether Judd had seen the message sent at lunchtime the day earlier of not, certainly at 01.38AM it had not been read or seen; it was a copy of a letter received the day before, confirming her preliminary appointment for surgery, the appointment which was within ten days. She'd very obviously hidden personal details, but the main gist of it all was legible and easy to understand. If she was going to check, it would be at 02.30AM and at 03.00AM and then again at 03.30AM, in case he was having difficulties using his phone privately, not to see if he'd read her letter, oh no. To check whether he was needing to source others who met him online there. And, or were his personal needs being met?

#

Regarding where the Ingagooks lived, it would be many generations after that the new chief was born, the inhabitants of those faraway lands believed it because of astrological signs and basically meteor showers the likes of which they had never seen before and because of the sound of their dogs just inside their enclosure barking and howling that was more than usual, it was something certainly thought of then by elders as a sign, that they used to encourage their people. Dogs had been proven to adapt to a more reliant friendly relationship with them, they considered the bonds to be strong, although they had not learned to use them like huskies. Also, the Chief had seen, because of hearing of unusual markings as the child was not formed as the others had been, or how they all had usually been recognised. Their present Chief was always happy anyway, until one day, noises could be heard, they had their spears and tools used for daily life, the old chief, and others, found themselves staring along the length of the barrels of guns. They hadn't the time or the inclination to do anything, but neither did they feel alone, not at all. Neither did they feel helpless, they just did not understand. The chief was recognised by not by his garments and some jewellery across a part of his face, they all, mainly all of them had jewellery across much of any visible part of their faces, except their eyes, some of the jewellery had slits across the eyes, they were proficient at understanding their senses in life and reliant upon them. Their jewellery was mainly made of bones and rock fragments and some minerals found in hidden ice-covered caves, but their worth was calculated mainly by their possibility to be used as structuring tools, some bones were more flexible than others and could be or be made sharper, and some minerals too. The Chief had elders and others closer to him when the intruders arrived. He of course and his close partner, were uncertain and now being pushed around, they were thankful quietly, as were them all, that the new chief, a baby, was not near them and would not be seen then. Even the child's parents themselves although now basically being shunted around too, unaware that their child was though of with such high regard. The habitual intruders were not interested in jewellery unless it could be re-used, their interest was initially in furs/pelts, and live food-stocks, survival and any trade options that may be before them, this did not mean that they were hoping to negotiate trade deals with The Chief Elder.

The ice was still ice and snow still fell, and the ice in some parts there always became more each year, then it would melt back at another time of the year, only a little, but it was an indicator to them, as the cunning hope-filled intruders just moved in, they didn't need to use force, so yes, there was maybe some heat forming in the atmosphere, although the old chief would not have fathomed it so readily, they moved into their various dwellings as they attempted to discover, rather than searching, for things they did not yet know about. Their way of taking was more skilful that just to wade in and pillage. There might be other ways to take advantage, their intention though was to be totally unscrupulous, and as unscrupulous as they wanted to be. Yes, they were surprised by this extremely passive nature they'd discovered. What did they see though? Despite their reasons or acts, would it be enough for them? What would they never have seen? Coincidentally, a bird dropped from the sky, they were quietly thankful, it was still alive although they knew they needed to care for it, an intruder shot it dead before them. The Chief and others saw a spear in their gun, that was far quicker than theirs or their bows ever had been. They needed to do nothing else, their communication was only empowerment.

Those intruders were to take hold of and coax and persuade, travel to another land, a land that none had heard of or seen, the intruders knew it would require food for up to a year, their own resources had been almost their quarters depleted, so they certainly had needed to find something? Whereas, they had not travelled away from the ice much, equally their guests had not travelled onto or toward much, and yes, they had travelled a year to eventually discover them, so they planned carefully for the right time, and when the sustainable would be sufficient not only to get them back, but also to afford their unwitting cargo on that very long journey. They also knew that they had lives where they came from, so their careful plan was being hastened and hatched, it wasn't exactly something that some were totally unaware of, they were though just peaceful and had become slightly threatened and intimidated, it wasn't as though they had neighbours they could call on, but neither would they be exactly asking for any spare teabags either. It was a serious and heavy basic hostage situation.

#

It was now 04.30AM of the Sunday, Pamela had decided that she would let sleeping dogs lie regarding Judd. So much had happened. Now she seemed even more convinced that she'd been too right about how he was and had decided that it was herself who would leave having an insight to move forward, as she just did not want him now, she did, but she could never trust him now, it would be like trusting to fate that in the lands where the Ingagook lived, as in generations to come, the ice continually melted, and in other places too, that rather than hoping that as with in the story of Noah, all of the sins of the world might be washed away, that too as they would be the sins technically and not of man's deliberate creation that rather than the structure of various microbial cells being broken down by the rising sea levels as ice melted more, to include animals and people from years before who may have even had things like smallpox and other problems, frozen then in generations of ice, the rising sea levels surely not would be the heavenly tear to wash that all away, and neither was mirroring going to resolve that either? Whether Judd wanted her was either of no importance or becoming that way. What he may have wanted of her neither was too. Why was he potentially meeting people for casual encounters so close to where she lived and indeed within a forty- minute radius, that she knew of, of both his workplace and his own home too? She felt as if she could not go anywhere without remarks at how she looked or potential comments regarding her countenance, she felt as if he was using his acquired prowess whether aware of it or not, to its full potential. But did any of them really understand, did Pamela, or was it a test to see if she would have any beans to spill? Or, whether she would remain untouched by others. If it was, certainly they may probably one day be silenced of their own accord and or doing. And besides, they were outside, she had not been permitted to accept any invite from them, neither should nor, could they expect to receive. This would now be Pamela's own choice. She did though know how demanding Judd's job was timewise upon him, at least this is what he'd led her to believe. So, as he'd said the week before that he'd just had a whole week off, and as he'd not long returned to work after the long break being furloughed, she very much doubted that even a manager could get a whole weekend off just the following week, for him, based upon what he'd told her, it would not be at all normal. So, whilst she did think earlier that it was as if everything had gone back to normal, had his plans been scuppered by his having to return to work, of was it a restructuring for him but on a smaller scale, or had he managed to get others to do his bidding in arranging, he only had to do the personal interviews. not that they'd necessarily have had curriculum vitae's, because she doubted that certainly many of those he interviewed were experienced enough.

Then, could the question not be why? Anyway, there weren't so any options, he was either lying to her from the start or had realised he was struggling to keep up with her, in which case, he could be just teaching her a lesson, which she doubted. Or he was with a new the Wednesday through to Friday meet had now been condensed to Friday evening and straight through all-nighter, to some point on the Saturday, when he'd have been released or had to get back to rest for work on the Sunday, or Saturday through to Monday or some part of Sunday. Pamela did not want her good feelings she had generally regarding others, soiled by hearing then the sickening jibes and jealousies of those who gained some form of pleasure from being able to seethe. She couldn't now remember exactly how things had been before, but she had no choice now but to note that he would not be online often, rarely not at all though. His phone too, was never switched off all night and until way into the afternoon of the next day before. Not ever, not even during the Wednesday situations when they were happening then. He also always checked and read her messages, even if he didn't respond to them. Sure, it was possible to read messages and not be seen, but that was not his ballgame, neither before though, had switching off notifications been. It seemed for her to hinge on what time and what day, he'd read her message. If at all. Although, it was Pamela herself smiling about it albeit sadly and quietly now. Not angry or concerned, not even interested in him, or those who considered maybe to be his, or that he could be theirs, disconcerted and trying to pull up from being demoralised. No longer able to find the energy to feel interested at all! With her letter from the hospital, now it was time for her, in his absence, or neglect or selfishness, to think only of the successful outcome of her surgery. She remembered a doctor asking if she'd ever or may become a feminist. Pamela was just a normal straight girl, despite many years of being called gay, possibly because she was always alone or had gay friends. Or because of how she was and her own situation, a situation few at all were fully aware of. She was aware all her life that her parents of course knew, that was why they gave her a personal name that was not her birth name, and the same with some other members of their family. Just because some did not have 'other' names, it never mattered. Not to them. It was never favouritism, not once and not ever. Of course, if Judd had been with someone over the weekend and wanted to impress them and keep his phone on, with 'no sounds at all,' other than those easily explained away, he could now, because he'd discovered a new trick since hearing her phone make a sound, switch all notifications off from any of them. Gone now too it seemed, were the days of him 'requiring,' to know, that some were waiting or just online for him. Had the audience changed, or was it always not quite as portrayed, intentionally or not, by him? The only way now that anyone could see her messages to him, would be if the interested eager viewer had access to his phone. But they'd have needed to be careful in case it registered that they had viewed Pamela's posts to him, he might see that too you see? Was the shrewdness of it all worth worrying about? It really would all depend on what type of cake they might be trying to bake and who might therefore hold even the presumed interpreted cherry.

As a final kick in the teeth from Judd, realising that Pamela was as down with wondering what the hell was happening. She didn't think she was 'losing the plot,' or anything like that, in fact it was only a few weeks before she had a few online conferences with a psychologist and a clinician because she had been concerned as to how it all may have been impacting on her, in spite of her bravery and attempts to smile through it all. They confirmed in writing after that they did not believe she required any follow ups until after her surgery as a post-operative and that their impression was that her situation would improve after the surgery anyway, the communication online and subsequently had managed to give her a greater degree of re-assurance, but what was the point in that if then she'd go somewhere and have it ripped to shreds by things she overheard from others, said in a way that she would be forced to hear it, and yes, Pamela had to even question now whether Judd had left his little mark there with them too.

She wanted to go to a local shop and checked online to see what time they opened, their website said 07.00AM, but she was certain it was 08.00AM. She got ready and went to the shop. It was a lovely bright day. The shop though had a sign up saying that they were open at 08.00AM, so she went to another shop having checked on her phone that they were open. Ther was a man in the shop who from behind resembled Judd, she thought that was nice because it showed to her somehow that it maybe wasn't so bad after all. Her notion was that even if Judd turned out to be bad, that too, there were other options potentially, thankfully. But wasn't that exactly what Judd had done to Pamela? She arrived back home at around about 08.00AM, a message appeared on her phone indicating that Judd had responded to her message. He had at 07.16AM he'd copied and forwarded the message from her that showed her hospital letter back to her and typed with it, "Cool, happy for you, smile." Unsure of whether to respond or not, she got a coffee for herself and at 08.10AM replied with, "You're welcome!" His phone was switched off again, it was so unusual, she couldn't work it out at all. She wondered whether his routine had been discovered and so he'd completely changed the pattern to confuse, but she decided to hang on and watch a while. An intuitive instinct suggested that she should. At exactly 08.16AM an hour after, she saw that his phone came back on. At 08.20AM she sent another message to him. The message read: "X." an indicator after advised her that he read that message at 08.30AM. So, it had gone from undetectable/ with phone switched off from when he sent the first message until 08.30AM. Intuition cruelly told her then at that moment too, that Judd and whoever he was meeting had had now avoided even idle chit chat at the bus stop, so he had quite obviously been to where he was going to before. She checked her phone from the week before when he visited her. There was a message from him at 09.32AM an hour and a half after leaving her referring to his bad back problems and exercising to attempt to fix it. She'd thought then that he was trying to be vindictive and generally just nasty but could not respond to it because it would have been as an accusation and guessing and excuse for him to block her. She decided to wait, hoping, but not desperately, that he would come online at 09.30AM. At 09.32AM, he did, only for a minute. She sent a message at 09.32AM but he didn't read it, meaning he was not looking at her page online. She copied his message from the week earlier referring to his back problems and forwarded it to his page at 09.45AM. She half expected him to go back online again at 10.00AM or very soon after, but he did not. So, his phone had been switched off. It made it impossible for some of the apps he used to say that he, 'the user,' was within a mile from Pamela's home. Or it would have been on, as it remained since 09.32AM. Then on his way to work from there, he called in to see someone else locally, in between where Pamela lives and his workplace. Then at 09.32AM, he left there with 28 minutes to get to work by 10.00AM. So, was he now staying locally as a convenience with one buddy, and just sleeping around with others locally too? All then within quite a close proximity to where Pamela lives?

Dear, dear Pamela hopelessly felt as though she wanted to destroy Judd, but still none of it yet, 'in her opinion' was deemed by her, as his fault. Pamela then realised again, that if she didn't look at his page or show interest again, whereas it had been he who'd contacted her, she could not be hurt by what she finds, or believes she sees. She'd walked around a little and wondered why although she'd seen attractive looking guys when out to the shop and lovely looking ladies too who were so smart and a couple who were laying in a shop doorway, they were all nice. why would it be so difficult for her to meet someone else if ever she wanted to? Possibly, because she appreciates. She hadn't been 'looking' as in searching for to meet anyone specific in that way when she met Judd. In spite of her experience, she had not studied as a Doctor or a Psychologist, it was her intention however her own experiences and those of a professional nature, had enabled her somehow at least a modicum of rationale, she was not going to allow her seemingly warped or jaded opinion of what she had become in recent times, during predominantly the past year, dealing with and having not only adjusted to the ongoing frustrations of her need for surgery, exacerbated by her having met Judd when she did, but then having met Judd. She had jokingly said to him once, "am I always to be regarded or considered by you as just left behind." And just as she would feel him smiling or sneering at that remark in months to come, she too had then.

Pamela was thinking of other times when he had met someone, and it seemed as though nothing else mattered at all. It was as if he had tunnel vision or something like that, or as if possessed. You see, apart from placing adverts a few websites, yes for contacts as in meets, not that she had, but she too had been deceptive, her own working had to be. Agente' provocateur in some countries, so and yes, she was wanting to meet someone but had been put off before. Often men would still contact her and send photos of themselves, she would examine them and question every little lump of mark or bump, believing that any of them could potentially go to meet someone for casual encounter and if for example it was a very dark room they were meeting in, they would not necessarily see something they may miss. Fairly often, of those who contacted, she would suggest that they visit a std clinic. Some were horrified, some were upset and some thankful, extremely. Usually or certainly the last time it happened, the chap was very grateful and thanked her, she directed him to a local hospital facility that was free. Unfortunately for her, she believed she had always been way too selective for her own good.

Anyway, a few of those who'd contacted her mentioned a website and asked her if she'd ever used it, she told them she hadn't. One day, not too long after she'd met Judd, they'd had a disagreement because he denied what he was up to, she told him she didn't want to speak to him again, he wouldn't listen at the time because all he wanted was what he was doing, and it wasn't the first or the second time, she knew when he was going to meet others, such was the situation on that day, she also knew he was about to go into the persons flat, she knew it without doubt, she also knew that there was no way she would be able to contact him for an hour and a half and then and what again would ensue, again that his moods because of guilt, would change again and exactly what she would have to go through, again, she decided 'no more.' She investigated the website that many had mentioned and still is a member today, although because of Judd and how she felt for him, she would not meet another man then, she simply never would have considered it. She was browsing through the website and who should she come across, but Judd, a profile he had set up for himself, it also said that he'd been on the site that day and had been a member for a year and gave a list of his friends on that site? It also said that he liked making videos, gangbangs, same room swapping, and other types of swapping, whatever they were, Pamela didn't know. Couples and all kinds of things. She was speechless, horrified. She'd presumed that he was meeting people from the far less busy and not sexual oriented site where he'd initially contacted her from? That's what she couldn't understand, how was he meeting sex contacts from the site where he said he'd got her contact details from? Then he asked her to contact him on another messaging app, other than the app they'd been using. She soon realised that it was purely for his own convenience's sake. After a while she realised again, that he was contacting them on the website and then giving them the phone number and app details, so they could contact him there and from there he'd arrange to meet them. In spite of warnings from the website generally about not meeting and that it was forbidden or in some context's illegal, he continued thoroughly, all the way through the four and a half months he was furloughed too. Unfortunately, Pamela had her eye on his movements on the website, even down to which of the newbies he was meeting, and he always went for the newbies. Sometimes, she'd see some of them and just have to sit back horrified, she knew he'd find them, and that when they weren't on the site and he was chatting on the app, precisely to whom. Then, suddenly after he disappeared for the first of a few days with them, and totally ignoring Pamela, their profile on the website would usually within the first 48 hours then totally cease to exist. Just as her own had. Although he didn't know about Pamela's fully paid up, as his was, membership of that site too.

The website was a meeting website where users say what they like and meet compatible partners Pamela looked at some of the newbies, females, because she knew that was what he'd be searching for mainly, or believed that then, she knew he lived near an airport and the amount of time it took him to travel from there to where she lived, so all she had to do was to do a search for the types of people she knew he would search for, because of how he wanted to be or was with her. Pamela saw a photo of one of them, and then told herself that basically anything between her and Judd was finished, there and then, it was over, there was absolutely no way at all that Pamela awaiting a surgery could compete. That same day, Pamela was aware that the person she saw a photo of was going on and off the website at exactly the same time as Judd and at various the times throughout the day, although he was unaware that Pamela knew, all Pamela could do was to lay in bed and cry, she wept so much, holding a sheet up to her face, unable to physically move, with her knees pulled up to beneath her chin almost, she cried into a sheet, so as to not make a sound. Also, when they left that website, immediately he would be chatting to someone and not allowing interruptions on the app, not because of switching off notifications, he just was interested in nothing else. Then unbeknown to him, Pamela would have to witness it all, every last detail in her mind because of how she was.

Pamela always knew that there were some things she could do as in a psychic dimension, she just was too shy to admit it to herself and too, she was not greedy or selfish and didn't want to appear silly to say it, mention it or ask. It was better for her to quietly integrate it into how she worked, rather than make a fuss about it. This though, this side or aspect of it all, was something extremely new. She also wondered more recently whether Judd wasn't attempting to copy that of it he could not fathom. The girl was twenty-four, she was skinny and had long blonde hair. Of course, Pamela was jealous, not of her though, not at all! Of the fact only that Pamela and Judd could not experience these things together. Then for Pamela to have to endure the pictures like it was happening in front of her, as if seeing through his eyes and even her eyes, but it wasn't his eyes, or hers, or anyone else's.

Judd went off to meet her at her place. They spent the whole of the first night together, he wanted her, but she wanted males or couples, plural, not singular. How he managed to get her to invite him, Pamela would never know then, maybe he showed her evidence of possibilities and arranged to meet her first, as a tester, a sample, to see how they'd get on, or maybe he showed her a video of him and the person he had been meeting on Wednesdays, and others who he'd invited to their parties. She certainly looked game. She also had a look about her as though she was looking for or waiting for opportunity to come her way, she looked keen but not eager, she certainly didn't look stupid. He went to meet her, and they had three days together. The Wednesday meets were on still then, the idea was that she'd be invited to that, by him. He arranged with her and accompanied her to there? To make very sure that she got there! But first he had to go to her flat again himself for that whole afternoon too. They enjoyed each other, why not? Pamela knew they would get on very well. Her name on the website profile was, 'Jenny C.'

(26 June). Judd, Pamela presumed or thought, might have felt, or harboured a subconscious resentment toward the person he'd been seeing in the past two weeks after he'd met Pamela. Especially seeing his new friend at one point lying on the ground, Jenny C, motionless during those few days. Feelings giving way to Pamela's presumption only highlighted by the look Pamela saw in the vision, that Judd had noticed in the corner of his eye, her grimace as he watched her offer Jenny C, barely then able to move, some water from an unclean saucer. He saw in them then, also struggles somehow with an embittered relationship he'd had for years and was still involved with that too, that was his regular Saturday and Sunday meets. Meets that now were strictly about personal needs of his partners it seemed, because he'd use such too, to meet his own need, to create a seemingly more gratifying sex scenario.

Pamela remembered again how he'd always focus on pictures at her flat and smile, as he moved from one to the next as though creating a movement or direction forward for himself, as though constantly in need, or with a desiring to progress and accomplish somehow, either that, or it was that there was not only always one picture to choose or decide from or at.

It also maybe had explained the relationship with his Saturday and Sunday meets, who he could not obviously live with, was he too busy Pamela wondered, or too old even, or was there another reason, or reasons? Pamela might have envisaged Judd carrying children in his arms, although she believed it was the spirits of children, guides, advising her in visions, as to what he, or they were up to. There were also those he met who he decided for whatever reason to keep around, like pictures on a wall, that he could change as and when he liked, to suit his own intentions, or to give an impression, or create an illusion and yes, should they look at his carefully placed phone, or should they have access to it, to others, or someone else. And of course, those he'd located, to perform, each time progressing that little bit further. Not that many of those would have realised.

So, when then, he'd ask Pamela to send photos of herself to his phone, obviously as they weren't meeting then, it was so that he could move forward, so the photos had a value, even if he traded them, or used a photo to encourage someone else, his next acquisitions, to them to better or improve upon it, so really, he wasn't actually going for look-a-likes after all, not as Pamela had convinced herself, believing he wanted her, oh he wanted her alright, as many as he could pull into one basket and put a lid on it, he did with them what he attempted with Pamela to get them there. It would be many months before dear stupid idiotic Pamela worked that out. Each time, when Pamea sent a photo to him, believing he wanted her and that it was just difficult, 'stringing her along,' he'd say to Pamela, "I want," it was an implication that in usual circumstances was a form of trickery, certainly a deceit. Letting her continually believe that somehow, he fantasized over the images and was very interested, when all along, an inclination was steadily developing in Pamela that he did not, she knew he did not really, she either didn't want to believe it or wanted to see how depraved he was, to prove something to herself, and it wasn't that she would love him anyway, despite it all, if after all of the problems they were to meet again, that was something she believed she was capable of, with him, how far would his abuse test that, and how? How long would he keep it up for, why did he need to, the answer was there but Pamela didn't see it then, she knew that she had to somehow turn things around, but that all, how Judd was, was unfortunately something Pamela could not have envisaged. She did though believe she understood the thought processes he carried with him, how true or accurate, maybe we'll never know. When his meet from two weeks after he met Pamela, in a vision, then put a dog collar on his new friends' neck as she lay on the floor and then pulled her up by it and said, "drink," he, Judd saw only his Saturday and Sunday meet partners and their small pretty long-haired white dog with a pointed snout,'Suzi-kiku.'

Something was happening at the weekends, and it was though the Wednesday night fun times somehow possibly compensated if they lacked at weekends, although there was often things Pamela believed she saw, it was just very difficult for her to fully contemplate, then recover from having seen some of it. She even wondered whether his weekend partner set him free during the week to allow him to just do, would it be a while before he learned how to get the most out of that too, or was that how they'd learned to make it work. And if photos were 'tradeable' where was that going to stop? Had it ever, was there a market for it all, somewhere? Yes, even Pamela's then, more innocent photos, innocent because of inexperience in matters of sex.

So, he was creating scenarios selfish, or was he playing a part similarly, but in manipulation, unbeknown to him? Granting freedoms to them, even if of sexual expression, however dressed, or undressed, that could seem to be. And whilst so many were in lockdowns too. Was Judd 'acting the innocent and corruptible,' or had his first partner he met after meeting Pamela, or his Saturday and Sunday partner realised early, or way earlier. His Saturday and Sunday thing he never ever missed, it was as regular as clockwork, even if he'd during the lockdown, where their meets, parties went from Wednesday right through to the Saturday morning, he first then had to escort who he'd picked up to bring along with him back to their home before he went on with his little bag of 'excitement or seeming mischievousness.' Certainly, to anyone, 'in the know,' who would recognise it. A real good little boy, some could think, for some too, it could also have the kind of ability make him look pathetic. Maybe that was where his cake was sugared? Pamela often felt certain that no one else was ever invited to those meets, she was so very certain, she named them, his 'chocolate on a mountain top,' meets and just how fine could those ultimately be. Strong manipulating some weak, just as he'd thought he'd had a bad deal with life chances, because his choices much earlier he'd believed, had never been exactly his own, he'd been moved from what he'd thought then was a more difficult life, or is it weak manipulating strong? But if it is based on lust and desire? It could be easy to presume Pamela thought, that an eager and willing 'supplicant,' could be pandering to the desire of a needy 'perceived' weaker person, who desires or fantasises, or what if they cannot usually attain or gain for themselves, is it still a service if growth is exponential, and if for example, no cash ever changes hands as such, or none that is located. Or was that covered now under the umbrella of escapism.

For sure, private conversations on media would have been different between Judd and the person he met two weeks after meeting Pamela, if not only because of Pamela's need to have a surgery that was now, or became after, then, impeded by an exponential growth of another kind, that of Covid-19. Also, they could have said things to Judd online that Pamela would not have been involved with, like, 'remember what you did to,' or many scenarios now. Was the person some desperado who just didn't want to let Judd go, or was he innocent and was being abused and used by that person who was basically very selfish and quite sadistic? Would that person ultimately be any match for Pamela? Would they try to think that they would not be found out and what would the consequences of that be, after all, Pamela was not a whore, quite the opposite, and there would be absolutely no mirroring that, however it looks, so they'd actually attempt to locate somehow, and take? Even Pamela had to smile at that now. And as it certainly seemed to explain his last meet with Pamela, who believed of herself, there was not a way then, to compete on that level. It seemed to have been the case then too, as Pamela and Judd had not communicated for a whole four days at all, total silence. It was Sunday June 28th. Judd had been furloughed since March; Pamela was alone all those months. Maybe the Wednesday things had stopped since, or they'd developed to such an extreme during those months when many of us were in lockdowns, that the weekend thing had been extended, or maybe he left one party to now just go straight to the other. He'd logged in online on the Saturday at 11.30AM, but was probably just checking or confirming arrangements, or thanking his Wednesday–Saturday meet basically, and certainly as that manipulative streak was concerned, planning the next.

Pamela had remembered how he was like a kid in a sweetshop when he visited her at first, so excited during his first and the next visits, she'd been looking at some texts from him sent back then much earlier in the year than March, and that his moves since their initial meet somehow became after, not wholly of his own volition, rather someone else who had a level of, or means to make him feel controlled or to influence him somehow, was it to be realised later by Pamela that he was still only actually, 'on the make.' It was also as though their messages had been seen, she thought, and that whoever was reading them might do anything to prevent him from coming to see Pamela again. Anything. So, the game had been 'upped,' but realistically though, 'if' such a person, or persons, would have, even if for their own gain, whether that be either sexually or voyeuristically, sought to prevent him from visiting Pamela 'so much,' even if it meant them seeing him or watching him now and encouraging in him, daily rituals and sex encounters with strangers, so they'd put him at risk, or was it to be that they didn't care quite so much, was their cruelty more tuned, or did they actually believe it was, that Pamela would never find out about it or realise? But that person didn't know Pamela? They'd watch Judd throughout the whole crisis that was the pandemic, as though dousing him with sugar, they though, could not have been sure as to his survival risk? Maybe they were Pamela thought. And if during those meetings they remained totally distanced as they watched him, then carefully chose who to bring to their very personal parties. So potentially, he was dispensable too, were they exploiting him or was it him making the most of it all. Such a naughty innocent Judd. And with no consideration of or to those he visited, their immediate families or children throughout a pandemic, if any of them had children.

The term 'if you love them, set them free,' to Pamela had taken on a new meaning, even if to put them at risk. Or were they, that crowd, still all-of the opinion that Covid-19 was not real. Pamela compared the annual deathrates 'in all settings' a week earlier, those recorded, 'as of Covid-19.' she said to herself, that even if there had ever been a psychosomatic element to any of it at any point, that was something she personally considered, too much of it anyway, would also have been unknown and guesswork, as the virus had been believed to have been an unknown entity. Were Judd, and Pamela who had remained totally distanced, and isolated for the whole duration of the four months and then until the November, simply trying different stances, and basically just as scared as anyone else maybe and some even unaware of whether anyone would survive at all. Effectively then, it could have been perceived that there was nothing to lose, and Pamela's isolation somehow, however stupid, and as much as she'd have preferred him to have stayed with her, that's why in March when he told her he'd been furloughed that day, Pamela invited him to stay with her only throughout the crisis, but he said he could not. He, especially having acknowledged that invitation, and so painfully, instantly after asking him, she was aware of it, he now had quite other plans. He planned to use that time, to utilise to his best advantage how he was being abused by the person who he met on Wednesdays. No more stuck within the restraints placed by what was his job. Gone were the one-night Wednesday night meets, those now became Tuesday until Saturday or certainly late Friday nights. And Pamela had to sit in isolation through it all, and often then, every last detail of it.

Were his Wednesday antics about to possibly sour, that freedom extended so kindly by the person who thought that by allowing him although basically leashed to her, so she thought, was starting to backfire. She was finding it difficult when he didn't turn up at their usual time of 17.30PM, but then he'd turn up with a young thing on his arm all smiles, particularly as he'd just spent half a day with that person, and then looking forward to the party provided. But his Wednesday meet was now beginning to feel used, and it was not sexual, and her happy eager to please and willing kind face started to not look so inviting and happy smiles. Their relationship was changing, yes, she gave him a long leash, only to then have to watch him hang himself by it and there was nothing she could do to change it without admitting or him realising that she had basically tricked him. She couldn't tell him that she cared for him, because just as she'd taught him regarding Pamela and others no doubt, it was possessiveness to do that. Before he'd turn up earlier in the day at 17.30hrs, eager only to please her, and then as a treat she'd maybe invite others, now and because she'd thought it would be easier if he interviewed them, thinking too that okay, it was what they'd attract, and she liked multiple guys, it kind of helped in her personal situation with her confidence issues, often she'd have guys pleasing her and she'd watch Judds expressions, or even deliberately seem to not watch him, he'd be sitting in the side-lines then, as they pleased her, it was all done in a kind of childish way, as though to make him jealous, or to make him then want to compete with them somehow. He'd sit and just smile. Yes, sometimes she'd even invite a male and female couple to join them, but it was quite rare. Although still pleasing her still, oh he knew how to compete, especially believing it was a free for all party, though pleasing himself far more certainly now having invited a guest of his own. His Wednesday meet did not like it now and she couldn't get out of it, now she was having to have sex with others, as though by force, and Judd knew, he knew all along, that she wanted him. He ignored her and just watched, and she did not want them. He was indeed a fast learner really, that was what he knew in Pamela, that was part of the magic they shared, but Pamela was never able to show him properly then. So, Pamela's years of yearning, some would now attempt to invade, imitate, and then mirror, or mimic? Pamela was not a type to ever use profanities fortunately, neither was that though or would Pamela's situation with regard to be or become something open to abuse. His Wednesday meet had underestimated not so much how things might potentially develop, but as much as she'd trick and scheme, she was never going to discover what Pamela had seen and dear Pamela was not going to tell, or have it known, certainly not in messages or in any way that could be intercepted. Pamela couldn't anyway, all that person had been doing was reading texts and messages between Judd and Pamela and trying by arranging these little soirees to pull him away from her. Did it eventually happen? Also, he was constantly logging into the website during their meets now, at very precise times, was it to invite others, was he not satisfied, or was he becoming in more demand than her? His logging in was only for a few seconds, never longer, so not even really time to chat. Was he reversing it back to her, or was that how they played? How they worked their little audience of those eager or those who'd fallen victim to them already. Or to him. She'd know these times when he'd log in, just as Pamela had, but Pamela knew too, he wasn't now speaking to her, or Pamela. And then, after, she'd now have to sit back, just as Pamela had. Whatever happened at their three/ four-day parties, she'd know that whoever he'd brought with him, he'd then very personally 'indeed,' escort them home after, for quite some hours in fact and even overnight, before his Saturday-Sunday regular, thing. He'd not be online during this time, and he'd never respond to telephone calls, they knew never to attempt that. That would be all, depending on how early he left there, she'd now have to remember him by, the thought that not even between then and the Saturday, she could not intervene at all after he left, but until the next week, and because unbeknown to her, he always went on another meet too, various, eagerly waiting, even on Sunday evenings when he returned. Then he'd be out of action until early the next week, arranging checking what had been arranged for him for the Wednesday, and in the meantime, he'd be first round there to see to any newbies that hit the website. He was hiding much of it from his Wednesday person too, it must have been quite frantic really. And not only for Pamela, who. Unbeknown to them, very sadly, knew what was happening, should Pamela have been happy about how she was. And more. Also was a real worry then, did he have a new accomplice or accomplices, it wasn't a worry for Pamela. Pamela would be surprised if his Wednesday meet now had any hair left on her head at all.

It was now still the last days of June, news continued of a possible second wave, and reports that the virus should be isolated. If psychosomatics came into it, Pamela thought, then it was about creating a situation, because no-one really knew how it affected health in a mental health context, to create a scenario whereby even if those who flagrantly were flouting the rules, who too, could be just afraid or attempting to test situations to form statistics, could see or realise realistic changes positively somehow, that could create natural means of resolve and ways forward.

The question on Pamela's mind more often though, was of Judd, whilst it's negotiable, that he'd have used them for anything other than mutual gratification, what could it achieve if actually 'bait,' for someone else? And who was that 'someone else,' and importantly, what was their ultimate aim really? And if opposites are their most attractive. A means to finding the right fit, without doing any of the work yourself, and having fun doing it. A horrifying thought occurred months after, that Pamela herself may have been used as a kind of bait. So, Pamela initially was, 'in the way,' a risk to that conclusion, if Judd was being used anyway, but not if a person wanted to see whether Judd would bite, and how it could be used if he did, and the effects of. That person had it seemed, found a someone who could get them closer to an objective of theirs maybe, someone capable enough and gullible enough, who'd recognise others like Pamela, 'gullible' enough, or so they thought, to treat them like some kind of pinnata, whether emotionally or physically, it wouldn't matter, to shake them effectively to the very core, and where if in doing so, in some cases, oh not Pamela's, it were to generate a link to their victims own paternal or maternal links, what if in some cases, it robbed them of for example their youth or innocence, where or in whose bag would, or could such an elixir if discovered, end up? And what if, he'd married the person he met at weekends at some point, and if the in-laws didn't like him? Did they see something or was it just that the spouse or partner had been playing it very carefully from the outset, indeed, 'sensibly' dressed always too. Could clothing on the washing-line of the neighbour of her parents, really have evoked him so much as he lay on a lawn or had his wife's own confidence worked. Could that be what her parents noticed, rather than her, or was it all part of a gloriously, with greater experience, compiled façade on his part? Could it really have actually been Pamela's innocence, because she'd done nothing because she could not for medical reasons, that did shut the door basically in his face and motivated him to not only go searching, but to learn from her innocence on precisely how to approach others similar who were not forced to say no, where Pamela did not have that as an option. Or that he, or he and his accomplice/s might allow Pamela to continue believing that she was responsible for it? Was there actually even more to it that any of them might appreciate.

So, although he paraded around acting like the village idiot, he actually claimed to be a hotel manager, or "working in the hospitality sector," Pamela believed it all anyway, especially that part. Not of course that he wouldn't have been spurred into action at the site of the right type of clothing on a neighbour's washing- line, the right type of dresses and ladies loose tops blowing in a gentle breeze, instead of the more formal clothing that Pamela also usually wore, although rarely with a bra, she liked the feeling of being more liberated, plus, she always had in her mind somewhere that she did not mind dressing for a man, but not to find, or with the sole purpose generally, to lure one. Pamela thought early on that his rushing around and sometimes, an almost slight edginess about him, seemed peculiar, she attributed it to nerves, was it his need for the fantasy of it all? The only resolution she could offer to herself as an answer to some of his antics, was to be somehow just that. She also wondered whether he was in fact very much trying to run away from something, also there was a thought that he, in spite of his claims that he'd stick by Pamela until after her surgery, that he was attempting to run to something, possibly even having met Pamela. Whoever he was meeting on Saturdays and Sundays though, Pamela was aware from the very start and although he never said it, those days were out. Pamela also noticed then that another barely old enough person had appeared on the website, the website Jenny C was first on, and that the times corresponded with the times Judd was on the site and when he used another site to arrange the meets. Jenny C of course, liked females too, or possibly even more than males, but Judd would still try, because Pamela knew instantly that she fitted his requirement perfectly visually, and when he brought her to that party where she was made to drink from the saucer by his 'accomplice,' it became obvious that one way or another, his aim was met. That girl was never seen on the website again and after two days, neither was the other newbie, he was obviously working quickly in all aspects now, yes, Pamela noticed Judds movements on that. A horrible thing to consider too, was that as not much was actually known about the virus, might Judd actually believe that where those like Pamela were in total isolation and adhering to the government rules, was it the virus being controlled by the isolation of those who got through it and stuck to the rules, leaving those like Judd and his pals to just continue to enjoy the greater freedoms that the chosen isolation of others like Pamela had presented. Had it all opened a free sex zone to those who knew how to and whose remit it was, to abuse.

It was then that the private online conference with a psychologist and a psychoanalyst occurred, she wanted to establish that her faculties were kind of 'on it,' and that she hadn't been in any way too affected by the isolation, although she thought it was more about the hurt, she was having to endure, she wanted to have some kind of confirmation from professionals that her scruples had not been too adversely affected or interrupted in any way. Also, from a personal standpoint, just to feel that she was ok, she'd wanted to feel totally certain regarding her decision-making capability. Also, there was the thought that she wanted to feel safer that as she was involved in a health advisory capacity, that the base elements of her mental framework were within recognised structures to be able to facilitate actions she might take, without causing unnecessary harm, especially to Judd. In a nutshell, she wanted to be certain in her own mind, depending on the outcome of the assessment, that any risks Judd might be placing himself in, that were of no fault of her own, and were of his own volition. He would never know how much Pamela cared. That Saturday there was some unusual action online, it was as though he had not been where he would usually have been at all, or if he had, Pamela strongly felt that he had arranged a meet and taken three hours out to do whatever, it was all the usual patterns, was it to fool her, she wondered whether Judd or an accomplice had realised that Pamela was on to them somehow, the feeling was of suspense. She even wondered whether the little game was another experiment of his, or well-practiced, and intended only to generate some invigoration for him? She'd been though thinking about the spots and pimples on his back, so many of them, so much that some could quite easily have felt their flesh seem to crawl after meeting him, Pamela would not have been at all surprised if some did think like that, more disgustedly, though chances were, that they'd find a way of ignoring that, it would not necessarily have been their general concern, his actual well-being. Suddenly, then Pamela thought only of a pit, totally full of snakes writhing together, she stood back slightly as if startled. One of the snakes then raised itself up, it's face, now right opposite her own and its tongue moving about fast as though very hungry and liking her fragrance, in front of her very eyes, it was big, it sounded like a rattlesnake, she looked at its scaly reptilian skin around it's face and eyes and the perfection of its shape, it's tongue and the sound it made, seemed to work together, as if to Pamela, some kind of dance. As frightening as it was, and it was, she smiled at it, she wanted to laugh, her face was beaming. She didn't question whether it was nerves making her want to laugh, but she did appreciate animals. Oddly though, it changed into a wicked stepmother image, a sword appeared, and its head severed before her eyes, and to her surprise, another formed in the exact same place where the severed head fell from, this time though, with the most vivid almost flashlight-like green eyes. Pamela was too disinterested though, to want to look at it, 'playing very stupid games,' she thought. Pamela turned away from it and it seemed to go around and over her own head, the to re-appear in front of her face. Pamela stared at it, and said, 'you have no place here.' It was a warning because Pamela would never deliberately harm them. She thought to herself, that she understood that times are difficult, especially presently, though she did wonder also, whether in meeting others or anyone at all, for especially if you engage in play, what exactly could you potentially be up against, or was it all like a smoke screen of a kind, a subtle warning not to delve too deeply. Was it to do with cultures, did any of them know and was it of their thinking and design, based on their backgrounds, or was any of it just there anyway as part of their being, constantly influencing, if the bearer aware, their decisions? But for who? Pamela thought, 'it could not be for I,' so something was helping it somewhere. Sure, some of Judd's friends may quite well have thought of themselves as evil or wicked, or even capable. She considered how humorous it now seemed to her, that she had offered to help him, if she could, with some matters, although uncertain then as to what they might be, confidently, based upon just wanting to offer help. It was obviously though, was not a concern for Judd, or the others, or anyone with whom he directly frequented? But if he was visiting others, each with their unique agendas, and telling them bedroom-wise how amazing they are, by his actions and words when exercising and stating preferences, what was he potentially passing back, back to where he'd been before, or those he'd been with. Was it important then to consider that what he passed back could constitute as an emotional parasite with possibly physical affects and that the handling was not necessarily even in the initial meet but what you'd be left to deal with subsequently and possibly without knowledge of, if you permit it to interfere with, or bother you? Did dear Pamela think like that then though? Judd obviously didn't, or he'd have said, wouldn't he? Did any of them know, would any of them know? Oh, my goodness, Pamela's own background prohibited her from blaspheming, though there might be some things some could think. A question then could be, would any of them have any notion of how they had decided to play? The seemingly lifeless body of Jenny C back then yes, had been nothing to do with Pamela. Had Pamela not been so shaken or disturbed, quite possibly, the conference with two psychiatry healthcare professionals might not have been required, as Pamela would have believed her mind to have been better equipped to be completely certain to have retained wit and faculties and for longer, she thought, 'then maybe the key is not to be alarmed or hurt or affected by it, but I have feelings she thought.' Had it by default, ruled out any element of discussing it with potential perpetrators, when you know that whether rightly or wrongly, you had been subjected to such a different type of abuse, and if offers from you, had been obviously rejected or by being ignored, laughed at. Or had it all developed that way, deliberately to safeguard the perpetrators and to fool victims to it?

Certainly, the dark character that Pamela saw appear on the night Jenny C lay on the floor helpless, the character that approached Judd, had been similar to that Pamela's friend Jean would have remembered and had mentioned to her in a conversation once before, although she must have been so caught up in wondering whether she was going crazy, such was how it was, that she never put the information together, although it was now as though somehow, especially as Pamela had been assessed, that somewhat leaner figure than that Jean had referred to, was now a dark cloak and named nothing other than very possibly 'belief' itself. There seemed to be no other logical explanation. Could it have travelled with them from all of those generations before, when floorboards or planks so neatly placed on top of each other would creak almost in tune with the wind as it could be heard hitting the flapping sails pulled up so high upon that mast? Was it the same icy caves Jean knew of, and that Pamela knew of? Could it have been the same cave? Sure, it was as much a stormy day that day of the invasion, as it would have been years, but equally though, none of them would have noticed back then as invaders, and certainly subsequently, not as they were about to set sail.

#

Jealousy yes, Because of what Pamela had offered him, deceit, yes. He'd taken the offer Pamela made that was totally genuine and of a strange but very real loyalty even and didn't care, he used it solely to his own advantage and to that of any accomplice he had, or those involved, whether unbeknown to them or not, Pamela didn't matter to him. With Jenny C, all they'd have seen was a twenty-four-year-old being offered, or was it that they had now incorporated other 'paying' guests? There was much more to be gained by them just to demonstrate effectiveness to those who visited over those few days each week. As to what effectiveness and to what end, hey, who'd really know? Pamela did not want to know. Sure, 'all' who attended during those few days were 'vetted,' Jenny C had only met Judd the week earlier, so it was too late to vet her. Yes, the cloak character, the dark character, the lean one, in those early hours, Judd was standing up against a wall, it had seen how Jenny C had been treated, it went to Judd, without touching him, Judd backed up tightly to a wall. It stared at him, Judd was unable to speak, it slowly moved its head within two inches of the contours of Judd's face, although not interested in Judd's smell, Judd could sense it and feel the anger in its quietened breath, droplets, not that anyone would have really bothered, particularly as lockdown restrictions were about to be lifted, were way too heavy for Judd to have breathed any in, even Judd wasn't that fast a learner, neither would he ever actually be.

The body on the floor was motionless, and yes, for sure, how Judd liked it. The dark character was seen by Pamela to walk again to where Judd was, and again right up to his face, he was still just standing against a wall wondering what had just happened, and even doubting that anything had. It quietly said to him, "now clean that up," then it left. That weeks' game did not fill Pamela with anger and not either with rage, for reasons of health she felt obliged to attempt to deal with though, the feelings of intensified hurt.

It was then that Pamela thought of parties and their velocity and lucrativeness, to be able to cream off and then preen the best talent, or what got the cakes baking nice and hot, had to be for some a more viable option. So, they enjoyed what they loved doing and in spite of restrictions, continued to thrive on it, and ultimately learned to put it to constructive use by making it financially viable, they weren't anti-establishment, they just were selfish? It wasn't even about making ends meet in difficult times or struggles, it was apparently just about sex and the rewards exponential, initially. Pamela thought of it as abuse but even by her standards had to feel somewhat sad for not having considered it herself. Dear Pamela, wouldn't, not with her morals. Or was her surgery having been postponed, awakening her to not permitting herself to be beaten down any further. In fact, she remembered something she'd seen once on an invitation regarding the millennium year and how then, she'd thought to herself, maybe regarding the words on that card, "it's not always about who you invite to a party, but it can be about who you choose not to," after all, she hadn't quite understood it then.

Was that now beginning to turn a curve of its own, was it all just a game and the person Pamela wanted, had been and had continued to meet others throughout and during the pandemic, as the restrictions were now being lifted, was it becoming prevalent, was it really, purely because of her surgery requirement, obviously it had been, she had to believe that, or the alternative was that he'd have just moved on anyway, to the next, as he had been doing since. Pamela could not conceive that she had lost out to someone who was simply more his 'cup of tea.' She'd punished herself and been allowed by Judd to repeatedly punish herself with it daily. Even afraid to think of the word 'spread,' especially about the pandemic, regarding her mind, seemingly at times being torn in half as though she'd become worthless. Then a system that albeit was doing what it had to amidst the pandemic, had further again postponed, without being able to comment on a date, her surgery. Wondering whether she hadn't herself become the pathetic loser, sticking to her precious stupid 'morals,' and showing no interest in others throughout, Pamela had always prided herself on how very selective she had always been, had she been always simply too selective? For her, it was more than that, it was just love unrequited. Could it change, and would she want it if it did, or had her own ego been kicked to the ground and violated and then trodden on and then humiliated. Was it all lost, as if she cared now?

#

That evening a person contacted Pamela, a message came through to her phone, they sometimes did even still, but she'd ignored them since meeting Judd. It was a little scary for Pamela to start a conversation and as result and for various reasons, also because strangely she felt afraid to, she was hesitant. Yes fearful, that was the strangest part, she'd become so scared that by speaking to chats with anyone else in texts, that she was somehow breaking some form of loyalty, or an intrenched loyalty, the type that might have been achieved by abuse. Pamela was happy about his calm nature and about how he communicated, it began to touch on inspiring her, but it was as it had been with Judd really, hence her scepticism. It did almost somehow let her believe that things could improve, he wanted to chat on the telephone and Pamela told him that it was not something she ever did with men. A strange coincidence was when he said that he lived near to Pamela, only a couple of minutes away from where Pamela lived, in an adjoining street. He offered to send a photo of himself via email, but Pamela thought very carefully about that too. Had the experience also made her display paranoia? And what if that person had been with any of the others Judd had been with? Yes, Pamela, she'd become affected, although preferred to believe what the professionals had told her after the assessment, something she wanted to be certain that no-one else would become aware of, it was nothing horrible, it was something nice.

Why did Pamela decide not to meet him though, "just for a chat and or a coffee," as nice as he seemed, it was mainly because he then told her that he was, "only in-town for tonight." Pamela thought of Judd again and questioned whether she had been so greedy ever to have even considered wanting a person that 'anyone,' else had, or wanted that much, enough to lie and cheat or deceive regarding.

Thinking of a card that had been sent to her years earlier, where a person had written to another and said, "In the still of the night, as I gaze through my window, at the moon in its flight, my thoughts stray only to you," these were some lyrics to a song by none other than Cole Porter," beneath those words it read, 'had Cole Porter not got there first, I'd have beaten him to it.' Maybe that's all it was, that someone else had simply beaten Pamela 'to' it. So, had even another curve turned. How could, or how would Pamela think to consider how she might be able to cope. The feeling of utter desolation, but she had been pushed to extremes emotionally and beaten with every step En route. Pamela also felt nauseas, having seen the photo of another of Judd's recent acquisitions and knowing his eagerness to please, what could have been happening over just this past three days now of this, another week of it. Initially it had been just Pamela and those he met at weekends and then Wednesdays, although she had guessed there was a little more to that then. Had the penny at last dropped, that Judd was not actually interested in Pamela at all? They could have blocked each-other, so what was it about? How would or could, the uninvited, have therefore ever become? Did he know of the suffering, his accomplice? Or was it, as they used their new invitees all about zesting up, or bolstering up their excitement? Pamela had already thought that what they were doing didn't need 'bolstering.' Judd knew that Pamela would have had many interested in Pamela on that website although only a face photo was visible, So, if she then became to him and his 'friend,' or friends, as though somehow 'waiting for a crumb to drop,' how pathetic had it caused her to become? How pathetic had she permitted them to make her feel and was there a point where she'd been worn down so thinly that it happened. She did not any longer now even notice it. But it was her who'd said to him when he first became furloughed, "why do you not come and stay here, you can use me whenever you want, however you like, and as often as you want to, at least we'll both keep each other safer together throughout it all." And yes, we know, he kindly told her then, "It is not possible, but thank you." When she and he exchanged messages after that, it always felt strongly to Pamela as though there was someone else listening in or monitoring the messages, always. Sometimes it didn't even sound like Judd responding, although the differences in how he would respond were slight, they were very noticeable, certainly to Pamela. Pamela believed that he and his Wednesday accomplice were very much at one point, working together, very much as a team. It was as though they were enjoying ridiculing her and that they then were using those experiences sexually. It was during those/these months that in conversations whilst Pamela was still very much isolated, that she asked him, after my surgery and the pandemic, what of you, will be actually left for me? Wasn't that the stupid question then?

The fact became that in the however many years before meeting Judd, where she had seemed to not be interested in men for meets, somehow, she felt uneasy about it because of what she'd seen or encountered by way of discussion with others, it had caused her to focus more on other things. To the point where, yes, she never chased up the situation with regard to having her surgery matter resolved, it had not mattered to her. Had all of this with Judd caused the same concerns she had around trust to now raise their very extremely ugly head again, but in darling Judd himself. And then and certainly until into just the beginning of the July of that year, as his personal net had widened further anyway, had it gone from Pamela not wanting to ever get involved, to now her feeling of absolutely no consequence, that thought was to bring Pamela to tears. That she could have allowed him or any person, to have or think they can yield that much influence in such a callous way and so selfishly over anyone at all. Pamela herself was becoming more disinterested. Understandably though, and because Pamela really had no idea about personal relationships, as in boyfriends, she presumed that because they could not 'consummate,' their having met, and wanting to further their personal relationship yet/then, that he'd somehow found elsewhere another array of other games to play, or that he had been 'biding time,' and so frustrated by it, or was, or had he become so intrenched himself during these months in what was happening, and yes, whether by default then or not, 'closer to home,' that Pamela had just been 'blown out,' he had confirmed her absolute worst suspicions. The saddest thing had become, that she could never tell him now anyway, and that was how he'd have preferred it at the start, though now because he'd have been aroused by it, or would have used it with others, as he had every other suggestion and photo and experience, she had shared to him.

#

'The britches up.'

Pamela had heard mentioned before "picking up britches," but had never imagined that she might one day say or think that herself. She couldn't get out of her mind how in such a short space of time, Judd's activities had developed and so blatantly she believed in front of her own face. Pamela had just woken up anyway, dazed, she kind of shook her head and felt almost drunk but she didn't drink so she knew that was not possible, she did think to herself, who on earth would ever want me like this anyway. Oh, my goodness, she thought to herself, she wiped her mouth and tried to gain some level or degree of focus, she wasn't usually that bad, but she had been dreaming, or having more nightmares, she must have gone to sleep feeling that she had lost Judd to Jenny C without giving it greater thought that he'd have met so many others in between and would continue to, and that she Jenny C preferred women anyway, and that his Wednesday meet wasn't short of guys she could meet. Was Pamela adjusting, or was there more to it? In the dream she was thinking about where Jenny C had been laying on the floor, and Judd against the wall. In that dream Pamela was now also there, she had heels on. In that nightmare, Pamela herself had walked in, she saw what looked like Jenny C on all fours on the floor as she had been in her online profile, and just kicked her so hard with such force in the side straight and completely out of the way like she was totally irrelevant, Pamela could feel now her own fingernails growing by the second and more sharply than she'd ever filed before as she then noticed the person, he'd been meeting on Wednesdays too, but she wasn't interested in that. Pamela was very slim and in very dark clothes and looked similar to a photo of herself she had sent to Judd although in that photo she just had high heels and a short black body stocking dress on. Not questioning whether he'd been fantasizing over it or not, that could have explained the vivid nightmare to Pamela, she nailed, with long nails, her ears to a wall before she had time to even think of anything or move, then it must have been a six-inch nail, Pamela pinned her head to a wall by lacing a six-inch nail into her mouth and just whacking it with the palm of her hand, Pamela had not even been interested in hearing her suffer. Judd was though, and not surprisingly, dressed as Pamela had been dressed in the photo, their attire almost so identical, it was quite amazing. The only naked person there was that Pamela had as like in martial-arts, maybe like a 'kung-fu' style, kicked, she had named it the HKP and seemed quite chuffed about it actually, for her, rather like one knee bent downward, fingers of both hands interlocked and a floorward lunge onto the bent knee, as if limbering-up to exercise, you could almost hear her fingers cracking as she stretched them, although of course this was not something she ever did. As she stood in front of Judd, she was salivating, he was quite still by this time, just staring, he knew something was happening because he tried to look down, presumably to see what the sound was as the saliva droplets did again hit the solid polished wooden floorboards in that very silent room, but this time it was Pamela? He knew something was there but just could not move, even the glance downward was tentative, it was he afraid this time, she saw his fear and was not concerned by it at all, she though said nothing to him in that nightmare. He must have worked quickly because it had only been maybe five or six days before that she'd sent that photo to him unless he had access to a wardrobe now? That day and having had that nightmare, she sent that photo to him again, of course it was now, way too late. For him.

#

One more word, (possibly). Or, for want of better (maybe).

After Judd had visited Pamela a few times a friend of Pamela's said to her, who at that time was unaware of the complexities with regard to her even having met Judd at all, complexities in backgrounds and destiny, did it matter in a slight change in destiny, if such were to be believed, altered or changed, did that happen every day or was that just like being in the right place at the right time anyway, were Judd and Pamela meant, and all of the circumstances, designed to prove or disprove and push and test and break lies, if it was true, into a million pieces, had covid-19 just been an unfortunate problem that no-one could have predicted safely. No-one could have really, could they, Pamela thought. That maybe Judd's background, possibly with an unusual though undiagnosed condition that Pamela believed she knew and understood, possibly because of her own birth situation, having been so very premature at birth then, and born in a place that had only just a few years earlier been a workhouse, designed for the very poorest of the poor. Anyway, Pamela's friend had said to her, "what do you know about love, you've only been together two months, I've been with my partner ten years." It seemed a fine statement to at least listen to, whether Pamela wanted to hear that was debatable, she found it insulting and as Pamela was aware of what she had done in her life around relationships, and more to the point, what she had never done, was unknown to her friend. Her friend would never have understood the real complexities surrounding Pamela's birth, and where the onus would then have been purely even then to attempt where and whenever possible, to save life. Pamela dismissed it, rather than to seem to, or appear to give the credibility she believed the person sought, by her believing there was something or anything of an authority in her friend regarding such matters, in Pamela's opinion, the only test of friendship by her having to listen to that drivel, was that she was as understanding as no doubt her partner was, who Pamela had known longer. Pamela was hurting and it even seemed as though somehow there could have been jealousy and cruelty by some who seemed to profess and during difficult times anyway, and whilst they may have been in the throes of enduring relationships, however happy they seemed, to comment in such a harsh way, or that to, "dish it out," merely constituted as nothing more and nothing less. Pamela understood too, some of their own habits. There was a blank look on her face then, that seemed could only be disturbed by noticing the natural pinkness of her long fingernails, there was no doubt as to her sincerity. Remembering a conversation between Pamela's friend Jean regarding a friend from a church, Florence Breeny, where she'd used the term, "woe be tied," some might question or wonder, how many times should anyone 'forgive,' or is it a daily thing and does it encompass everything? Was it like a car warming up on a winter's day, with the window wipers trying to move on the windscreen that should, or could have been wiped or scraped a little first, or was it like hearing a racing car revving up, and getting ready or more like a double decker bus sat in a derelict yard, you could look at it and almost hear the sound of its engine, but it was still motionless? Pamela then thought about how churches were probably the place where you could go and pray in a designated area rather than trusting it to the elements or neighbours who might hear you, and who might not feel the same way, or who might exploit, or say that they feel the same when maybe they actually do not, and how much of such prayers, could be influenced by bullies? At least a church or private space did allow such, but wasn't your own home meant to be such a private space she asked herself or had all of this become how erratic her own life now seemed to be. The fact was, it had always been like that, certainly for Pamela. So, regarding the forgiveness question, how many times and how many individuals and how many scenarios, and what depth of reality to it all, as peculiar and quirky and ridiculous, although not in a condescending manner at all, because all too easily it could be perceived as such, and far more stupidly on her part ultimately, Pamela had been more in favour of trying to live by example. Now, if the only contact Pamela had really, 'as in,' a close contact, a contact not associated to immediate family or close friends, or medical personnel Pamela had been in contact with luckily, throughout her life, had suddenly now become that person, 'Judd.'

Thankfully though, on his part, as he became more intrenched 'apparently,' in either compliance to, or in the whims, of a selfish few, who seemed somehow too, not really it seemed, to care about Judd at all. Or was it love; did they love him? Was it about how he made them feel? Had the balance of the lost hard done by, overworked, suffering, struggling kid, still been, 'bringing in the reddies,' it was still his gameplay and as lucrative for him as when he met Reverend Prewikk. Or was it the arrogance in knowing that and that he was aware that they all knew they would never have him totally? Was that why some he knew then possibly had been scared by Pamela who had become at first, their unknown entity, would Pamela see what they never could and never would, though they would try any means they certainly believed were possibly available to them, to find out. It would have been integral to their discovering why and how, as lying and deceit had been then, in the furtherance of their objectives? Or should Pamela have just trusted them? And let them into, or even close to her own intellect. If familiarity had bred contempt before, was praying that they or even Pamela might change ever going to really accomplish that now, certainly as Pamela didn't know what their belief structures were, only that they seemed conditioned around a pure unadulterated selfishness. Were they simply attempting to be confidence tricksters? Pamela thought that notion was funny. That they knew very well that they could never have him totally, not them. Did Pamela realise in time? Or had the furore of it all, deliberately and very intentionally, even without Judd realising, eventually put the blinkers, so selfishly and totally on it all.

Some had been certainly pulling out all of the stops recently, and especially during the newfound twenty-four-hour availability where he had been furloughed, they tapped into that child within his soul whenever they could and as shrewdly as it was possible to. "Isolation of cases breaks transmissions," so was he the carrier and those he visited like the outer shell of the virus cell? An interesting thought, but that holiday was then, at a hotel. For Pamela, it required specific in-depth thought to attempt to work this one out, and not for those whose sole remit seemed to be how to fool or keep Judd somehow. It all seemed so ludicrous.

Pamela's decision not to want, but not to have resolve or, resilience personally tested by unquantifiable, was an easy decision, to trust that those involved in procuring a vaccine or vaccines, became an even deeper relevance. Forgiveness, would forgiveness have achieved anything if in a circumstance whereby it was, he, possibly being manipulated so unaware anyway? And what if there had been even more to it? Would destiny surpass their selfishness and greed? Or would they attempt to alter in favour of themselves, irrespective of possible harm or dangers, because isn't that what such selfishness, in those circumstances, is? Could Pamela forgive those he visited so easily? Would, to do so, not be like an open invitation to them to play more of their games, and yes, albeit of a rather primitive psychological type by way of its somewhat sinister approach, Pamela although oblivious and that was a wonder of it, seemed to naturally understand, but, of course, Pamela eventually was to. So, they, some of those Judd knew, had decided to attempt to play those type games with dear Pamela. Pamela's own decision therefore was then, to do nothing but to hope, although of or about what, she was not going to say, not even hint at. Pamela sat by her window and moisturised her hands with hand moisturiser, then she put her hair back and fastened a hairgrip to it at the back. She removed the clear nail varnish from her nails, it was so finely applied by her that you'd hardly notice hers at all, only someone discerning would have ever noticed, not even Judd ever did. She then went to wash her hands with soap and water and upon returning, sat down again and pushed her cuticles back and in total silence. Then as carefully, she brushed nail oil onto her cuticles and just remained seated for five minutes. It was difficult for Pamela because she was usually never able to allow herself that kind of time for herself. She then wiped her fingernails and painted each one of them with varnish straight off, then she waited for them to dry and varnished them again.

Pamela had been thinking about her vision whereby she believed thought she saw the person, Jenny C lying lifeless almost on the floor, was anyone really all trying to get ringside seats for further upcoming events? How hard though, were they actually prepared to work for that. Gratis? And were the bookings already being lined up over the weekend? And all Judd had to do was turn up and do what he did best? Cajoled by those, who even if they were not interested in the females, were interested in the males they attracted. It was then that Pamela gazed through the net curtain in her room, she moved a large curtain slightly to allow her to see more, the light shone in through that small space so much that it made her feel dizzy as she almost had to try to regain composure. It was as though she'd blacked out, or something, or was it just another horrible dream.

#

Did Pamela remember overhearing a conversation that a cousin of hers owned a hotel, having progressed from a small bed and breakfast hotel years earlier, she was impressed by the location then, as it was in the most prestigious area possibly known, but she was so young she did not fully understand what was going on, certainly not regarding business things, she thought it was something to do with a perfumery, because they would often give her samples of perfumes and sometimes, a little money, she would use if to purchase items to keep her fingernails nice. She remembered how they laughed and how they would have thought it somehow funny, some even said then, "Pamela and her hair and nails, and so young." She now wondered though, and it was not such an amusing thought, had they somehow known how lonely Pamela had been, so they sent that guy Judd, she didn't want to believe that they or any as a joke even might have learned of her being on websites and arranged for Judd to call on her, to cheer her up? She just wasn't sure what to believe anymore. Did Pamela visit the hotel in a professional capacity and advise her cousin, knowing how one hotel senior can sometimes now others in similar networks, to have all staff tested for Covid-19 prior to re-starting because some were obviously so unhappy with their work, that they could risk bringing the whole business there into total disrepute, even by association if facts were known, did she mention that some of the staff, certainly one of them, had very possible side-lines of his own, and annoyed that she seemed to have been herself kicked into them, details of such activities by personnel which could be viewed, if accessed she'd presumed by her cousins phone, as long as Judd hadn't changed his phone number. No, because Pamela knew that they were doing nothing illegal. Even her thought that all staff be tested was basically as far as she saw it, 'of no point,' because then, not enough was known about the virus. Or did she simply go onto her media account then, where she knew Judd made most of his meeting arrangements with others and remove all conversations by deleting the account and re-installing it. But she'd just heard on the news, that very minute too, that a person had just awoken from Covid-19 after being in a coma for six weeks. Pamela, stupid Pamela, the innocent soul, wanted to believe that friendship somehow prevailed in all things, she really did. Were some pushing a little too hard, or attempting to further wake her up? Or was she being again, typical charitable Pamela by allowing herself to believe any of it, especially now? Was it not something so sweet at all, that some of her family might have arranged it for fun, her enjoyment, however peculiar or odd it could seem and certainly to Pamela. It had been solely, that the person Judd met on Wednesdays liked very particular types of guys, So anything or anyone that posted whatever ads on those sites, she wanted then completely taken out of the picture, unless she could use them personally 'to attract,' and then Judd would scour through who they both and theirs had got to attend their party and others, to take those rarities and they really were, on at weekends, out of actual view of the Wednesday meet anyway. He'd said to that person he was married, but even she knew it wasn't to a female. So, if she, was able to get him to bring younger, it kept him away from Pamela and the likes of, and helped her too, and ultimately, unbeknown to her, it then also helped Judd at weekends. His role had been 'to work, watch and be rewarded.' Judd would forbid those younger from contacting the Wednesday meet people after, and they could not because they were not allowed to, speak whilst there. Any friends of those invited, Judd would pick and use 'if they were younger,' he had effectively, by inviting them to invite their friends to a media app, managed to get them to do his bidding for him, all he had to do was initially interview them. It also kept them away from other websites, that he and his accomplice were then free to manipulate, hence his 'pouncing,' as soon as anyone new and young enough joined. Those invited to the Saturday and Sunday meet were Judd bringing "something special," along, and hand-picked by a person who once had been there himself. Then all he had to do, was to somehow remain, 'innocent Judd,' watch and be punished or rewarded by them sexually for his work or effort. Even his own job, he'd even been told to get a job in a hotel by them, and to work his way up to bring in some money, from a very young age. He'd also been 'told' by them, never to seek medical help or attention for anything ever. He never did. So, if a day came where, even if his Wednesday accomplice and Judd had been laughing and using the fact that some, including Pamela were eager to get a response from Judd, would it actually mean that maybe it wasn't his Wednesday accomplice who might only be tracking his phone, and that those he was involved with on Saturday and Sunday might be tracking all of it? And should they discover that for example, Pamela or anyone had got close, by way of tracking his moves, or if Judd became aware that his moves were being scrutinised and that his movements were to be found out, what might he have to do, and would he respond quick enough? How quick would he respond and how? How angry would that make Judd, just to have to change then all, of his phone details etc, if that were to ever happen, and how would he explain the need to. Maybe it was all just normal practice after all?

#

So, by meeting the explicit needs of those who would 'sugar him up,' by punishing him, and watching Judd in depraved acts, he became a 'sugar-daddy,' but never actually ever needed to put his hands in his pockets ever. All he had to do was turn up with the goods, he was doing the interviews and testing, he had their photos, and then, thanks to Covid-19 methods and the means to even do conferencing to show 'some' of his interviews, and then other channels to sell the videos. So, if his remarks to Pamela that he was concerned for her actually had any credence at all, were they really just lies, for him to come in and use her? Maybe she was just a stupid insignificant stopgap in-between his visits. Fortunately, her telephone number was neither connected to, or online associated to any of her personal media accounts, nothing personal in fact, she didn't even tell Judd her full name and she didn't tell him her name was Pamela. Any personal papers or documents were completely out of his view whenever he visited her, as sad as it seemed to Pamela, no doubt he'd have tried hard there, painfully even. Were the constant emotional pushing, to get Pamela to forward documents or photos of, that had personal details on them, she; known not to. Because she had dealt with scammers before. Somehow by default, that Judd and his pals caused so much hurt to Pamela, out ruled the more stupid idea, that Judd had been asked to contact Pamela by anyone, because anyone felt sorry for her, where she was never meeting anyone.

Pamela went into a trance-like state just for few moments, although she thought she was dozing off, she visualised a man and a van, he looked like an honest man, he was older that Pamela and the older version of Judd that Pamela had seen, in back of the van, the man stood, he had younger lads helping him load the van with furniture. It was very obviously their line of work; she noticed that the drawers on the floor by the van were from her own chest of drawers and was puzzled by it. She'd put them accidentally outside her home when cleaning apparently. It seemed odd, that she would do that, but it was a dream. Pamela said to him, the older man, who had guys helping him that they were hers and that she had the original chest at home just a few houses away from where the van was parked, that they were made for, his reply was, "we've got a similar piece of furniture at home, and they'll fit." The lads working for that guy weren't being mistreated at all, especially if they were good lads, and they obviously were genuine lads working for a genuine bloke who'd have probably given his right arm to keep them of mischief, possibly because of his very own background too, he knew exactly how tough it was. Precisely as Rev. Preuwikk himself had seen however many years earlier.

The person, his Wednesday meet, of course she knew he was playing the field, to find, and she would do anything possible to keep him visiting her, because she knew that in time, he'd open up to her, she'd seen the signs, she recognised those signs and knew there was more to it. They'd told Judd that they 'wanted to see Judd with someone of his own age,' although his Wednesday meet, had only seen the younger Judd. Pamela's own potentials had not been realised even by herself, Pamela always saw much more, but in a different way to that of just selfish feeling.

Wondering again, whether he'd just been totally lying to her from the outset, even with all the facts, she still bothered to think about it, to give him some legroom, she thought again about the real age differences between the three versions of Judd she had seen. Then she thought about her birth and although by her thought of Judd, she thought she'd met the love of her life, whilst happy of course, that the surgeons and medical team were able to keep her alive back then, and where some decisions would not have been easy decisions to make, she could not blame them for behaving as they had, just as they acted how they do when the Covid-19 thing happened, Pamela knew the protocol. They did what they were meant to. As some presumably would have in other countries with the various birth conditions, even unusual ones, when they occurred, finances permitting, so it was difficult. Pamela thought, 'am I supposed to say, or think somehow, that Judd and I got back together, if it broke my heart to think it, or lie like that about it. Or to appreciate others more for their understanding that I cannot lie.' What if Judd had been born with an unusual condition, she thought to herself. As uncanny as it could seem, it was not as though she could argue or doubt without casting aspersions such possibilities, even if they were only, however vague, possibilities. It for Pamela certainly might have then explained to her why she had believed she had seen him in three different guises, and they weren't three different people, they had been Judd at three different stages in life or a deception or possibly an undiagnosed issue maybe, and possibly another reason why he'd been told 'never' to seek medical help or assistance. Pamela wondered whether he had a rare condition too, as she did, and that maybe he was actually even the same age as Pamela, and that this was the reason she felt as though he had been her soulmate, as though they had somehow travelled through destinies to meet each other. So, it might not have been therefore, that Judd 'liked them young, 'if,' he had a condition possibly, or, certainly had picked up a rare condition from somewhere, but was disliked by basically 'his own captors,' as his true age, and he preferred the younger fun loving and having Judd himself. It was a case of 'finders-keepers,' although stupid Pamela hadn't realised it because of inexperience in guys. He'd been in a relationship and had been playing the field but wanted real love. Quietly she herself also then thought, that had he in fact been sent to Pamela for reasons untrue, that they at least got a better deal than half-price.

104360

So, the furloughing came to an end, much to Judd's disappointment, hotels were re-opening. News indicated that they'd be open again within two weeks, could he have condensed into those two weeks, all those meets he'd arranged prior to? His holiday, however needed, Pamela had always thought in their initial meets, now quite concluded, still though, because of all that had happened since, that even dear Pamela hadn't anticipated regarding what he was really like, and any new bits –on –the side or even those he'd already met, now free to remain whatever they claimed to be to get him there, although now, without him, but to them, would it really matter? Had he been capable enough to win Pamela's heart, would she want to be bothered? What might Judd's reaction be when the full realisation of the extent of what he'd done hit him, after he started back to work, and how neglectful and cruel he'd been to Pamela. It had seemed sufficient that day for Pamela to send him a message, however he'd abuse it, to simply say to him, "enjoy the sunshine," She hoped that every time he saw anything reminiscent of or heard of sunshine, or cold, from then on, it would serve as an intense reminder to him. Had he been similar to Pamela or aware, he'd have known that whenever he met any of his contacts, Pamela was reminded physically too, of her own need to have a surgical operation, because it prevented her from participating normally. Pamela eventually, although months after even July, would realise one day how he would have noted her eagerness when and as she waited as though with bated breath for news from the hospital during those months, and her disappointments, as would anyone else looking at his phone, his friend/s or 'accomplice/s.' Even that, Pamela's pain, had become an account of a kind, he learned to manipulate, she imagined him and how she knew he was laughing at her in messages, and his over-confidence on rare occasions when he'd message Pamela on Wednesday evenings, as though they were enjoying every last second of it. It must have been for them like, sucking egg yolk through a small hole at the top of an egg or breaking into a beehive and invading the hive cells where the young, too young to move, were establishing, and just taking. Whatever, even if nothing as callous, maybe just like removing the top from a chocolate and spooning out the filling for themselves, leaving behind just an empty shell. In some cases, hey, why stop there, have a box, she thought, but he and they had worked that out too. Of course, she knew that he was a cocktail shaker some evenings, yes, Pamela, she had been forced to watch, because of how Pamela is, unbeknown to him, every bit of it! Blending cocktails to form the right kind of party and initially at Pamela's expense? And the longer some were made to wait or were played with presumably, the better it became, or until they had all they required, or only until they started to become aware that there was possibly a greater chance that their game was about to actually be realised. And the sexually inclined hello messages during the week, or when he was in need, to 're-stoke,' and always the same pattern, then he'd go and meet someone, or just stack it all up again until Wednesday or Saturday. Just as the desperation felt, affected, when Pamela knew he'd arrived at a place and what he was about to do, because often she believed she saw it, even down to the colour of a padded bed headboard and it wasn't a usual colour or a colour Pamela had been accustomed to seeing, every detail. And Pamela knowing that there was nothing Pamela could do, she tried to dismiss the visions so many times, but they would never leave her, she even knew what time his phone would switch on again, it was often that precise, sometimes though, rarely, he obviously was enjoying himself a lot more because he stayed longer, as he once did with Pamela, it almost destroyed Pamela, but it all became very normal over the months though, Pamela had hardened to it, was it to be to the detriment of anyone that she'd been forced to suffer in that way, and during a pandemic? After his visits to whoever, it would be as though Pamela just no longer existed, Pamela had to continue to let him believe that she had no idea. Then another profile on the website appeared, another newbie. It was standard, they 'collaborated,' any usual texts or messages from him totally ceased, the person's profile too, vanished overnight from the website, Wednesday chats online stopped, he wasn't chatting to anyone at all. This time, it was obvious that whatever he'd found, he was not letting anyone close. So, he knew the game, he was a user. Pamela had checked a photo on his profile and remembered a bike company he'd used, there was a bike company in the photo, she checked aerially and located the street and what hotels were on it, it was such a surprise to Pamela that they were the very same hotels that some of her cousins lived near and where her father had worked with an architect some considerable years earlier, as they'd have been being built in fact, but Pamela was so young, she loved the architect's garden and remembered visiting there with her father. He lived in the same street then, as her other uncle, her father's youngest and the only surviving brother, the uncle who shared the same birthday as Pamela. She always thought of him and the other five people she knew who shared the same birthday, every year Pamela would do that. She did wonder though, if those Judd met had partners, what might Judd be passing to those partners via his conquests, but his advertisement said he liked couples anyway, so it would be their own fault. None of them would ever be told by him, his address details or name, if it wasn't his real name he used.

#

Judd needed to stay youngish to please his partner, who was being pleased elsewhere too. And to ultimately get his own reward. Not from that thing he was meeting on Wednesdays or the cronies there, however up to it they might think they were, or have been led to believe they were. Oh no, there was more to it than that.

Little did Pamela know on a particular day, she had no idea, when Judds phone was unusually registering as switched off until 08.30AM on the messaging app. That the reason would unfold as the day ensued and that from 17.00PM onward she would be tested again as to how much emotional carnage she could handle from him as yet another scenario, similar to that observed with the Jenny C situation was about to unfold before her. In the afternoon at about 15.00hrs, she looked at the newbies on the website that he used. There was a newbie, a CD again supposedly or allegedly twenty-six years of age. She was a petit five feet five, or 1,65m though, and very slim. It also said he/she was a smoker, so he was bending one of his rules for a change as he claimed his own page said he would not meet smokers. That's how slim she was. The ad word for word said: Seeks males/ MM meaning two males at once, (There were also photos of others on the page of similar ages, early twenties)." I am a naturally genuine & social person, and have great people skills, I am easy to get on with and I assure you, if I arrange a meet but prefer spontaneous, I will not waste your time. Message if you want to find out more, I'm a feminine tiny pretty Tgirl, I love any party, (no quickie ficks or quick mouth chat oral). Then was said: Who has qualified: 1. Distance / possible meet up for meet ASAP (Max 40 minutes waiting). 2. nice & fit body/perfect figure/gym body/no big belly. 3. Good looking / attractive/friendly / polite / the same interesting / good personality / honest /genuine person. 4. Tall guy 175cm up. I will give you my app number (It was the same app we both use) for video call and swap live location for make sure, please accept this point *** if you knew me, please contact on app directly anyway. There were also lots of toys and the ad said adult parties, gangbangs. The list was extremely thorough. Anyway, he couldn't have verified live location from his home, it would have demonstrated that he could not get to there within the allocated time. If he had in fact gone there this morning just to test out the possible spontaneous quick meet suggestion, he could then have arranged to meet in the afternoon. Pamela noticed that ad earlier in the day and had wondered if he'd gone there in the morning, but she didn't want to believe it with it being the same postal address code. She also noted that on the advertisement it said, "Looking for local hot guy to hang out with me tonight." Pamela only went online for odd seconds at the times when he would be on but didn't stay because he wasn't. She presumed he was at his work. Then she went to the meet website and noticed that the person was last on at 14.00hrs. He sometimes after 13.30hrs, it was a thirty- minute journey. She checked again at 15.30Pm When he would usually always check in. The phone wasn't switched off, so she texted a short message to him at 16.00hrs. At 17.00hrs, he must have quickly checked his phone and realised. He blocked Pamela. AT 18.44hrs, the persons website profile advert still indicated that they were not online. It's possible that just as nothing would prevent him in times past from getting his needs met, especially if he thinks there is something to be made from such a meet, and more-so if there are some of similar ages to the person, he met who can be invited to, he was not going to allow any interruption whatsoever. When this had happened before, sometimes it would last for days until he had been somehow very totally satisfied, or until the guilt wore off. Mostly it would last a day or sometimes two, then he would expect Pamela to behave as though nothing had happened at all. This time though, Pamela doubted that it was an option anymore. Maybe he might reconsider when he sees her photos and letter regarding the hospital etc, again when he has got over the guilt of being caught out. He'd have also realised that Pamela could have tracked his phone and the person he visited via the information freely available as a courtesy via the website. It is a vile feeling when this happens. Totally horrible and nauseating. The thought that he was with others used to virtually crucify Pamela, it ripped her to pieces. It then would become just a dull sickening pain. And an exercise in emotional damage limitation regarding combatting possible effects of, if or should these issues cause problems.

Pamela, deflated as per usual during those days or months, later in the evening went to the bathroom, as after walking from the bathroom into her small hallway, she pulled on the bathroom light cord to switch the light off in that room, something on a wall directly opposite caught her attention. She switched the bathroom light back on, particularly as what she thought she noticed was a little too close to the hallway light switch. She wasn't wrong, it was the biggest spider she'd ever seen in her flat, she'd seen similar ones and didn't mind them, even putting on of them in her small attic space because it was wintertime then and she hadn't wanted to go outside in the cold or put the spider out into such harsh conditions. It looked as though it was having difficulties feeling its way up the wall, almost as though a person who would use a stick because of sight issues might. It to her looked as though so apprehensively it was putting its long spindly legs forward on after the other as if to establish whether the next step might be safe or not. Its body mass was not so big, but the legs made it look very almost as big comparably as the light switch itself. Pamela went to the kitchen and located a plastic food container which had a separate lid, then promptly popped him inside it. He must have slipped through a small gap she'd allowed for him to breathe and dropped to the floor, even in that dimmer light cast by just the light from the slight space under the bathroom door she saw it run so very fast across the carpet. Not like when she'd seen one of those exact same spiders less than a week earlier walking so slowly, being careful not to harm the spider, she managed to get it back into the container and then, so as not to alarm him, rather than trying to find her keys to her flat, she put the main entrance door on a latch and pulled the coconut matting doormat up to keep the main front door from locking shut behind her. She had a very short gray lace nightie on and flip flops, it was raining outside, but not uncomfortably so, she put the spider outside and hurried back, as she stepped over the doormat decorated with a huge heart design, she smiled and thought 'he was a sweetie, Judd too.'

Then it was coffeetime, the night before, she'd enjoyed some small boiled potatoes with some couple of spoonsful of a cheese and chive sauce added to them after, mixed with the very remainder of a jar of tartar sauce, only one spoonful of that was left but it was sufficient and it was about to go over, she thought that the tastes would complement each other and was not incorrect in that assumption. Above the saucepan there were a couple of small flies hovering and whilst it almost made her feel nauseas that they might have got near the potatoes, she was nonetheless thankful and thought to herself 'well, I'm very thankful that I placed a wire gauze over 'that pan.' It's easy to imagine, 'for some,' that even twenty-four, or twenty-six-year olds are innocent, especially in photos, she was experienced enough to know that those photographs of the person and group he was visiting, were not innocence, would he be discerning enough to know that seemed a silly question as he'd have read the profile she hoped, or there would have been no point either of having such written on his own profile page too. Or were the photos, so tasteful in his opinion that he felt assured that he could basically just take it for what it was, such was the precise innocence. During only the first few seconds of viewing that profile, and we must remember, it was Pamela who'd only met him, there had been no others, because of difficulties presented before with her need for surgery, she was though whilst sickened by what she read and the person's lack of knowledge of written English, confident that he'd be doing no videos there, to further his ambitions, very probably too, not unless a fee was paid by him first, such was the extent of the innocence as Pamela perceived it, for dear Pamela, there was no doubt about that aspect whatsoever.

With the confidence that those locally would get no further with him than he had ever allowed her to unless as part of his own groupings, on what was the Wednesday thing, or invites to other parties, now, even at theirs. She gathered quickly, that those he was visiting or involved with there, could have absolutely no qualms in just accepting that he was, married and that no doubt, it could, or such a presumption had they been told this, would help them greatly in their personal fantasy. Realizing that, Pamela, now more amazed than ever, too, that they all seemed so unaffected by risks associated with potential health complications. Knowing now that she'd never meet Judd again, she remained resigned to the understanding by herself, that her health of those she knew was of a greater and wider effectual importance and considered that those he'd visited, and if only referring to that little grouping, with others he knew or other groups and their potential diversity populous-wise, who might she now, ever be able to meet? If they were involved with things like that and whether she could ever trust any of them, in any way at all. She, also, now unaware having looked at only a few profiles, that they were not a 'minority group' themselves, they are a minority in life she thought. Or was Pamela unbeknown totally, even to herself, just so very innocent herself?

Where some illnesses can be brought on and even worsened psychosomatically, so was, she thought, how much involvement emotionally you allow for whatever reasons, usually financial, which strangely then made her think of the title of Jean's book 'Nom Penny,' was it all about finding a way of life that for you was safer and securer and if married or in relationships, or even considering your friends, how foolish would you really be, or influenced by those other factors, and more, the possible causes of those factors, such as poverty to allow yourself to be dragged into and consumed by it, unless if you'd been kicked out because you now were just too old for their tastes, how would you pursue something new and cope with such a realism and if having been exploited by them, you sustained a damage of a kind. Pamela thought, 'was that what it' all about darling,' not that Judd was a spring chicken himself, was his need that great that he was doing what he always did, to visit therefore for no longer than an hour and a half and not to give out any personal details, would he keep them all at arms-length or only some, like Pamela. So, whoever he chose, would only see, or feel in that brief time, whatever he wanted, creating a need and even a vague to Pamela, though real to some, mystique? It was as though at that point, she realised and regarding the Covid 19 situation, it should not be the general public afraid so much about consequences of, but of such groups and how far could they go and how soon before their bubble would shatter, although they obviously did not care, neither were they concerned it seemed, the only reasons many places had closed and remained shut, was now because the law decreed it. How far could those die-hards, or greedy selfish individuals be prepared to push that and who else apart from them alone, were likely to feel it more? Pamela could say, "I never drink wine." That they would consider beginning to dare? Certainly, when Pamela had attempted to alert Judd as to the risks even before the furloughing started in February/March, he was totally blaze about it and said to her then that he did not care. So, did none of those he was visiting care, if they were seeking encounters with different and many? It certainly looked that way to Pamela when she checked, and they weren't searching and available just daily she noticed, it was every few hours of every single day? Or results, or did fortune favour the brave, could it have been that they'd already isolated themselves, so their unit or part of the world had already become as much their own fates, as their destinies. Pamela, unsure as to how she felt to have been excluded was also neither concerned, nor worried totally about it, in fact, she felt more contented. Totally unbeknown to them she had by far, bigger fish to fry anyway?

Yes, she had some ideas of her very own, unfortunately her ideas since meeting Judd had been 'put on ice.' Now though, she could dream again and want, instead of experiencing a continual nightmare, and remembering the look on his face in one of the photos he'd sent to her and recalling the image of himself on that photo he sent to the person bogus account, that was where she really believed she saw him? She'd had another imaginary image of him since, but he was much older, in a restaurant with a bow tie on and he wore a moustache and had put on considerable weight that suited him. Possibly it was in Germany or somewhere similar because of the attire of some, or just holiday makers in the vision or somewhere on the Mediterranean, but she'd wanted him then and didn't mind, she thought how she still would love him then, although dancing with many women there too. It was how he was. Maybe she'd just considered being with him and staying with him that long, but he was not wanting that? Maybe the image in that photo or something associated to it, was what he was running from or really trying to. Or was he trying to pass what he was running from on to others, like creating labels that he could then conveniently, of course at his leisure, as long as he remained aloof, then walk away from? She briefly thought of him and even wondered if he was dying, but he'd blocked her. She told him before in March that she was ok to discuss anything he wanted and at any time if he wanted to, thinking that he might be HIV+ or something like that. Would he even remember that conversation, more to the point, especially now? Maybe she was thinking about him too negatively, but there weren't so many options? She just had to get on with it as she had before with him, though this time, without him. She had on her mind the song Teddy Bears Picnic, undoubtedly these teddy bears had certainly had and were enjoying theirs.

When standing in her own kitchen preparing some orange tea, she surprised herself and thought with regard to a reference to and of a slang word she'd never used before, 'those slags, and they are' she thought, are and never will be interested in her or anyone like her, or the affects upon her or any of them of their actions, however they might lie and attempt to dress it up, or misguide. Not only did she peacefully calm herself down having even thought in that manner, aware that she was in fact, after realising, using the term as a verb and 'slagging off,' she also was aware that their mere and meagre existence was now forcing and had forced her very own hand. She didn't want him to further influence how she'd been or how she was prior to meeting him on those websites, if she'd been a positive influence, she even wondered whether Judd hadn't been sent by someone, as if to 'check her out. 'Or did such a person think they were being somehow charitable, to cheer her up somehow? How disgusting she thought. She even had a pathetic notion that he knew because of how her advertisement was written, that she was not so confident, although awaiting surgery, and that he, as a hotel manager, would have had experience in planning, she even crazily wondered whether all of this was happening, his seeming to be meeting people close to where she lived etc, because he was somehow trying to let her know that he was getting closer to her as if to say 'how lucky she was' and because he didn't want to cause any possible harm with her preparing for to go to have surgery? Sure, her imagination was often vivid, she sipped her tea and then as if from out of the air itself, envisaged some Indians of a very native type, dancing and chanting and her with her legs open wide and from somewhere although unkindly possibly, from a distance a tomahawk being thrown in between her legs, this to her was a kind imaginational aspect and was to signify personally and that her surgery would be an absolute and total success. This of course had been something she had thought since her childhood anyway. Hoping and trusting unreservedly the expertise and determination of trained experienced medical staff, which was so much more important, that the outcome could and would be, most certainly because she was not tackling it herself, and therefore to become way much farther from that which could be even remotely considered, for the same reason, as a hatchet job? She was very, humbly then appreciative of the kind gesture in encouragement-sentiment wonderfully thought, so much that she very almost shed a tear. But it was ok not to shed a tear fully too, to have almost done it was felt, recognised, understood, realized, and known.

Pamela went to nap on the Wednesday afternoon, she was exhausted. She woke quite suddenly, on her mind as she was sleeping even, was not that he had gone with others for sex, but that whilst he could have met others from anywhere at all because they were available, she'd seen this herself, yes, he'd deliberately decided to meet some who lived so very near to where she lived. It seemed to her to be the most hurtful thing and unforgivable by design. She checked on the website to see whether the local person had been online since 16.00PM when he'd usually have finished work. The website indicated that the person had not been on the site since five hours before, it was now 21.00PM. Although coincidental, it was not the best Wednesday for Pamela who sat by a window listening to how windy it seemed to be outside. In fact, it was very windy outside and had been on-and-off for a few days. She then remembered that even the postal worker had mentioned it, so there would be no point in attaching or associating it or attributing 'as peculiar' in any way to such other quite minor occurrences. The only consolation for Pamela about having seen that person on the website at all had become the certainty now that in Pamela's own opinion, she would not meet Judd again now if life itself depended on it, and certainly not if any of theirs.

She went into the bathroom and could only think with utter disgust about how often that person had been on the website displaying open availability regarding sex unprotected- and that Judd was now visiting there or had invited that person or been invited to a new Wednesday show, where he was to lay a leading role. The thought of it gave Pamela stomach cramps, but with that thought, she also realised that similar in a way to Judds lameness, much of it was actually gas, she did though notice just how very tight her own ventre, or her tiny belly, was now becoming, her actual thought was 'remarkably tighter.'

Pamela had switched off a table lamp and was quietly sitting by her window, there was a net curtain, so she wouldn't have been seen from outside. She believed that she could hear voices or a conversation in progress and it seemed to be coming from a little further along the road. One of the voices said, or shouted, not in what seemed the friendliest sounding way, "I know who you are." It was enough for Pamela to use her remote control and turn the volume right down on her television. She wasn't a 'curtain-twitcher; as in always at the window at all, in fact she was often too busy anyway, but out of interest she thought she'd listen, particularly as for once, it seemed that the tone had not been angled toward her. Pamela, sometimes, when she could remember to and as with other situations sometimes too; remembered how she enjoyed laying with her head resting on the back of the sofa with her eyes closed, only when she was doing it? Almost as though constantly busy and never permitting or granting for herself, that moment of peacefulness and calm. Hearing the trees and weather, the wind was not howling but was certainly heard blowing through the tree-lined street. She actually thought at that moment of some of the television advertisements where such relaxing moments were appreciated, or exploited to the full, she thought how kind it or everything seemed, or was, to hear the trees and wind like this instead of or rather than to have been forced to think of Judd and his new friend or pals.

Pamela imagined that on the wind almost, the person Judd was with had sent her a message to say 'sorry,' and had with that forwarded or sent too, a kind of gestural essence of a kind as a potential compensatory measure? Such messages Pamela would learn eventually, were not worth a light. Pamela didn't even register whatever it was, she visualised instead, placing it beneath her right foot and squashing it. It was at that moment that Pamela remembered another guy engaging her with conversation on that website months earlier. She'd forgotten about that conversation completely because she blocked him believing him to be potentially perverse. He'd told her, after she told him of the location where she lived, not the address, that that he met a person near there and mentioned the road where Pamela lived. He also mentioned a derelict building and that he'd had sex behind that building with a person who also lived locally and described that person. The description she recalled, seemed uncannily like that of the local person she believed Judd may have been visiting. The location all seemed to fit too. He said the person lived in the street next to where Pamela's place was. She knew that the person had to be reasonably familiar to the actual street Pamela lived on to know of the derelict premises, because it was a one-way street and quite away from the main road, so the derelict premises would not have been seen unless you'd been a visitor to the street, or had passed through it, or even who lived on it? As in very close to the derelict premises to have known that it even had such a space, a car park, to sex behind it, as the entrance to that space even visually was on a no-through road. Pamela also recalled seeing a person scuttling by her one morning whilst she'd been waiting for a shop to open and considered too as they resembled a lot, although clothed, the image on that website, the direction she was walking in. There was a man standing by the shop waiting too, he was similar to Judd as well Pamela thought, only bigger, she remembered how the person looked down sheepishly as passing as though that storyline usually worked so well normally, the guy even stopped looking at Pamela, so obviously it worked. Was it a pre-cursor, because now Judd would be similar in stature build-wise, to how that bigger man would have been with Pamela?

Pamela could not believe that she for a brief moment, imagined a sheet of glass decapitating that person, and then staring at her lifeless eyes, but then she thought how stupid it could have been to imagine such awful things as it probably only actually meant 'that person,' would lose her head to Judd, as if 'head over heels' as she had. Agreeably, and noticeably she realised, it had seemed to be his penchant so far that they would, anyway? What Pamela and the person Judd was with, had not been aware of then, they could not have known, although had she taken the time to somehow read darling Jean's book, she would have, was that the survival of many local self-help peer-led support groups whether either of them used them or not, for those affected by sexually transmitted diseases were at risk of closure and had been since just before the covid-19 epidemic began. Sure, they had money on reserve, but the situation then caused many places to suffer financially, including the company that was coming up with the money to support the groups. Would their very own actions now affect permanently the futures of those organisations, would that they didn't know save them? It didn't matter whether it did or not. Dear Pamela on that day, felt as if Judd had stuck a knife straight into her back. If their actions caused Covid-19 to re-escalate because they simply did not care- and by too, those who know them and knew of them, or were meeting them- by default the company would very probably cease trading anyway. Pamela though was oblivious, so much and to the point whereby, she could overcome their such trivial games. Good old Pamela eh! So, was it about not so much where you were coming from, or what you'd left behind, but where you were going? How far could that go back and what exactly was Judd running away from?

A question could or had become, so if Pamela had been on those websites and was a regular just checking them out and advising some on where to get free help who contacted her, if she identified a problem or even just to suggest to some that they should consider getting a check-up, had she been doing wrong to have shared her experience in such a way, if for others just 'getting down to it' and having a good time had become an income or was a reward? A kind of 'breeding' facility where breeding risk and the gamble involved in it had become or was anyway, the risk involved. So, that services were in place and good she thought, and preventing a person from spreading a disease or infection to the partner of another and potentially any future offspring they may have, was not? It had been Jean herself who she'd recalled having said to her before, "where there's muck, there's brass.' Were those who wanted to keep it so dirty, doing so because it was 'their thing,' because it could only therefore become more depraved. Because they or others could make money from that, and why those like even Judd had said that they; "don't care about the virus." Were those hiding something? Possibly too afraid to go and have std tests, or maybe they had and were just so angry. The fact was that there would be no way of knowing the if's, but's, maybe's or why's. Possibly it was where Pamela was not drinking alcohol. But then where did that place Judd who claimed not to drink anyway? The photo Pamela saw of him on the page she discovered of his on that website had him sitting on a balcony with blue canvas boating shoes on and tight jeans and a neatly pressed blue shirt with his feet up on a deckchair holding a glass with drink in it and obviously sipping, looking out to the sea, it was a beachfront hotel. There was a bottle of gin on the table, only one glass though, that which he held. Or was all, that things were so very tough, that it was convenient for some, seemingly to allow some 'unfortunates' believe they were getting a favour. Could it have been just about condition, or conditioning, like ploughing fields.

Pamela also wondered if his actions to her had not been to warn her or to advise her, or to alert her, he obviously didn't have much time for her. Or was it her own intuition and interpretation that was very much in effect, was either though prominent, and did one, by or during its own lifespan deplete the other?

In a somewhat hazed state, her mind as thinking of nature, she could hear rain outside, it sounded like water trickling along a small stream where silver birch trees could be heard in the breeze. She thought then only, 'if you plough a field, what do you leave in its place?' Then it was as though suddenly she was in a subway; she'd gone down some steps and admired beautiful carvings in the stone walls, carvings or sculptures of torsos of notable persons of times gone by and then, once walking through the expanse of the empty tunnel, there was no-one there at all, not even a person who could have been homeless. She imagined that she might see a coat or something, an indication that there might be rough sleepers, either sleeping or napping there, or something, but nothing. It smelled as a tunnel usually would, not an unclean smell because it had a flow of air throughout. She did notice the graffiti, on the wall particularly to her right, she walked along a little further and then up the steps of the entrance on the other side.

#

Regarding that person in a neighbouring street. if it had been or was the same person referred to by that chap, process of elimination alone said that the person could only live at one end of the adjacent road, it was also, if not in the road where Pamela lived, in the same direction of where the voices were either coming from or were being directed at. Pamela put some heels on and a micro-short skin-tight lace dress, then gelled her hair back and applied some red lipstick and some mascara, then grabbed her door keys from the small brass oriental looking hook in her kitchen. She wanted to say hi to the trees, she intended to head in a northward direction along the street, as she left, she noticed that the time was close to 23.40PM.

She slowly walked down the few steps at the front of the premises where she lived and immediately turned right, observant and listening for any sound at all, as a feline might stalk prey and be mindful too of potential predators, Pamela though, wasn't thinking predators? She'd believed she'd been suffering an ongoing trauma repeated emotional abuse, and was trying to make how things had become, seem more acceptable to her, because she felt as though she'd very much got the wrong end of the deal herself so far. She walked past the derelict premises that she knew was now boarded up, Pamela herself has rather liked the look of the premises herself, though it hadn't been part of any personal plan to shag men in the car park, not at that time anyway. Her idea was to return it to a hotel status, a respectable premise, with lavender and the likes of to attract bees in the carpark, now though, regarding that car park, she could only wonder what was the strongest disinfectant available and that maybe with boiling water too and the strongest industrial bleach, it may resolve it. Wild animals would be cleaner, she'd thought.

She walked the length of the street, which is crescent shaped, so it naturally turns to the right from outside where she lived and to the left if turning left after leaving there, as where she lives is central in the street and was the first premises there to have been built. Road traffic though only comes from the right and through to the left where it re-joins the main road. However, Pamela. Walked to the end and took a sharp right turn into the adjacent street where the man she'd chatted with, claimed that the person he'd had sex with lived. As she walked, the thought that at any time Judd might have bypassed her property to reach where the property where the other person resided, had made her feel slightly angry? Also, the thought that immediately after leaving her flat the week before, he could have just checked on the website and then walked a few minutes into the neighbouring street infuriated her. Pamela had a strange feeling that day and even wondered if she should not have followed him discreetly just to check if he was going to the train station or not, it was all very strange for her, but somehow it was as if she had an idea that he might be up to something. She'd turned the corner and a little further along the road, she could see the flashing lights of what looked like a stationery emergency response vehicle but at that moment, it was not so much as to determine which, it was parked on the opposite left side of the road. Traffic on the side of the road Pamela was on, was oncoming traffic and all with headlights on because of the time of night. She got nearer to opposite to where the emergency vehicle was, then slowed down to not display how angry she was and to appear calmer. She naturally was inquisitive as to what was happening, but it just seemed to be an ambulance with lights on top and on the sides, all flashing. Not wanting to seem un-natural and although she couldn't see whether there was a driver in the vehicle or not, she winked, just in case. Any anger she felt was certainly not directed at them. There was no other movement apart from some people looking from or standing at a third-floor window. Pamela moved just a few yards so not immediately opposite and then spun around on her heels as she turned to face them, she just stood there staring. Ok she wouldn't have known who they were or whether they were the persons Judd had visited but there were not many other property lights on, that she could see along that part of the road. It would be a while after, when she wondered, what was tidying up after Judd, so was Pamela a witness to something? Was that what he meant when he glared so angrily at her and said, "nice to see you." She was also aware though that his recollections of photos of her and how those photos might be perceived or interpreted could potentially have been abused by him. Such would not have been a new concept where he was concerned, how he attempted to deal with those thoughts could have become so though, they were private photographs. Or had he dealt with it; in the only way he knew how? Certainly, if Judd had been in that property, he would have certainly seen Pamela across the road opposite. She remembered thinking 'how very almost southernly park,' it all was, she'd remembered seeing a brochure selling properties about such a resemblant place. She headed back, turned right into the street where she lived and then as she went to approach the few steps outside, she was greeted by three people leaving who each had woollen scarves on pulled up to or past their noses, and all were wearing nylon fur trimmed coats. One of them said, "Good evening," and Pamela thought she heard one of them saying, "never seen her looking like that before." Maybe though, she imagined it.

At 01.35AM Pamela decided to very quickly just check online, the person was on the website, this indicated to her that things were ok. It was not Pamela's fault that nowadays and particularly recently, she could not permit any longer, herself to be as trusting with some, as she might otherwise be of others. It would be soon after that she seemed to 'without warning' doze off, seated upright on a sofa, she hadn't been tired but sometimes this happened when certain unusual situations had reached a crescendo, it was often too, one of her in-built defence mechanisms. As if in a semi-conscious state, she imagined that person, and Judd trying to penetrate her, but her body, he grunted and did not understand the body was quite lifeless. It was slightly unlike with the' Jenny C' episode, this time it seemed even more lifeless than then. She wondered about his personal perception of them, and their intent or mindlessly unquestionable mode to entice at that moment, but herself was too hurt to really want to be considerately thoughtfully, or even remotely charitable in that to any of them.

An hour after, the person was still on the website, Pamela had no intention of fuelling or adding any weight or credibility to what they might be, or were up to, she wanted nothing to do with it at all. She imagined or visualised very strongly, him putting his coat on and leaving there, as though fully intending to permanently. Oh, he'd spin every yarn, and of the desperate cringing facsimile of a desperate or loving girl, he'd be flagrantly aware that the latter did not form part of any, by his standard, actual respective own equation. He'd also have been aware Pamela knew, that even though he hadn't unblocked her on that app since a few days now, maybe he wanted to get Wednesday out of the way. By past experiences, she'd estimated that she'd probably be blocked from contacting Judd for possibly a week to ten days, or even longer, until he'd moved on from his new so eager fun friend. Maybe it would happen quicker, was she hoping or dreading? The thing was, that there were issues, he'd either presume things were unchanged between he and Pamela, or he simply and plainly, quite totally, wouldn't care a damn anyway. It was obvious that she missed him, but what was the point if she could never tell him and because she didn't need to and because it was her having let him become aware of it, that had motivated him? Was it not about her wants, only his? Her mind by this time, no longer wanted or could attempt to fathom it. As difficult as it was for acknowledge it completely, he'd gone a little too far this time, the fact remained that he probably would not care, even if he did completely understand, he didn't need to. Pamela and he were quite similar in some ways, maybe too similar, Judd and Pamela, both knew it, just a little too much! Pamela logged onto the website again a while after, although this time, to check whether there had been any messages to her from any of the site users. There was a message from a guy who'd joined the site just four weeks before that she thought was encouraging, but she felt unable to respond to it. Again, rather resentfully, she checked the neighbours page again, the page displayed that they'd logged off ten minutes earlier. Pamela then listened to the wind outside, she thought it sounded lovely, she was grateful that it would do greatly to carry away all or any oddities in the air, firmly too, to a quieter space somewhere in oblivion.

#

Pamela had imagined the person who lived locally all too easily saying to Judd that she'd never met a boy like Judd before, and that the person was quite accustomed to earned and deserved loathsome thoughts from others and how then to, or not to deal with such thoughts, Pamela though, decided to let her think that such thoughts or ill feeling would be from his so-called wife. Pamela might have been only a few years older than Judd at a push, but the local person was half his age. Pamela knew she wanted him then though, as soon as she set eyes on him, it was unfortunate then that Pamela was maybe a little too giving and careful not think on the rare occasion, rather on the few times he visited her. When he'd leave her home, she would hear others saying, "how handsome he was, and horrifyingly for her, so readily." If he, because Pamela had she hadn't met any guys yet and because she wasn't able to have normal intercourse sex yet, and because of the circumstances, if he took from that because of his experience with women, he was banking on her need and wanting him, even though disinterested now. He wouldn't realize that whilst he believed she was just waiting, that she knew, because of her experience's professionally, that his behaviour, if he banked upon the reaction and would use it for his own gain, 'the price,' to be paid for that type of abuse, was nothing like he could imagine regarding 'that trash' he'd been with, or 'Jenny C,' and certainly more than the heap of fakedom, that might have charged for any video. So, no, Pamela didn't care anymore. It was her who really didn't need to, and she certainly wasn't waiting for him, in any capacity. She hoped, that as difficult as it was to consider it, that he wasn't aware, she knew somehow that it would be better for him if he didn't know? 'If he does, he does,' she thought to herself. But as she'd said in times past or certainly heard said, "you can trust a thief to a personal degree, but a liar you can never." She painfully had to ask of herself, what then was he?

#

Judd was leaving, neither he, and certainly not dear Pamela, he'd certainly blocked her and she knew, just as the other heady play games had instigated, he'd enjoy having done it when he did, were to know that another gruesome scene was about to become unleashed in her imagination she hoped, and not her mind, and yes it seemed, for her, in her mind she hated it so much, Pamela had wondered always, whether he was somehow aware and was subjecting her to it deliberately, as if waiting from their last meet for just the right moment? His 'not so' manipulatable friend though, would be waiting immediately outside the door of the person he'd spent hours with. The same character as before, wasn't salivating, no, not this time. Not such the older dog now it seemed, but certainly with some new tricks of its very own stood there, not as it had been before, Judd felt it staring although surprisingly, not even slightly angrily, just staring as if to ask, "mmmm, yes"? The person he'd visited, unaware totally of the presence, or it would again prove, fate, could be heard saying, "are you sure you don't want to spend a while longer darling, I'll get online and arrange for more others to come again too while you play, like before"? He said "sure" to her and turned around and went back in, but this time it was he would not be exactly alone. The person he'd visited then removed seductively she thought, a gown, and was down to just the bare underwear, and very sleazily and almost pathetically got on all fours, for him. "I thought you'd injured yourself darling, wow you recovered quickly didn't you." she said in a soft and so well-practiced voice. She'd turned her head away from him and was looking at his reflection in a large mirror, unaware though that there was an invisible mirror moving around the room and an invisible glass pane object that seemed to somehow now, unlike before when Pamela had these visions, form part of the presence of his 'friend,' that too, neither he, nor she could see. How impressive Judd looked in the reflection in the large ornate framed mirror, he picked up one of her toys, it was a very large Pamela thought, in disbelief, black rubber phallically shaped object and placed it directly beneath her open mouth and said to her to wait. Before that she said to him, "wow babe," unaware that at this point his hands were very much being guided. He had finished with her after all. He then got another toy, the same one in fact that she'd actually much to his dissatisfaction, surprisingly used on him, on their first meet when he was eager but thought she might not be interested so much, and placed that near to her rectum, he smiled at her in the mirror and asked "do you want plenty of lube on it babe?" The same presence that poor Pamela had seen approaching him after the Jenny C scenario, it didn't even look at her, it grabbed all of her hair and pulled it all out swiftly by the roots and then held it in front of her face just for that moment, staring at Judd watching her expression, pushed her head so far down toward the ground until the whole rubber toy was stuck inside her throat, of course she tried to scuffle and her legs splayed outward, all at that same time, simultaneously like a splat. Judd pushed the toy she'd used on him, it was the biggest sex toy she had, with such force straight all the way into her. Her legs looked as though they were still even then trying to move just a little and had tried to stretch outward, but Judd at about that time was already poised for her, as she liked, as if about to penetrate, so they didn't go too far? Judd then was told, "she had such a lovely big mouth too and especially for one so young," Then another two toys were squeezed in somehow and pushed full pelt right inside her mouth and throat. Then Judd looked up at the presence and said, "don't you just love latex." It then told him, "Pick up those tissues you used from the floor now and you get out of here, take them with you!" Fortunately for Judd, the toys had been cleaned after use by another of their visitors that day and he wore gloves and a medical mask anyway and he never touched anything when visiting anyone and had said he didn't smoke or drink. They'd also had some fun in the shower before, that she adored.

Although the sound of a helicopter flying above the property was the only sound that could be heard, and very loudly throughout, that had been the only sound that anyone else would have heard. As he left, the character that was moving around so fast as though it was using the invisible circulating moving mirror and glass panel. The person now splayed out on the floor motionless, had smoked and did drink. The ashtray had some half-smoked cigarettes in it and some of them looked as though only one puff had been taken from a cigarette, there was though a remainder of a smouldering cigarette too, the character lit another cigarette with that and stubbed that out. Then it stood in front of the face of what was on the floor and crouched down, it moved its head from side to side as though trying to hear if there was a squeak or something, then it lightly touched with the lit cigarette the flesh just immediately between the eyes, then pressed it very firmly into the forehead until it did smoulder no more. Then via an open window, it jumped from the ledge and upon touching the ground outside it vanished, along with the mirror that moved twice as fast as the pane, they'd disappeared at precisely the very same time. Before getting onto the ledge though, the character peered round at the mess, and said, "so selfish darling, and during a pandemic too?"

Had he created a hotel, where it didn't matter what the cost of each different room was, how inexpensive or not. Where the filthiest meant he spent less, but each time, he was moving in an upward motion by way of scoring goals as if on a football pitch, where basically by moving the new hits, moved the goal post each time and every time a different application, but each time, the most important thing for him was that each time, the accomplishment was his own, was there a dynamic recognised by certain types of individuals, was that in his mind or was it just about not losing. But there were no goal keepers yet, not in his games, he would be rid of them very quickly if he even thought they were 'getting close' to him. So, he thought he was an only player? And competition he avoided and blocked? Because by not doing so, by default it made the room too expensive for him? As clever as it had become, was it about control therefore, or seeming control. Was Judd adult enough to admit then that he had just lost, or had he just moved onto the next as he always did and even managed 'to boot' to then put it all, down to a bad experience, because the next experience could and no doubt would always be new and exciting anyway and totally devoid of any 'complications,' welcoming and just free for the taking.

Pamela again just remembered a photo he'd sent to her on the phone of himself, he was laying provocatively he obviously thought, and to some obviously would have been. In the photo, he was also in front of a video or television screen, Pamela after tried to locate the video or recording from information within the subtitles but could not. It was of a person with blonde hair stood on a round stage, the person's head was bowed down so you could not see a face and the person had blonde hair that could have been a wig and a type of dress on that most could have worn well. All around the stage were people seated, but neither could you see any of their faces either, and because the stage lighting was only focused on the person on the stage then. Beneath, the subtitle when translated read "where do we go from here?" It no longer mattered to Pamela, where he thought, he might want to go, but whilst quite bored, she hadn't disposed of him so readily just yet. Neither as some were being re-infected with Covid-19 then as news implied, neither had the thought that a percentage of some who'd 'go with him,' and, or theirs could probably die. Were there limitations and was he only thinking of doing what many others presumably had done already before. How expensive, or inexpensive had those rooms now become? Were the Judd and accomplice/s thinking more along the lines of 'highest bidder,' or doing it just because it had become their sexual fantasy, sex in domination and submissive roles. Surely in some places, a line surely would have been crossed, if some unbeknown to others started making money from it. But could there be a situation where, if some could disappear for a few days and be coaxed in the meantime to remove their details from meeting websites, just as Pamela had, who'd miss them? Who'd miss them for a week or even two, if it effectively became a paid holiday? She thought carefully about how much of it could be just about greed, or whether it was about just addiction itself? Or is it needs-based, or insecurity based she wondered. She found it difficult to believe in some of the circumstances, that it was insecurity, in spite of the bondage scenarios and thought more that it could be even 'weak, not meek, manipulating the strong, and neither, inheriting.'

She'd imagined Judd had stood on a precipice before, looking into her room, and whilst her situation was as it was Healthwise, easily reaching a conclusion that there simply was nothing there for him. He could always find better and younger by way of choice and availability and nicer, those who would never question. He knew that more than most, as did some of those. Few were to become as adept at choosing guests than Judd. Meeting Pamela then, for Judd would have been like him being asked to repeatedly suck on lemons, he wasn't as keen on lemon juice as Pamela although rarely was. He had diversity in his life, yes, his weekend supplemented by his weekdays, and rarely and giving reason to the diversity itself, the twain. He overworked-look, was it where he was now just rushing around so very much, from QR codes on phones to phones being monitored, the parties on Tuesday-Friday, and those then setting up their own parties, and whilst everyone else was then lockdown, and sending invites too, choices, demands, needs, parties with videos of Judds visits now being streamed as well, ultimately to paying clients too, maybe those who in time might book a room in a hotel to view? Mortgages being paid. None of them though ever got involved to some of the very select after-parties, and never to those at weekends, Judd himself was reliant on an invite to that himself, Judd learned to keep that very much to himself too.

So, the lad who had been brought to this country by his Saturday meet, had to find a way to stay young to compete with others his captor and friend had managed to secure.

Although, his role then was as a submissive slave to a male and his own other 'conquests,' The Saturday and Sunday thing, and the actual holidays albeit not really needing to go very far at all. But certainly initially, they all believed and would continue to, that they were so very involved. Belles of the ball. And to think, the video he'd asked Pamela to do was not even sexual. But her refusal was actually what he needed, and her reaction as though it was a cheek to ask that of her, yes, she felt used and had an idea that he would only use it to spur himself on to somewhere else. It did. It catapulted him; he knew all about abuse. He'd simply ask someone else, that was why he said to her "xxx you bitch, don't do it then, I ask you for one simple thing and you cannot do, ok." Pamela knew him better than she then actually appreciated or was to realise herself and then learn regarding her own learn of previously before never so required personal strengths. Ther would be some, unbeknown to Pamela who would be very upset if they knew, but also, they'd have trusted her too. Then, after switching on the television to see some of the news, she'd just made for herself a coffee that was on a tablemat on a sideboard. In a large white coffee cup, the coffee even she thought looked nice even if from a purely photographical standpoint, maybe that was why she liked it, did it make her think of his preferences and the importance of her surgery, yes. Especially as out of the corner of her eye, she saw a small fly divebomb it. In disbelief, she couldn't see it because it had obviously dived into the bubbles and where the coffee was very hot, she found the fly, obviously it did not survive. It made dear Pamela very sad indeed! Had Pamela actually caught a rat by the tail she wondered and was dangling it and just staring at it and listening to it. Would she have understood that such an image could be useful, 'if 'she realised, even if not a wholly conventional approach.

She remembered too how the last time they'd met, when he was getting dressed, before he wiped himself off, and away, he stared up at a photo of her with her father. She was a bairn and being held in his arms, it prompted her to investigate slightly some matters, where he said he was from, it said: Religion, Unaffiliated 34.5%, Roman Catholic 10.5%, Protestant 1%, Other Christian and Jehovah's Witnesses 1.1%, other unknown 0.7%, believers, not members of other religions 6.8%, and undeclared /no answer 44%, and of how very extremely angry he looked that day as he left, and no wedding ring did she see.

Was the person who had been overheard by Judd whilst standing-in and serving at a conference where guests were discussing money from profits and costs regarding changing from use of some plastics in their company only thinking of his own salary and not necessarily thinking then of the longer-term impact of such changes, or maybe he hadn't heard that, or it was just the figures mentioned he heard. His attitude, very much 'we're only here a short time, so let's make hay while the sun shines,' so he presumably, by how he worked, thought he was that sun also? Pamela had known too well, that when she said to him after, "enjoy the sunshine," because of his selfishness and greed, it would have roasted him therefore from inside out. He wasn't afraid of the virus either, although that was on her mind, hence her saying it, not that he'd have realised, because of what he'd heard about 'building communities,' by way of catching and spreading it, he gathered this information by his own interpretation whilst working at the hotel, ears and eyes everywhere listening to those from health and other organisations who had been staying there prior to him being furloughed. He just had to catch it, it was as important and as integral to him and with regarding his 'on the back-burners plan,' as meeting Pamela. She'd learned since that him having his 'ear to the ground,' or so to speak was something else he'd become 'quite' accustomed to too. It was like a house from home for him. Ultimately though, as his preferences changed and he became more ageist, would or was it to work against him and affect how Pamela was dealing with matters. Pamela thought about plastics in consumables herself and wondered about those that somehow might or could even get into the food-chain itself and believed plastics surely would not join or fuse together even if inside a tummy, but En masse,' not like a length of plastic that she imagined that could be somehow fed into until eventually it could, if pulled or exertion applied, just rip that the insides, inside out, when attempts were made to remove it. Plastics in consumables would probably be more like a tapeworm, she thought, although it could not re-grow if broken, as a tapeworm does. Surely though, such, where people change over time, less hair, more hair, teeth, bones etc, plastics in a food-chain must create DNA structure change eventually, that could prove harmful in many areas. It would be something reversible though. Pamela wasn't too worried because there were companies already working on enzymes that could break down structures of some of the plastics in oceans. There had even been research on discoveries regarding leaves that had been heated to ninety degrees centigrade and the affect enzymes from this had on plastics.

Rain had stopped play for dear Pamela regarding the Covid-19 situation and the postponement of her surgery and everything else that had followed. Now she was further excluded from taking part, because of greater or better understanding? The whirlwind of a romance had gone to a kiss of the wind and then been demoted to nothing more than a storm in a teacup? Not even a storm if truth be known. And then, to finish it all off, his dirty unclean for him, sad excuse for an ass she thought, had to be cleaned yet again?

Poor Pamela couldn't even eat a baguette without thinking of him. It wasn't other women he'd turned her against, but some of those on their unique journeys who hadn't been diagnosed as gender dysphoric yet, and whose personal habitual lifestyles, were not always quite as tuned as they like or might prefer to have others believe and because if they were, it might not have paid for them? Surely, Pamela would be totally stupid to believe that he was still actually wanting Pamela?

#

Next visit to Jean

It was time for Pamela to visit Jean again, they'd texted and agreed to meet for an hour the next day just before 11.00AM and arrived five minutes earlier. They greeted each other in what had before been a normal way for them both, smiling eyes and a wink. Jean made tea, didn't ask this time whether Pamela wanted tea or coffee, Pamela hung her coat up and then promptly slumped like a heap on the sofa. Jean asked, "are you alright dear, you look troubled slightly," Even Pamela knew that there was no way the Jean could possibly have seen her fall onto the sofa like that because from where the kettle was in the kitchen, she quickly recomposed herself and blew slightly as though saying, 'phew,' then replied with "no I'm quite fine Jean thank you, but how are you"? This time Jean wasn't wearing a long gown frock style dress but a pale sky-blue mini dress with cork wedge soled shoes of a similar colour that were adorned with large flower applique of the same blue and pink. The shoes were made that way, it wasn't one of Jean's personal creations. Pamela was quite transfixed on the flowers briefly, almost as if she'd seen them before, but it wouldn't have been possible, the flowers were similar in the centre to a large poppy but also like a hydrangea but much smaller and there were two on the front of each shoe and they were the peep-toe style of shoe. "I know you Pamela, what's up, she said, oh you like the flowers on my shoes, these are my nautical shoes for when I'm boating, should one day I ever."

They'd already started drinking their tea by now and Pamela asked, "Is it always about moving forward Jean?" The response possibly was unexpected, though not too, had Pamela read any part of her book. Jean replied, "do you mean like replacing a door on a protected building with something of your own choosing without acquiring the correct permissions?" Pamela could not respond, it was as though she didn't want to hear a response, even a response that didn't make sense to her, not much could have on that day. She was staring through a gap in a curtain and at passers-by outside, now again thinking of her surgery. She was not feeling pessimistic, because of Judd and his 'developments.' She in that split second harped back to the last time it happened with Jenny C, she also wondered whether it might be about to be discovered that it was all about who was the 'centre of attention,' where he would be the person, they all 'waited for,' to arrive. So, he'd duped Pamela. She then had to show the same acumen regarding. Not to him, she owed it to herself. Jean said, "are you sure you're ok Pamela, you really shouldn't frown darling, drink your tea lovey, and don't worry, really, that ids the very last thing you need to do or to even be concerned about, you really do not need to, not at all!" Pamela turned around to Jean and said, "so sorry, what, what, what did you say, I was thinking about something, sorry!" Jean smiled and said, it was a creaky old mast darling, very creaky, but don't you worry. Pamela smiled.

#

There was no doubt about it, Judd had seemingly infiltrated her world, because of his own habit and the sneakiness and secrecy of it all, it seemed that there was nowhere she could look, think of then, or be, without thinking of either him, or what he was doing and how he was doing it, somehow he'd floated her boat, he had managed to become her daily fix, then his habit and the realisation that he could no longer do it without then being reminded of his own had caused him to cease ties with her. Now she had to learn again to start doing things again for herself, on her own too, and sadly and similarly, on her own terms too. Would she one day turn her phone on and find that he'd unblocked her, would she eventually buy a new sim-card as she'd done before 'twice' and go online and say 'hi' again, was he expecting her to, or was it now his turn anyway? His turn to make amens or make peace with her. His turn to patch up their indifferences, or had he in fact moved on too, had what became an obsession for her, because she felt that she knew, become just too great for him to handle, or too worthless for him to even be bothered. Yes, it kind of gets you somehow, the wrangling, or mangling, and desperation of it all. Certainly, something was happening, but she was never totally sure, not of precisely what it was, did he simply yearn excitement and have an abnormal boredom thresh-hold, was it 'work hard to play hard,' or just a release from working such long hours and she'd threatened his coping strategy? For poor dear Pamela though, with the very nature of that game, her loss now, was no less great than the tedium's of parts of his own or what had become his then present routine. The only person really who could change it, was really him now. This was how she felt, and he didn't seem to be interested in commitment before anyway? She very much further doubted now that even her surgery would have any impact on how he felt or was, he'd just abuse it, or say 'no I don't want,' but she wasn't having the operation just to please him, whether ultimately, she would have or not with everything that was happening then, and would her views on him change and she then become relieved that they would not meet again? Of course, she wanted to though, very much. She had a nap for a few hours and woke up thinking 'guys like him are ten a penny,' she seemed to feel, from within her very soul, that somehow, he was, or had been, more than that, certainly to her. The saddest thing of all though, it also 'seemed,' that not many were happy about either her choice, or was it that she and he might be able to achieve that degree of happiness? It was as though everything, or much had seemed to be almost acting against them, but they did not meet Judd then. Would he realise, or maximise on it, had he already done that, did he know by experience anyway? Each time Pamela checked his or that person's profile before, was she giving them a sip of her own cup of actual and real innocence to immerse themselves in? And, whilst Pamela had been using her skills as a statistician throughout the pandemic, was it to become a string in her own bow, or basically, just 'another' sword of Damocles? Was it about time for clawback, payback, or something else completely? Pamela asked herself.

#

True, she had seen much since the beginning of the year, deciphering fact from reality was never going to be easy for her and possibly was the very reason she found herself in the predicament in the first place. Had she just discovered that she was older than she believed she felt, or had he indeed just now made her feel older, or had he made her feel 'unwanted' and hurt? Why then should she even consider, to begin to even desire to hold back now? Pamela decided to take the rest of that day to realize a way forward. But she was far from happy, she was alone, hurting, her neck hurt, the insides of her arms were hurting, she felt nauseas, she felt cold, desolate, and quite livid? Also disappointed, in a way that could have led to feelings of anger. But no, she was hurting way too much for that. Taking a very deep breath, she pulled her tummy right in, her chest stuck out quite some, she blinked a few times and held the breath, then exhaled very slowly, and in her flipflops and nightdress, then went to her small kitchen, to 'fix for herself,' a very nice, very welcome, cup of coffee.

Pamela braved the website to check to see whether any messages had been received from others, there were a few requests for photos, and she was happy supply because the covid-19 situation was still under some restrictions. She'd hoped it would help prevent them from taking unnecessary risks. She replied to all the messages, one of them was from a person who was barely twenty-one, he sent a photo of his face, a very handsome chap and six-feet tall too, she thought he was quite a looker, she would not personally entertain meets with any person who'd been wearing a school uniform within at least the past twelve years because they had to legally, whether of legal age of consent or not. She sent some photos to him and a message, it said; "Hi, darling, here are some photos for you. I know it's fun, but all that glitters 'aint' or isn't always at all real in a safety way. Think of yours. Just for now." A message came back asking if she would meet him, he said I can come tonight (Sunday) or Tuesday. She thought of Judd and then of that guy, and it was as if Judd was kicked out. Then she imagined Judd as if he was looking at her from above, singling her out or cutting around her as if to remove her from the equation.

Just before that, only moments before, it was as though she started to piece together bits of what had happened in the months between January and August, was he visiting that twenty-four-year-old and others not for sex? Was there something more behind it than even she could want to attempt contemplate? Or had she blocked it out herself, true, the velocity of what she believed was happening had traumatised her, maybe the fact that Judd had then very much more recently blocked her was just because he didn't want anyone keeping track at all? She was now feeling very uncomfortable indeed. She looked at the website moments after, there was another message from that young guy, she was glad and felt confident that he could, by how he spoke, handle himself admirably. The message because she'd said that she might meet him on the Tuesday simply said, "Yeah go on"! Of course, he was nice, but she wouldn't dream of it. She was glad that that a message appeared on his page saying, "Safe-Sex ONLY."

There was more to the Judd situation, she somehow really knew it, but it was though her subconscious mind had been impacted too, as she from very earlier on was becoming aware of risks he imposed, and her processes, unknown to Judd, threatened and similarly, as unbeknown to Judd too, that were coming out again of, or from what became her intrinsic personal secure mode.

September came, although some had been venturing out, Pamela often was still, pretty much stuck indoors. Glancing down at her fingernails, she'd consoled herself with the idea that, 'it is better surely to be more concerned with your own progress, rather than checking profiles on websites regarding what seemed then often to be the lack of progress of others, it had been some three weeks since checking on any of those websites. She decided to move on from that, even the small plant on her table she then thought looked happier.

It seemed a truer justice that it had found its way back to it's not so isolated place of origin as though banished back to there by news of a kind, a fate of its own' or a pre-destined route, or a precaution, set by something else? An awareness somewhere else, not to condone, of the atrocities un-associated, most certainly wholly, to whatever seemed to almost guard, as some might want to keep something so wild or dangerous chained or kept away, or hidden? Yes, back to its cave. So good was good after all and bad wasn't truly evil though it had the propensity to be.

Pamela was focused on healing, so although any of that was quite unbeknown to her, it did allow her to achieve with those likeminded even though admittedly too often, she had considered herself to be, and was more of a loner, her own sense of tranquillity, or as she perceived, 'generative tranquillity,' as in her mind certainly like waterfalls would spurge and cascade down from the bases of lines of beautifully heavenly trees, regenerative also.

It would be five weeks that passed, before Pamela realised that the reason, she hadn't written in her journal at all, was because in the sub-conscious part of her emotional well-being, she was still piece by piece also removing the spaces she'd safely afforded Judd from her thoughts. A realisation of, that as it was sudden and unexpected, where she'd believed she was keeping herself somehow busy, although she had not been busy at all, as though unable to do very much. The total lack of physical motivation and personal willingness, it was a frightening for her to accept this. It was a Sunday, neither had contacted each-other, now while she was lying on her bed, she decided that it must somehow be properly finalised without any doubt in her own mind whatsoever. Was it already and how foolish could she possibly have been being? Pamela had become very resolute, she certainly seemed confident in her own mind and on her own unique part now, and by her way of thinking that she wanted to not even ever think of him again, not under any circumstances at all. She'd just eaten an apple and had placed the core on a saucer on her table and was thinking of how the apple was so crisp and fresh and wondering what part of the season where they harvested and stored because the apple seemed harder than any she'd tasted before, more condensed, but it was very nice still. She started at that core and thought of Judd and only of how he is and was, 'rotten to the very core.'

Now under the impression that what they shared was neither a love nor hate thing, she was at least certain, and it pleased her, that there was by how things had moved on in that miniscule moment in time, absolutely no love wasted, or lost at all. She hadn't resented meeting Judd; she just didn't want to further feel nauseated by even the merest thought of him now. Was it to be as simple as that really though?

Pamela then visualised all memory of him, though only the memory regarding their having met, going up in flames, similar to as you might imagine a genie appearing from the inside of a bottle, although it was just a heap of odd wood pieces and hay and flames like a small fire up to maybe just above five feet tall from it. Then as if from no-where, she visualised what looked like his charred lifeless body, or certainly a body, bound at the feet with thin rope, being dragged by what at first looked like a spider leg, it was a day before she realised after what it was or what it actually was more like, it was like a huge spider's fang, but only one of them and it was black. It just pulled the body that presumably was that part of that memory toward it from her right side, by hooking onto the ties around what were possibly she thought, his ankles, they were charred so she couldn't actually tell, it looked only like a way over cooked piece of meat to her, but in the form of that which could have only been a human corpse and where rigor mortice had obviously set, it was just deceased. The fang, as long as his leg, but in a hook shape, just appeared in a downward motion and hooked and so quickly seemed to drag his lifeless body across the floor, then out of view. At first, the speed of it was similar to the dark cave banished character, and it was a little confusing for dear Pamela anyway, whose frayed tattered soul had already presumably been torn to shreds, she just accepted what she visualised as normal and didn't even question any of it, unperturbed, or possibly because she just couldn't anymore? It wasn't very long at all though, moments in fact, not that Pamela considered ever that she was delving into anything, she'd always been like it, so it was nothing new, she saw another vision. Simultaneously a voice could be heard to say, "stay away from her, do not involve yourself with her." Pamela didn't know where or whom the voice was from or who the sentiment was directed at, particularly as the image she saw was of a female looking person dressed in widows' weeds. They were long dark clothes, and the person did not look particularly tall, but not much shorter than her either, it was a feint image, as if from the smoke itself and she could not see a face then. She was not silly though to guess, that the face could be something of great distress, the feeling was from Pamela that the image was neither of this world or of this time by her attire. Pamela felt a deep sense of sadness of the character and even days after when recalling it was unable to prevent herself from shedding tears. It was as though the character was troubled, or maybe she was warning Pamela, particularly as she'd seen that image of a dark-haired woman, hair just past shoulder length possibly and maybe even with a scarf or head covering of some kind, not lace, in very long dark woollen type clothing only the day before too, a voice from that character Pamela thought, was then so very quietly, almost a whisper, and she wasn't bothered by it at all, apprehensive, but not bothered, heard to say; "You got here."

Pamela's wrist on her right hand, was very strangely then suddenly feeling as though it had been burnt and there was a muscle aching on her wrist, the left side of the inner part of the wrist if looking at the palm of your right hand. It was slightly reminiscent of blood pooling that can be associated with rigor setting in once a person becomes deceased. She rubbed it for some time because it felt very tender, it was a burning sensation that she'd not experienced before, similar to if you were to scold your wrist accidentally over a hot saucepan, but apart from the superficial feeling, it also felt bruised slightly as if knocked and even an hour after, it still felt hot to touch.

Unafraid of that character seemingly then as if from smoke whereas the day earlier not, but the former had seemed to remove notions of the latter explanation being of validity. Maybe a pencilled etching could have portrayed it better she thought and could even quite happily consider despite feeling tearful. The vision of what pulled Judd away so quickly, it sounded like a sack of coal or gravel, or shingle, being pulled across a concrete floor, but very quickly indeed? It was just normal for Pamela. Generations before, many, and as one of her own ancestors had apparently been slaughtered as having been believed to have been a witch, it was not something ever spoken about, couldn't possibly, how very well she knew though. 'Nanne Fich,' but it had been changed, certainly then remembered as Nanne Fitchurch, she'd changed it she said, because she saw a fish in the sky. Her husband died some years before leaving her with one surviving daughter and what small piece of land they were lucky to live on. Nanne had been born with a birthmark on her posterior, a small almost diamond shaped though quite flat mole, she'd have been killed had anyone known about it, they were killing people then, females just for possessing a cat, often they were poor, and often went through horrid torture such as 'Caspi claws,' leg irons heated over a brazier, or 'pilnie winks,' those were thumb screws. It angered and hurt Pamela beyond belief to know of this, so much that it would make her hands shake and tremble, and it would hurt her composure to the extent that it almost immobilised her by the sheer horror of it, she would hold back tears of such overwhelming hurt and resentment to the aggressors, to prevent even them too, now from harm, despite the very real understanding though not in fear, that even her hands trembling would then have had her hanged back then. Even tactics such as iron rivets 'pinning' into unmarked graves were used, the rivets pinned through their joints to it was said, 'prevent them from returning from the grave,' if you had a wart or a flea bite, you could basically start singing to the lord there and then, or hairs near your lip if female, a three-inch-long needle was used that retracted with some kind of mechanism, if the person made a sound or indicated that they felt pain, they were, to their captors, already quite gone. Their land or property, if anything remained, would be as gone as they were.

Pamela was glad that she had the image of the memory of Judd being prized away in such a way, because her preference she jokingly considered, was to have had him fed to wild dogs. Though with anthropomorphism, as "the attribution of human characteristics and emotions and behaviours to animals or other non-human (including objects, plants, and supernatural beings) playing purportedly, such a role, certainly recently in the country he 'claimed' to have come from, she wondered whether there much of a difference anyway? Her intuition indicating that the character visualised was wearing widows' weeds didn't happen until a few hours after the memory of the meet between Judd and her had gone up in smoke. She'd been trying to describe the uneasiness about it all, that, to herself, to rationalise, or attempt to somehow. But even if she had, with her frail mind as it was still in recovery, and amidst the covid-19 situation and with all that was happening or not generally, and the balancing that with her own interpretation of events, would she ever really get it totally, right? Was dopey Pamela who was a descendant of, her ancestor, Nancy, 'Nanne' Fitch' in 1646, yes, who was burned as a witch, just in for yet another surprise? Would the realisation of that surprise be as recalled as the sound of the charred corpse being just dragged and kicked and hit with objects away, or was she about to go through another totally drawn out fiasco, would she one day have to question over all that happened then, in those days, where supposedly, "the mark of the devil was seen on skin," but pre–paper, scribing had also been done on animal skin, whatever, she was determined that the sword was very firmly secured in the stone as it were, and the handle way too scorching hot for darling Judd, if he'd even heard of such. Whoever he'd been frequenting with, was no longer Pamela's concern. Suddenly in that split second, the widowed weed character seemed to appear again from nowhere, it lunged forward to her and as if very angry or upset. Not with raised hands or arms or anything, it just seemed to move toward her quickly, Pamela blocked it with a transparent dome forcefield, a security measure she'd learned to attach and was already applied. The forcefield of course was electrified and although she wouldn't usually consider killing flies, she'd seen one earlier and imagined it being pounded on by a bug as it disappeared out of view behind a cupboard, not that there were bugs of course, it was how she sometimes thought, who knows, maybe protectively? Of course, dear Pamela stopped what she was doing, the crazy girl she is, walked across the room and so cautiously still, as if playing with the fly, not that she was, peered over the cupboard, it was still there and there was no bug or bugs, but she was afraid enough or the fly, to check. As then with earlier that day, the visual where a fang pulled Judd away by his feet, similarly the character in widows' weeds was zapped and vanished. She then heard a voice saying to her, "you're so horrible," her response in thought was, 'I know I am.' That voice Pamela thought was quite effeminate, and as though he was speaking directly into a small empty can, the remark was said almost as if in some way anticipatory of such a response or reaction from her, but also with a doubt as to whether she would bother.

Had it all resurfaced as a defence when threatened after trusting Judd to that extent, how she'd adapted and learned to deal with what he was doing. Especially as during the afternoon of the day earlier when she visualised the fang, she thought of him again as if he'd been lurking waiting to pounce in from within her memory, hearing that he wanted more, had he learned somehow to fester within a person's psyche and then feed from the manipulation of the hosts imagination? So technically would it determine on her strength personally or his prowess as to his continued success, how tough was Pamela? Could he be allowed such influence after, when he'd behaved as he did, without initial permission other than that gained by trickery. No doubt he'd smirk and plead guilty if asked, and yes, Pamela had 'got there,' but not "there"! And after, her then remaining seated, unable to move even a millimetre, to endure the thought knowledge wise, even if unbeknown 'possibly' to him, of what he was doing and that those, or that he visited were and would be unaware of the extent). The next day when sitting at her table thinking about it, she noticed then a very tiny fly walking around the rim and into her coffee cup and back out again, yes, she smiled and noticed that classical music was on the radio, she'd been listening to it and hadn't actually really hear it, so deep in thought, she laughed just a little to herself, knowing it was time to make a fresh coffee. At that very precise moment, the very small fly flew from and away from her coffee cup and across her face and off away.

That afternoon, after doing some light shopping, Pamela had planned to call in on Jean, at 16.00hrs, when she arrived Jean had already made tea and which was waiting in a white porcelain teapot that had a small blue and gold motif on in it and a coffee pot was there of the same design and another containing boiled water, there were two coffee cups and two teacups too. Jean poured the tea as Pamela was removing her long red cotton coat and hanging it. She sat opposite Jean, distancing was still the order of the day too, but Jean said to Pamela, "oh you know a person killed themselves in a street not from yours today. They were seen by public attacking themselves with a knife apparently." Pamela then put her hands to her face and burst into floods of tears suddenly. Jean didn't walk across to her from the other side of the table, instead she asked, "are you okay dear"? Pamela replied, "I've blown away my whole weekly budget on a signed picture of some teddy bears, you know how I love them, I couldn't resist it, Jean." Jean then asked if the picture was very expensive, Pamela responded by saying that it was yes, and that she'd be on lentils for at least the next nine days now as result. Jean smiled as she sipped from her cup, holding the saucer in her right hand, with her eyebrows raised slightly, said, "is it a nice picture dear"? She replied that yes of course it was and mentioned that she had attempted to purchase a print signed by that artist before, but each, and every time she checked after they had gone sky-high pricewise. I was thrilled to get the opportunity Pamela said. Jean then said, "drink up dear, there's more in the pot, help yourself to a scone if you'd like, there's butter and home-made raspberry jam too." Pamela got up and walked to where her coat hung, to fetch a handkerchief from her pocket. It was very neatly folded and obviously unused, she apologised to Jean for her outburst. Jean then replied telling her that she was obviously overwhelmed by her acquisition and said Well done! Their meet was for fifty minutes that day and it seemed to go quite well. Pamela had got up to get her coat and she stopped suddenly. Jean was watching her though nothing out of the ordinary, she wondered why she'd stopped quite so abruptly as though something had tapped her on the shoulder. She looked around at Jean and so very casually said, "I have a message for you," Jean didn't say anything, she stared with interest, "I had a dream, and a message came from your friend, Davinia, there were quite a few men carrying a coffin and a person being laid to rest finally"? Jean said not a word, unable to, as Davinia had been cremated years earlier. She didn't question Pamela, who then was so precise about a few words, she said, "the internment was fully paid up in front, in full." Jeans face beamed with utter delight; she knew what she was talking about immediately. Pamela smiled then and said, "thanks for the mention, so you were nineteen then were you"? It was as though Davinia was saying it herself. Jean didn't respond. Pamela went on to say, "she looked happy, but I can't say more than that." Of course, Pamela had noticed a receipt for three internments fully paid for in advance years earlier at Jean's, when Jean was Jon, they weren't anything directly to do with Jean or Jon, but she couldn't say that because she wasn't meant to have noticed, or were they, and was she? It was all slightly confusing sometimes at Jean's then. She then asked Jean, "is that a new picture on your wall there or have you moved it from somewhere else?" Jean remarked that it was indeed new, and that it was a print, and that the original art was by an artist who'd lived for a while in France. The sons of the painter watched the precision with the brush. Especially that work could describe that seen by the painter although sometimes can be abstracted from actual sources. And that even abstract work, deliberately painted as, was a beauty also to behold to those who may seek or understand an even broader and different depth and sometimes, also, or even to help them through challenging times. And to suggest that perception is one's own version of events, and a confirmation that not everyone is always the same, and of how tastes and experiences themselves, can lend themselves to, without taking from or destroying, though for some as complementary and for others a possible solution themselves, and each a potential pathway with decision making doorways to pass through, and open discussion with those you meet on those journeys and should choose to shake hands with cordially.

Pamela asked, 'did it ever have glass on it Jean, the print,' she replied, yes, in fact it, did, but I was so excited trying to open the parcel it came in, I accidentally put the pliers through it, luckily the print itself wasn't damaged, Pamela stared at it print and replied by saying, 'yes, very lucky indeed.' You see, the print in an original signed lithograph, from an original by an artist who then had been born near Sacre Coeur, in Paris, or certainly was from there. He'd often painted females and occasionally landscapes, one of those he was known to have painted more frequently, gave birth to a son, it would have been the child of that son who then have travelled at a young age having been approached when in one of the harbour towns, he'd been a bit of a rascal with a reputation and when the opportunity came, he took it without a second thought. As for the girl in the print John had, the sad thing Jean thought about it and the reason he liked it, was because no-one apart from possibly the painter would have been able to put a name to her, possibly she thought why she'd been painted in the way that she had. It would have been a son of that painter, he didn't marry, but brought the two boys up himself and continued painting women until almost before he died in 1876. The lithograph was dated 1903, it looked like a watercolour, it was so impressive she thought. That son, one of them who was said to have had a vicious temper, the rascal, ended up doing similarly when he met a twenty-year-old in 1787, he was then thirty and she gave birth, he by then although not very wealthy had also started painting too, and worked on farmlands, belonging to a local doctor, he was actually regarded as a surgeon, those he worked for allowed him to bring the child up as part of their own, pretty much as in exchange for his labours, although they had recently been bereaved of a child themselves. Ten years after, the farmhouse burnt down, there were no survivors, they weren't a large family anyway, four of them including but none survived apart from the painter's son, who'd used up some brandy given to him by those he stayed with and had been given some laudanum by his nibs, because he'd injured himself, his back. The only part of the property that wasn't ablaze was a downstairs room, there was nothing there left for him, he picked up whatever he could run with, even some of his master's clothes and bag with some things he could try to sell, and he ran. He didn't even take his paints from the yard barn, and he just ran and didn't look back. He was never actually heard of again. The mother of the child was hanged in 1798 and the lord judge or judiciary of the day in his words, said to her that, after her body shall be "dissected and anatomised," for killing a woman. In fact, it was the friend of Pamela's friend Jean, who'd mentioned when intoxicated once, that her great, great, great, aunt had been a 'scullery-maid' to a person who'd been hanged. Maybe there was a connection?

Pamela then said quietly, "It's extremely smart Jean." Then she said, now maybe you have an idea as to why I bought the picture showing lovely teddies, It's enough to keep me sane 'jokingly,' you know I love them, I seem to no longer be able to find the time, or an inclinational desire these days, to run around trying to catch laughing gnomes, not every single day anyway." Jean was somehow astounded. Before she left, Jean asked Pamela what her plans were for the rest of the week, she said that she was going to visit Euphoria at Grimpmoor Farm, they both knew of the area of Grimpmoor, it was to the west of Braithfurling where Pamela once lived and Euphoria of course, was Lady Broadley of Grimpwater, she lived in the farmhouse and Grimpwater Farm Manor. Jean said please convey my regards kindly, Pamela replied, 'sure.'

#

Pamela experienced again a very unsettled night that night, having been woken up and was then hearing loud banging on the ceiling of her flat from the apartment above. It reminded her of a dog with an itchy back leg and as it was trying to gnaw at the fur, was kicking its leg then involuntarily and against similar. a table leg or something, or that a kid was bouncing a bouncy ball on a wooden floor repeatedly for ten seconds, every twenty seconds. It seemed odd that she would immediately equate the banging with Judd, but she did, and she attempted to alter her thought regarding it. Somehow, she was still affected considerably by the real the fact that she knew that what they shared, those moments, had seemed all just too good to have been real, based on her own experiences of him. And that it probably only meant that she'd allowed him to come into her mind again somehow. She felt very uncomfortable and not only because she was itching in a very unusual place, she had odd itches sometimes, but this was more, and sore. She was itching externally from the exact precise location on her body where she knew the surgeon would be using a scalpel to start to operate on her, she felt it with two fingers, it was almost as if the scar that was there since the time of her birth or very soon after, which was never explained to her, and because it was too personal a thing for her to ask about it was open of its own accord, it was only a few millimetres but she didn't know how to consider it, the realisation that a very possible earlier surgery and yes, now needing to be reversed, although it did not affect in any way her actual medical diagnosis, was something for her to cope with emotionally again, although it wasn't a problem because she had done so many times anyway, it was a visible scar and not like anything she'd seen researching. She applied some anti-bacterial and anti-fungal cream to the area and because in the night as she slept, moments before she woke up, she'd imagined him pressing against her there, in exactly that spot, it was mainly that which awoke her, the noise upstairs was coincidental after, otherwise she'd have probably slept through that, she wondered whether somehow, because he was smiling, he was aware that she was closer to her surgery date now, or was he vindictively comparing it to the ease of where he was? Although she got back to sleep again, the time she woke up was 00.10hrs, it was a Monday, remembering the day before how she's imagined something dark dragging him away by his tied ankles, she realised, visualising again, that imagery was to her right side. To her left though, his face and him, she briefly wondered if he might be missing her? But she didn't want him. For her it was all a little strange as she then pictured herself covering him in a very binding web, and with her face only some ten inches from his, staring straight at his eyes, not into them, then she regurgitated over only the part of the web that covered most of his face, then she saw his 'unflinching' eyes staring at her. As precisely as that surgeon's scalpel she knew would be, none of that she'd regurgitated would seep through that web onto his face, not unless he attempted to move, then it would consume him. Then she moved back, thinking that yes, someone else had simply snared him again. And she now knew not only the tactic there, but also their very probable dress code. Then as though very quickly it had pulled him, Pamela could see that it was as if Judd now had wings, sure they'd become entangled but not of Pamela's doing, he was pulled in, maybe it was a flying visit, and although there seemed like there was a struggle, it would only be as only as those very deliberately clad legs rolled him up and spun him around, then stuck what it actually believed was venom in. Pamela pulled out from a drawer her dressmaking scissors and recalling clearly that memory of what looked like a fang and as it very suddenly and thankfully she thought, had seemed to re-appear to her right again, and as we all already know, Pamela would not hurt spiders, not real ones, she used those scissors to snip right through two of the very thin hollow tubes of legs attached to that fang, severing them completely. Then, as fluid seemed to gush at first and then dripped, it retracted as a direct result and pulled without hesitation away from her. It wasn't that she, Pamela was hurt, she just wasn't going to be used again, unless on her very own terms.

Was it that Pamela stupidly thought Judd might be too confidently presuming that he could still get to her, knowing that he'd find that amusing, or that he could still abuse? Or was it that she, Pamela still thought about him, had there become that great a difference even between thinking of and about? Had there always been? Okay, it was odd thoughts whilst sleeping, had it become subconsciously so upsetting for Pamela, that he may be visiting someone else close to where she lived again. Barriers that had taken her more than three weeks to put in place, whether she planned to or not was irrelevant, she hadn't though, it was quite natural, she definitely did not want him, but still he seemed to be able, just by her thinking about him, damage. Only the night before Pamela had questioned of herself, she was very new to relationships and certainly of this type, had Pamelas total naivety when they first met, awoken that child in him, maybe this was why she wondered whether it was possible then, not to want a person who stupidly you'd believed was your soulmate. It was enough for her to want to immediately go to her kitchen to remove her white cotton laced trimmed nightdress, the other from the night before was still on the floor waiting to be washed. Before taking it off, she'd found a very rough feeling towel, it was how she liked them, she put that in the bathroom on a hook behind the bathroom door and walked back to the kitchen and scrunched the nightdress up that she'd been wearing and placed it into a plastic container, then she put the container into the microwave and heated it on the lowest setting for fifty seconds, she hadn't wanted to look for something else to wear, she was feeling totally lousy. She wanted him gone. The nightdress was warm from the microwave, and she watched it to check that it did not catch on fire, it hadn't been in the microwave long enough to burn anyway. She hung the nightdress on the hook next to her towel, then dropped her panties off to the floor, it was time for a nice hot shower.

#

When she remembered him pressing against her, she was very aware of their bodily differences, it was unfortunate though that because of present limitations, he had not been able to see with her beyond that anymore, there was and wouldn't be unsafe penetration. The water from the shower was hot, all she could hear was the sound of the water splashing against the bath from the pipe because the shower head was broken so she could only use the pipe. She knew it wasn't exactly the nicest surrounding s to have anyone call in, but it wasn't as if she was a slut and she had other priorities. She had attempted to repair it on numerous occasions, but the threads had gone in the shower head itself. There was more to that than had met the eye too, shed at one point wondered. But then where did that place those in other places who did not have showers, they still had great and loving caring relationships. Just listening to the water and unable to hear the extractor fan in the bathroom, she momentarily wondered then whether he hadn't walked past where she lived and had noticed how overgrown some of the shrubs had become and whether that was why she'd had the image of the spider and web, because he'd thought that in passing, of the front of where she lived? Had he been stalking her? She doubted that, but nonetheless it was a thought. She wet her hair and lather it up, then used a rough feeling burgundy wine-coloured red face flannel, to clean her ears and neck with soap, not body wash, not even some of the more citrus type, she loved them, but it had to be very neat soap today which she did not rinse off, as with the shampoo on her hair. Her eyes remained closed throughout as she used the located very abrasive feeling rough flannel and rinsing it often and adding more soap to clean so firmly her whole body. Starting from shoulders and arms and under arms, her tummy, under her breasts, everywhere, pressing so hard, that it caused her to tear one of her fingernails. It had hooked onto the flannel, so she had to be careful after, it was one of her longest nails to, so she was now even more far from impressed. She then lifted the shower pipe up with her face pointing upward, let the hot water just rinse all the shampoo and soap off. Only then, at that moment, did she realise that she exhaled, she'd obviously held her breath throughout the showering. Then as she opened her eyes, she could see in front of her the glass shower door panelling through the steam from the hot water, as she'd exhaled, she was met by a strong smell of onions and garlic where she'd inadvertently burped too? Then almost nervously, she laughed out quite loudly, almost, just for that moment, as though she hadn't been allowed to before, she picked up her underwear and took hold of the dressing gown and walked to where the other dressing gown was waiting to be washed, then put them all immediately into the washing machine and put a clean dress straight on.

Not so long after showering, Pamela did look out of the window, she'd wondered herself whether a spider had built a web across some branches of a shrub or on her window as the right bay window was set back slightly and formed a neat cove, where the shrub had sprung up in the garden there. Instead, and not that her eyes were drawn to because there was no visible spider web, she noticed a young blonde lad walking along the street and thought nothing of it, she was also somehow mindful that he should not notice her having noticed him.

A few hours after, of course she'd wondered whether Judd had gone to someone else local again anyway, she was glad to have felt rejuvenated from the stresses of it all. After she'd sat down, of course it would rarely be when she was staring from the window, momentarily, she thought she heard someone shout out, "he's just a happy boy ok!" sure, Pamela had thought that the lad she saw was happy and was glad for that, but also, she immediately thought of Judd too. Oddly, the accent of the voice she heard was not dissimilar to how Judd speaks, and he was not from this country so whilst it may not seem totally unusual, it did create an interesting prospect, it was though whoever, or whatever said that, maybe it was something simply travelling on a breeze, which was why she'd liked to have actually seen whoever spoke, it sounded very inter-mingled with Judd indeed. In fact, Pamela did recall hearing that exact voice before, although the dialect was much stronger and more individual than she recalled. She had often thought in times past that individual dialects are very special, maybe that had made her more attuned to noticing changes, how widespread had it become or was it? The removing of individualism, or had it become a new realism and was it based on excitement of achievement, even if such was not necessarily from what many might consider under the circumstances, exactly the best circumstances, not generally really. And where did that then place that young lad having to walk through it, if of course he heard any of it at all. Pamela hoped that he would be gaining his learning experience from school. He certainly looked capable and unassumingly content. Pamela, afraid to refer to herself in thought as third person and if using the pronoun 'she' now was afraid, because by default it linked emotionally somehow, and because possibly Pamela's brain had not been enthused with endorphins associated with meeting someone you care about, with that which Judd may have visited, Pamela vehemently disagreed with and did not want this association at all and certainly not where it by sheer default, removed her choice to refuse. These feelings were normal for Pamela and she knew that it was nothing serious and that it had no real credibility in an honest sense, true though, Pamela had been worn down to some extent, had that been deliberate and for the reasons she'd considered, to then allow such, or had her barriers down simply been kept there and then abused and repeatedly and continually in an attempt, to those unaware or too trusting, or so very inexperienced, to weaken them, the barriers needed to be up, yes again and in full working order, did Judd think it had exposed Pamelas vulnerabilities, but he was supposed to have worked in a hotel as a manager, she could hope he would know better, as she always had, but he wouldn't when it came to meets. Deciding again to attempt to put an end to any notion that she might have thought he had, but probably didn't as obviously and quite possible she now even considered that too, neither did she, was she just trying to forget it all, to just blot it all away? But Pamela believed that she really could feel that he was aware of the hurt he'd caused her, or was she feeling just hurt, knowing that in a more direct personal sexual way, he was hurting someone else, was that a part of the wearing down process, creating victims once access achieved. Regarding the voice she heard, Pamela heard, she was pleased indeed that very obviously some seemed overjoyed with that, that some were so happy about it, very pleased.

She then slightly filed down her chipped fingernail and buffed it off, and whilst seated, applied a layer of nail varnish, then got up whilst it was drying to put the kettle on an make a coffee whilst in the meantime, she brushed her teeth again. She then considered again, as though she was at a point now where she was almost obsessed with him, or had, during these awakened thought moments become so. Another thing to think about for Pamela was now, because of his sleeping arrangements, did this mean he could always get to her whenever, or if he ever wanted to, or was she now being paranoid? Had she been affected and to what extent, 'or why' if he did understand? She checked her phone, a text had come through at that moment, the identity and text message looked and sounded as though it was from a male, although, these days, was she ever totally sure nowadays, had he finished Pamela off? Did he hate her, had he been taught to hate her, as though doing someone else's dirty work? The strange message asked for a 'Pam Toros,' 'Toros' was part of a name he used only once when he first contacted her, it was an account identity. She'd been confused when it seemed to change to something different quickly although hadn't questioned it then, she decided then not to enquire about that very quick account detail change, would that she did not, have been something he'd have instantly picked up on? Sure, a thought crossed her mind then, she also did think then that she was being somehow tested by him, but too, she didn't want to believe it, that there was or could be anything then 'going on,' other than what was presented or how it seemed, she was trying to be not in any way doubtful, when she saw his photos, she knew she wanted him immediately, she certainly would never have guessed then, what she was to ultimately endure emotionally. The message on her phone from a person mentioning, 'Toros' and coincidentally Pam, he was not from any Spanish speaking place she thought. Or was he? Could he have been, certainly the image of him in the boating shoes sitting on a hotel balcony could have placed his origin there or in a place like that, in spite of what she'd been led to believe by him and for sure, that was nowhere like where he claimed to have come from. So much now again was being thrown into the air for her consideration. The horror that it might have all been an act on his behalf, seemed comprehendible. His hair in that photo looked well groomed, no more than an inch at its longest point and tapered slightly at the back of the neck, it was combed across and looked a thicker type of hair, not fine, or the type that could lose its shape easily once styled, with a very slight barely noticeable fleck of blonde that she picked out where it was a sunny day, fair skinned, but in the photo, very slightly tanned. His hair then in that photo she now realised was definitely dark, not the blonder hair he had on the few times they'd met and since they first met, or was it a very well concealed gray? Something else no doubt picked up from one of his conquests. Then she remembered the last time he visited her, when he said to her, "nice to see you," that's what was different about it, his hair was dark and he was not clean shaven, totally opposite to how he'd been before, blonde, and totally clean shaven. Pamela had been too shocked when they met that day to have met him again and more-so concerned about his perception of he, it was just after the lockdown, months had passed, she'd just thought that he'd been through the mill and had been meeting lots of people to look so rough and unkept, very much as though now more accustomed to pleasing, 'certain types,' he might casually visit and very often by the look of it. Just as he'd forgotten her address that day, had he very stupidly indeed forgotten slightly himself? 'Oh, my goodness,' she thought. Had his act at last finally caught up on him after all, as he'd been meeting so many often and months had passed, he'd forgotten his image with her, or his plied image. Was that what he'd meant when he said that he "couldn't handle this anymore," he must have realised and hoped that she hadn't, though it would amount to nothing more than a complete fool that might chance to believe that certainly Pamela, never would? And then the block? Today though, it was the day after Battle of Britain Day, the news channels were pretty much all about the possibility of another lockdown in the UK.

There had until then been a recurring possibility in Pamela's mind that he did work in a hotel as he'd said and because, he mentioned something about overheard conversations once, but he wouldn't speak much about it at all, oh no. So, his visit to her was somehow still to touch base? She wondered why, especially as he was obviously meeting others, why her, but it was short lived anyway. She heard the postman posting mail into the communal letterbox in the hallway, at that moment, or only seconds before, she heard someone shout out, "she must have upset everyone," although there was no indication though, thankfully as to who or where the reference was to, or about, Pamela was upset by it, or was her desensitized mind becoming sensitive again? She was hurting still, that's for sure and the remark because it was so early seemed odd though not totally unusual. Some mail had been posted in the letterbox, which was addressed to a neighbour's property, they'd been having work done. It was very rare that mail found its way into the wrong address, but too, sometimes letters got mixed in between others by mistake, probably more from the sorting office end than the postal worker himself, it was one of those days.

Pamela had a knee length, loose-fitting, grey striped dress on, her hair, she walked to the kitchen and wet it to dampen it down a little to reshape it, she was wearing tan-coloured heels. Sure, she was upset and borderline angry, she hadn't fully realised the implication then of her having discovered that he'd tricked her again or tried to. She hadn't realised at all, so yes, she, whether the comment was intended for her to hear or not, because she felt as though she'd been whacked around the head, that many times, still had to emotionally deal with it, even the admitting of that by her, hurt, as she felt as though she'd had her brain demolished. Taking the mail and finding her keys, upset but not unhappily, with no make-up on too, not even a smidgeon of lipstick, she went to post the misdelivered mail at the neighbours. Surprisingly, although there was quite a lot of activity on the street, none of the voices she'd hear could be heard there, those were silent. Not looking at anyone, she walked briskly the few yards to the neighbours' address. There were workers indeed busy there, he stood back as though shocked as she clambered under some scaffold and then leaned forward to post into the letterbox of that front door that was left ajar to allow access to those doing work there. The workman stood only two feet from her with his hands in the air, neither had health or safety masks on. She then walked back to her own flat, of course she considered whether he'd noticed her own perfume, but was not concerned. She did then realise upon getting back into her flat and throwing her door keys on the bed that, she'd held her breath for the whole time, from leaving her apartment until she returned, she didn't breathe once. After calming down for a few moments and deciding not to be concerned with any antics and certainly not Judds foibles, she smirked and thought only of her large metal hoop earrings, then smiled slightly as if to obliterate such emotion, and any thought of who, or what, might next be on his list?

#

An hour or so after, Pamela was on the loo and thinking only slightly of the poison Judd so freely finds it acceptable to administer. She recalled watching him from a window the last time he visited her walking along the street to her home, her imagination must have either been over-active or he was on the street, it was as if she could feel his presence somehow. Maybe this was how he was working, the more he slept around, the greater chance that he could achieve a prominence, and if he was meeting those who lived so near to where Pamela lived now, it was also a way of keeping her in check or manipulating her imagination and by way of abuse of other 'trophies,' to have her believe that he could. The feeling was very strong and unusual mainly because she didn't want him, unfortunately, her being on the loo, served as the greater importance as much as she wanted then to look from the window. Just as before where she had to remain seated though and endure, it was then the older image of him in her mind, he had his back to her as if purveying, presumably as the younger version of him did what the younger version did, this time, it very conveniently was the younger version of Judd she envisaged. When she'd finished, she washed her hands and walked into the room where the window is, as though afraid, maybe for her life potentially, and, both scared and afraid to be noticed doing it, she moved the heavy curtain back so very slightly, only one inch of a gap initially, she had to focus through the net curtain because there were beams of light reflecting on and into the window where it was sunny outside, it wasn't a warm day, but it was certainly a sunny day, weather reports said it was 11c that day at that time at that location. She of course realised anyway that even if he had been walking along the street at that moment, that he'd have been gone out of sight from her window by the time she got to the window and no, thankfully he was not there.

Pamela then fixed for herself some toast, it was unusual that she had any bread but deliberately bought a brown multi-seed loaf of brown bread a week earlier and treated herself to some crunchy peanut butter, she'd kept the loaf in the freezer to prevent her from binging but Pamela as she was, soon grew accustomed to the taste of the rare treat of the peanut butter, to the point where she would eat it on frozen bread quite easily, even if there was still ice on it. The toast was very lightly done, although she liked it that way, it was because the grill on her gas cooker was not the quickest when it came to cooking. She didn't have a toaster because she rarely ate bread products, unless she could heat them up in her microwave which even, she knew, was not the best mode of practice, but it was quicker she thought. So, with coffee made whilst the toast was cooking and then a larger than average dollop of peanut butter spread across her two pieces of toast she went and sat down, breakfast was nice she thought, and very yummy, tasty. Within an hour she was lying on her bed responding to texts from a health worker who often usually started work earlier than most. She imagined that whilst standing in her kitchen though, waiting for the toast, Judd could see her, she briefly stared at herself in a mirror in her kitchen, her very pale pastel shade mint green dress clung to her, and not that she was particularly vain at all, and certainly not with restrictions or limitations imposed by her medical situation, she did notice how her nipples stuck out prominently because she had no bra on. Still with the hoop earrings from the day before. She imagined and believed that he was trying to push himself against her, closer then, at that precise moment. It was not sexual, more devotional than sex. He was and remained fully clothed and even had a short jacket on, something he didn't have on that day, she'd not actually seen it before? Noticing that he was being very sweet, too sweet in fact, her glance having been therefore until that moment quite distracted, it was too in tune with his manner, to presume anything other than his left hand was far busier behind his own back, indeed it was, he was trying so hard to pull that sword from that stone. Realising immediately that he was surely toying and applying some fool hardy trickery, she thought of how it could only burn his hand now as she'd realised, sure enough it did, though it wouldn't have marked it. Not yet anyway. Then he placed her very forcefully on a seat and whilst remaining directly in front of her, quickly walked backwards, scattering in front of him, between Pamela and himself what looked like gravel in a three feet wide pathway, obviously he was well practiced she was admiring, to have done so with such accuracy. He moved speedily from left to right and then right to left, thorough and fast until a distance with the gravel was some 6.096 metres, just under seven meters, or even precisely that. Was it to create a distance between them, she even wondered peculiarly and optimistically on his part whether he in his imagination was not trying to create something for others to feel, or see? She watched him from that distance then, was he trying to demonstrate this. So stupid she thought, as he now became almost confrontational in his stance and yes, as though performing in front of a different kind of audience. Had he realised her experience? Or had he known all along? Was it something he'd observed or indeed was advised about by someone else, she incautiously thought?

Then suddenly, he was standing immediately in front of her, she didn't see him move, but it didn't matter, he'd expect at least that much of her. The seat became like an altar, she recognised that much quite immediately. She was pinned back on her back with her arms outstretched, then he held something or the remainder of something directly above and within less than twelve inches from her face, it was a carcass of some kind, something that he'd quite obviously had sex with, he wanted her to see that. She was hurt so much by what she witnessed then, it was not like things she'd seen before with him, it was not normal. It was potentially obscene. He threw it to one side like he was throwing a stray hungry dog a bone quickly, discarding it as though of absolutely no consequence to anything or anyone at all, he was staring straight into her face throughout and he said quietly, "you can do nothing to me now in the slightest, nothing at all."

Pamela felt her fingernails extend, although it would not have been necessary and certainly not reliant on anything he did, she told him, "Get real you idiot, why attempt therefore to change your very idiotic and stupid habits of a lifetime." It was though of course only Tuesday and not Wednesday as she'd thought, so he hadn't, he'd have been at work very early then usually, and wanting to get away even earlier. Had he 'deposited,' only to collect or pick up later?

What he discarded, made her think of complications she'd heard of regarding her birth, she was disgusted by it. But it surely had to have been only her imagination? At least she hoped, but all the way through the furloughing, she hoped. So where was the consequence there? The fact that he couldn't have known that she'd already worked it all out, every bit of it, whilst he was furloughed, now she only hoped that the same not only would not but could not happen again.

#

Had Judd believed himself or considered himself to have been so clever that Pamela required an explanation. She realised then, that if she 'pictured' him in her imagination, and suddenly for example, he might, be holding two children in his arms, all that meant was that he was having a threesome or planning to again, with two very much younger than either he or Pamela. He would never fathom or contemplate the knowledge Pamela possessed, or her capability. Would it become his eventual downfall? Did anyone really understand Pamela quite as much as dear Jean, and why Jean? Was it something to do with their backgrounds somehow or that they'd known each other a long time too? A few hours after Pamela became very quiet. She was in one of her almost trance-like states, these had never been witnessed by anyone. Stupidly, it wasn't that she didn't want anyone to see it, it was that she never had the company of anyone immediately closely enough as in an actual relationship, to show them and she was always slightly too embarrassed to volunteer information without being asked. She visualised Judd placing by her to Pamela's left side, Pamela was lying down as she had been before on the altar-like arrangement in her vision, he laid out, the person next to her very carefully who he'd been with for those few hours, or a couple of them. Pamela was not looking to the left or right, she was staring straight ahead and could only see him smiling and that he was laying someone by her side, but she did not flinch one bit. What was placed by her side was quite lifeless it seemed, or certainly unconscious. As I said, she did not flinch, she just could see Judd staring at her face throughout. Pamela's left arm then moved upward and dropped it across the neck of that laid by her side with such force and so quickly that all you could hear was the head of that she'd hit dropping to the floor where Pamela had decapitated her. She then stared at Judd; he knew she was unimpressed. Realistically though, Pamela knew, and not as sadly as Judd liked to believe, that all that amounted to, was that whoever then he was with or had been with was or had become quite besotted by, or with him.

There was nothing that dear Pamela could do to loathe him more, and nothing he could do- as there was legally by normally accepted channels, still no contact between them to believe, that she herself, wasn't completely and utterly in love with him still.

Staring from behind a curtain through her window again, as though pathetically hoping somehow, for something, although there was no hope, because of her requirement for surgery, she saw a few men rushing around as though in a hurry, one of them was using a broom and sweeping very close to where she was standing, but he was outside, he was sweeping the steps. Even he, because of his hairline, reminded her of Judd slightly, but she wasn't as stupid as ravenous. The scary thing was that if he didn't have a wedding ring on, she'd have made a play for him at some point had she had her surgery, it was something she was trying to gain a level of greater control over and in a very dignified way. She was the marriage type but with a wild streak, something that she'd only share such a partner who could run and pass the gauntlet. Pamela was capable of being very emotionally hurt because she was capable of such trust, equally though, she was not only a shrewd and tough cookie but also sometimes quite vulnerable too, as she was discovering. Apart from the sound of the broom touching the metal gate now and then, and the ground being swept, it was very quiet.

#

Wondering whether Judd, with his background or his habits, or those of others he'd met more so, whether at some point, one of them might have actually put a jinx or curse on her, or if he'd somehow partied with something that might. She could only then think with her own ancestry, that it would be an extremely foolish individual who might consider it, lest of all, attempt to apply. But dear Pamela was discerning, it was a quality, not a hinderance. It would be the very first time in her whole life that she had ever questioned this, however vague possibility. That would have been fine, but if so, that they didn't know her, or anything about her, seemed to be more the paramount concern for her. So, how would darling Pamela who'd visualised herself decapitating someone, 'for whatever reason,' deal with such a fool-hearted notion? What would she do, it wasn't that she didn't know, it was though that she was not bothered by it at all! In fact, she laughed quietly to herself, maybe not quite a laugh as such, in what for her was one of those 'disbelief moments,' although Pamela thought about it quite intensely for only a minute, her own thought was that it was more a eureka moment and concluded with 'goodness, gracious, are you really sure about that'!? And to boot, with the mere fact that this time, even dear Pamela, albeit in her own imagination, had she been driven to such a level of debauchery, or extravagance, or teasing, and in such a callous manner, you could be forgiven for thinking surely, 'was the gal thinking at all'? Or what, was she thinking of. Had Judd with his dyed hair that she believed whole-heartedly was natural blonde, driven her around the twist totally, and of course, if he really knew she was aware and almost, though not quite as seething as he could have hoped, that he'd have even thought of it as funny anyway. But if he'd blocked her, had he driven her to it prior to that moment anyway with his falseness? Or every time he moved on to the next, was he just passing the rubbish back somehow. Pamela decided there and then that a clean break was the only solution, despite his carefully structured escape leaving her again to deal with all that he'd hoped and said to her, she might be able to, "handle."

If he was often focusing on 'new arrivals' anyway, how could Pamela and he, or anyone he met and he, reach any ultimate good conclusion unless ignorant or oblivious or just in it for sex, emotionally, mentally, because whatever way you look at it, could anyone have been so selfish and thoughtlessly inconsiderate? That he knew that he wouldn't have got a look in with Pamela had he been honest with her from the outset would become soon realised by Pamela. Had the lies affected her so much, because of how she was, and her expectations having allowed herself to believe she could trust, created an unsolvable dilemma in her mind where she was forced not only because of his ambitions, but also her own inexperience and very trust itself, to blame herself until she could at some point work out what had happened? So, his "nice to see you," remark, should have been where she picked up on it, but she was still too affected, and having spent all those months alone and having been put through his antics. She was certain though, that what was Judds should remain totally Judds and similarly, the baggage of others he met, that he hoped to rid them of with his charm offensive and his strategy, should return to them or Judd, the great heap that it must have now become, and that of anyone he met or should in future meet, ideally should be for him to face. 'Was he running away from something else,' had been a constant thought of Pamela's. Was she near to discovering what it was, or possibly is? Was he about to jolt off again, did Pamela realise in time? Was Pamela and quite inadvertently and in the same way, where she just didn't understand, soon to prang him so hard, that he would not know which way to even turn?

The thought that Pamela was or had become like a bird in his eyes that could not fly because of her requirement for reconstructive surgery was not pleasant for her, she imagined herself as or like some ballerina, hair up and just stuck, complete with a tutu adorned with plumes and even wearing white tights, then just sat on a floor holding a tissue as she could no longer cry about it, as he seemed to be able to just gallantly parade around directly in front of her, she could do nothing about it. It was as though it had become certain somehow, that he had every intention of laying every conquest of his before her very eyes. If she no longer wanted him, and it was contentious an issue for her, was it just because he knew he could? Was it part of such a so-called curse if there was such a thing, was it possible she wondered, for what, for what reason? None of it halted the covid-19 situation and there was still a wait and a queue for surgeries. Had it all caused her to lose some focus, as though her surgery whilst she'd certainly 'appeared' to be consumed thought-wise, by him, had become a secondary concern. Not that she was having the surgery for him anyway, he played no part in that decision at all as far as she was concerned, the matter had already been decided upon by medical professionals too. Even if he'd have said to her, and it was a thought of hers, 'what if you don't survive the surgery,' and had he pleaded with her not to, it would not prevent her at all. She would not spare such a remotest thought, and besides, tests were being carried out and changes had been made to give greater chance to the outcome being a success, she was not in the slightest bit worried about that all, or of the professional standards. It was a borderline despisal she was feeling toward Judd now, nothing more, nothing less. It wasn't though, that she could do nothing for him, oh no. It was very much that she felt deeply, and sincerely, that her initial pre-furlough concerns regarding his 'ardour,' had come to a very real fruition and now as result, he could do nothing for her anymore, a fruition in more ways than one, did, whether sad or not for some, became a reality.

Had he required Pamela to have made that initial emotional connection though? Was it how he then 'pounced' on locations and was he almost done and about to move to another location anyway? It was certainly something she wondered, although more likely, it was just that the gap between them, had now widened more. Yes, her opinions on why back then he seemed during their initial meets to go for those who very strongly resembled Pamela's photos, or knowing him as she did, had also progressed, it was probably just his way of saying to her, 'no I don't want to screw with a swan or another animal Pamela darling, you bitch.' It was obvious then, certainly for that part of his trip, he wanted someone like a ballerina to die in his so wonderfully and superb gallant arms? The fact still remained at least, that even if Pamela, by her words, thoughts, or actions had driven him into the arms of such a person, she could think 'oh well,' I can now move on too and be happy for them both. She visualised him then, at that moment, as they'd held each other in such loving embraces, the person he was with, taller and short 'fair. hair, they skated around so impressively, she could see his long calves, he was wearing dark navy trousers and his skates were dark too, the blades on the skates were a standard chrome colour but she could see the precision in the workmanship, as he moved so well, covering such a small area really, she went beneath his legs as he held her hands and then stood immediately upright behind her until they swung around and faced each other, and all with such an undoubted accomplished accuracy, she would see no bad in him them, none at all. Of course, it made Pamela sad, irrespective of how they themselves had not become. And because with his lifestyle, as it was, she may as well have left that skating rink and tripped off a kerb and been accidentally flattened by a steam roller and yes, leaving poor Judd standing there. Pamela imagined him with his mouth open this time, although she didn't know why. Yes, like a little boy, lonely and lost, what was next though, would usually be very soon on his agenda. He was not interested in the flirtations and sex, he knew that. Did he know that Pamela did too? Had he actually realised when he last visited her, and would he have had very good reason to want Pamela to believe something so ludicrous, had he really thought then that she was just very stupid, or totally unaware, as in naively so? He knew something was up, he could tell by how she'd and repositioned pictures and replaced some, each of the few times he'd visited. Did he realise something, or anything, 'Mr gameplayer?' Or was it that she had somehow put him in the picture too much too. So, yes, there was obviously more to it, would it be that it might ever prove enough, that he did believe she loved him, and knew that she did.

Pamela slept all afternoon that day and awoke by something causing her left foot to itch so much, that she pulled the duvet back immediately and using the torch option on her phone carefully looked to try to see what it could have been. How idiotic had things become that immediately from her waking, her immediate thought on discovering that there was nothing there should be, 'oh, it's only Tuesday.'

#

Wednesday came. She was surprised in her imagination, to visualise both the older and the younger Judd together. He did what he'd done before with what looked like a bandage tied around a stick, the type of stick that you could imagine in some films, that could be on the wall of a cave possibly and lit up. He unravelled the bandage in front of her, but maybe he didn't know she could see him, or was it to gain her attention span? Or was that her making herself invisible in such circumstances, as her eyes suddenly became drenched and welled-up with her own tears, tears that she could not allow to fall, to become something she hadn't known she could do. Poor, dear, Pamela. Then the two supposed bodies, the first who'd been decapitated anyway and the ballet-dance who'd been flattened, he picked them both up, it was at that moment, in her vision, he was still where he was, but on a horse, and as a Knight might raise a jousting pole in supposedly a competition, though from her perspective, he was, or that part of him she believed she then saw, became to her, nothing more than a child playing or exploring, or pushing his luck a bit too far. Raising the jousting stick high, to above where Pamela was lying, above her there was what looked like something Japanese and possibly even so wonderfully and delicately made with a so thin dark wooden frame and some rice paper, a sail of s kind, it was attached to a mast and was spinning. It was spinning around the tall mast so quickly at that moment, he pushed his jousting pole into it, bits of the pole were seen to break off until it got inside it and having wedged it, stopped it spinning. Was there more to that she would wonder much later. Then as though he'd picked the two bodies up again, he then opened two long doors that seemed to appear beneath the backs of the ankles of Pamela's feet and took the two bodies down into there. Pamela didn't see him get off his horse, but of course he must have. She then moments after, saw him engaging in sexual activities, although the person at him was very much alive, naked, but alive, it was a dark-haired person, like the person he used to visit on Wednesdays but not quite the same, it was not as easy to determine because she now had more make-up on than then. He said, and it didn't make sense to Pamela, not that she wanted to acknowledge, "they are all dead anyway." As he'd taken them it seemed, 'underground,' had he found somewhere underground, to have his little parties? One of those with him, was heard to say," I'll do whatever he says until midnight tomorrow." There were lots of bodies down there Pamela noticed, not that she could see too much, it wasn't dark, it was just an expanse of an area and lots of bare flesh, only that closer to him was moving, the rest seemed to be totally motionless, there was no sound at all, other than what had been heard then. He stood up, then naked and was doing something with a reddish tan coloured polished wooden panel of about one metre long and with a depth of no more than an inch and a width of possibly eight inches, but she couldn't work out what he was doing with it, he was using it somehow to block out light maybe, although it seemed as though it was to bolster something up as though to improve the integral structure down there, possibly even to prevent soil from falling on them, and then them getting dirty she wondered, but she couldn't work it out. It was at that exact moment, Pamela realised how stupid her imagination was, she noticed on her phone when a message came through, that it wasn't Wednesday at all, it was only Tuesday. This could have only meant that he did not know, or was unaware that she'd seen him all the way through the furlough then? So why now? If he was focused on those meets in that way as he was, like a one-track mind, he couldn't see her at all. She could though see him, what he was doing, and she could feel him smiling, but not at her. She licked her own dry lips; they felt plump against her tongue she noticed. Then she ran the tip of her tongue across her top lip from right to left and back again, she sucked on her top lip for a moment, then her bottom lip, then her mouth opened, and her tongue very slightly tipped on her upper lip again, she thought, 'you are in for it Mr, truly in for it'! Though she actually thought, "you little get."

Judd wasn't about to leave her alone, there was a point where 'she believed,' in her then, 'fragile' mind, fragile and inexperienced in matters with relationships with men, that he was saying to her somehow that he'll do all this beneath her feet, "with your radar off, 'you'll'' never touch me. Horrified, because she felt a great respect for, 'all those that had perished,' she wasn't sure what to do and even whether she should lock him down there forever, just to get him out of the way, but Pamela knew it would be cruel and she was more for giving or allowing opportunity, not deliberately creating it, Judd though was certainly another of those that some could have perceived by her, as worth giving such opportunity to, just in case she was wrong about him, and even though every sign had said to her, don't get involved, including how he would call her a bitch, for example. The problem had been that she had given him opportunity initially and then time and time again, her decision to have a clean break had to be achieved in order to rid the traces of him from her imagination, it was as though he had invaded it, or much of it, or was it the rubbish he'd been passing back as he moved from one to the next, set or that naturally possibly would have done nothing but create a havoc. As long as there was something left, even if it was her work experience and training, things should turn out fine, something left of her own mind. For a moment, again, she even remembered saying to him, 'what will be left for me of you, by the time I have my surgery if you are doing these things with many others,' also it was very unfortunate that Pamela could still remember how he thought that remark was somehow amusing, as though he knew it was her desperate plea, so poorly it seemed to him then, weighed against his desires and habit? Moments after, it was as though he was no longer down there in that hole, but was again somehow watching Pamela, he was on his own now, but watching, Pamela was rubbing her legs as if she was now quite tired, she was seated on the edge of a sofa and placed the palms of her hands on her knees gently but firmly, as though it was chilly and she wanted to try to warm herself up, her very smooth legs pulled close together, she pressed both palms down on her knees and her shoulders went back a little, she outstretched her arms, still on her knees and pushed her shoulders forward as far as they would go as her palms moved to in front of her knees, she felt her fingertips as though they were extending then moved her palms to the outward sides of her knees and moving them fairly quickly to her ankles, slightly pulled her ankles in and then sat as if in side-saddle on a motorbike, she felt her hands rubbing gently her ankle and then her shinbones as the pulled her palms back up toward her knees as though applying a moisturiser and realising that she need to anyway soon, she hadn't for a few days and had noticed too when walking to a shop the day before, how very pale her legs had become. Pamela could though, all too often also imagine the others touching him, she then saw the person from the smoke again, the imagined apparition appeared before her slightly ahead of her though to her left, if looking at the face of a clock, she'd have appeared at where the 10.55, or 22.55 might be, this time though, there was a face. She was on a very small wooden raft, that was no bigger than a dustbin lid in size, she wasn't smiling but held in both hands a wooden broom, the long flatter type, like the type presumably that would be used in a garden to sweep up leaves not a standard household broom that had shorter bristles, she was using it as an oar. There was no rush about it at all, you could almost imagine a swamp of some kind or some dark dank depth and that she had found reason to emerge from it. Why though, Pamela wondered. Very slowly almost ghost-like, she passed by Pamela on her raft as though Pamela was moving forward. Pamela who at that point only, realised that she was not on a similar boat at all. The sadness Pamela felt was so intense that she could neither smile or say even a word, she also knew that to be moving forward, 'because she cared somehow,' if she allowed the apparition for one moment to believe that she was not happy to, and especially as she was still so shocked by the difference in their boats, although Pamela could not bring herself to lose focus from moving forward and remaining attentive, she had to ignore the fact totally that there was a golden glow from the boat she was on and although unable to determine for those reasons, not that she wanted to or had inclination to because of fear, that it was a boat and not a raft, it did not men though, although the glow she could detect seemed to be coming from the sides of it where you might put your hands if resting then, to peer over the edge at the water, that the apparition was not actually at a different level at all, would that be a problem for Pamela ultimately, was there something in that which even dear Pamela hadn't grasped yet? The fear and lack of comprehension as to attempting to decipher what was happening, had luckily caused Pamela's face anyway to remain motionless throughout. Fear alone dictated to Pamelas mind, that along with her own instinct, made her quite aware, that if for even one slight moment, she allowed herself to display at all, that she was, 'in any way, that the face and tone generally of what was on that raft using a garden broom as an oar, could change into something so uncomfortable and horrifying, that they would not allow her to pass or to move forward at all. Pamela hadn't noticed sound during those moments, because she was afraid, but after, she thought she heard the deep exhaust sound of a moving racing car, suddenly, not that it was possible that she would hear that, as though something was rumbling in depths somewhere, was it with a happiness, or was it she thought, as a groan, from the very realms of the darkest of the most amazing forests beyond, or even she wondered, from way back when, the Ingagook Mountain Forest maybe? She was always amazed, often quite sad but certainly amazed! It also made her think more about how lovely the sound of a local bird chirping truly is. Judd yes, he hadn't remembered where she lived when he visited her last, she knew somehow too, that whatever happened, neither therefore would he, because he'd been putting himself about so much, be likely to appreciate how much she understood things and depending on the outcome or resolve, from where, or how that might come?

#

'In way too deep.'

Some of Pamela's ancestors from farther back, were said to have been from Egypt, strangely for the time, especially for that time then, Jean had mentioned to her that hers were too, although they never touched on it even once. Pamela was convinced that Judd had not established a link to, or of any underworld- as she perceived,' or knew to have been, or might be, become, or was. He hadn't made her aware in any way, that things might be possible regarding, but of how very much more careful she had to be in future, as she already had her very own understandings and felt that he'd affected her sub-conscious mind, somehow, and had,' in making her aware of his antics, and knowing how invasive he's certainly liked to consider himself to have been, by doing precisely that, was determined to attempt it. She though remained aware, even more now, that his little space was his very little space there, his hovel, however substantial it had in his perversion, or fooling around had become. How deeply he'd plunged was indeterminable to Pamela, then anyway. Unbeknown to even her then, was it a challenge? Would she see beyond that challenge before her? Was she finding parts to a puzzle, could Pamela realise? In the back of her mind somewhere, whether correct or not, would she think that the challenge was literacy based somehow, whether lack of, misinterpretation, understanding, perceptions regarding aspects of, needs and priorities of, ignorance, choices options, struggles, habit, fear, and survival? Had she naturally just written his attempts off and not even spared any slight thought, even that he had any chance, before he had chance to even consider possibilities, as though she'd instinctively somehow managed to put blinkers on him without him knowing, in which case, what else was she capable of? Pamela could differentiate between respect and dignity, and abuses and would never have permitted the latter in a general sense. Neither did she agree with grave robbing, though she was understanding.

Pamela was blushing a while after, to believe that she was on a boat from which there seemed to be a golden glow, she'd noticed it but was in disbelief, but as though unaware and unconcerned, as she was thinking of matters more important to her, like the sadness she thought she felt, so too blushed out to even look at it therefore because of what for her was the embarrassment of it, she couldn't look at it further to see exactly what was happening there. She'd have felt like a right twit to be honest and just gone along with it. Or maybe it was just clean she thought, and possibly sunlight was reflecting off it, the effect could have been too, she was aware, very similar to if a passenger, such as Pamela herself; was just too terrified to move anyway? She thought a while after that she found herself sitting on a seat on a wooden deck as she thought she could see that ahead of her and without thinking about it, sound knowledge that such a vessel would have been constructed this way, she'd have wanted to say standing instead of seated, because she would not have wanted to seem condescending, as after passing into that far brighter space, yes, it was a indeed a lovely sunny space, beautiful blue skies, the slightest of breezes although the water perfectly calm and totally quiet, it was like a lake or river and they were only some four metres away from the edge that was raised slightly as though a mooring place. There were thin dark green reeds growing form the water, not many at all, although and this was possibly why she noticed one bunch of them, they had grown maybe fourteen inches above the water and there were maybe twenty of them. It was not a place she'd recalled having seen ever before. There was a girl standing on the boat very close to her, it un-nerved her because she'd seen images similar in visions of a person like that. Her hair was thick hair, as in strands thicker, and dark. Standing in what looked like a white Grecian garb, drinking, not sipping, what looked to be water from a white utensil held by both of her hands, seemed natural and not because the cup did not have handles on it. She wiped her mouth after drinking with the back of her right hand, Pamela didn't want to think it but there was an almost peasant look about her. She appeared to be looking at Pamela as though quite surprised, that anyone might be there at all, as though she never expected anyone to be, maybe she'd felt that there was, Pamela thought, because there was a vagueness too, indicating that all was not exactly possibly as Pamela might have imagined. Pamela remained silent, the look was as though Pamela's appearance clothing-wise, she thought, could have been possibly very different to hers and because she seemed to be still actually wondering what the glow was all about and whether her own clothing that she could not notice, was reflective of that. There was also a look as though she shouldn't have been drinking from that cup because there was a slight apprehension, but the action was overcome by the thirst and it looked to Pamela, like a desperation. She didn't look underfed, though she looked hurt and afraid and starved, and as though recovering from severe personal hurt and had not been allowed to display anger about it? Pamela knew all about this, too. She had a red mark near her lip, like she'd fallen or had wiped her mouth slightly too hard after drinking. Her garment looked perfectly clean and with no creases and her hair was not dishevelled, Pamela did not like her, but neither did not understand why, maybe she knew that there was more to that being presented to her. She knew! There was a look about her then, 'possibly' because of hurt, that Pamela did not trust. Maybe she felt uneasy because under normal circumstances, Pamela would not be in such close proximity to those she did not know usually. Now, these two, however Pamela was dressed were on the same wooden deck and presumably it seemed at least, face to face. Pamela's immediate thought anyway was very plain and equally simple, 'do not dare to come, or consider it even appreciable, to venture anywhere even close to me.' Yes, she was uncertain, in those few moments, scouring through the many visions she'd had, she tried to recall having seen this person before anywhere, there were many real similarities and even coincidences, although none of those had been so close, not close enough conclusively in Pamela's mind, to determine satisfactorily. Whether it was or was not someone she'd seen before, as much as she wanted to, because she wasn't unfriendly by nature, she refrained from even saying that she had a very similar, almost identical dress, in the colour gold. Had they been the only two to have outsmarted Judd was also a thought of dear Pamela, had he thrown them together another. Or was it just that he was busy with his ballet dancer now? Possibilities were indeed bountiful, and she chose to believe; that was very probably the reason. If he'd just put them together as a game, was there an audience, would there ever be, and to what? What was he making from it, Pamela just couldn't work that out? Did he realise much more about Pamela and wanted to see for himself, he'd have wanted to give that impression for sure, 'the ley of the land.' Pamela thought about that and her mind suggested to her that if they were indeed on dry land there might be some weight to that as a slight argument, but now whether anything directly to do with him or his over-confidence, or trust or not, if he was capable of actually displaying that at all, had they been placed there by him, or whatever likelihood there could have been, even if it was to create a distance between him, his now friend and the two he didn't want around, which as Pamela knew was how he liked to get involved, or to involve himself more directly and focused with his newbies, the fact still remained, those he should have pulled closer to him, were now on water, he was not.

Then there was the thought that the image of a person on the boat could easily have been another more visual embodiment somehow of the character from the smoke, the character who looked as though they's drifted by just moments earlier. So, when Judd was playing with a tan coloured piece of wood, was he thinking in terms of a lovely raft for a ghostly Pamela figure to seemingly haunt from and float around on? The thought didn't exactly fill dear Pamela with excitement, in fact she found it beggared belief. But as she'd said before, too she could imagine that he would find that funny, she however did not. As far as she was concerned now, two crooks, namely the older Judd and his alter-ego hadn't known about Pamela at all, she would work out how to deal with it, maybe she already had. She could not say anything about it to anyone or let him believe or have any inkling that she had. The last thing she could do was to show the character with the handle-less cup that she either cared for what was past, or that she had any intentions of dealing with matters. So yes, that he did not remember where Pamela lived and that she was no longer traceable 'on the radar,' even if it was only something he'd thought, suited her privately, very well indeed. She slightly almost giggled to herself about it, but it was weird because she didn't make a sound as though holding it back as though she started to feel free, and more importantly, because she knew, he thought he was disabling her ability to track him?

Her first move was to ensure that he would gain nothing from his so-called conquests, this also meant that later, as things progressed, he would have absolutely no idea at all within any or a spiritual realm, absolutely nothing at all! Pamela was so determined and thorough that she even thought, or considered, that should he, or in the event that he did, attempt to intervene in her life from now on, he would only gain greater coverage than his own present antics if he were to become hung drawn and quartered, and his body parts then scattered over four nations, doused in noxious liquid that even the wildest of animals would never touch.

#

After sleeping, it must have been exhausting for dear Pamela, she woke up, they were doing a new type of party. She saw an image of a deity and knew that they should not be doing this kind of party in front of that, however they might attempt to disgustingly make it seem, and even all with such masks on, and so many of them, because it had been stipulated that only so many were allowed in any household at that time. The deity moved to Pamela and was happy, that party was folded up. A very important person came and saw to this immediately, he a friend of Pamela. A golden coloured elephant procession could then be seen by Pamela coming in her direction, the character though who was from that party where Judd and so many others were, could be seen riding or trying to ride on a shimmering golden elephant, but in the thigh length boots etc kept slipping off, not that the elephants were aware at all, they did not know that, unlike when Pamela saw them again and they her. This she believed would bring a wealth to the whole area and not just those greedy few, the elephants were shimmering so brightly when they came to her, she bowed to them so gracefully.

It was decreed, that no-one should harm those from that party, because by their actions, as long as people were doing shopping and certainly as some seemed to be buying more, to stock up, that any price on their heads, presumably for their acts beneath such a deity and trying to then mock it with excuses, was being met by those purchasing shopping and goods. This meant that the only way they could change themselves, or their acts along with themselves would perish with their own kind. The continuance of their lifestyles would also free anyone else from that day on, from the control that they believed they had on others, should by 'luring,' they be able to pull out from the minds of those they played their games with using trickery. They had been blocked permanently, although Pamela thought it seemed harsh to be honest, and that it should be only whilst and especially as the pandemic was happening. Deities are deities though, maybe things would calm down a little, or other resolves found, but Pamela did not want to argue at all, and it resolved the situation for that moment then, because it was very serious. Although it was part of the decree apparently that; "they had been blocked permanently. Any continuance of their own activities, or actions as they were, could only worsen their own personal situations henceforth." And as for the older imagery of Judd, he would serve only as a block and with his back to Pamela, blocking the younger imagery of him to her, and no matter how far together they looked at the earlier image of the sea from that balcony, the sea would be all they would look at, because there was for them now, nothing more for them. At that moment, a telephone rang in the room of that apartment, Judd stood up and he ignored the bottle of alcohol on the table on the balcony, closed the door behind him, his taxi had arrived. He'd been to the hotel lobby that day and said, "I'd like to check out now please." They said to him, "you don't have to vacate the room until midday Sir." He then left alone with only the suitcase he'd come with. This was Pamela here, and Judd, would he be lucky to have walked away with the shoes he came in, it was still early days in a funny kind of way. Was dear darling Pamela in for the bigger shock? Was she still upset though, that he seemed to be able to casually just hitch another ride, is that all it really was? He shouldn't be able to just do that she thought, no one really should lie like that, and certainly not to the discredit of anyone other than themselves. She was her own worst enemy sometimes, true. But Pamela thought she'd been totally fair, she believed it, as painful as the reality was becoming, she had to drop it. Oh, she'd argue, saying 'if they, presumably Judd, chose to in future abuse any part of that, it would be their or his own choice, maybe then, she said, it would prove that by his having met some with such traits, that he certainly believed he'd learned now to fool the water. Did he really think that she wondered? And that he could even fool dirtier water than where he'd been? Excluding her of course. Had almost a slight resurgence of a concern for Judd again just occurred, like something of a strange, peculiar vaccine that would save the day, or a guillotine, removing her thoughts of loathing, to replace them with her unique version of unbridled lust yet again, even though she was awaiting surgery. Had a so heavy sleuth gate just dropped down before her, she even quickly moved her right foot slightly to the right believing that it might have done, in the hope that her big toe would not be in the way, yes, to stop her in her very tracks.

There was of course, a possibility that Pamela hadn't been seen at all, the surprised look on the character sipping a drink on the boat could just as easily been because of the stillness water, having come through an ordeal and was wondering now or had wondered whether it was actually okay to take a drink, hence the expression, was Pamela seeing his, 'old flame'? She did remind Pamela somewhat of the person he'd usually meet on Wednesdays, or the image she believed she saw then, maybe she was just taking some fresh air was a thought Pamela tried to come to emotionally wrestle with. Or had she been put there to watch? A reversal of technique, or a new skill gained by the careful expertise of the temperament of dear Pamela herself. She was undecided as to whether to quietly watch from a distance, or whether to just push her into the water. Pamela did not trust her at all! Then she thought better of it, presuming that with understanding of how Judd thinks and no doubt her too, if they had met regularly, pushing her in, would surely make her an old flame no more? Was that why she stood so close to the edge Pamela also wondered, was she wanting that to happen? Pamela didn't really give a hoot about it all by now, the whole fiasco was becoming way too tedious for her, and the uncertainty even though there was no contact had become frustrating because she felt let down. Maybe he had moved forward from those Wednesday meets as she'd earlier thought anyway, or things had become more lucrative locally. Had that been put there to confuse the issue then, as it was still only Tuesday? Pamela thought about it only for a second or two more, then she decided. She sent that character to the very same place where Judd last positioned himself so 'admirably and preciously,' to join with his own so-called "dead anyway," friends. As she did so, Pamela said, 'fire you can handle at least for a while, water you cannot.' The funny thing was Pamela felt as though she'd done the right thing. She imagined the older Judd being moaned at by her lot though, and often being clouted on the back of the head by her. Pamela didn't like that and had never seen it before, but it looked normal for them, especially as he had to then explain the so rapid expansion of such a relatively new personal play and personal entertainment area to her.

The next day, although obviously a coincidence, Pamela was saddened to hear on a news item that four hundred pilot whales had been found dead or 'stranded' off the beaches of Tasmania, it was said to have been one of the worst stranding's on record globally. It would be months after that she would actually say to herself, why did I ever want to bother with this lowlife scum, but was that not what Judd was saying about life too? Or was the scariest thing to be realised, that should they ever become together, who else would hear those claps of the purest thunder and lightning probably on record since records began. And then there was who? "Me"? Would it come on rye, maybe that was the real question there, wedding hat at the ready? But he's already married, isn't he?

#

No longer would dear Pamela allow him, she believed, or anyone he knew, or could be likely to have met, whether directly or indirectly, to access and cause that kind of interference in her life. Where he had been with so many she presumed, not even he would be able to properly ascertain from where the end or when the end to it might come, or from where or when an origination point might begin, this was unfortunate she thought, for him and his. Had it already begun she questioned, it was even more sad that there would therefore in such circumstances, really be nothing anyone, and certainly he, or they could do about it. It was a horrible thing for her to have to contemplate. And it was good for everyone though bad for him? That was a harsh pill to swallow. He didn't know Pamela, she tried to dismiss the thoughts as though they were nothing, after all, he only treated her as he did every other woman presumably, she herself hadn't done anything and was only thinking it as she thought it could be or may be. Had they been in contact with each other, it might have been a conversation they could have, but he made that decision too and without notice. For some reason she wondered whether she was better than him in some way or lesser, because neither would be of any relevance and neither would in such circumstances, either or anyway, become the reason for his ultimate downfall anyway. It wasn't even actually anything sacrificial or anything like that, but she loved him, she loved him so much.

'Voices like bluebells.'

As far as Pamela was concerned, it had been Judd who'd slipped 'under the radar,' long before he'd attempted to block it, she was glad to be even more aware of his sneakiness and of what would not happen again, and certainly not by him. He'd not made her aware oh no, neither would his tricks have any leverage now, she was glad to now realise in her innocence and his abuse of that, the full extent of it. The very and only innocence he would not have time to learn to regret screwing with. Pamelas chromosomes were extremely real and very much his opposite, unlike those, of those he would have unbeknown to himself and probably them too, have so often been meeting, this was something that Pamela thought was personally important because it said how Pamela personally considered herself, it was not such a big deal though and at the end of the day, even if those he went with had male chromosomes, as long as they looked nice, it, and for a variety or dare Pamela think, 'a host,' of reasons, as if it was ever going to make any difference to him, or potentially with hindsight, any of them really?

On the Friday, of course she'd imagined him again the night before, this time with another woman, smarter in appearance, but although her sleep was broken and even though the next day, it was as if Pamela could hear him saying that the person was a lawyer, Pamela shrugged. She then thought, 'no self-respecting lawyer would have been doing things those she'd imagined the night before, even with Judd pinned down as though being forced to watch. She was certainly sure that no money was being exchanged there. As it was not too dissimilar to the other occasion during the furlough, it only demonstrated again how devious, or deviant, Judd was, to have even maximised on that, again, to his quite personal advantage. Because she refused to accept any credibility in the realism of such a suggestion or implication? She thought very clearly indeed that he then said to her that he 'deserved a medal,' to have met Pamela when she was before the date of her surgery 'you bitch,' he then said. It was either just too similar to something he'd said to her on a few times before, so it was no worry to her, or that he would have realised, had he known, that there might be something in what she'd thought. The rain had been pouring down outside, trickles could be heard almost tinkling as the rainwater ran along the gulley's of the edge of the kerb into the drains, she imagined Judd, not standing so proudly now, but trying to swim in that very rainwater and not successfully at all. His arms and legs almost flaying about as he tried to stop himself from being carried away and unable to prevent it. Pamela walked outside and yes in her nightdress that had since dried, she saw his face staring pitifully from beneath the drain looking up at her, his hair drenched and his face wet, and his fingers almost trying to grip, holding on as though it was really tough, had he been duped by someone else and he'd only at that moment realised it? Pamela pressed her right foot onto his fingers, she could feel them trying to move beneath her shoe, but it was impossible. She pressed really hard, then just as he was forced to drop yet again, it had hurt Pamela so much, and she felt so callous herself, but she said to him, 'piss off and meddle with that you fool.' Knowing that she wouldn't have put her foot on his fingers had he been excrement, she didn't need to smile, she wiped her left hand across her right as though feeling that she had achieved something, she wasn't sure what or whether she had at all, but she knew that she felt just so sickened by him and too, that he was now by his own actions, certainly trust-wise, that further step farther from her.

Judd would never understand that Pamela role in it all, not if for him it had been a casual hook-up, neither did she though, and she certainly didn't imagine that all that had happened could or would have, neither was he meant to, that was another reason why she loved him, but presumably he'd never actually truthfully know. He made her forget for those moments when they were actually together that she had any kind of a role at all, the rest after, was her exploring situations that she'd never been involved with before, was there much to sort out, or had it all just snowballed, what would the outcome be, and would it be good? No-one knew. After her surgery, could she forgive him, would she ever want him near her again. Would they ever meet again if she didn't want him now? If that locally was regarded as, or thought of as, by Judd, or anyone, including itself, as like a 'black widow,' it was now to become nothing more than a carefully scribbled decoration applied to a pencil, to be then placed into a lidded papier mâché' long box pencil-case of dimensions one and a half inches depth, by approximately eight- by three and thrown into the back of a cupboard and as far as Pamela was concerned, forever more.

#

Pamela had found those few recent days to have been tiring, yes, she had separated from him, but it was a though whenever he could, he still was there in her mind, the difficulty was weighing it all up and asking herself, what do you know of him really? Just like when she saw him clinging on beneath the drain cover, she still had feelings for him. Just a while after, whether she'd woken up then from a dream, or was still in a dream, she was embroiled in, as result, a new vision for her to fathom, it involved everything from ocean and plastics, and as far as Pamela was concerned, even possibly monarchy.

Again, as though with a quick reaction or realisation or as the trickery in her dream, on his part, she saw him disappearing down the drain hole, maybe she thought, he'd noticed and latched to the sympathy she'd expressed before. This time though, she saw the exact same face that she saw in the earlier photo he'd sent to her of himself, the scary face that immediately caused Pamela to become hesitant, but he would not have noticed, he was too excited that day. He certainly wouldn't have seen then what dear Pamela could not believe she saw, and then it would have been too late for him to do anything apart from slowly attempting to destroy her from inside out from that moment on. What had she seen in that dream though? He then said, "Mary didn't know either." His hands at that moment seemed to come up and try to grab hold of her ankles, water by then was splashing against his face, she said nothing but thought, 'that was your second and very final time, you had me waiting for that? This time, you'll still inherit nothing, bye. Whilst any prophet, the saints and apostles may well possibly be busy with more important things, May God, have mercy and pity on your putrid soul.' Then he disappeared.

Was he simply rejuvenating himself with newbies constantly, did he even need to inherit, or was that how he inherited, if they'd become in his opinion 'dead anyway,' was that for him it? How many would he corrupt and have corrupted, and to what end really, apart from, to satisfy him and whether indirectly or not, his own. She hadn't put the pencil case into a cupboard yet, but packed that image into it too, and closed it shut. The funny, or odd thing was though, with how they were, you could still, even though all seemed lost, never be exactly sure how things could happen further.

The true fact though was, with so much uncertainty, Pamela already had her understandings of snakes and serpents, as we know. So, when he turned up with snakes around his neck and with their fangs in his forearms, she looked up to him with a smile, as she always did and would. She tilted her head to one sider just slightly and licked her lips a little, stared as though to say, 'oh my goodness,' and said: I can give you something for that darling. He smiled. She knew that his own attempts with the bandage around bits of wood, could potentially, by her interpretation, not his, although he'd have relied upon hers, have been caducei, an ancient Greek or Roman herald's wand, typically carried by the messenger god Hermes or Mercury, or had he been doing things correctly, therefore the presumption on his part that his hands were tied may not have been totally incorrect by his standard. She did however, already set that, "something," in place, and regarding those, everyone who have families and loved ones too, she 'hoped' that her actions would help them all.

Before the snakebites, you see, yes, he'd 'seen it all,' and what it had done. Ultimately, was he when his back was to Pamela, was it decreed somehow somewhere, or destiny. That yes, he would go with many everywhere and fend off in doing so, others. With his back to her, guarding her, not letting anyone close at all. Would, or was it to be that he didn't want someone who could give him fire, it was someone who could give him water.

#

Euphoria's Grimpwater

Pamela arrived at the train station of Braithfurling and managed to get a bus that went past the farm. Grimpwater was not a large farm, it had been, but some of the land had been sold off by the late husband of Euphoria, they no longer had chickens there or livestock. Some of the land outside the farm of Euphoria's small farm, supported crop growing, She arrived and unlatched the gate, there was no actual road to the farmhouse itself still, as in a pathway of cement or slabs, but she could still walk it even in heels because there were lots of small stones and it was quite dry on that part, traffic could certainly drive over it easily without sinking into it if it became wet, although no path as such, as in a path made of paving slabs or cement. It sloped downward on one side and there was a dug-out gulley for drainage from where thick grass sprang and the hedgerow began. You could only see over the hedgerow by standing on the slight hill opposite the hedgerow. There wasn't much to see over the hedgerow as it had all become quite overgrown now, what once was a lawn area was now just grass and at least twelve inches tall and the hedge itself looked as if it had been shaped by the wind itself, there were some rose bushes around the lawn with large blooms where even they too had become very overgrown and there were a few fully grown trees. As you walk toward the farmhouse you could see the top floor window through the trees and the pointed roof of the main part of the property, the roof sloped down on either side of that window, where-as the roof of the outhouses sloped in the opposite direction, so if the main building sloped North and South, the outhouses sloped West and East. The few outhouses that were adjacent to the main building, it all sounds huge, sure it was large, but it wasn't massive, they'd utilised the space well. It was a lovely bright day, the sky looked beautifully blue against the dark green of the leaves on the trees that were still very leafy for the time of year. Pamela let herself in and walked through a long wide hallway and called out, 'I'm here Aunt Euphoria, it's Pam, do you want some tea?' A voice was heard to say, "no I have Pamela thank you, but help yourself if you'd like." Pamela walked to a room at the far end of the hallway on the right, it was where her aunt usually sat, and sure enough, after knocking and as there was no response, Pamela turned the small doorknob and walked in. Hello Aunt Euphoria, she said, I shan't kiss today, so you'll have to imagine it, how are you? “Ewww I'm fine darling,” she said, then she asked, ‘how have you been and more importantly, how are you today?’ Pamela said that she’d experienced ‘kinder times,’ and asked her aunt, how many minutes are there in a day? Her aunt responded by saying, one thousand, four hundred and forty, there always have been and always shall be, are you questioning my sanity she asked? She glanced at her hair, it had been combed and had a hairclip in it as it had been placed high, then she said, “of course not Aunt Euphoria, would I ever.” She said, I dare say you would not, though there are some, you know Pamela, she said, that’s one thing I have always admired in you, your ability, to seem too available, that it can easily lead some to believe that anything is always quite achievable. But you still have those faux fur lined boots Aunt Euphoria, she said, ‘and don’t you know it,’ she replied. There was some mint cake on the table in a clear loosely knotted plastic and the remainder of a chocolate covered soft sweet was on a side plate with a small chef's’ knife beside it. They did have tea, and it was nice that Pamela was able to concentrate on more important things.

Very briefly though, if she thought of places where there were wars, she remembered seeing a man on the news amongst a crowd, he was waving his fist in the air, she saw their bombed and damaged houses and thought very deeply about them. She thought of Judd and about his seeming to have become empowered and coming from his background, and from being teased too, and understood why he might think ‘yes, I want a piece of that,’ and yes, why not also, in his quests, wanting to stay younger, or was it need, was he chasing the dragon because he had to stay young just to stay in the game. Or was it that his options had been streamlined to not much actual choice, what were his own achievement options apart from that job? Pamela herself knew what it was to have ideas and not to be able to move to the next step, especially when all personal steps seemed to lead to nowhere and when opportunities and often for those same reasons, seemed to pass you by just too often. It was like standing on a blue counter and so much wanting to step onto a red or yellow counter or a green counter, but not knowing how to or whether it would be worth it, usually because there was a fear, not in her case of the unknown, but that everything would still be exactly the same as it was anyway.

She sat with her aunt Euphoria by a window at the far end of the white painted square shaped room compete with picture rails and photos and a few odd paintings of her Late husband Bertram and one of her twin sister Phenomena, they said nothing, and just each sat staring at the sun seen dipping behind some tall trees, as though that wanted to say hello, then all of a sudden Euphoria said, ‘haven’t been affected by gravity too much yourself have you,’ you look very smart and neatly proportioned Aunt Ephoria, she replied. It was one of those moments when they both wanted to laugh but were just enjoying the moment far too much. Pamela always appreciated seeing the sun as did her aunt. Her aunt said, the sound of the harpsichord on the radio suits quite well too, don't you think Pamela? She said yes it certainly does. Aunt Euphoria said that she had some records that were harpsichord records but that since Bertram had died, she didn't really bother with playing records anymore. She said, he was the real enthusiast you know, especially in the garden too. He chose plants that looked as though they'd been windswept to create an illusion on a still day you know, some of them will last another seventy years she said, because they were planted thirty years ago. Some are to keep unwanted out and some to keep in and some to mark boundaries, most of those can be treacherous should you catch your tights, she said. Pamela didn't enjoy these conversations too much because she felt somehow that her aunt was feeling way too sentimental, so she laughed at the remark regarding tights, 'and the roses,' she asked, which said Lady Broadley, Pamela referred to those on the other side of the hedgerow on the way to the premises, as they were looking from a window at the rear of the property, she smiled, and said, the old fool planted those for me, that's, The Keanu Lawn Pamela, she said, I named it that. Then for quite a while the only sounds heard were the sound of the radio and the sound of China teacups being carefully placed onto saucers as they enjoyed tea. It seemed for that moment there, that even the breezes were stilled, as none could be heard, not even through those older windows, and no leaves could even be seen falling from trees, not that they were particularly close enough to see them really. Pamela was appreciative of the time to sit a while as they did, and because she knew that it helped with digestion and posture. Then Lady Broadley said, "your dear late uncle often said to me, and sometimes he even said it quite loudly, especially if looking through the window at me from outside, we'd stare at each other as though nothing could ever separate us, you're like my own cool mountain breeze above the sea," he'd say. Always wise therefore to keep your mind balanced, and your feet firmly on the ground Pamela, she said.

#

Pamela was still in, 'avoiding' meeting others mode, and waiting for surgery, there still had been no word from them since more than a month now, so it was difficult again for Pamela still not having a fun time at all with how she perceived it, the intrusive nature of the covid-19 scenario fiasco. To her, it seemed give some nothing more than an excuse to take advantage of, or abuse her personal circumstances because of the mental and emotional challenges it presented for her in the state she was in. In the earlier part of the year, some governments had filed, and others were considering taking legal actions against China, not that she considered that those cases would necessarily accomplish much, apart from propaganda and a sounding board to express the flavour or poor taste and attitudes to a stronger level of consideration in the future, of and for others. She was wondering about contacting a lawyer for herself or was it just desperation. She was upset too and questioned why she should basically, 'bust a gut' for those or to help those who choose to behave like that. And why bother not having a boob job, 'to stay natural,' because it seemed to help maintain the status quo!?

She felt as though she needed some quiet time away from thoughts of Judd and everything and was thinking of the land of ingagooks, she'd also had a vision that a person she did not recognise then had died it was a young man, he was near the age of eighteen or just over. She paired the person with someone else in her thought, the girl she'd seen Judd with, she didn't want to frighten him because she knew nothing about him, in his desolation and bewilderment, it seemed to have been done without interference of normal practices, or familial belief, but only with a hope that their service went well. The amulet, as he'd have become empowered now, she thought, was to bring him back. She knew he was in a world of his own believing, not a world of hers, so it was for him insurance while he checked it out for himself. She went back and looked forward to the farthest part of her own past world, as she chosen to remember it, she did not want to bring him back, because he had created this for himself. But or his saving grace had been, that he had once met Pamela too, there would still be something in a deep part of his sub-conscious, even if that something was not freedom, but hope he did not know of. Had he lost hope? He would have and wanted from his world now, having realised it was a mistake to be brought back using the amulet, into Pamela's world again, but she had encompassed her world again. Would he now want to be brought back simply to re-surge – in her world and take control. Pamela had seen in a vision a person who had died, it was a natural death, and did not want to intrude, a young person, she put with him a spirit guide because he looked quite lost and alone for a while, then a while after, respectfully separated the two she put together and left no trace and thanked them both as the person who died then went on his journey, but not now so alone. Pamela would not allow interference by Judd or anyone he was associated with others, and certainly not in death and certainly not of one so young. She left the person who died with his own family. The girl Judd 'could' have once been seen with, who in Pamelas mind could have tricked and taken on therefore, the guise of a spirit guide, she returned that to Judd. The strange thing was, the clothing she had on when she met the person who died, it was the exact same style of dress from the girl seen on the deck of the boat, but now in gold colour too. She remained determined though, there would be nothing he could manipulate, splice, enter or control. Nothing! Also, this did not mean that he was to be 'brought back.'

It had become important to Pamela now, that what she deemed as the five and six worlds, and beyond, be kept separate, because of, as she believed and considered them to be, their demonstrative capabilities. She knew that there had been some element of possibly of a set of confusing factors, and that they may not be realised yet. She also knew that it would be important that the returning of all involved aspects, to their own worlds clean and cleanly, was important, not that they would remember how or that they had been there or what they had seen, neither would any entity or force be able to tell them or remind them, or mirror or use any form of trickery to, or cause them to visualise or recall in any way at all, any part of it. No part at all. Neither would they be able to remember how to return to any part of, or able to retrace or retrack, or speak of, or draw upon or feel where they had been.

Neither too, would anyone or entity, or spirit guide have any idea or vision of what Pamela had seen, done or how she achieved it. Neither would they in any way at all, be able to visualise or remember seeing any part of it or hearing her words throughout. She would not be considered by them as anything other or more than that she had always been to them. No part of what had happened was to play any part in further development of ability other than that she had learnt, and this as it had before, should, would and was to remain as it always had been, even after her surgery. Neither should anyone upon operating on her, have access to this information. Though this did not mean that they would not find or realise answers to questions and involving their own world, not universally.

That, that was part of themselves in other worlds should remain theirs and no footprint either way remaining, or evidence of any voids that happened as result of their ventures into those realms or worlds would be replenished and vice versa, with no traceable element at all.

You see, she'd been woken from a dream, having felt unusually drowsy hours earlier. She dreamt that she was laying down but from under a door beneath her feet, someone she thought she recognised was trying to cut by, slicing very, nicking, quickly the soles of her feet using a long knife, from under the gap at the bottom of the door. She had a cover on and tucked her feet into it and tried to move up onto her pillow more, she was not frightened by it, but had she been awake properly, she'd have felt annoyed more-so, that possibly Judd's more horrid face, or some other quite unfruited fruitcake of a total twat of an idiot, might be still attempting to aggravate or provoke her somehow. Moving up onto her pillow more did prevent a further occurrence of it then, but she'd been very woken up by now. It did not mean that the experience had not shaken her, in fact, at that moment, she couldn't have gone back to sleep again even if she'd been too tired to stay awake. It was the type of startling moment that just left you feeling stunned.

The notion that whatever face Judd was thought of by, not that they, the three of them were too dissimilar, that maybe he'd thought it convenient to possibly believe he could seemingly disproportionately just dive into oceans and take whatever he wants and leave destruction in his wake by his actions, then return whenever he wanted to, to do the same again, if it were so, she intended to deal with this too. She'd realised in just the twenty-four hours since leaving Lady Broadley, her aunt, that there had to be a way to stop him from 'lurking' in the mind. It was then that she believed she'd realised how he'd achieved it. He knew that Pamela was capable of doing things that he could not, or that he had in the past failed abysmally. The amulet, it was nothing like those she knew, it was a game to him. He knew when he turned up, that she'd know what an amulet was, irrespective of whether she'd recognised exactly what, or if anything, that item symbolised. By association, he used it to link with her own interpretation of an amulet and its use. So, he tricked her again. This time though, he inherited everything, because he had his freedom, but nothing, because he'd exploited her kindness. Pamela was Pamela. Did he have everything if he no longer held her desire to want to trust him, or nothing?

Pamela noticed on the news that a storm was about to hit the region, the whole country in fact. Storm Judd. Her immediate thought was 'oh well, and not that there is any association there, at least that was all resolved just in time.' Also, about how amazing some coincidences can be, and she thought of herself and other coincidences, then decided that she hoped it would not be too long before she worked Judd out of her own system completely even if not as quickly as he more evidentially had, whether deliberate or not, or because of his personal recognised advancements in that area of prowess. The rain had been pouring outside for some thirty minutes and suddenly she heard the sound like a racing car in the distance again, though this time hastening at some speed. It was early in the morning, so generally, apart from the rain, it was quiet, she then heard what sounded like plastic post being strewn along the street outside, and the trees took on a huge surge of wind, you could hear the leaves so much, it was just on 07.00AM, she opened the curtains and looked up at the trees, the only light very visible was from neighbouring property windows or doorways as it shone against and up the trunks of the trees, the streetlamps at that time had turned off . Looking up at the sky she could see the leaves waving as if to say, yes, it is autumnal now, as if in a very beautifully romantic way, they were waving goodbye, or at least if Jean's French origination print,' was to have a kindly say she thought to herself, certainly and amazingly, thankfully appreciably on her part for sure, of them; 'au revoir.'

Maybe where there was need for clarity in her mind because of waiting for surgery, Pamela although not wanting to offend anyone, had thought if life or any small part of life, had somehow eluded her, as she having taken steps, waited to discover her real self, all that had only seemed so far prohibitive in some ways, or ways of whereby she could meet those or someone of the opposite sex, it would also show her an unkindness, if they were, by their lack of understanding and tolerance, not. Her having met Judd was only to serve that none had, and that Judd then when they met, was or to her became for that moment, her superman. In what was left of the wind though, and yes, the silhouettes of the leaves, they looked amazing as it was just getting light outside, though a darker shade, still you could see that they were still darkish green against the beautiful sky that was then, a lovely grey colour, about to become a very hazy looking, subtly barely gorgeous pale blue hue.

Within the same hour, more news, this time though that two senior global figures had been diagnosed with Covid-19. Pamela saw images of their aeroplane and the insignia and had to take decisive mental action, to separate them from any similarity to amulets. This made her feel safer that things were better placed for a successful outcome. The wind still howled through the trees then well, not quite a howl, but it was trying to, and what sounded like an empty paint pot could be heard being blown along the street could be heard too. That was soon to be dampened down by the sound of car tyres on the wet road surface. It seemed that Judd had become nothing more than a mild breeze and a whimper after all, she wanted to think or say that he was 'all piss and wind' anyway but couldn't bring herself to such levels. She made a point to go to the window to see the trees again, to sneak a quiet peek, the trees were now almost motionless but further along the road she could see that branches there were waving simultaneously like formation dancers in a swimming pool as the trees re-balanced themselves. Then it seemed to calm, and she heard what sounded like a large aeroplane and the racing car at the same time. She tried to establish whether it was an aeroplane or not, but very honestly could not.

#

Pamela realised that Judd had, because of the mundanity of his work, been running away from that, the mundanity, this was why he always sought new experiences, it was nothing to do with romantic notions that only Pamela could have. Any meet like the few meets they had would have been just normal and same to him. Pamela decided to turn that around now. She knew he was with a person somewhere, not that she was into tit for tat regarding the knives on the soles of the feet thing, she summoned the blackness character to visit him Pamela alone knew exactly from where and what to do and more importantly how, that's what she thought although she hadn't known it. Jean could have guessed that she knew. Oh, she didn't want to harm Judd or who he was with, she just wanted to freeze him. But just before, she had Judd consume that he was with. That Judd was with was angered, but there would be nothing they could do from that day on. Judd and his existence, whoever he met would be new each time. He would think only that it had all caught up with him, the boring nothingness. The fact was, she 'summoned' nothing for him, This Pamela, the Pamela who knew Jean and whose aunt was Lady Broadley whose birth Christian name was Euphoria, was quite capable of dealing with this by herself. His meets from now would always be same, not same as. Every time he was near where Pamela lived, or with each new experience, if he had them at all, he would become burdened, by how he had lost Pamela by his own deliverance and actions. His own life now returned to normality, and Pamela's, as she did not want him. 'Storm Judd' never would be anything, she didn't need to summon darkness even if the storm had persisted, which it did not. Judd had proven himself not even to be compared to the tail end of the ultimate of miniscule drizzles, and throughout their alone existences, they's be grateful to mental health services, for as long as they could remember, though oblivious as would others be, to their fates, or their destinies, within their new individual fates. The only recovery they would know, would be, is that they shall know of others, whilst only they can, and neither shall they hear or be heard.

Because most Judd favoured often were likely to have been illiterate anyway, they'd never know why he behaved or did not, as he did. And by the time they found out, they'd be frozen in the past of Pamela, frozen in ice and time, and with any swords or weapons of any kind, or assets of any kind, or items containing mineral or minerals, metal or stone that for any moment of time, might conceal or generate heat or attract, as their actions were ill founded, then such items, to be returned from whence they originated, or can be safely applied.

Their heads and hands severed, and after removing their tongues 'totally,' their remaining carcass then to be cut into five pieces, straight down them, then across. Their blood and bodily fluids then drained, boiled, and returned to soil, yes to parts of the earth where it was heating up where it should not. Such were about to become quite cold again too. The insides of their ears to be seared with hot pokers. Most of their teeth to be removed post-mortem, and ground to fine dust whereupon the dust would be put into their mouths. Their front upper incisor tooth if in the middle to be left as it is with a space on either side and one other tooth left there, to show where they had come from. Seared poker would be applied to their brains through their eyes. None of this was to constitute as torture and as they were considered dead anyway and because it was post-mortem.

Whatever Judd would or might ever think about it, whether he liked it or not, whether happy or sad or however, Pamela did not want him or his, even as prisoners. They were now, not permitted upon his demise to wander the earth forever, and neither theirs from nor held within the ice, now much colder there. Neither could or would, they seek, or gain any credibility that good had ultimately have been achieved. And neither could they, hear or bear associations by way of rescued, saved or any joint actions and or meets, they shall not ever recover. In the event of his death, he, and they, should forfeit from revelling with others whom he'd so carefully placed there upon his or theirs. Their skulls, teeth removed, except for their two upper middle front incisors, or middle tooth if only one tooth was there. Then a gap either side and the adjacent next tooth, only one, the nearest on either side to be left. If they wore dentures, they should be put in instead, then their skulls to be placed on spike poles facing the forest as a forever respect to and of Ingagook land and the peoples, who were.

She could hear the rain; it sounded like a trickling stream in a bluebell wood.

Yes, dear Pamela, as stupid as Pamela is, did forgive them.

#

Do you like that chocolate cake Pamela, Jean asked? 'It was shop bought she told her; Pamela said it was delicious. A double layer cake, moist with cream through the centre of the two layers. The fact was that Jean had made the cake herself, but just didn't want to say, she'd been an expert at cake-making for many years. It was a slightly unusual cake for Jean, both appearance wise and flavour wise, because although a chocolate cake, the top had not a vanilla cream that was on the lower sponge layer, but a light creamy chocolate fondant cream. Then it was dotted with a few pieces of candied green angelica that she had sent from France. All exactly and precisely trimmed to the same size, of no more than a quarter of an inch, there were none shorter and none longer. What had happened, was that on the same very normal but busy day, when Pamela returned from visiting Lady Broadley, she'd called in at her local supermarket, where she'd purchased the washing up liquid. Later that day, her phone rang, it was a person from the supermarket, he asked her name, she said, who are you and why do you want to know that please? He said he was from the supermarket and said, you bought a raffle ticket, yes? She remembered that she had bought a raffle ticket from there. He said, "congratulations, you won the raffle." Thinking that she might have won a bottle of cordial or something, she didn't know until he told her "you won the hamper, can you come on in now/" She explained that she was exhausted but that she had a medical appointment the following day and asked if she could call in then, he said, yes, and asked her what time would she come, she told him either at 09.00AM and said, 'what do you prefer, then, or after 09.30AM?" He said, "ok see you then."

The next day, she went to have a flu jab and then nervously, because she didn't actually want to win the hamper, she'd only bought the ticket to be supportive because she liked the shop. She wanted to ask if they could do the raffle again or give it to a charity, but when she saw the effort that had gone to, she was too overwhelmed and embarrassed to say a word even. Plus, she'd also done her shopping the day before. I was a lovely hamper and the items all placed so beautifully in a wicker basket tray, then covered by a see-through piece of plastic wrapping, the basket dressed and with then a thick blue band around it and the whole thing then with a huge light blue ribbon on top. She must have been in the shop an hour almost as they wondered how she could get it home; they eventually tied it to her shopping trolley. They did some photos with some of the staff, "to show that the prize had been won, should anyone ask." When she got back to her home, it was quite a walk from the shop and she felt as though she was blushing all the way back and especially with a bright red floppy felt fisherman's hat on, tied under the chin because of odd winds. When she walked into the front door of the premises, a neighbour was remarking that some letters had been mis-delivered, "they were addressed to the church she said, it's so unusual." Pamela asked, "do you use alcohol." Her neighbour said yes, then Pamela pointed to the hamper and said would you like that. There was a large bottle of something alcoholic, a celebratory type of drink. She gave that to her neighbour and asked if they were going to the church to correctly deliver their mis-routed mail. The neighbour, looked at the hamper and said, "you should do it," Pamela asked, "oh please, can you do it," but no, the neighbour again said, "no you should do it." She popped her shopping inside the door of her flat and walked along to the church that was in the same street where she lived. She hadn't been inside the church hall for a few years and was very impressed walking around it, at its size and scale and the beautiful windows and the plants in the tended small garden type areas, rather like a castle with a very narrow small moat, where the moat would be the garden and the entrance to the main door where no plants were obviously, might be like a drawbridge descriptively. It all seemed quite shut, there was a car near the door of the church that had the rear door open wide, there were many boxes on the back seat, but no-ne around at all. She walked the whole length of the church and around to the back of the church, there were some private residences attached to it and at the far end a charity had a base there. She also saw at greater detail the scale of the carpark behind the premises that had become vacant, she was for that moment in awe but couldn't focus on that too much because of personal reasons, it would have made her feel sad.

She stood next to the charity premises and squinted to see whether there were any opening times, thinking that really it wouldn't matter if she gave it to them. There were none that she could see properly. She looked to her left at the length of the church which had been modelled in the early 1800's on Tintern Abbey after all, it was "unified by a single main roof and lit from a tall clerestory running the whole length of the church," itself, there were three pointed sets of double doors along that wall that she'd counted, to show the length of it. She started up and through the clerestory she could see a lightbulb on, only one solitary normal lightbulb on a cord. She said to herself, there must be someone in there and with her shopping trolley walked back. This time there was a man by the car, he walked in the direction toward the main closed door of the church, at least it looked closed, as did they all, she never checked them because she was in awe anyway, before she even saw the other places, the plants would have done that for her, however few, because she knew their impact for helping bees and others and all generally in a wider context, however quaint it could seem. He was a bury chap with what sounded to her as though it had a hint of Gloucestershire about it. She asked, are you involved at the church somehow, his hands looked dusty as though he may have been doing building work or certain that he had been or was a very hard-working person, not that such are necessarily always a great guide of such, he might have been doing heavy work that day or recently, or it could have been from handling the dusty looking boxes. I've been helping out a bit, he said. She thought nothing, but inside smiled, thinking 'well, I'll not comment on that, though I'm grateful that you have and do.' Pamela said, I wondered whether you could use these and pointed to the hamper, and then said also I have some mail for you, or certainly to be handed directly into to the church premises. It wasn't that she did not trust him, on the contrary, she wouldn't have minded leaving the hamper with him, but oh no, certainly not their mail and not at all because she didn't trust, it was how she always had been. He said to Pamela, 'maybe the vicar would like to accept these himself, hang on, I'll go and get him. As she stood there, she recalled an occasion when she went into that church hall and was sitting down listening to their service. That door he went into slammed shut mid-way through the service, of its own accord that she was embarrassed to be there. She was thinking, how could I have slammed shut then with such a velocity, if it remains closed now and if there was no-one that she saw that day, not from where she sat, and she was quite astute, holding it open? It was all a little odd to dear Pamela, the door opened, and the vicar walked through the door, that this time stayed open, she didn't see his foot holding it open and he couldn't have picked the hamper up from the shopping trolley as she loosened the ties, if it had been holding the door open? She said to him that she had won the local supermarket raffle and asked, 'can you use these, pointing to the neatly wrapped He thanked her, and she told him that the only thing removed from it was a bottle of alcohol that she'd given to a neighbour. Although looking at him, she noticed his teeth as he smiled, she wasn't sure whether he was thinking that she'd removed the alcohol for herself, hence the smile in that way, but she was glad to see what she thought was his humour. His attire, a black suit garment with white collar was spotlessly clean, she was a stickler for that, certainly impressed by it. His hair smart and a little whiter than before whereas before it looked more gray tones, it had been some years, but he somehow looked healthier, taller, and less stressed, despite his deep faith and commitment than before. He asked in those so brief moments, "how are you," Just before she'd walked close to the door, walking along the length outside, the church bells had started, so it must have been almost midday and they were still ringing as he took the parcel and their mail, that could demonstrate how brief a moment it was. She replied, "not too bad thanks." It was all just very normal; he was still smiling. She asked, "how are you, and said his Christian name and addressed him too, formerly, he said, "ok," and walked back into the church, the church doors closed and se walked back to her home.

Jean asked, 'how was Lady Broadley when you visited her,' she said, 'there was rainwater gushing from a blocked unfixed gutter right by the entrance to the GP Practice where she got a flu jab, there were holes in the ceiling at the supermarket and three buckets on the floor there.' She then mentioned the washing-up that had to be done at her aunts, and that she was grateful to have done shopping before because of the washing up liquid situation and to be able to do the washing-up in a sink. Jean smiled and looked at the angelica on the cake and said to her, "a little bit goes a long way,"

Pamela suddenly remembered that years earlier, a person had said something to her, though she'd never met Jon, or Jean as she is now, she thought it was an odd coincidence again that Jean might know about that or, say something quite so similar. It was when Jean said, 'as sure as chicken's is chicken's, and hen's is hens,' and eggs are eggs, some bells will never stop chiming.' Pamela then asked Jean if she'd heard anything about something he'd been involved in and some folk from way back, for some reason she'd thought her name was 'Ditty Dotty,' or something like that, although she didn't say that to Jean, in fact she wasn't exactly certain herself if she recalled anyone saying that particular name, but it seemed to be on her mind, like as though chalked or etched somehow, Jean responded by saying 'no, I haven't checked,' then Pamela, just as she was leaving, stopped and stared at Jean, it was one of those rare indescribable moments that you sometimes had with Jon, though it was the first time with Jon, as Jean, a moment so unusual in its absoluteness, where you don't know whether to turn left or right or exactly what to do, or even what to think. Jean had her reading glasses on and was writing something on some papers that were on her lap. She didn't even look up, or peer over the top of the glasses, at all. Jean asked, "anything wrong dear," Pamela couldn't move or even flinch, she then moved her head from side to side as though saying no, in disbelief, it was one of those Deja vu moments, then she breathed in deeply and as she breathed out, turned her head back to its normal position, she regained her breath and said to Jean, 'nice brooch.' Jean said, 'thank you, hope to see you again soon.'

Of course, on the table and Pamela didn't see it was a document stamp, neither would it be too long before Pamela was back there at Jean's, the following day in fact. The base of the document stamp was shaped like the base of a pyramid, so just a small square. Jean knew that if any man, she didn't know of Judd, because of Pamelas insight by birth, ever positioned themselves as a rocket launcher near her, presently they'd only ever be somewhere behind her, the only people they would hit, would be those around her as the rockets fired over the top, they'd always only ever be nothing more that critters trying to scratch at the back door, though first whilst scrambling and clambering against the brickwork, they'd have to actually first locate the entrance. That was something, anyone, and because of the circumstances surrounding her birth, not the circumstances of, prior to her surgery, was never going to achieve, and by the time that happened, it would not be worth the wrong type trying. How much of how Pamela turned out could be attributed, as with anyone, to those circumstances regarding her birth, and had the percentages, created something within her, or those around her, percentages that Judd may have been understanding of, had he known, did he feel it? At first maybe, but wasn't it all somehow about survival anyway, but some hurdles just kept getting in the way of what could have become their own possibilities, certainly then. Was that survival now, somehow part of a peculiar possibly quite imaginary elixir now with Judd, on his search, or had his confidence sent him to new climbs and adventures, now with tools and possibly better reasons to continue. And so, the biggest help, 'or failure,' may be possibly Pamela's surgery itself? When for example, she became then, like a 'normal' woman, was there anything special or unusual about Pamela's visions, were they just not being utilised. It would be a few years after, or a couple, that she would remember a photo of herself she'd sent to a former colleague Stan, it was a shame that at this time she had forgotten that. Just as she felt normal, she was, could anyone suggest had she been used properly? Did, or could the other person who'd been on that boat realise? Was she waiting around, or helping Pamela really, or hoping that dear Pamela might drop somewhere a handbag she could just happen to be near with dear Judd, should after Pamela's surgery, Pamela be as some other women were, or had been suggested to be. There was no coming back. She was ready now. And besides, unbeknown to even dear Pamela, one of the incognito workforce personnel 'of a kind,' associated to dear Pamela, had met Judd very recently, and had purposely discovered his first. As for darling Pamela, in her quiet and so peculiar way, she was just carrying on for now, obliviously, tending to her somewhat, what had actually become for her, a normal lifestyle. She presumed that Judd had been lost in a desert somewhere, in the brightest sunlight, you could say he had and very much so, not that his feet touched any sand. Pamela, thoughtfully, always had a focus on the wonderful trees. She couldn't help being who she was, neither could she allow herself to be repeatedly punished by Judd emotionally, because of how and what or who she was, he would never understand, because they never spent long enough together to get to know each other. She did know though, that had she behaved any differently to how she was behaving, or dealing with matters, that it would have been an insult to her feelings regarding the very fact that they'd ever actually met at all. Darling, darling, idiotic, stupid Pamela, she believed that he couldn't bow his head down in shame that far if even he tried, but neither was it any longer, actually as though he had that as an option, or could. There was another thought, that if Judd had based his survival on trusting Pamela, should there be only two options when a vaccine is found, those being take it, or perish 'as in die.' If Pamela is unhappy with certain things, where does that place those, he slept with? With news even if in continual visions most horrible for Pamela, somehow, that as all the hopes even of the quirkiest kind somehow became located and painfully pulled, from every possible recess of your thinking ability, then became smashed and shattered into a thousand pieces and what had been your own dreams became no longer a cherished option, yes that very day would for Pamela signal the final goodbye. She thought, whatever was going to be the point, if they just keep on doing it and by doing so, it basically, with ignorance and deceit and greed, and abuse at its helm, disguised by bravado in whatever guise by.Judd, simply destroys what fragments remained of Pamela's soul. To have been so downtrodden to fear thinking 'fragments,' should it pave the way for more. It no longer mattered. Any notion that in a more 'natural world,' other than that she'd been in, whereby it could have been considered by some that her meeting Judd was somehow a means for her to 'let off steam,' as she waited for surgery, was she'd have thought 'utterly disgusting? They'd have had absolutely no compunction as to what she went through, and neither she, then of the damage that he could have caused to her, damage that could have potentially killed her during surgery, or caused serious complications affecting the rest of her life after, thankfully that had been explained to her by medical professionals in September. Thankfully, Pamela had practiced yoga for many years.

Pamela slept and then awoke, her neck felt very stiffened, it caused her to think again sadly of blood pooling. She checked that website though and there was a message, a lovely message from a so handsome man, so they were coming, now and then anyway. He wanted to meet her within the hour, but she told him no. It had been too how Judd often secured meets this she knew, so it was easy for her to realise how he would have been at those moments and how such availability would have then worked so well for him, it did put her off though. Whether she met him in the future or not did not matter anymore, it somehow served as a tonic to her, even though she did not, maybe that was how Judd operated, although he would never not turn up, he'd never miss those opportunities ever. Her thought after went from 'hooray,' to 'time to get the bunting out. 'In her mind again, yet again, Judd was 'permanently' gone?

Pamela mentioned to that guy she was in a queue for an operation, and that she didn't want to risk harming medical staff by taking odd risks now. He asked if she would 'add him,' she wasn't sure what he meant, he meant add to list of contacts, but then he replied and said, "I added you." As very sweet as the gesture was, she now knew slightly better, or had become even more selective than she even ever had believed or thought she could ever have been before.

The very next day though, Pamela arrived at Jean's place, Jean hadn't even had time to shave but it didn't bother her, and neither was Jean so concerned, only about why she'd needed to come again so soon, it was not really like her at all. Jean said why are you all a dither and your hair, what have you done to your hair, or what haven't you done, she said, sit down, Pamela looked quite flustered. She said it's a long story Jean, but I'd been seeing a man, but we stopped seeing each other, well, we did continue but not in a normal way. Jean didn't know exactly what she meant but was by then making a hot drink for them both. She then explained that in a dream the evening before, she had seen some of her aunts, her mother was there too, briefly in the dream, but only from a distance and not directly involved, the aunts though were all from her father's side of the family. She said that one of her aunts was a feisty woman and not to be argued with at all and that she had confronted Judd, the man she'd met. She said it was unusual because although I had a good relationship with my aunts, there was an aloofness and a distance sometimes, unlike the night before where the presence was in defence of Pamela, to Judd. It cornered him into a very tight spot where he was forced to acknowledge the harm he had been causing. Then almost immediately after, she saw Judd fly off with one of the people she'd seen him with before, they both were holding hands and almost nymph-like and winged, as though in the throes of love, or infatuated, but not bothered. They looked happy, she told Jean, and seemed unperturbed by that. I had put some things in place, she said, but in the dream myself and my aunts and some other members of my family all linked arms over the smoke from a fire, a fire that was not burning, she said. Pamela had presumed that it had been more indicative that there once had been a fire there. Then we all said, "they cannot be blamed for battles they had to fight to keep them there." Then my aunts were all happy, we all were. Then Pamela said, 'it will be important to secure that wherever they are or wherever from that they all had good and proper burials, she said. Then in the dream, I was standing in front of what looked like a large-heavier than usual metal manhole cover that had what was almost like a kind of turnkey pole attached to it, that was some four feet in length, I had to push and even pull it around, such was the weight and thickness of the cover that so slowly turned. It was so heavy she explained, but there was no doubt as to whether, or not I could move it, it was strange she said. Once the lid released, the cover itself was maybe some four feet in diameter and the lid that secured it was maybe some seven inches thick. Then from inside it came a really big hairy creature, dark haired and you could see no skin at all and the hair was so very thick, possibly three inches long, what came from the hole was the width of the hole itself, though he seemed to have no difficulty pulling himself up, no difficulty at all she said, and climbing out of the hole where he stood in front of Pamela with huge horns and very shiny clean feet though they were hooves, very shiny though and not dirty at all she said, he looked so spik and span really, it was as though he knew me she tod Jean. He was really happy to see Pamela again. He dusted his hooves off and just stood there happy. "I wasn't exactly sure what to do," she said, and you know I am not exactly personally partial to hairy types, or certainly not when they are that hairy. He looked so impressive and clean it was amazing, she explained. She said, the only way I could explain it would be if we were watching a theatrical performance, he'd be like a dancer, but way taller and real horns and you could hear him breathing as though he was hungry? He then said to Pamela, 'they are all ok anyway, you needn't have bothered.' He was referring to those who'd died, she knew this immediately, the Pamela laughed so much. When they flew off, I didn't let them run away with anything, she said, yes, I let them believe they did, because it's how Judd is. Let's see how things are tomorrow, it's Wednesday she said, now quite as though alarmed, 'it is Wednesday isn't it Jean,' she asked. I did check twice, really, I did. Jean, now seemingly astonished, said, "yes, it's Wednesday my dear." But I don't care for Judd anymore, said Pamela. I don't want what I see of him, and yes, he'll fly off like he's a sprite or nymph, but I know he's nothing more than a too challenged individual she said, a person with problems. I feel as though he will keep returning to my thought and doing this, I do not want to allow it to continue, I must set a trap for him, she said; a trap that would keep him away from me. She stayed at Jean's for the remainder of an hour, and they agreed that they may meet again on Thursday, if Pamela needed or wanted to, and that she would contact Jean by phone beforehand.

#

The Snare

Pamela wanted, not decided to set a trap for him, to keep hm away from her. She imagined it could be financial, but then imagined garlands of flowers being placed around an about her own neck. Believing it could all mean something 'strategic,' and because she was not worried, she permitted that part of it. She visualised a circle, as wide as the utility access hole thing had been, open, as though in the air, before her eyes, it was also very similar indeed in a way, to that seen above the trees, by those who discovered the skull of Juk so very long before. The circle then became flat, then Pamela could see or imagined herself seated there in a nice seat, the type of seat that swivels around. Then a neighbour, who the night before had said good evening to her when Pamela returned from where Jean lived, seemed to cause an interference, it wasn't a bad thing, although it was unsettling for dear Pamela, because Pamela was trying to focus without distractions of any kind. It was sad, but it was how Pamela was, for her, it was not important that anyone should guess what might be going on for her, and because Pamela also knew, not that her neighbour would have, that some, especially if Judd had been an example, could manipulate, and how some might, just because they decide they want to, however innocent such interventions may appear to be. Basically, Pamela was more private lifestyle- wise, and had also relocated for very specific reasons on more than one occasion, she certainly did not feel that she needed to give any explanation on that, not to anyone. Pamela blocked that person out of her vision. Then, from some thirty feet away, she heard two very quick bursts of what sounded like a flute or a piccolo, on right to her but ahead of her and after her neighbour had gone, though way behind and out of view or sound by that person who'd driven off by then anyway. It turned out to be a warning to Pamela, though Judd would not have heard it, he'd of course flown away and was nowhere to be seen at that point. Judd though, certainly by now, was apprehensively very much waiting though, for any form of a trap that dear Pamela might set. But, just as Pamela was Pamela, Pamela knew only too well, Judd, was Judd. Pamela was then undecided as to exactly what to do, she thanked the piccolo player though.

When the hairy character had been released from beneath the ground, he seemed to mirror everything Pamela did for a while, she thought it was strange and even in fun tested it, she raised her hands above her head and swayed from side to side, and sure enough, without a murmur, it copied her. It wasn't playing a game, it just did it. In fact, although Pamela did not have that image, his movements were so precise in copying that she just couldn't understand it at all, or why. It was like a mirrored image, she was though wondering, now thinking about the weight of the cover and how much effort she had to use to turn it, and why was it there at all, now, what had she done? But it wasn't as though there was a sign on it saying, 'don't touch,' to her it seemed as though she was somehow meant to, or she really would not have considered it. She decided to let that character play and entertain itself somehow, because she wasn't certain how to respond or react. Then, as another surprise, who should go and sit in the seat that Pamela had been sitting in, the swivel seat, of course, Judd. He sat in that seat with one leg on top of the other so casually, just as he had in the photo looking at the sea wearing the blue boating shoes, but this time, he had a snappy pale grey suit on. He looked very smart; he was totally unaware that Pamela could see him. Whereas in the photo on the hotel balcony, the view of him was the left side of his profile, though from within three feet away, with him looking at the sea, this time, the image was same, but being viewed to the right side of him, him was staring straight ahead, so to the far right of Pamela. Had he been looking at a boat on a sea for example, it would have been the far right of Pamela who was observing him, and he, so very focused on that boat, just as when he would put sex before anything priority-wise, he did not see Pamela. He wasn't meant to. Of course, Pamela wanted to confront him herself, but he looked so accomplished, she could not. The hairy character with horns had been seen by Pamela going into and welcomed by a party on her far right. Judd was now watching that party on the swivel seat; Pamela had sat in.

Then she realised something, and she knew that he was aware, aware that something was not exactly right, as though a bounty-hunter had found a predator's lair, or was that delicious part to become realised later, considerably later by her, although, and naturally, 'pardon the pun', she may have eventually considered, he couldn't think of Pamela because he was too busy watching the fun. Did she put that on ice and look ahead? He was anxious though, very anxious. Pamela knew it, and more-so, that because of what usually happened around Wednesdays, and neither that it would be the first not the last time, that too, it would be a few days at least, before he re-surfaced or appeared again. She wondered about the time-machine thing but as nice as it was, her own opinion was that this required something completely unreservedly tamper- proof.

#

Jean's friend 'Bernadette,' had mentioned in a telephone chat to her that it could be exciting for them to try to go for a day out somewhere and to maybe visit a cemetery even, where it could be quiet, maybe Jean sensed that Pamela had been struggling recently or that she had become distanced, so she mentioned it as a gesture to her at one of their meets, Pamela though didn't give it a thought, her friend had mentioned a Mausoleum and because of its interest as in how it was constructed, it struck a chord within Jean somehow, not that it was in any way cloak and dagger stuff, or that it necessarily was caped in mystery, so certainly not achieving partner–in–crime accreditation, as it was commissioned and all 'in kind,' and probably she though more 'tongue in cheek,' that something dastardly set out to achieve ultimately any harm at all. But somehow, just because of what seemed to Jean, of a pure design integrity and even because of ancestry personal, worthy of at least a glance positive, an homage of a kind, for the sheer consideration of it's ideal and construction. A few days after, and unplanned, it was very early, the local shop had only just opened for the day, so it was 07.30AM. Pamela saw bags of nuts and seeds in the shop, one of them was quite a large bag, and some bread rolls that had multi-grain on top of them, she quite liked those, plain, nothing on them, sometimes with feta cheese, or rarely, a delicious tomato with a squirt of tomato puree too, but to have with water only. Yes, she'd decided right then and there, to pay a visit to the Chaltentnar Cemetery, she'd never been in the cemetery at that time before and didn't know whether it would be open yet, but it would take her twenty minutes to get there anyway. She didn't have her reading glasses that day, she'd had to squint so terribly that it embarrassed her should anyone have noticed, not that they would have, to read the bag of seeds information in case they were salted or flavoured, that they were not, she'd forgotten to bring them, so she couldn't read the instructions at the bus stop, neither did she think, 'well only certain buses go that way and there weren't , that many and there were no turn-offs where buses go in different directions like crossroads, that she could think of, so I could get on any bus presumably?' It was a tough trudge but eventually she arrived at the cemetery. The particular cemetery was opened in the mid 1800's and has an impressive gatehouse at the main entrance, then the whole place is fenced with such tall black gloss painted metal railings around. Then, where there are residences, outside the cemetery along the far side, tall walls had been built in between their properties and the railings, she was very interested in those and that they were nicely almost slightly angled walls, they'd been built that way deliberately although correctly proportioned on either side, she thought it was stunning although stayed a few meters away from them, just to appreciate them, the walls are made of old red stock bricks and had some ivy growing on parts of them, but you could still see that the brickwork although slightly naturally weathered was quite intact. Pamela was surprised that permission to build such tall walls would have been possible, or maybe, it was just where she'd re-discovered another nature wonderland. It was just getting light as she walked through the main gate, trees on either side, so tall, looked as though they went on forever, the sky was just brightening up from a red glow, apart from woodlands and forests and seas and oceans, Pamela was again in her element. If there were bees, she was just 'gone,' there was no other word for it. Uncertain as to what way to go, whether to take a left turn or right, or whether to walk through the middle and take one of the paths on either side, as they all had the potential to arrive at the same place, it is a big cemetery, she decided to take the middle path. Sure, some of it was overgrown in places but, it looked fine too and it complemented the structures beautifully. A few people wandered along the path ad a few joggers passed her, but she was listening and wondering what to do and where to actually go, it was as though although she was content, and she appreciated where she was, there was still a feeling of knowing exactly where she was, as lovely as she could believe it presented in a picturesque way, she knew that she must be totally respectful, she looked at the names and dates on some of the tombs and plots and felt sad.

Her being there could not have been more than it had ever been when in a cemetery, and that was do things that proved or demonstrated respect and not to alarm of think to consider any actions that might cause any distress at all. To consider it at all, would have been the farthest thing from her mind or her thinking processes. Never, never, never could she. Some of the grass was shorter and when she ventured onto a path to the left, she noticed that in some places the grass was getting longer, possibly twelve inches tall in some areas, and taller. Daylight kind of happened as the sky brightened and there were no traces of red in the sky at all, it had become a pale blue that seemed to complement the pink sweet pea flowers that were growing nicely across the far-right side of the cemetery, not tall or bushy, just now and again, Pamela would think, "how lovely is that' when she saw them, and how beautiful for the bees, she most definitely thought. She did bend down, although it was more of a bow, to smell the fragrance of a sweet pea flower, but was also thinking that she did not want to take. She glanced her nose just across the top of a flower that she held in between a couple of fingers and so not to dislodge it at all, and said to herself, 'oh my goodness,' she was so humbled by it all. Some birds ran quickly across her path just in front, as though as day broke, their playfulness too was being shown. She pulled from her shopping trolley the bag of seeds and started scattering them in places where she thought birds might require them. Then a squirrel came, it was so playful, it jumped onto a tree right before her and looked back as though to say, 'can't catch me,' Pamela smiled and thought, 'how cheeky,' the squirrel stopped and gripped the bark of the tree trunk and stared back at her, he placed some nuts and a piece of bread into a place on the tree where he could get to easily. A while after, just scattering a few seeds here and there, she stopped and gazed at a Mausoleum, she'd been there before but had never noticed it, it was to her, almost as though it suddenly appeared from no-where. There was a person standing by it, right next to it in fact. She said to Pamela, "no gain without pain," then she ran off, she was dressed in a tracksuit and had been exercising. Pamela smiled, and was surprised too, although there was no reason to be. It had seemed peculiar to Pamela coincidentally, that although there had been just a few people on the main central path, she hadn't noticed any that far in, but it would have possibly seemed as strange to that person, she thought, that Pamela might have been there at that time and had stopped immediately in front of the tomb, Pamela even wondered whether the person had seen that Pamala possibly looked astonished, not that such a structure was there at all, why not, but that Pamela was impressed by it, though she could not understand why? It was of course the mausoleum that her friend had referred to. It genuinely looked as though it had just landed there. Pamela walked around it and sat in front of it, put some food out for some squirrels and scattered the remainder of the nuts, not so near to it, but reasonably close to it, four or five meters away from it. She looked at the markings on it, and though some things a while, she felt as though, she was meant somehow to be there at that precise moment in time, and that what she did there, was, although respectful to the inhabitants of the tomb undoubtedly, she paid her respects. She looked and listened, the sounds of birds heard in other parts of the cemetery, she could not hear them there, only the sound of a slight breeze, the sound of crickets that she giggled quietly to, that she'd heard and that evoked such great memories of childhood for her, she could neither hear them there either, it was a structure on a huge marble platform anyway, so the grass would not have been sufficient for crickets there. Pamela removed her coat and sat on a step by the mausoleum just for a moment. Then she put her coat over the handle of her trolley, and went to walk quietly peacefully further, it had been almost ritualistic she thought, though she had no idea why, she instead thought of it only as respecting. The silence of it all and the almost mystique, was broken then as the trolley wheel accidentally went in another direction and scraped so hard along the ground, yes only for a few seconds, but it seemed so loud, she felt so embarrassed, but also was aware that it would never have been deliberate, not ever, not in a million years would it have been, not in ten million or more, that was how strongly Pamela believed this, and that that would be disrespectful. She went along a few other paths, just to honour those in a way, who had passed, and then thought that she'd like to go to the mausoleum again before heading back to her home. When she arrived back at the tomb again, she had to take a photo of it, because it was as though it had changed colour somehow? The sky was blue, but it was as though it had changed colour to shades of green, though nothing at all unnatural about it, but it to Pamela looked as if it just didn't look like the same grey granite type of stone as it had been, Pamela propped her camera on a tree and did three photos of herself there too. and did a few photos of herself standing and sitting next to the mausoleum, she had on a short cotton dress of brown and black and white ornate looking large diamond patterns that had a thin white lace collar and just plain shoes. She hadn't considered either personal significance in them, or the photos then, or whether there was any at all? As she walked away from it, having said thank you, she looked back and t it, to briefly smile, the person who had been standing in front of it when she arrived, was gently joggling back along the path to it again, Pamela smiled ever so softly.

When she got home, her fairy brooch had arrived, she put it on herself and went into the bathroom to look at it, on the television that had been switched on, there had been a news article about terracotta soldiers, she thought immediately that there must be something quite strange happening to her, because she was certain that she saw a green sparkle in the eye of one of them. Very certain. The mausoleum, many believe certainly does house or may even be, a time-machine, some often spoke of time travel, and of its Egyptology inspirations, maybe Pamela didn't know that though? So thankfully neither would she have taken from, attempted to borrow, or more to the point, intrude upon.

Pamela noticed when the hairy character walked into the party, it was as though it was a warrior returning, welcomed, gleaming and bright, she really thought that was very impressive and in a nice way too. That it really seemed to appreciate her so much too, as if it had waited for ages and ages to do only that, and for that very moment, Pamela knew too well how sincere it was in that too at that moment, so much that at that point, she did not need to give it a second thought at all. Okay, she did not know what it was, but it looked kind, that was for Pamela the main thing. Things dramatically changed though, withing only a few moments, she saw it staring at her from behind metal bars, caged, staring through directly at only her, despairingly, and Judd, still in that seat and watching that very party. As crazy as it may sound, Pamela didn't wonder, she hoped then, that if maybe an ancestor of 'her own,' had come to her, through those visions she had of Judd with that amulet that day. That somehow deeds were to be placed, and that amulet, a key, the key, she said to herself, then she said, no it could not be? She presumed too, that a likeness, being that hairy character, she'd released by her, and 'that she'd have seen it,' and that there were similarities.

Pamela like Judd, and that character, although very possibly a re-creation for her in different ways. The charm and suaveness, and perfection and smartness appealed to her intellect. She could not go back in time and present the deeds to Judds own ancestors that Judd had left that day, so they would pull him to them. But she did see then, ice cracking before her eyes, so much that Judd could not be seen through it, she saw Judd then, still seated enveloped in ice, it became like a globe of ice and he still in that same position unable to move, in the middle of it, still as though touching his chin too, he looked so proud of himself, it made Pamela very happy. The character that stared at her from behind bars, and those it was with at that party, although she imagined that had been made a captive alone, she moulded too, though it did not look like ice there. She moulded it big enough, or small enough, just to be able to place them where they'd come from. Then she put the screwcap back on and with so much might, pushed it closed again. She wasn't sure whether the whole party were put down there or just the hairy character alone had been put back down there but certainly him. It was as though by default she thought, he seemed to find himself being misled as though natural for him. As for Judd, the ice-ball and he inside it, appeared as though it moved into the sky where it became smaller and smaller until it seemed to almost vanish. Then the question for Pamela became, 'what of those deeds'?

She knew that if the ice Judd was in had gone into the clouds, that there might be a risk that it could melt into water vapour somehow, this would not be good, because she knew it just wouldn't, not if her plan was to be rid of Judd, he could re-appear as and whenever it rained. Not such a good thing for dear Pamela, because she did not want him to taint those lovely experiences for her too. Instead, she sent him then to way beyond the Ingagook Mountainous land, as if his head on a stake was never to have been quite enough, she wanted to achieve a happy ending too. She did love him after all or believed she did very much. She sent him within that ice form to a place where the temperature had been measured at minus 133.6 degrees Fahrenheit. From where his love, for Pamela, could be a beacon for all to shine forever. And from where her love for nature could reciprocate and always guarantee him, not so much as the centre of attention, but certainly a player. It would give him the attention he deserved and there would be no coming back. She felt that he was kicking the ice now, inside that ice cell, and then inside a wilderness of far colder ice, the difference this time was, that of course she was watching him, for a while, it was very sad for Pamela. Was lovely Pamela smiling though, as he always had and certainly was not now? 'Kick as much as you like, she thought, kick as much as you damn well like.' Knowing that whilst he thought he was enjoying watching his Wednesday party, soon his body would go into shock, whether it was after of before he'd suffocated horribly, she didn't actually consider, he would harm no-one ever again she thought, and certainly not Pamela, of course, Pamela knew too, that he'd flown off just before all of this, with his new found supposed lawyer friend, who by now was resemblant slightly of the ballet dancer who got flattened by the steamroller, even that helped with 'their' imagery in conceptual flights of fancy, Pamela said to that, 'see you in court babe.'

So, Pamela seized the opportunity, yes, she'd seen them fly off, like etchings lifting themselves from a piece of paper, sure it was a 'blood sport,' and yes, they'd be together now, the rat had been caught, and just as the hairy character nice shiny hooves went to that party, only to become 'snared.' No more would it be Judd snaring, and the main thing, he could not bother Pamela again, nor cause disruption, 'anywhere,' Pamela did though think that he was probably making the very most of that situation, his baggage gone, handled by dear Pamela like any baggage handler at a hotel. Maybe he had simply bedded down for winter. Now what would Pamela do with those deeds? And what were they? Deeds to what, of what and or what involving? With no idea at all, neither did it really seem to matter. It just didn't matter.

Had Pamela learned how to move from one coloured counter to another, fact, fiction, imaginary, and her desire, if there were only four. Could she prevent them from becoming overlapped, say for example, quite hypothetically obviously, if Jean was still Jon, as she had been, and say, if she was Pamela too and if Judd had been a friend of hers from years ago, Florence Breeny, and say if Florence had given Jon then, two watercolour paintings, 'The Rockery and The Garden Path,' and had given her a brass vase with a small cross imprinted on it and say for example Jean still had that. What if, the penny in Pamela's mind, only dropped when she'd sent dear youngish sometimes, 'stud Judd,' to the farthest cold regions on the planet, what if in a dream, Florence still saw Jean as Jon anyway, or vice a versa and although they lived hundreds of miles apart now, Florence appeared in a dream to Jean and touched the cross on that vase with her finger and was not harmed by it, and that Pamela saw that, she would have, if they were one and the same, and what if after as Pamela lay in her bed, her hands across her chest, the very tips of her index and forefinger of her left hand held the tip of the index finger of her right hand as though they were that very cross.

A while after, Pamela dreamed again that she was on a bike and ass he stopped off somewhere it was stolen, but parts of her anatomy in that dream had become for that brief moment, as parts of a tree. Was it that her imagination was becoming fertile, had Florence waited all these years, never or rarely contacting, politely, always courteous, and polite? Then Pamela knew as would all of Florences friends, that she had done nothing improper during that time, was it a courtship. Pamela also recalled that Jean had said, one of her close friends from way back, said to her, something so 'out of the ordinary,' when Florence accompanied her to visit that friend, that it shocked her. Not that it mattered now, one thing though, Pamela was forced to ask herself, if she was Jean too, if her surgery was life-threatening or dangerous, and if Florence said it doesn't matter to her, would she still go ahead with it. At that moment and having just woke up, she said, it would not matter, that was a mark of their friendship. It had even caused Pamela to question strangely the smile on the face of the vicar when she handed him the raffle prize that day, so genuine was it. The fact that less than an hour after that dream, she had wondered why she was being tested in this way and dismissed it all, kind of, although Jean was going to ask Florence if she wanted her to cook for her, that was already decided, chances are Florence would say no, but she felt it correct to enquire, also because less than a week earlier, Florence had mentioned that she was 'now on microwave meals.' And because Jean hadn't considered Florence to be the serenading type anyway, and certainly not for that long. When thinking about it all, she that her feelings might carry well and somewhat wholesomely, if it was possible, with the season to come. One of the amazing things about fact, is that it is, knowing what your fact is, that can be important Pamela attempted to tell herself. Hearing a phone beep when you know there is not a phone on that side of the room for example, because your phone was directly in front of you on the table, and it did not beep. Understanding biology today was paramount on Pamela's mind too. She was also sad, because she'd heard that day that dozens of mummified penguins albeit from five thousand years ago had been found in the same area as ice was melting, where she'd sent dear darling Judd to, though they were found the day before, so maybe it was to all become a hopeful conclusion somehow after all. She'd not thought of cryogenics, the thought that even by what had happened, she might have been doing him a favour really crunched her peanut hard, so she did hope though that the ice would not continue to melt, mainly because, she really didn't want to see him floating along any stream near to her again, the thought of it to dear Pamela had seemed an almost crucifying thought, so we can only pray and hope too, for the actual best, at any time. She was feeling love, and it was important to her in a way, that if it was personal that whoever she might reciprocate that to too, unless generally, had a name and if possible, even if they never told her it, a date of birth. So, who at the moment was it, Florence, Florence, or Judd, it for her certainly couldn't be both? Would there in her mind be any doubt really, or was she fantasizing? Would things change dramatically after her surgery, she'd received acknowledgement of the appointment she'd had in September less than twenty-four hours earlier, and confirmation in that document that surgery will happen as soon as it is possible to do it. She was thankful that checks would have been conducted to gain an understanding as to levels of potential risk factors, there were a few, how would it fair, not that she would joke about it at all, 'altar, hence her avoiding Judd more. Potential aisle, slab, or just thankfully, the operating table. Would there be some, somewhere, who wanted neither, and if so, what might their reasons be? If ultimately, it kept her single and productive and free of sexual activities, associated risk and even at her age, becoming hurt by it, were there some who did not feel she could handle this? But what about what she wanted, whether it involved sex, marriage, or whatever, however? True, she wasn't sure what she wanted now, not that there were choice options there, apart from her imaginary ones. She did like clothes though and looked forward to a day when she could just put clothes on that she wanted to wear without hiding, or however accomplished she'd become at it, without knowing that she was not quite the ticket really, as she always knew she was. Back then, it was "it's not as though anyone is going to get that close, I'm always busy anyway." First though, it was going to be an inevitable further wait and whether those she knew or thought of, were close by her or not, she was still alone at her home every day, apart from her piccolo player and the likes of and the forestry and other amazements. Did any of those who might wonder whether the surgery could lead her to things objectionable, ever consider whether she might do things better after? Had some already decided how she was going to be, without even asking her? Based on what? What was there 'anywhere' in her existence, that might cause them to imagine that? Were they hoping that if they say, or thought it of her enough, that she may as well do it anyway, because the result surely would be the same? Some were referring to her as a whore when she couldn't have sex, and none of them had ever seen her with a partner for that very reason. Was the greater risk therefore, not in keeping her as she was? Because she hadn't built those close nitty, so gritty sweat based and almost incestuous relationships that prior to Covid-19 and distancing, so many others had become affected by? Did some think she would just jump on the first person who came along after? No-one thought that she might just want to work with a bit less physical pain. And work for what? As a buffer for angry guys who ejaculate into jars to provide sperm that unlike Judds, points in the right direction to provide to infertile couples, so Pamela is a punchbag, for those who might accuse her before the surgery even happens. And for those who since the pandemic started Pamela had worked as a statistician to get and keep the projected death rates down and as low as possible, and who saw Judd go from what she thought she knew of him, to what he became, because she could not meet him, because too many were still obviously doing what she never could? And then making fun of her because she could not and because they were screwing up her man, maybe normality for some, but not all. Let's put that another way, they were, "keeping him 'single' and safe until after Pamela had had her surgery"? So, they actually thought dear Pamela would want to go there too? To mix with that. So, what would that become Covid-20. She did gain a greater understanding throughout it all why his Wednesday arrangements were so important to him, it wasn't about age after all, it was about abuse and total availability. They were looking out for no-one except themselves, Pamela knew that all along. So, what was their problem? The fact was, Pamela did not want to meet anyone, though she appreciated things like nice genuine smiles and quirky moments, but they with their suggestions and implications were trying to chip away at that too. Or was that still so very much 'it'? They wanted to turn Pamela into the tragic case, they knew so well. It made them seem better people in their own minds, almost as though it became a comfort within itself, to their tragic egos. But dear Pamela was, and remains oblivious to it, especially now. Had life eluded Pamela, or had she already distanced herself, and not so recently, because of enduring so much of the exact same emotional abuse, where she never seemed to quite fit in, why should she want to know, certainly now.

And now, that choice is not theirs, it's Pamela's, it's not an 'ism,' of any description, and why? Because she herself would hate that, she does not need either be told that or to with respect have it droned into her or ink-stamped on her forehead or her forearm. And yes, she may get her hair totally shaved off immediately after surgery, but neither for you, or to offend, to attract, or to run away from, or divert attention elsewhere, or because she does not fit in, or cannot 'deliver' if she alone decides that she 'wants' to, and that she is and always has been naturally so selective, shall certainly not be a problem for any of 'those.' And if Jean, should end up with Florence, neither there shall that be because, or as result of, her being forced to, and definitely not for the sake of 'the egos,' of anyone!

The flowing day, whether Judd had frozen or flown away to new heights, Pamela certainly felt as though her own better and honestly good spirit had returned, it wasn't that she felt happier, but she'd had a dream again and dreamed of red pencils, she could not understand the significance of that only that she knew they were not the pencils that were in the lacquered pencil box, now in a cupboard. Also, before she'd actually woken and for moments just after, she was thinking how she could not dislike anyone again, or have bad feeling towards them, and that women, girls and ladies men too, and as the day before even research she saw in a press report was indicating that babies were less likely now to be born with wisdom teeth and remembering seeing the size her own were after they'd been extracted, that one day, they would not require surgery, certainly not of the kind that Pamela needed and was required to have. Pamela thought to herself, that, in spite of any perceived or any actual personal accomplishments, that she wouldn't wish that on anyone, not even dear Judd, the jibes, they were kind of like having rats in your hair but then telling others whose hair might not be well-groomed that they needed to consider purchasing a comb or hairbrush. Sure, she had an impressive work accomplishment record, if reliability and determination were important to any new potential employer in the future, should she be forced to change after surgery, as nothing yet had been confirmed as to security of her position, if problems did occur during and after surgery, but she wasn't concerned about that. So, in generations to come, maybe those performing such pioneering surgery work, will always be able to move on safely and with an element of absolute pride and accomplishment. She phoned Jean that day and they had a lovely conversation just for a short while, the thing gleaned from that conversation, was that Jean's friend Florence Breeny, who she'd chatted to that day, so she told Pamela, besides everything else, very probably never had and neither would consider ever doing ice-skating anyway?

#

And just when you think it's safe to go out, as if Judd wouldn't appear again, Pamela had slept almost all day, except for one moment that must have zapped her because her thoughts were quite serious about the lawyer-like person Judd claimed to be with, and who she'd happily for him, seen him conveniently fly away with. It was a Sunday, and it was unusual to be so sleepy for a whole day for her. She'd woken up briefly at around 16.30hrs and thinking of that supposed lawyer person, she thought that for him to have flown away with that so easily it would surely depend on whether the person was a defence or prosecution lawyer, and whether a criminal lawyer or civil, and whether he would have had the nerve to lie to a lawyer, or not about his personal circumstances. Pamela then awoke at just have been 19.30hrs and was imagining that she saw Judd clinging to a thin strand of metal, it was like a very thin rod that appeared, now though, he four large feet which was unusual she thought, because he was obviously attempting to be a chameleon of a vivid green colour. She stared at the rod and imagined it becoming electrified and he vanished. She knew though that all that would have done was to make him feel somehow electrified and enthused. While Pamela slept, she dreamed of a pangolin, and thought of how they pretty much got the blame for Covid-19, those, or bats, it was suggested. The pangolin would have been slaughtered and cooked, she imagined herself climbing down the scaly steps of the pangolin's back as though saying farewell to Covid-19 then she thanked the pangolin and apologised to it should it have been cruelly slaughtered and should it not have been responsible for Covid-19 at all. Then she thought of Halloween and that people should feel safe to hang their plastic or home-made bats on dangly strings from their windows now, if they wanted to. Then almost 01.43AM if Judd didn't appear again, still 'attempting' to be a chameleon, it would be very important that she noted 'attempting,' because she thought it alarming that nothing seemed to stop him, then something far bigger appeared and not the same colour at all, it was a darker colour and not like illuminous or vivid in any way, that 'may' have been a chameleon, but Judd, he was too busy watching Pamela. Its long sticky tongue moved so fast; Judd was gone in a flash. She heard it burp, then Pamela said an oh so very quiet; 'thank you. 'She wasn't the type to make fun at something like viruses, not ever. Thinking briefly of Jenny C and how under usual circumstances, she looked the type of person or probably was, the type of person who would not give someone like Judd the time of day under usual circumstances, Pamela went and did something to something that had belonged to her father, then a while after she saw that imaginary animal that made a meal of Judd, digging into soil as though starting to and burrowing underground, Pamela thought nothing more of that. But what it left behind changed colour, it was blue with red feelers, it looked to her like a big covid-19 cell, she moved so fast with what looked like a sword, then stopped suddenly within certainly less than a centimetre of it, she tapped the top of it so lightly with the edge of that sword, it was like a large water melon, but it fell apert before her eyes, her intent was to disable it to ultimately prevent anyone from consuming or taking it into them even before they might attempt to, even if anyone had inadvertently accidentally placed it, thinking it was a lovely water melon near them. The sword was so heavy that her shoulders ached, so the last thing she needed was another challenge immediately after. Of all things, a deck of playing cards then appeared. Her father had always told her they were, 'the devils' playthings,' she never took much notice of it because she didn't use playing cards ever anyway. She shuffled the cards and tapped the pack on the table, just like she was a croupier, then dealt maybe eight or ten cards in a circular motion across the table, well, the cards flew through the air as she seemed to somehow turn them over with two fingers and look that them quickly, then flick them, they-all of that few cards landed in a circle on the table and each one landing face upward, she then said to whoever she believed was there to see them, 'take your pick,' a man appeared as if from no-where to the right of the table and put a knife straight through one of the playing cards and into the table directly in front of her, he leaned across to her, it wasn't her father, he would never use knives, but he said, "what do you think you're fracking playing with lady," then as he stood back, her eyes left the cards on the table and the handle of much of the knife that was sticking up in a card to her right, her eyes slowly moved up his body, just as her eyes reached his face, something grabbed him around his stomach, it pulled him so tightly as it gripped him and his waist immediately shrank, he stared unable to speak as his body within a second just doubled up like an overcoat thrown over an arm, he was pulled without time to think, or even a moment enough for her to respond. Had she bothered, though, she wanted to say to him, 'now you're not part of the lovely team who come to collect the recycling are you, and you are certainly not a number-cruncher,' but he was pulled away into obscurity. She did though after, think about it all to herself, now slightly perplexed, seemed, 'I know I didn't eat cheese before going to bed, because I didn't have enough to buy some, and I brushed my teeth just a while ago, I had tea because it's too early for coffee should it actually affect my metabolism, she then thought about the new lip moisturiser she'd recently purchased and licked her lips very slightly, then she said, mmmm yummy, now that was really quite tasty. Strangely though, Pamela, she knew she'd sliced to covid-19 cell into two, she also knew, maybe because however many generations back, some of her family had set up an orphanage, maybe her love, not taking from that of his own mother, was a different kind of love, guessing that it was his trust in her, that actually kept him safe possibly, in spite of all that could happen in imagination-land, that critter, that ate up that darned chameleon look-a like, yes that Judd posed as, if that rascal hadn't been so dirty where he hadn't been home or probably hadn't washed, sure he shook off the covid-19 for her to deal with, he fed that back knowing she'd be waiting, and with a sword of her own, that critter burrowed underground and it moved quickly, yes, even that sensed something was about to happen, it had to re-surface somewhere after, to basically throw up. But, you know, it didn't matter so much to Pamela, yes, he'd slept with every girl basically he could find, and guys who dressed as girls too, if they made the grade, she knew he would. He knew she knew from their first meet, she cried during those times more than anyone probably ever would, having to live through it all, she didn't expect that. But when you cut through it all, she knew he'd be safe, as would any he met, yes, the truth of it all hurt beyond hurt. Would she ever want him now? Her own stomach felt sick to the core with it, and how they laughed when they bedded him, did any of it matter now? Of course, the real prospect now was, that somewhere he was basically lying-in vomit, yes quite lovesick himself. Pamela was so hurt by it now that she could not be bothered or want him or anything to do with him, it wasn't their sleeping with him she despised, it was that they thought it was so very funny. She flicked a coin into the air and said to herself regarding all of them, " heads you win, tails you lose," it went so high, she didn't need to look up at it but she did, it spun around and even in that room that where the ceiling was so high, she thought that she hoped it wouldn't hit the ceiling because it would have seemed to Pamela just all way too typical if it had, it landed back in the palm of her right hand, without looking at it she then placed it across into her left hand and held her hands firmly together on that coin for a while, just a few moments, her mouth was quite wet by now, she sat down almost afraid to raise her right hand and look at the coin. She clasped it with her right hand and so ballerina-like, stood up again, it was as though she'd lost a penny and found a pound, then she walked across the room and so very gently placed it into a pink beaded clasped purse, with the coin having been placed so carefully that it should remain undisturbed, she very quietly closed it, and noted only the pleasant sound that the clasps made, then, as she looked at a photo of her one of her aunts and her father standing by a swing-park where that particular aunt worked when she, and her father were still alive; 'only swings and roundabouts, I think it's coffee-time, and after I have some pots to wash.'

Pamela had a coffee then a shower, whilst in the shower it was as though she asked herself, but how could that be if he'd said, 'they were all dead anyway,' my past work is my past work, I knew enough about these websites. He wanted to have sex with me, we did, though not as he wanted, because I could not, he was happy. He must have been fairly happy as he came back certainly here three or four times despite my need for surgery. He would never know understand how I work, bravado or not, plus I had dealt with internet scammers for years. My only concern was to save as many lives as possible. No-one knew anything about the virus and my own work, and all that happened since, all my records and during are documented thoroughly, my primary and only concern was to try help save as many lives as possible. My caring for him did not matter then, just as it does not now. It was a fait accompli. Nothing further needs to be said really. I do not need to want him, and I have no desire to want Judd, I don't care whether he knows that or not. I really don't.

#

It would have been in 1665, that a couple then were to be blessed with childbirth, in fact they had twins. The father of the twins was not considered as 'educated' and was at sea from the age of eleven to eventually become himself though, and grateful of the opportunity afforded him, a Master Mariner. Where they lived was close to what became a main port linking that area of ocean to others of the sea where it was dense enough for traffic, to other regions and too, to the colonies. It would be difficult to ascertain exactly which port Fich arrived at as what eventually became the other larger port with the capacity regarding distance to travel, was some one hundred and forty miles away, and where who later became his wife, Nancy 'Nanne' Fitch was eventually hanged and rags tied to her feet were set ablaze as she swung, fortunately she did not survive, although fully clothed as the flames engulfed, before the rope eventually burned through. The location and surrounding area of one of the ports had been more remote and certainly more densely forested in years gone by, and each area not short of their sieges, rebellions and strongholds as the political scene was very awash with battles galore anyway, some women had even dressed as men there in an attempt to fool the invaders that such battles, or should they consider to dare attempt, would not be exactly the easiest of options at all, there were only four remaining strongholds at that time in an area that at its longest point covered some three hundred and sixty-two miles.

One of the twins went to sea also at the age of eleven. The other, was a birth with some ambiguity regarding the birth and sex, such were the perceived deformities, that the child was upon death buried, it would be unfortunate then, that the birth was not what you might consider 'a natural birth,' in fact the responsibility of helping fell upon what some might consider a rogue, although, unbeknown to the family then that persons own way of thinking was not of any religion, rather that such deformities were or could present as a cancer to, or in, or on society generally, and as such a polite thing, was that when the family were told, you have a son, there either were no witnesses or in spite of seeing things happening, they simply accepted that they had been blessed with a son and they had. They were overjoyed, and because they already had a child, a son aged two years, 'Caelin' Cottingdon-Woolsby. It would be their uncle Kaleb, now twenty who also would take to sea, and he who eventually, on a journey from one port back to that where his home was located would meet a homeless and destitute Mildreth. It would have not been easy to have foreseen their size, how menacing they'd have looked, but more-so if you'd never seen a ship before. Before the birth of Kaleb, there had been more to be had from utilising certainly the skills and prowess of some privateers to loot foreign ships, so the ports had become necessary hubs too. Kaleb's uncle was a humble man, aware of position and responsibility, and indeed, just an accomplished Master Mariner, he was said to have run an orderly ship and was fair in his dealings and instruction. His ship had a very special name, and that name would always be known particularly as some could locate the information, and some one day, although he did not think like that at all then, that some would indeed check, known more-so then as a very good ship. And there would be none ever as meticulous as Pamela.

#

Nanne Fitches' daughter, 'Mildreth,' although she was basically illiterate, as were some many women then, a small percentage had been taught how to read cookbooks, but not how to write them, and men did not cook anyway. She'd understood from her mother that things written, 'however they were done,' was special to be requested to and allowed to do it, so that as the cost of writing paper then was around four pence a 'quire,' somehow that had been considered humbly, also although she was never told so much of them, she was never to forget the mountains, and although she never thought of anything other than kindly, or considered anything other or with regard to unless, because she never saw other, she was known as, 'in the lineage of a daughter of.' A quire was approximately twenty-five sheets, an average labourer earned the equivalent of ten to thirteen pence per day and the cost for textiles foods, oils and candles had increased by more than fifty percent, more than sixty percent even, it wasn't an overnight increase, but there were no signs of things easing up, and presumably to cover all of their many problems, it wasn't until 1604 that an actual overseers to the poor and impoverished law was passed and it was needed too, the population on those islands alone had risen from four and a quarter million to almost six million in just a hundred years. Piped water in some streets hadn't even happened properly yet and gas streetlamps not until eighty years into that hundred and they didn't give out much light, so good trading was very important for the economy. And there were the plagues, 1603 and 1636, the last being 1665, although it was never understood why it seemed to stop there then, yes, the same year that the twins were born. Then during those years, poor lighting or not, at around 1640, did the dear King himself, not see fit to confiscate all of the gold that had been deposited in banks by any merchants. Merchants then started using goldsmiths who then in-turn provided promissory notes that again in time would become tender and exchanged by the wider community. It was difficult for some to fathom but generations before, coinage was measured by weight and type of material, so eventually maybe somehow the inevitability was that there would be changes to somehow attempt to balance things out.

#

Writing a book had required four or five hundred sheets, so access to any formal education was limited anyway, life systems much presented then as those involved in agricultural labour, there were those who fought, those who work and those who prayed. Not so long before, people had been speaking of Latin tones and phrases taught, common English had been unknown, whereas before they'd spoken in French, which was certainly the language of the lawcourts of the time, and those who could translate French were few, not even one person in twenty, so there was an overlap of Latin and by those who couldn't actually read Latin, then of course there were the other nineteen people of twenty, how were they coping, well, if you went to buy a candle, you might say, 'good day, can I purchase one candle please,' and the person selling would respond, 'yes kind sir, 'or madam,' you may,' to say certain words even if they were trying to learn a new language would achieve an objective, these were 'fixed expressions,' a bit like if you phone a phone company and they ask how you are, they very rarely in many cases might vey from the track, invariably too, time and motion wise, it actually was and is quite effective in most circumstances of trade anyway. Honestly, kindness and reliability and reputation established would eventually then help you along more as relationships continue or develop. Maybe seventy years earlier too, those who lived on and worked and managed the land, hadn't technically owned the land, but were noted as landowners, so it would not be long before use of writing and records would become a necessity in all society levels, Nanne Fitch knew only of beasts that congregated like packs of wild dogs, she said, with saliva dripping from their mouths, pacing and circling, waiting for a moment to strike, that was why she said to her daughter that she needed mushrooms that could only be found in a certain place, to prevent them from returning. There too, were those 'brighter' beasts, although far less friendly referred to them as and said, "you'll never put rope around their necks, they was and are was too slippery for that," who would and could and did recognise and identify by smell alone, and destroy, or make new of documents and charters written in French or Latin, and yes, especially if they felt they somehow infringed upon ancestral rights. They might even use the marks of what were conditions like syphilis on soles of feet as an excuse to indicate falsities, behaving as though they might never have seen such before, of course punishable by death unless a confession could be secured and should the marks then disappear. Her daughter was recalling the banner seen somewhere of presumably Vikings although yet to be determined. Women had been thought 'only' to be good for helping before and in many cases were taught by the said clergy of the day, not of course, that it would protect them, should it have protected them in death, maybe in those few rare cases, somehow?

It would be sad that Pamela's own circumstances were to bear some similarities although there were no documents and medical records were only kept for up to ten years in many places after that and at that time, in fact there were so many wonderful development changes to the facilities since, that it would be difficult to think how to keep track, not that anyone unless Pamela or someone else who did not quite understand, or maybe they did, would one day understand better.

It would be Pamela taken through a sea of depravity, in one brief sleeping moment she was to witness sadness that to many would beyond understanding, she tried to make sense of it, she knew she was the same because of her difference, although she looked different, because she had been given an opportunity to see this place. She seemed to glide through this almost darkened space although it was as though somehow a light was guiding her or she herself was being seen by them, more importantly that they could be seen.

When she got to what she thought was the end of that place, a place created by only a few who thought they were basically 'doing good,' as was 'their own real belief, generally, not knowing what they may have been creating, or maybe the child had not received a proper burial and it maybe set a precedent and of hidden guilt and sometimes shame that could remain in the subconscious of innocent minds for a lifespan. She saw standing on a slightly raised platform, the brother of the twin who survived all those generations before, she recognised him instantly. He held her hand and she looked back, she said to him, some of my relations are back there, she went back and found them and pulled them out of it, almost as though he'd pulled her up, although it required considerably more force on her part, it was as though they'd not been waiting, they were surprised, and they knew Pamela immediately and maybe possibly because Pamela had survived, she then saw a person and behind that person a light of some kind shone, she wondered how to set free those still down there, it was not a place of poverty only because she recognised various situations, but of depravity, even if a depravity of mind by way of a possible lack of a broader understanding, not requiring justice, but resolve, they were not hurt, some looked like archaic medical experiments that had gone wrong, although they actually were not, they would not have known any different. She could still see sadness in just an eye that stared at her down there, she didn't see a brain attached to it, just an eye with its various attachments, she thought of sinusitis etc, she would also be aware of its pathophysiology and that the costs of treating just that condition, if it was anything to do with it, ran into many billions. a sat on her bed and wept. She said thinking of them, 'I am so sorry that you had to go through' or were put through' or just went through this,' then she saw the whole place clear as though it never happened at all.

They could not have been medical experiments, because of those she recognised from there, not that they would not have consented, but because she knew some of them hadn't. They were free now, and no harm to anyone, as a kind of film ball created around them, like a huge balloon, they ascended into the sky, to a brighter nicer, less restricted place, minus feelers and that their loved ones too, might experience a great and sense of wellbeing. It was only the, just before Pamela had thought of the wellbeing part, that it seemed it all somehow cleared up, as though it had seemed unkind that they were there, although it may not have been.

She even questioned stupidly whether she had been deliberately kept in the medical condition she herself was in, to prevent her as that which would have been the eldest daughter basically, from ever bearing children. Of course, Pamela's immediate family knew that she did not particularly like children anyway, it wasn't that she didn't like them, it was for Pamela, very much that there were places for them where she would not have to listen to them crying, because as a child, it always made her feel so deeply sad that she cried too. She'd always thought they were in pain, and it made her end up not being able to tolerate the sound of children crying, it would be years after, that her mother told her that it usually happened if a child had wind or were teething. It was news to Pamela then, but it already had affected the poor girl terribly, she was distraught by it. Easier after to think if she should hear crying, that maybe that child is teething," before though it would tear dear Pamela to emotional helpless shreds. She'd realised that it would surely have been a quite unjust supposition entirely, she also outrightly refused to acknowledge any possibility, that anyone she knew, could have knowingly been involved; therefore, in any such preposterous a possibility at all. Whatever way anyone chose to consider it, she thought it worth it anyway, to have been able to be a part of that she'd seen. Then the twin from generations earlier bowed to her, as did others behind her and to her right, males with black well-suited garments and black ribbons tied in the backs of their hair, or short wigs possibly, bowed to them both from her right side, he immediately in front of her to her right, though mainly it seemed, as if they were with her, at him, and possibly as he had been Knighted and was now Sir. Cottingdon-Woolsby. The Cottingdon-Woolsby Orphanage, with having worked diligently for some twenty years, and after gaining support of a considerable few personages of high esteem and rank, because in his travels, he had seen so much suffering, corpses of children on streets and children starving in, streets where many were stricken, by poverty and disease, It had been Pamelas maternal ancestor Kaleb who took his own brother, of influence, to let him see for himself there, that which he might not otherwise seen in any haste and appreciating his astuteness and forthrightness, care and charity, then he did go on to form the place for destitute children. Kaleb and Mildreth eventually had two children; Mildreth remained a homemaker. A charter was signed making way for the particular children's hospital and orphanage to be built in 1739. This after the founder, in his own name and that which was the maternal name of Pamela's female relative who'd been down there, in that place, totally unbeknown, to them all the whereabouts of them, and innocently, yes, by design of historic misadventure in the name of protecting the general public, they had been somehow 'tarred with the same brush,' as their so distant ancestor's twin sister, yes, Pamela's own maternal grandmother and too her husband, her grandfather. It looked as though as a good will gesture of politeness, he kissed what then became a white gloved hand, although she'd had no gloves on beforehand. Pamela by then was back sitting on her sofa anyway with the back of her left hand on her lap, and her right palm placed on top of her left palm. She had cried, and was snivelly slightly with emotion, but was thankful that he and his twin, they had at last been re-united. She then heard him say with a somewhat jovial tone, 'blessed.' And of course, that started the waterworks off with Pamela again, as she could not hold back floods of tears. A while after she saw her very distant relation and his own twin sister again together, though both as though now smiling back, but facing now a tearful Pamela, how beautifully elegant they looked too; she thought. In 1744, he was, 'ousted out,' because of his 'critique' by a majority that had formed, a majority formed, of his own undertaking. His understanding when the hospital was founded, there too, was that, as boys were said to always be more favoured with education, his over-riding principle was that should and when girls gain eligible status in the same manner regarding education, that they upon often becoming mothers themselves, would then be far better placed to impart such experience and knowledge to those children and that would be better for the public at large in achieving such. The hospital was to be known as an institution for children and orphans who could not be properly cared for. The hospital today is a museum, mainly because great works were very kindly gifted to there for the benefit of the foundation, it still operates today working as a fostering and adoption centre and has many groups these days for both parents and children, also support for separating parents and parents of particular faith or ethnicity, they also work with adolescents. They also work in collaboration in some areas of health with the very same Trust where Pamela's surgery would eventually be performed, although they don't actually know that, not that it is of relevance, except for Pamela, it would seem way too embarrassing to even mention it to them, therefore. They campaign on behalf of children and visit children in psychiatric care and residential care too, it provides much for those who may seek. Pamela has not been to the Museum or any of it, she would like to visit but it really would be way too much for her to emotionally, and that's not such a bad thing you know, she would indeed think precisely that. And yes, her own grandmother had the same maiden name. The name of her grandmother's other parent was Wren. When Pamela reads of their progress in the work they do and achieve, it makes her cry too much as too it humbles her, she just could never go there, the emotion would be too much for her. And she always actually hopes that everyone is ok, everyone. Was dear Pamela an example herself, by thinking that to her uncle when a child herself, not an example on nurturing and education, and astuteness, and trust. Pamela's own failing therefore was that she never spoke of what happened apart from one time, and that was all fine, because of the level of understanding and trust between her and who she told. There was nothing that could have been done about it then anyway because Pamela never told anyone, not until considerable years after, that uncle died. As an example, last year, the organisation had forty-five thousand teachers subscribe to one of their programs, two thousand, five hundred and fifty-four schools were reached through their education program, helping one hundred and eighty-eight thousand, five hundred and five children and parents, and more than five thousand of their amazing volunteers helped more than half a million children through younger children services, to education, and more than eight thousand professionals trained or advised a little more than four million users online by way of their specialist advisory services. Pamela would never ever allow 'anything,' to interfere with such work and ethics. Pamela would probably advocate children's self-defence classes, believing that not much more than a very swift kick to the throat of an abuser could suffice. Not that her distant relation would have ever thought like that, or in any way be of a mind to choose violence of any kind as either a viable, or indeed and acceptable solution. It would make Pamela laugh at least a while, imagining an offender receiving such a blow, and very possibly another reason why Pamela's suggestions were not always the most 'appreciated' by some.

#

Soon it was Tuesday again, 'Pamela,' telephoned the hospital where he was to have surgery, near to where to check whether there had been any progress made. They advised her that all surgeries had been paused again, she was distraught. She imagined herself in her pastel green summer dress climbing onto a bridge and stepping off into the deep river, but she knew it was only a thought. That in the same afternoon she had to put her family through because there was no available help around, the stress and hurt of what she was going through upset her so much. At first, she'd asked them, can we go and get a copy of my birth certificate to show them the weight I was as a child in case not all departments she had been speaking to not so frantically but just hurting could access that information, she was told that information as to birth weight does not appear on a birth certificate. Then intermittently, she cried spontaneously through the rest of the day until she cried herself to sleep that afternoon. Judd was the last person on her mind, she didn't think of him at all. She had a dream though, that she was with a man, he was naked, it was not what she would call an adult themed dream at all, he said that he didn't mind waiting until Pamela had her operation, he told her that it didn't even matter whether they did anything or not, he didn't even have to say to her that he wanted no-one else, she knew instantly, he did let her know although not by saying it, whether she trusted or could trust him was not even a thought in her mind, and neither was it of her, in his. She had realised that day that the Covid-19 situation was fairly much at a catch-twenty-two situation. Any effort to write letters of complaint, would be a waste of resources, she even advised medical personnel of that, despite their kind gestures that it could help. One of them even said to her, you must write a letter of complaint because if no-one writes a letter of complaint then they don't make changes, and no-one moves forward. She explained to him, and said, "sir, my letter, should I write such a letter, is not on this occasion written plurally, it would be written singularly." She then thought that it should not be necessary to write such letters these days, the service should be better placed by now and effective, she understood that letters sometimes are important to maintain stimulus, but because of her own background, also realised that the response was likely to be the same as before, in spite of the letter now being about a slightly different aspect of what had been happening. She thought about that man in the dream and although she could not see his face, she knew that he would not go looking for someone who resembled her, because he "didn't need." Neither did he need to go from one to the other after, running through other look-a-likes, making a fool of her. She then started to wake up properly, it was exactly 23.10hrs. She said to herself 'oh it will be 11.11AM in one minute, and then at that moment that minute clicked onto the next and it was, the date was then 14th October, so it was 11.11.2020.14.10. She thought of Judd and said, now you cannot frack with Covid-19, now covid-19 fracks you, and all that you have been with and continued to throughout the crisis. She saw him halted in her imagination, he stared at her, it was the unattractive face she knew he was running it started at her desperately. She said to him, "you can no longer harm me or anyone now. You and your 'friends' and certainly you, had better bend over and learn how to take it, because Covid-19 will now complete, but only you and those you are close to sexually in such relationships. He was then told by someone else, "that's it," they either told him 'You're finished, or we're finished, and that he could take nothing more' from certainly Pamela. What she'd realised in that dream was the cell that he could not penetrate. Pamela could have died the day before, she had to put her family through hearing her pain, this was in her opinion, the latter with neither regret nor, thought to want to, forgive, 'unforgivable.' She saw Judd, it looked as though he was ransacking a place looking for something that might help him, he was pulling drawers out and scattering things, he knew his time was up, there was nothing that he, his lies, or his selfish deceit now could do. Then she saw a member of nursing staff who she knew in that dream. He was standing as they would, he said to Pamela "we have an onus of care Pamela." Judd was standing behind him kind of, though he wasn't smiling at all. He felt safe. he said, "no, this one's mine." Then it was as though the member of nursing staff watched on as a large dark covid-19 looking cell, but it was like some dark thing, started to build itself behind Judd, then Pamela was in a situation where she was stunned because he started smiling smugly as it kind of caressed him, He stood there with that look on his face and Pamela could do nothing, the member of nursing staff looked on astonished. He was speechless. Pamela wanted to laugh and say to him something like, 'ok, now what a fine mess you have gotten me into this time, and what the hell do we do now Mr.' It was as though for that very brief moment, time stood absolutely still. She though, that it would consume him, but felt that somehow, he was safe too, she could not argue with that scenario. She could find no reason to. Then, the man in her dream came and joined her, their bodies in trust merged into one light golden colour, but there was no doubt about it, it was a metalic looking golden colour. His face merged behind hers, that honesty was the cell that in Pamelas mind, could not be touched. The large dark covid-19 cell seemed to then push not so much push, but it moved away slightly from Judd, he them moved away from it to the left of it. Pamela then walked to the covid-19 cell and stood immediately against it, with her back to it, she said, "you cannot harm me now, and neither will Covid-19 harm anyone else again. It didn't cuddle her, as it did with Judd, it knew that she would not worry about it and for that reason, it would somehow melt away, but it was not an unkind thing and neither was her act in any way to provoke or evoke such from it, she smiled at Judd, she just knew it. Then she saw some mystical looking characters appear from the shadows behind Judd, the nurse was not noticeable in the dream at this point. They dragged him away, he made no sound at all, neither did then, they dragged him lie he was a piece of a dark dirty blanket across what looked like a wet floor. Pamela said to them, "stop," But they had already encased him in a tight wooden box, so tight was it that his he could not move his arms or legs from side to side, and he did not have time to push them upward, because large wooden stakes were and had already started to be driven through the sides of the wooden box to prevent his movement, starting from his feet, all the way up directly into his legs and waist and arms and even his shoulders, they were thick wooden stakes, he was still alive, Pamela said nothing but only saw that stakes were being driven into him when two final stakes were about to be driven into the sides of his skull through the box. He was neither moving, nor saying a word. It was a look of utter disbelief on his face. Pamela went over to him, even his own family members or any, if there were any close to him could not intervene now, Pamela didn't even need to question this, and not because she was afraid, far from it. She looked down over his face and stared at his eyes. There was nothing she could do, but she did not feel anything to or of him, she turned away, because she could not look. Then she walked a few paces, and turned around, he was now totally covered in and being consumed by scarab beetles. She said again, "stop, please stop," and then said 'back,' it all stopped. She herself had stopped too by this point, then went across to him, he was still alive, and it looked as though the stakes had been removed, his face was motionless, but normal again, but not even as though he looked glad or relieved. She stared at him, and said, "you have one chance to redeem yourself, and one chance only," The tone of her voice changed to almost whispers, though with a depth to it even she could not fully comprehend though she was not affected by it, as though it was natural for her, she said to him slowly, "you think you can trick me or try to trick me, I just this second realised that it is not Wednesday morning, it is Thursday morning, the time 01.11AM exactly, at 01.12AM, she said to him, 'if last night you were 'not' having casual sex with others, 'anyone,' under whatever guise you choose to name it, if it was penetrative sex, you walk away totally free now.' Then Pamela herself, slowly turned her back on him and walked away. He obviously was. It was weird, she then felt as though he joined her, but she no longer wants him. She felt as though he was trying to put a ring on her hand, or that was what it seemed like, or was being made to look to her like. Then she realised, he wasn't, it was her right hand the fool was attempting with, he was scraping at her skin, trying to get beneath it, to reach that within her, that he'd witnessed, he could not penetrate. Pamela looked at her right hand, it was unblemished, then she smiled, and said, "not this time, you don't, because there is nothing you can do to change my mind now, now you do actually die." Get used to it she said. You, and yours, are permanently gone! The fact remained that there would be nothing he could do, not even if he wanted to, and not that he did. But he was gone, and now quite dead. Or at least she wanted to believe that. She did believe it, even if he were able to somehow copy her or parts of her, sure he could do that, but she knew that yes, he won, but so did Pamela, that it no longer mattered would no longer be a concern for her. And he hadn't been able to get under her skin this stime, of course she could think of him, but he was only destroying himself now, Pamela no longer wanted him. He got caught out. Finally. The scammer got beaten by his own scam, he knew it, and maybe he knew she did, but it no longer mattered.

It's fine to think, oh in stories, the good guy or the good girl came out on top, sure Pamela's surgery was no nearer, was Pamela to be consumed by that, or was Judd feeding from it? The fact remained that there was a part of her, he could no longer now reach, even if he wanted to. Neither could he try, without self-harming, only achievable by attempting to form a genuine relationship with Pamela in this circumstance, not a look-a-like or resemblant person. If he tried to mess with her again, the next card dealt by Pamela would slice his head clean off his shoulders. No, she said; he has no place here. The choice is his, he could try to cuddle up with covid-19 again if he chose to, or even with Pamela by means that were of imagination or in dreams, but if he did or does, neither she shall, and certainly he could not, prevent what would happen to him and all of those he personally knows and frequents with. And it would definitely not be because she cares for him in any way whatsoever. She smiled and said to him, "Covid-19 is ready and waiting for you baby, I am not waiting for you. And no, you never shall, never can and can't."

Pamela no longer had to worry about it, did it mean then that others Pamela knew might, or that some Judd knew could interfere? No, it did not, the same fate awaited them should they attempt, Pamela was forced to witness an image that she never imagined she would ever see. Pamela then imagined herself on all fours, she squeezed as though having a baby, she said, Covid-19 may not be your personal biggest worry, I can remove you myself. As she squeezed, she did just that, what was very possibly him, now a mangled and wrangled contorted dark mess, then shot across the floor still struggling to twist and turn to develop itself further. Then, Pamela, totally unharmed, stood up and walked across to him, oh it was Judd, wanting so much to just say she forgives him and believing that ideally it would or should put an end to I and his games, but she knew in her heart of hearts that it would do nothing and the level of risk from him was way too high. She stamped on its neck, the whole length of her the heel of her shoe pierced through it, she heard him gargling as though he was still trying to breathe, but she knew that whatever it was, was also enjoying every second of it, it was disgusting. As the heel of her shoe went through his scraggly neck, until she felt her heel touching the ground. She said, 'for those I know, you'll now be thankful eternally that I do not use swear words, you pathetic excuse of nothing but a facsimile of a man, you could never be good enough, not even in your own dreams.' Judd was now quite, and very 'dead.' Then she without touching it, bagged it up and threw it to covid-19. She was sure she heard it burp, the piccolo player dressed in green and even with a hat watched from the side-lines and with its head tilted was cleaning his musical instrument with a cloth. She looked across at him, he would of course, once upon a time, have been associated to spirits of the forestry, very much indeed she felt humbly proud to know and be able to say, she asked 'are you ok,' he replied, oh I'm very fine ma'am. Then he paced his piccolo to his lips and his right leg kicked up and he was heard playing into the distance, or certainly into the night. He turned around though, for just long enough to wink. She then winked back and thought, 'I am glad that you are.'

They were to be consumed with hatefulness, although by virtue of their experience that was not as Pamela's was, or could ever become, although they disguised it well, to have been referred to as, 'hags,' but that was all by day to day they would now, with any or every word from their mouths or them per-se' however they chose to imagine it could be, now become. It would not be as result of the works of any great writers that they were as they'd become, but sadly, just as Pamela had been, they were victims too, not of cruelty, though some quite callous, carelessness and mistrust was to become the thing that would eventually change them, they would not even know it was happening, neither would they feel that they had lost out, how could they if they weren't aware? Any void potentially created, being replaced with a nicer understanding. Even Pamela would smile if she knew that an explanation of them would be, 'like they were being retired off, but they didn't know it.' And for dear Pamela's sake, with no harsh mind-stripping swear words. There were some psychological arguments that had considered the prospect that swearing can actually help in a healing process, though presumably not if swearing 'at' someone else. Their unacceptance of change would only be the defining factor as to whether they became anything other than harmless hags and of the simplest kind. They knew it well, if they did not, there was nothing that could prevent them from finding out from this day forward. And everyone apart from those few by what would be their own abusive words would live happily ever after? Is that how it's meant to be? Arguably, they could have paid visits in their haste and fear or a worrisome awareness that things might be different for them, but they really would not know, to some localised self- help centres, and we know where the salaries for the staff of some of those were at least coming from. Jean, with her background knew the advantages to careful and fair staff recruitment structures and policies. Dear Pamela, though, bless her, she was just happy in her quiet way that so many, though not Pamela obviously, had ended up becoming so reliant on Judd, even if they were just angry upset about having been basically lied to by him. She'd want to say, 'like lambs to the slaughter,' despite in their cases very often, it being inapplicable, and now irrevocably removed from the equation. They'd have to be very sure to remain gone, because if Pamela ever mentioned it to Jean, all that had happened, Jean would know exactly what wheelchair to put them all in and now, even which cliff edge to position it by and not so much who not to invite, but who might be required still. Of course, if Pamela did ever mention it to Jean, that possibly- they used the same group now as Clara Gringold, it could present a further dilemma now, however tenuous the thought had been before. Jean undoubtedly would say, 'maybe supporting those groups is actually a good thing then.' Although somehow, I think she'd probably use a very old pram rather than a wheelchair, something they'd at least remember as they dropped. Jean would then be forced to appreciate that maybe how Clara was, or is, or is, or was, quite normal? After all, Clara Gringold is a volunteer at a church in delightful Matlin. But then, of Florence's "golden oldies," comment and that piccolo player, if it was a piccolo and not a flute, was it all to merely imply indeed that there was many a good tune that could be played on an old flute after all? There it seemed, were too, to be no word, or name association further, possibly because of the pandemic. Neither could Judd or his associates or colleagues or meets, substitute 'any' imagery, or visions, at all, whether they were aware of their actions or not, or any consequences of, should there be any, and certainly not to victims, not even by way of passing back the baggage all too conveniently. The same applied to anyone he knew or touched, or who touched him, or who might view them in sexual or lurid or depraved acts upon or with another, particularly as their world fragments.

#

As if Pamela could cope with one more second of him, it was as though even though her most recent having finally found something that he could not penetrate, he still tried, she laid in bed and imagined him kicking at her, but he could not penetrate because she knew that he was not who she imagined he was. He'd even said something to attempt to gain her attention like, "who me." She'd heard it all before, though whilst her normal reaction would be to be in pain, as like a headache, this he knew too, he knew it caused Pamela to frown, that type of repeated abuse could have that effect, a bit like if you were hearing a tap dripping in a room that echoes if you are trying to get to sleep. Pamela rarely smiled, as though laughing but with a huge smile across her face, she noticed she was very much, actually smiling, it didn't mean that she had never before shared or experienced happy times, but she imagined that her operation had happened, and that Judd could not now get close to her and she meant herself, no-one else. She knew it was herself, and he recognised it too. Maybe there was something in that he hadn't then seen her before when they had met, there was that in it, but this time for Judd, it was just too late now. The day before, thankfully, Pamela had removed the plant that had not survived from the table near to where he had stood, although he'd have not known that, it didn't bother her, but she was aware and was thoughtful of how he might respond, even though she was really scared to meet anyone and not just because of Covid-19 and the lockdown measures etc, but because it was as though he, by his neglect during those months had caused her to retract back to where she had been before she met him, as having not wanting to meet anyone, other than those she had to work with, since eight years.

For Pamela, it was one thing and the choice of the individual, to believe that Covid-19 was not a problem. Then though, to have different sexual partners daily, and where those involved would not be aware of his games and the risks associated with that from the outset, in order that they make an informed decision. Judd, unfortunately, was not wrong to have believed that he was safe to have trusted the Pamela he'd met, and not someone else similarly named or who might know Pamela's name even if he'd mentioned it, or if her image had been seen before by those hangers-on of Judds, not because he was stupid, but because he was greedy. If they'd continued with their acts, however cleverly staged, and should it encourage others, around covid-19, neither should any religious minded person or background be able to forgive them. Also, everyone surely would guess that they might be responsible somehow, Pamela thought. And what of the industries themselves, even the industries they were trying or thought they were helping, they would not survive, and for what? Surely no forgiveness should be acceptable, not if granted to them, should they continue to operate, certainly with the present situation she thought, it would be counter active. Judd, by his actions, had risked ruining it all for everybody, and Pamela's surgery, and what if it were ever discovered, yes, the sickening thought entered her mind, although only a thought, it was then dismissed quickly because Judd could not penetrate any longer. That Judd was a married man, married as in how any reasonable person could understand, whether they approved of marriage or not, after all. Or did that say much more about Pamela too. Even at the shop she herself was seeing Judd look-a-likes, although when noticing that she did at least believe wholeheartedly that they were kind and not like him at all, it was encouraging, although hurt, she was no longer looking as such. And on top of it, because he was seeing so many, along with that was the baggage he carried. Something that lingered and could not be wiped so easily off, as he departed so eagerly and speedily. Was it to have become baggage that would never permit them to have amounted to anything, just as the foul odour he carried with him had resonated? It might have been easier for her to have accepted that he had been married anyway, even if he had not been, then effectively it becomes totally uncomplicated, she should have just thought 'ok, he's married,' then though that would mean that she was lying, it hadn't though given her an indication that it was why he might have told some he was. Pamela had thought that if or when in pain, or when for whatever reason, you have trouble seeing beyond those circumstances or a regime, or a combination of regimes, that keep you there, the continual compounding of circumstances, especially of those that can she believed cause debilitation in some, can and could further hinder any notion or consideration of being able to formalise some form of process through it all. It could give way certainly to a feeling of feeling trapped, and even that all of the circumstances combined are 'hell-bent' on keeping you there. True, some people may have an angle of their own, but if you are in pain, that there may be a hope, if the shock of it does not harm you, should be a small part of the way to regarding helping you get better. It is though not easy at all to think of these things so easily she thought, when in such a place. She even analytically compared circumstances whereby for example if a person was available in an advisory capacity voluntarily, to help with the general good and to also try to attempt to not only maintain healthier minds, but too, keep minds healthily active, in a situation whereby benefits of such were suddenly stopped, would it be like invading an island and removing their livestock and slaughtering their food stock to basically furnish fashion-houses and then once the land had been pillaged, the chief, or so to speak then forced, 'to sign away' in submission, because lives had been lost, and this was not foreseen, and their simpler lifestyle destroyed, for enough food, because their own stocks were being seized, and they had not enough to feed their own, many of their people were to actually die over months there, forcing their chief to beg, in the name of what? And then even though they left with children and whatever they could take as they had been planning to return to their own lands, they went back and slaughtered those who they'd already decided they did not want to take by marking their wrists, it was for the others, not about wanting to leave voluntarily. Those unable to be of use, they cut their throats or shot them all, there was nothing left, and they had surrendered?

Many died along the perilous route, also they were not accustomed to such heavy work, their decedents though would eventually find themselves generations after in a place more like a fortress, and living on the ice, as constantly kept busy, too busy to think sometimes, a distant memory for them, but that child did survive as did the progeny of, it was a long journey. The fortress was thought of as a natural fortress, it was not a place that was of aristocratic leadership, it wasn't as though it needed to be, they by the sounds of it were doing reasonably well without. And then on long trips, returning to various harbours with acquisitioned loot. Of course, there was also the grapes and mulberries, and eventually an ongoing ever-increasing growing profit in meeting demands for, over those of others for such produce, probably by some less scrupulous in their dealings. As such, they were often also believed to have been by some 'morally deficient,' especially too as there then became questions raised as to fulfilment of obligations when in one instance, some created a new fort, believing they could cultivate more locally grown produce and it was not as successful as they'd hoped, it would be very difficult for everyone concerned, their capability then for providing the likes, of oranges, silk, wine, pepper and ginger, and sugar by their wealthy and often notable commissioners with testing trying palates became doubted too. It would be a few years after that because of the internal contradictions their fortress collapsed, this left them vulnerable, then they too were invaded and 'all of them' taken away in chains. A lad named Fich, he was sixteen so he said, and had worked on boats and was 'a scrap of a lad,' full of cuts and grazes too, but he kept himself clean, having pleaded with a ship's captain and having said that he had no parents, and under the promise of him "catching any rat they heard of" and repairing sails, and doing the things not others would like. He was so thin and so small, and obviously knew of rigging by his speech, he said he'd worked on another ship and pointed to it, there were many lads working on it, Fich although young, certainly seemed of age and honest and there weren't many as discerning as the Captain, he was quite renowned for it, Fich, in 1623 was allowed to travel with them, that Captain had only happened to dock there just the once, to collect one single cargo of mulberries having collected a larger consignment from the other neighbouring garrison some four hundred and fifty miles south of there. An honest man, as was his own father before him, his son also worked on that same ship, as for young Fich, well, he was eventually taken under the captains' wing, although none of them would ever have opportunity to return to that fort in question. Years later one of that captain's own descendants did visit but to the other garrison in the south. It was probably a good that that it had been so too, particularly as that fort would become heavily invaded by some having lost a lot of their gold, to others, not quite as thoughtful possibly, who had been involved at that very same fortress.

The southern more 'affluently fortunate' fortress soon became the main distributor and learned from the poor experience they'd heard about and giving way to a very much more orderly and governed structure, it would be to that place having after established a ship building company, that his own would eventually return, expressing concerns over mistreatment of women, their rights to inherit and slavery. His concerns were certainly heard having become quite philanthropic by then and having been involved in ship building, although they did not always appreciate his views at all, the latter was noted.

#

Pamela was unsure where these thoughts came from, but she saw places in a vision, a mountain. Often, she would hear, 'oh it's not our fault, it's government,' but who put them there? Not that she was anti-establishment, other things she often heard were, 'school chums with other school chums.' Pamela could not chat to those such as her friend Jean about these things, for fear of what it might unleash, but she did go to school. Had it though all somehow become media with media, she wondered? Money made from it, reputations, and bravado filtered through to the masses, who might otherwise sometimes really have not much of a clue, or idea, going with the flow. Then Pamela herself thought, but isn't government is separate from all the other things and people? She even wondered whether government were needed to deliver fairness now, or she certainly did at that moment.

True, when he appeared to her home in a car in a dream with new clothes too and threw himself on a bed in her room, and some of her own friends from many years ago who she had not seen for a long time came in that dream too with him. In the dream he had asked her for money to rent a car, it was the type of car some would use for weddings, a neat trick, and the deposit had been, in the dream, in cash. Were the friends saying to her, that he was the one for her, or was he using the mirror tactic on her because days before when she'd imagined she was laying inside a sarcophagus for safety, and because she knew she was safe and because of her lineage, that he could not now get close or near to her, hence his kicking the sarcophagus. It wasn't a huge sarcophagus, it was long and thin, and had a face painted on it and other details, it was as though she was saying to him from inside it, now copy that, but all he could do was kick it softly, almost as in disbelief, yes almost. He knew it would now be impossible and he knew that he had lost out, his trickery, in whatever guise would now no longer be effective. Also, with every passing moment and as his attempts further fail, however he dressed it, in whatever clothing he could buy with the stolen recovered cash deposit for that car, that he seemed to feel as though he could keep, sure he'd moved up to a new level, and possibly found new accommodation, but the mirror cracked like ice she'd once seen cracking, before her, he put his hand through, as though trying to grab or even possibly to punch her in the face, it was his ever rapidly deteriorating horrid expression she could now only see of him. She then saw a shard of the broken glass mirror slash cleanly and without hesitance, across his whole throat, she could see him looking tearful, as though holding back more tears than allowing to fall, she was tearful too, but she'd seen it all before, afraid to even suggest, 'time and time again,' with Judd, the blood gushed from his throat, there was nothing she could now do, they both knew it. Then she woke up.

And incidentally, it was when the whole situation was weighed up, the exact same amount, he'd asked Reverend Streuwikk for, that he'd, recently 'borrowed' it seemed, to acquire the car, or lodgings, he now claimed to have. Pamela knew that it was another fake, attempt, yes, somehow, he'd accessed by way of the mirror he must have remembered, some of Pamela's own memories of friends she'd not seen for a while, or her past. His mistake was to think that she would not know that another two people, she did not recognise, would have been placed in that all so convenient grouping of his too. She would have wanted to say, 'idiot,' but she really couldn't be bothered.

#

An uncle in cellar dungeon scene

Pamela heard, "you were a sick child, look where you are now," it wasn't Judds voice, it sounded like an uncle of hers, because Judd didn't have an accent like that, had Judd been trying to punch her, put his hand in to reach her, or to reach something for sure?

It did not mean that their families drinking habits, should they have been caused by abuses, would mean that it was the same generally of course, Pamela herself has friends who just like to drink occasionally as a means of a more pleasant outing and socialising. It had made her think of how some would go to church and pray for forgiveness, the uncanny thing was, that Pamela did not feel it was wholly appropriate at all, and not in a disrespectful way at all.

The county had been awash with folklore as had where Judd was from, Pamela knew of the reputed mischievous behaviour traits of some of them, and was aware of, in some scenarios certainly, even why fairies were in some folklore placed. This made her think about the sick child term used. She was not totally sure of how to handle a suggestion therefore, by implication, that some would attempt to denigrate the fact that she had been a sick child, with misconception in an attempt to then mislead, and however plausible even to dear Pamela, by her way of thinking it had seemed almost laughable. Pamela knew regarding the image that Judd sent to her of himself in the earlier days of their initial meets, to the fake account she'd set up to find out what was going on with him, that certainly dear Judd very probably liked them young and it had shocked her, although she obviously had blanked any notion of it out, as a way of her trying to deal with it emotionally. He would not have known then, the full extent of how Pamela abhorred abuse, and whilst she might not have been the quickest thinker under those circumstances for sure, she certainly did not like being abused herself. She, Pamela, wasn't to comprehend the depths of it, and how it didn't help her, but as a way of self-preservation and sheer determination, caused her to create as a protection, an additional element to the foundation she already had in her very soul, he wasn't to know though, that from her own Father, she learned how to lay paving slabs from a very early age and there not only were not only no gaps that needed filling, but too, that there was precisely and accurately enough lime added to the mix from the outset, not intended for dispersal.

#

It was October 18th, Pamela decided to go to its lair, not such an easy thing to do, and not for the fool hearted. Not knowing what to expect at all, there could have been anything down there, but she soon found herself in a place and knew that she had found 'his hang-out,' there was in fact very little and really nothing down there at all, nothing at all. It was just dark.

Pamela as she walked into that space, immediately had huge horns on either side of her forehead, totally quite huge, she'd seen it before and didn't think anything of it, her face also became so gaunt as she walked forward quite slowly, glancing from side to side to what must have been the farthest part of the space, listening for even the slightest sound of or any movement at all, it was as though she'd have heard the heartbeat of a mouse, had there been a mouse down there. There was not. It was a dark damp cavern, although she was wearing a long black garment, because she knew that she could, the whiteness of her face and the horns would surely have been seen, even in that dark. Still slowly moving forward, with her head and those horns tilting so slowly from left to right, as though trying to give the impression for some reason, to focus more clearly and hear, should there be anything down there presumably, she didn't stay. Once away from that space and the heavy doors closed firmly, she bolted them shut, she realised that she had in fact seen him, although having given the impression that she did not, not because she was afraid, oh no. So as not to disturb him. She was certain that the things that had happened, happened only within that family, they were certainly not things that happened to others by his hands. Pamela wanted to find out more, she felt obliged to somehow, she felt as though it was something that he himself wanted her to look at, if she wanted to, but at the same time, neither was he really bothered at all, whether she actually did, With Halloween not too far away, Pamela decided to wait until after, because ok she may not have been afraid to visit that lair, but she was afraid of Halloween, it was never an easy time for her, such was how she was, it scared her to pieces. Oh, she could look at the masks in the shops and think, 'how sweet, and how nice for them,' and she'd smile and genuinely mean it too, but no doubt about it, she did think Halloween was scary.

Pamela thought of her paternal grandmother and then seemed to understand more why she was how she always seemed, reserved, and amazingly kind, and of the broken rosary that was found wrapped in a tissue in an etched patterned pickle jar, and whether there was any significance to its being broken, other than that in Pamela's own imagination. She certainly could never imagine that anything in the whole world could have made her grandmother break a rosary, and neither her father. And of her cousins from their childhood who'd died not long after, their father would have been the youngest of all the boys, and very recently when Pamela had visualised somehow whether a dream or not, that same cousin running toward her with open arms, it had been unusual too, Pamela thought, because the father of those cousins was with them, he was still as far as Pamela knew, alive, although she could not allow any indication of it to show, did he somehow know that she was dealing with matters she wondered? He may not have known Pamela so well, but he knew her father, his slightly older brother, and was it coincidence too, that Pamela and that same uncle shared their birth date.

Yes, thinking of even Judd, Pamela knew that she'd seen that face somewhere before, she'd just forgotten where. But Pamela was so young, she wouldn't have thought of it like that, not in any way. She'd have thought that he was older or that it was effects of drinking too much alcohol, but he was a light drinker, he certainly wasn't drinking like the others, similarly Judd, apart from the bottle on the table in that photograph of the balcony scene, he didn't either. Maybe their tastes were different she wondered, and very possibly Judds were. So are mine, she thought, though not as yours.

Heraldic shields would not have been ever something thought of by the family as they were growing up, it was as though they were too busy trying to survive and cope, it did not mean that there were none, they were just never spoken of, not ever. Would he in the lair have known of the relevance of their family name? She could almost imagine him then, but she was laughing, he said, 'there'd none as a finer laird as he,' she ignored it completely of course. She placed albeit an imaginary shield of their family over the handles of the large, certainly heavy, steel looking doors, where he was. He then said some unpleasant words regarding excrement, this pleased her, oh he knew that it would, indeed he knew that! Of course, too she knew that from where he was, he'd not be able to touch it, or even see it, she wasn't interested in whether he could or not. So, the shield, if you looked at the two doors that he was behind, now stared back at you, it also kept those doors very closed as the doors were in-between, she and he and although they'd not been totally sure which way to place it at all. Then she saw him, he was like a little boy, well not so little, way over six-feet tall and very thin and with very hairy legs, he had some clothes on, but it was as though, they'd gone back in time almost, she saw a young lad and struggles, real struggles, not identity struggles, but fear. It wasn't anyone she knew or had seen, but he did remind her of the grandchildren of the third youngest of her paternal grandparent's children, the uncle who'd have been the next older brother to her father. Not that Pamela was aware of it, and she even heard him from downstairs saying, 'oh, she is most definitely not, believe me on that, for god's sake and in Jesus name believe me on that,' a contentious issue was or became in those few moments, that, in rank, if there were such a thing in their family, her remaining cousins, as siblings to that uncle, of hers, would outrank her, if they were older than her, which they were not, as none older had survived, and neither would their surviving children, should out-ranking ever become a thought, other than stupid thought, she thought. She wasn't happy to have to consider that, and she hoped that none of the others had, not in a horrible way anyway. The main thing was, that it was a family resemblance that she'd seen in what was in the lair although seeing him from way back. Where her uncle was, was more secure than any sarcophagus, it was similar in some ways to where her maternal grandparents had been until she located and freed them, though a dreary place, it somehow had been intended in kind even though possibly ill-guided for the time. Where her uncle was, was somewhere else, and he was alone, as though forced to endure for an eternity. Imagining herself even splashing him with holy water, that would have been a sacrilege to her, in her own opinion, he wouldn't have even looked up at her and those chains were very heavy, they were huge. He'd have looked then up to her, and said, 'you wouldn't do that to me, I am your own flesh and blood.' It was at that moment, Pamela didn't make a sound, her face looked as though she was trying in disbelief to force a smile out, she imagined her uncle saying to her, 'you cold faced whacko, there'll be no smiles there.' She wanted to use a swearword then, but it would have insulted her paternal grandparents who that rosary had belonged to. The thought that he'd have probably grown up looking at that hanging on their mirror. Pamela then put her own hand over her own mouth, the fear, and a realization, that he'd destroyed that rosary, she could handle. The possibility that even sibling rivalry could have been pushed to its limits, to have resulted in anything such as that brought tears to her eyes. She heard her uncle again saying, 'you'd get more tears from a stone if you were to squeeze it,' she then said to him, 'shut up you please. 'The fear in a realization, she had to handle. As unkind as it could have seemed to her uncle, she decided because she may be over-emotional, she decided not to do anything further about her uncle until after her surgery, nothing about it at all. She'd waited her whole life it seemed for surgery, although had worked through most of it, her thought was, that however difficult things had been since January, he'll not be harming anyone where he is and that just as she'd waited, or been made to wait, and that was an even worse consideration for her, his wait was nothing at all by comparison.

Pamela then thought of the uncle who was the brother one older than her father, he'd passed away only in recent years, he threw some notes at her of some kind, it was unusual to see him looking happier she thought. Thinking of the two of his own eldest children who had died. Thinking of games and sibling rivalry, if the uncle in the lair, had been the eldest, and where the eldest of his youngest siblings had all, including Pamela, either been born with disfigurements or issues, where those two female cousins had died, and where the two nephews of his had also died, the eldest sons of the uncle older than Pamela's father, an as all of those children apart from Pamela's own brothers, two of them then, had been the only children at those alcohol infused gatherings from years before in their childhood, where she looked at him and thought, 'leave them alone, take me instead,' those older cousins were all dead now, and

Pamela born with a deformity that could have put him off? Those cousins with their skin issues and one in a wheelchair were all of them, the oldest children of the youngest of his brothers, and therefore potentially most at risk from him. She then thought of the uncle who'd been the next older to her father, and thought, 'had he been abused by him too,' that was what she could see in that semi-naked, not in any way naked, image of a lad, it was underpants and a thin vest, and his knees were pulled tightly right up to his chin on that floor and his legs still chained. Pamela did not like these visions at all. She'd never seen her uncle's bare legs, neither had she or did she ever want to, she had recognised their appearance in his offspring and theirs, the uncle in the lair though, now too just looking like a scared boy himself, similarly unfortunately, but with his own hands now covering his own whole face as if possibly weeping into them, but chances are, he was just bored. It was at that moment, or just a few moments before then Pamela saw what looked like a turnstile, she moved it around, it was a kind of flap thing, she was dumfounded to see a few, only a few children run out from beneath it, they disappeared, it was almost as though they'd been somehow trapped there with him, in horrid memories of his, presently at least, that much could be construed, as Pamela was not a happy bunny herself. She felt disgusted, she was too scared, and because it would all have happened long before she was even born- to wonder what it was all about. Deciding to attempt to check what might have been happening in the part of the world at the time when her uncle, yes, him in the lair, had himself been conceived. That not attributed to fiction, fable, or myth, if it was possible. If it had been for Judd in the past fifty years, as it had been, why should it have been for her uncle, ninety years ago

#

Whatever way you look at it, something, and it wouldn't have been a piccolo player, had shaped their destinies and tastes back then, moulding them, and pushing them, and shaping, then re-shaping and pushing further, further away than maybe her uncle had seen etched on the fields of those he'd seen who'd passed maybe generations before. It was not to condone the actions, oh no.

Had any of it been any different, would any of them have met the partners they ended up having partners with and to. On her mind, was the crest placed over the locked handles of those now considerably thicker doors, keeping them shut closed. The crest of course had been given to her by her aunt Lady Broadley, she felt somehow that she wanted to add even something more to it, to the shield itself somehow, to give it a more yielding and longer lasting strength, a greater strength, when she awoke at 03.38AM it had seemed as though everything had changed. She thought of her uncle, the uncle in the lair and of how tall he was, and of the tall character, the long-legged character that had mirrors floating around it at some speed, and that had jumped from a window a few floors up, he had obviously been protecting Pamela. She wondered whether that as a child had been fashioned somehow, not so much by the elf or the goblin with a flute but had somehow strewn those clothes at an early age too, seeing the graves of family members who did not survive. It didn't make it right. Imagining him, knowing he was there in that dark cell, or lair, the then heard a fox squealing so loudly and shrill, it seemed to go on for ages, certainly a minute or more. Had he been fashioned by those sounds she wondered, and was unaware of what they were, and it could not have been explained that they were mating foxes, possibly so as not to generate thoughts of such. Before she'd gone to bed, apart from having remembered oddly, a reference her aunt had made about a clearing in the woods behind the property there, she wondered had her uncle ever been in the woods or in the forest so late at night and been so terrified by that sound and others like it, yes, only the sound of foxes mating, from the snare, to the completion, as the vixen almost screams to get away from its captor, indeed foxy, foxy. She almost felt achieved to realise that there are things in nature that can help explain, they don't need to do bad things at all and that just learning and listening and understanding what the various sounds are, could for some, maybe become helpful.

She remembered the time on the clock where that officer had approached the metal bin and a conversation she once had with Jean regarding wars and allies, in particular how during the first of the world wars, she knew this because Jean had told her, although it had been Jeans grandfather who'd told Jean, Austria, Germany, Hungary, Bulgaria, and the Ottoman Empire, these were the central powers, they fought against Great Britain, France, Italy, Romania, Japan and the USA, who were the allied powers, Pamela thought of where Covid-19 had seemed to hit hardest, oh it could never be proven. And during the second of those world wars, where so many of the various nations' treasures 'disappeared,' although the main cause of those world wars, was Imperial Germanys determination to become a world power, by crippling Russia and France, hopes by Germany were that it might or would become a self-decisive war as the Franco-Prussian war had been, when it was being explained to Pamela, she kind of lost it there that day and opted to remark about Jean's deliciously tangy fruitcake. Such was Pamela. Jean asked Pamela then, "guess what's in it," she smiled and replied, "nice things and beautifully created but surely if in moderation? She then said, there are some things we are not meant to know though, as tempting as it may be to discover or how much we are pushed. Jean smiled.

Something was agitating Pamela, when she was to later realise, what if when Judd had visited her and smiled at her pictures, and of the photo of a WW1 Officer given to her by Jean, "to look after for a while," and the prints of flowers that Judd smiled at and pictures of clusters of flowers, had not been perceived by him as groups or how many he might meet on his next excursions, but potential disease explosions. If he had been told since a young age never to seek medical advice and believed that his life somehow depended on I, he, when meeting those individuals or groups would or could have been responding to the effects of disease on them, especially if they were the type who'd been conditioned by whatever means, to, 'keep it dirty. 'What if their mentality caused them not to keep their innards clean, or had their minds become affected to such an extent, as Pamela's could have, had she not had the experiences she'd had, and the initiative still to seek a professional opinion. If it was in any way connected to wars of those mentioned, he needed that town because of the hospital for veteran soldiers located there. In a way, had the whole world somehow become united again?

Adjacent to where her uncle was, in the lair, there were other cells, empty, she focused on that metal bin and the time and what it said on that clock and it was as though she re-visited it, strangely though, the girl she thought she saw the girl she'd seen on the boat, the girl who'd been floating around on driftwood near there. It was odd, maybe her and the feelings Pamela had for Judd had all somehow been binned. However, armed with a mini car upholstery hoover she lifted the heavy lid up and whatever was thrown in there, was sucked into her little hand-held hoover, without her even needing to touch it. She smiled and then was back at her own place, she then placed the hand–held hoover into the cell next to where her uncle was and closed the door quietly. Then she got the plastic bag from on top of the microwave, the sealed plastic bag containing the cloth Judd had cleaned himself with and placed that inside a cell two cells away from that, so three cells away from where her uncle was, separating them completely. Then she bolted that door and sealed it shut. She planned to make and place a crest depicting the face of a Faun on that door, as a Faun she knew, was only an untamed spirit of the woods. She'd learned how to make plaster mouldings as a child when visiting the architect. The handle of the cell door, she planned to have made onto it, a number three but facing the wrong direction. As for the contents of the hand-held hoover, believing that it was all somehow an attempt, merely to have a covenant of kind broken open somehow, she would release the hover contents back to the forest where it would restore and where it would not be abused by those such as Judd, anyone, or anything, when the right time came, although it would not prevent good continuance within forests or woodlands in the meantime. Unfortunately, though, it also was, just as neither sadly, would it necessarily prevent presumably then, Covid-19, re-infections.

#

As if it wouldn't stop there and not that dear Pamela would even imagine that she might be somehow 'on a roll,' then she had a vision as clear as day itself, of her uncle sitting in the lair, on the floor with his knees pulled up to his chest, but this time he was reading a large older type of newssheet, a newspaper. Unsure of what exactly to add to the crest on his door, to strengthen it, it then seemed as though it had already been done for her. What looked like a letter 'O' had been put onto the crest, with a letter 'A' superimposed over the top of it, though it was not too easy to know which letter had been superimposed over the top of the other. Pamela recognised or believed she knew this as alpha and omega, they are the first and last letters of the Greek alphabet and they have a religious meaning too, she knew this so was not worried so much, although her new calmness and thoughtfulness regarding, she considered it all, to be representative of a much more tranquil oasis of calm.

Pamela knew that on Sunday nights, Judd would have returned from his weekend jaunt, usually it seemed as early as he could, then he'd be out on one of his treks until late in the Sunday evening or past midnight, presumably if travelling to locations that had trains running all night, and she knew he had that very firmly in the bag too. Pamela could picture a person with a lampshade over her head, with musical notes as though printed all around it. It also looked as though with the amount of make-up that person had on, he'd managed to even find a sarcophagus look-a-like too. Ye, he knew he was safe with Pamela, and Pamela was safe from all of them, and they were safe now, from her uncle. It was then a lighted doorway appeared before Pamela, it was way taller and broader than Pamela, just an upright oblong shape, a doorway, with beaming light shining through it as though at Pamela, or certainly it had appeared for a reason. She thought, 'well what am I meant to do now?' It looked like a doorway and even had smoke or dry ice near it, or mist, Pamela walked close to it, you could see Pamela standing in front of it facing it, Pamela was totally naked with her hands by her sides, she asked 'what do you want of me,' then she thought she heard a few feint sounds of a muffled trumpet, in fact they were so feint you could barely hear them at all. She shook her head as though shaking her hair slightly, from side to side, and said, 'now isn't that just so typical.' So, Judd hadn't necessarily changed, though he had been warned, not that he'd believe Pamela's threats. Had her uncle shown to her that he'd changed, did Pamela believe any of it, thinking of that doorway, to have sent him into yonder? What though, if it by doing so, risked upsetting the memory of her humble paternal grandparents. Pamela trusted somehow that they knew everything any and of where she was with it, at least as fine as it could be for the present.

#

In 1929 though, a major global economy had collapsed, that was then of course there had been The Second World War, succeeded by a worldwide depression. 'Woman of the house,' in the location where her father and her paternal uncles and aunts were from, was then expected to take care also of small livestock such as pigs or calves and any poultry, also they'd have been responsible for vegetable and fruit growing. Sympathy for the general workload had not been a factor then, not until around 1940. Pamela's father had been born in 1942. Her thoughts then strayed to her uncle in the lair, and she thought to or of him, 'so, no electric or running water either and poor sanitation,' she felt that he replied with, 'yep,' but she wasn't sure, and of course he was considerably older than her father, there had been quite a few more children born to them between when he was born and 1942.Pamela was taunted, on one hand she could almost hear another of her aunts saying "blaggard," but so slightly smiling and also with a discontent, as though aware of quite mischievous goings on then, but Pamela was uncertain as to whether she'd have been saying it to her, or to or of, or whether she hadn't said it long before then, to her ancle in the lair. You see, none of her paternal aunts were still actually alive. Pamela wondered that if her aunt had said that to her uncle what his reaction then, knowing her tone etc and smiley understanding voice, might be. On the other hand, Pamela was thinking, 'who am I to think I can keep anyone as a prisoner, especially considering how my own circumstances considering my body and how it has been all of my whole life, and especially my own family. Again, she thought of him in that dark place, how many rooms did they have, she wondered, it was not as though she could ask any of them now, she didn't know any of this. Potentially, it could have been horrendous at night anyway, hearing things like, 'get off me,' or' be quiet,' and 'be quiet in there.' It was all contentious alright, she did not want the likes of Judd or anyone or anything he'd become familiar with, to be able to access visions or imagery of any off her loved ones, or family, or those of anyone else's. The crest now became a further shield that he could never penetrate. And whether, or not, though hopefully now a huge disappointment, to some who Judd might 'visit.' Momentarily then, was it to become a calm before their storm, it was as if she herself heard some shouting "no." Pamela then imagined Judd, as then he flew backward toward that doorway of light she'd seen, his hands as a reflex opened so fast as he tried to prevent himself from being sucked into it, it was pulling so hard around his waist, the skin on his fingers was tight and his hands were like clamps as he tried to grip and hold on so tightly, trying to hold on, did Pamela pull out a sword from somewhere and slice straight through his waistline, cutting him I two and sending him sucked into the light, now definitely gone forever? Her uncle could be heard saying, "well done you," then she slipped the sword in behind the crest. It wasn't that it all happened so fast that she didn't see any blood there on the sword, instead she walked across to that doorway of light and oh, he was hanging on, for sure, Pamela put her right hand up to the right of the doorway and switched the light down to a flicker, it was 04.00AM after all and October 19th. Judd fell to the floor like a piece of rag, she also realised somehow that Judd was actually afraid of the dark, maybe he had reason to be afraid, to have kept himself so busy in the lights of others, she wanted to say to him, 'get up you pathetic wimp,' but instead she briefly glanced at his dilapidated skin as though it was an inconvenience for her to even look at anything resemblant of him at all, she picked it, or what was left of him up and threw it outside with the rest of the rubbish, then she said to him, 'no, not actually quite so lucky this time.' Thinking of her uncle in the supposedly soundproofed cell, Pamela thought, 'I won' offer you a coffee because I'm sure that you don't.' There was a reply, it was, "oh don't go worrying about me, I'm quite fine here."

Where Judd liked his conquests if you could call it that, young, it was not like how growing up had been for her uncle, as difficult as it must have been for them all. Pamela chose to believe that at least, she even wondered whether any of it had been about inflicting pain, or a revenge? By her thinking that of and to her uncle when she was a child, had she herself set a game or a challenge in play unwittingly. Was it a game within a game within another game just waiting somehow to be played out, but she was a child? Or was it about to begin? In her mind, however anyone decided to consider it, it was abuse though, the crest was not being removed. Similarly, though, and awkwardly, it was obvious that Judd just didn't seem to be stopping, as though the pests he was visiting, kept somehow sending messages to Pamela, some of them quite intrusive too. A message that day from a person she'd never heard before, said, "you need to co-operate," to Pamela, whilst Judd may have thought the 'chipping away' at her, was helpful to him ultimately, or funny, saw only something that she couldn't be concerned with or by, as tedious as Judd himself was now to her, yes, Pamela disagreed.

That day, she visited Jean more of what had been happening and said to her that although they by continuing with their unwelcome jibes at her, would not prevent directly Pamela from having her surgery, he had before said to her that he did not care at all about Covid-19. Jean then remarked how sad it was that Judd had not bought for her a present of any kind, and then said, 'don't worry dear, those types habitually never do.' Pamela asked why? Jean said, 'well you know, it's still basically a pandemic situation, if he was putting many others at risk, all of those he'd met would presumably somehow share similar DNA possibilities now, and maybe there would be fingerprints on it still, they would be able to check that, ad especially where some were dying because of operations and surgeries having been cancelled, that they could track him, if the situation were to worsen, via his medical records, under security laws if the right people were approached and if it were genuinely serious enough a concern.' Jean explained that it would be an integral part of the nation's security surely, to consider things extremely serious in some circumstances, and particularly as there was still no scientifically known cure as such, and because science was what the authorities seemed to be focused on. Then she said to Pamela, but the rotter didn't, not even one present, it was only a thought though." Don't worry dear, you'll sort it out," Jean told Pamela. I have no doubt about it, she said. She said to Jean, yes it was a shame that he did not.

#

That evening, she was at her home, and she looked above he microwave oven, she'd looked there almost every day, there was a grey plastic bag, sealed with sticky celo tape. Then she remembered, it contained the wet wipe he used to clean himself that day when he came around to her place and looked so filthy and seemed so smelly. Pamela must had put it into that plastic bag and sealed it, that was it, she'd done that because she wanted to remember the wonderful moment they shared, it was as though she could smell him on it as she put hit close to her face that day after he left. Dear Pamela, must have forgotten all about it. She then saw Judds face, it was the older and horrid angry face now together. She smiled and thought about Judd very carefully. She said to him, 'one more move out of you, my friend Jean can have you sectioned, or something similar, especially during a pandemic, should you persist. She held the plastic bag up, he knew exactly what it was, she said, this is being posted by mail to another of my friends so that they can look after it 'today.' She said to him, 'co-operate, or don't,' it's your choice. The covid-19 virus ends here, she said. And if you go with anyone else, I'll know you know, that I know, but you won't know who I am. "Your choice," she said. Then she said to the others, 'goodbye trash.' But wasn't PPamela effectively sectioning him herself, not in medical terms, but she had certainly achieved regarding socially distancing him, by removing him, were the signs there all along? Were they signs of an authority? Pamela didn't know, she was just doing what was natural to her. But was it almost like saying "by the powers invested in me," she asked herself quietly. She said it to Judd in a way that he'd feel that every one of them he'd tricked, she then told him, 'Do you think I'd say it if I did not mean it,' she then thought to herself, happily, that countries around the globe could start saving money and rebuilding as from today.

Of course, it could not end there, how could it, although there was now, absolutely no coming back at all for Judd, or his so-called 'acquaintances,' from and by, thanks to Jean too, her decision. Pamela thought she saw a huge guillotine-like weight come down on the grey sealed bag, it was like some huge thunderous foot as though to slice it in two. Not this time

Judd, she thought. Instead, Pamela went to it and with the underside of her smallest fingernail, she lifted that huge weight up, then imagined she'd placed Judd beneath it, his neck just where the blade would fall and with him staring up at her. He knew it was his lot this time, his time was truly up. With Pamela's upturned smallest fingernail on her right pinkie finger being the only thing preventing that weight of a huge blade from sending his head to the basket, and she wanted to hear it land in it, she said to him, 'I don't need to, on your way little boy, and don't come back.' He'd have realised that he'd have lost everything had the matter escalated, his family, his wife and too his job, if he really had any of that at all, all of it, and let's face it, none of those he visited probably really would have known anyway whether he had or not. It was then as if an upturned piece of sticky celo tape, where the sticky side though was place and now faced downward upon soil, though Pamela did not tell Jean about it until a few days after, it was as far as Pamela was concerned, Covid19 being consigned to history, and Judd and his associates, all of them. Beneath his feet therefore would be the shiny side of the sticky tape, he wasn't totally gone, she called to him, he stopped and stared back. On her mind was, should a question ever arise where she might have to be forced to ask herself, should she trust Judd over her uncle, should the answer not be that she should more-so trust herself, especially where there might be doubt, as to whether Judd was the good apple, or whether Pamela had been captive all these years, and whether her uncle had tried to save her. She told Judd, 'Do be careful not to slip up now, won't you.' He didn't move and she imagined herself pressing so gently a large crucifix onto, so it was just touching or just close to his forehead, she heard his skin sizzle a bit. Then she said, 'the honeymoon is over, 'babe.' When Pamela mentioned that it all had been "consigned to history," Jean replied, 'of which dear Pamela is not.'

Pamela wanted to prevent Judd from turning up anywhere with his own personal form of trickery and deceit, or friendship as he liked many to believe. Turning up and knocking a hole in her wall basically, then placing two swords in front of her, because he'd probably have mastered that by now too. Then the older Judd, as though running off with one of the possible child spirits she'd seen released, and what if inadvertently or accidentally, he'd somehow managed during his pathetic game, to run off with the child spirit of her uncle in the lair? She was determined that she'd also block Judd from accessing via any sources or senses whether known presently or not, also to prevent and block him access of any kind, through time portals. him known sources. She would achieve this by using swords she believed he would by now have learnt to acquire, and without his knowing that or being able to access information, or any code or secret or formula or means that may assist him in such furtherance, or any kind of secret, and thinking of dear Judd, there would be no point of having secrets otherwise would there darling, she thought. His friendship was like a huge liner, built on nothing but fake trust and selfishness, yes it had the size to make a hole in a wall, but not the real strength to hold totally firm, he knew that very well, but to him, it did not matter, if it got him to where he thought he was headed, he was potentially therefore the most loathed person known, and they would never realise they were helping him, by even loathing him.

Pamela also wanted to relinquish rights of ownership he believed he had, to anything he has taken, whether directly or indirectly, habitually, and to remove from Judd, any successional rights, regarding anything from anywhere or anyone regarding his activities, if accomplished not within lawful means. Anything decent taken by him even by way of suggestion or where there would not be legal and just means, would now be returned.

She then thought about Judd, she said to him, "go knock yourself out kid."

It was then that a soldier appeared, he was an older man with a full uniform on, possibly even from one of the World Wars, definitely an officer though, he was slightly un-shaven and he wasn't a thinly built man, he had a flat officer's cap on, it was all like a very dark grey colour with possibly some blue, he had an officer's coat that went down almost to his knees, he picked up what looked like a child but it was not, it was more of a shadow of some description, whatever it was, it was motionless, it was as if he'd travelled through time itself, As any respect and certainly and dwindling remaining affection and trust she actually had for Judd, had been now destroyed, having itself been crushed beyond any recognition in Pamela's opinion, neither was she bothered by it, as though a destructive force of disrespect had just ravaged it all somehow, and that was nothing Judd could bottle up and ell on, though he tried, as if much could bother Pamala now. All Pamela had to do now was to see what was happening with Covid-19, it wasn't even as though the onus to be careful was only on Judd, but those he visited too, they'd lose him forever, if he wanted to play with Pamela, she would have him caught, it was simple. She watched him march through what looked like a yard and past a clock, Pamela noted what time it said what was on the clock, the language particularly, she was so surprised. Then he walked behind a very tall solid metal bin that had a large heavy lid on it, she knew it was heavy and the style of bin, he then threw whatever it was he held into it, shut it and walked away, it was as though he was almost accustomed to doing it, but saying too, "don't go there, you don't want to know." It was maybe how some health conditions were dealt with then, she wondered, so far back, by how he dealt with it, she even wondered whether it could also have been because of lack of finance somehow, to investigate unusual birth situations in some countries.

Then she heard her uncle say, "told you so, but do you ever listen." Pamela said to him, "shut up you, and be just as careful, you might be going on a one-way journey to a very sunny spot yourself very soon. "Then he said, "and so early on a Wednesday too."

#

That day, Pamela had to go to the post office to return an item, she got ready and although October 21st put a very flowy but not loose spring-summer knee length dress on of bright colour and a red coat and a hat, of the same colour, after going to the post office, when she came back to the street where she lives, there was a slight moment when she felt as though she could feel Judd, she felt him smiling, then she walked into the gate where she lives. As she did so, immediately as she did, a man who must have been paces only behind her walked past, Pamela stared at him, as she was putting the door key in the lock of the main entrance door, she thought, 'that's Judd,' he must have been standing behind her, less than three feet away and until she walked into where she lived, had not recognised her. He did though, as passing make a comment about certainly someone at that location being too old for him, then he walked so fast to wherever he was going. If it was him, Pamela knew that eagerness only too well. Timewise it was not the right time for it to have happened, not before mid-day on a Wednesday. she was slightly confused by it and alarmed by it. Her ideas though, or all that she'd decided, had not been changed. It was the angry horrid challenged Judd she thought she saw, or someone very much like him, though she thought he looked slightly taller, but it was disconcerting for her, she was quite tired by the thought that she, having changed all through the summer to what she'd become, after 'toning it down,' to please him and make him feel more secure about her, that he would then make such a remark, she was not surprised though that he went on.

That afternoon, she dozed off and woke up at 21.30hrs, it was unusual. Immediately she thought of Judd and said to herself, I hope he is not up to anything with any of them, because they will be fairly much sealing their own fates if they are. She could not visualise anything with regard to him, apart from at one point, the girl who'd been on the deck of the boat, walking quietly out onto what looked like a stage and wearing a gold-coloured dress. Pamela was happy about it somehow. She imagined that their games had all stopped and because of their all stopping or being forced to, it had brought about such a change within them, that there was an unsurmountable brightness about them all. It was like the light that was shining through the doorway but not quite the same. Pamela had realised that day what that doorway was, it had been the doorway to the mausoleum she'd visited earlier in the year. It was safe, had she not had the family background she herself had, she would not have been able to have been so surprised by what she was to find. Pamela knew in her heart that as much as she loved Judd, and she truly did, she could not even think about it without wanting to cry, she knew that she could not give herself to a man who did not want her enough and there was no way that she'd want a man who might be married, and if he was in an affair, Pamela was not going to play second fiddle to anyone, not anymore. It had been as though she thought that maybe those he had been visiting, had all been so afraid of being the first to die, that they didn't want to let that go? It was never like that, she was certain. Or was that Pamela being charitable again, very probably yes, definitely charitable. Pamela thought of Judd and was tearful, slightly, she smiled and thought to herself, and to Judd too somehow, that light that encompassed you all just then, was you being loved.

Pamela then went to bed; it was as though emotionally she couldn't handle any more. Judd had seemingly become replenished again as she could imagine him smiling, whatever he'd done or whatever had happened had revived him somehow. She didn't want to have him on her mind even though smiling constantly, yes it was nice, but not if he was only meeting others until her operation had been completed, why should she still want anything to do with him? She thought of how she'd once been and her online profile and about how his work was, and how unattainable she could have seemed, just like now the person in the gold dress on that stage. Pamela lay on her bed with her head resting on the pillow, she though how it doesn't matter whether he or any of them know what involvement she'd had in any of it, and that it was neither important that Judd knew at all what she'd been through. Before tears welled up inside her, she thought 'it doesn't matter at all,' and I'm certainly not bothered by something on a stage in a gold dress, then she cried, she heard a tear hit the pillow, then another rolled down her nose, she didn't think it dripped but she checked because she wanted to see what a tear on a pillow looked like, there were two tears, it was then that she thought, how amazing, tears must be a uniform size because both tear marks looked identical in size, then she thought again, 'no, I'm certainly not worried about a person I saw in a vision wearing a gold coloured dress like my dress on a stage, they have no idea.' She didn't hear her uncle then, but she did think he'd missed an opportunity to say; 'they needn't think those tears were for free.'

Pamela then heard a loud noise outside, it was as though someone had forcibly kicked a wheely bin, when she checked, there was no-one out there, apart from a streetlamp on and a light in a window across the street, it all seemed quite normal, it had rained quite heavily that evening and it was all quiet now. She glanced at her hands and noticed that her fingers looked slightly puffy, it was then she realised where Judd had been that evening, she'd wondered if he might have been local beforehand but didn't want to believe it. She'd even wondered how the Wednesday usual antics for him might pan out, he seemed to be passing back the crap again to

Pamela and having fun at her expense. Pamela decided once and for all and having realised that he was using his smile and that feeling generatively to transfer the muck back. In order that it not become a recyclable energy force, as she did not want to help them anymore, neither did she feel it appropriate for Judd or anyone else to comprehend or wonder how she might herself, not use such rubbish, but see it recycled or binned, and she knew how to have that done. Oh, she would pray for Judd and his friends, and for them under whatever identities or names they chose to probably fool people with too, because she knew now, that their time now was truly up. She hoped her prayer might be answered.

#

Even though two hundred years before, it was only a hundred and twenty years earlier than when her uncle was born, so it would have been probably within her great, great grandmothers time (paternal) and a hundred and twenty years before that uncle in the lair was born. As their own paths too, were to further develop, to result in what? Pamela thought, 'surely not Pamela, who loves woodlands and who cannot have intercourse with anyone because of an issue at birth, even if she ever did or ever would now want to. Saved from making wrong decisions and choices with a man she loved? She might not see those horrible visions now, but Pamela wasn't in so much of a hurry to notice a leaf fall from a tree that day. And as for the scene on the boat, there was no cabin on it that Pamela knew, so Judd wasn't going to appear on that unless in his wildest dreams, and he knew nothing about it, Pamela was sure of that now, hence "wildest dreams," Pamela had been on that boat longer than any of them could have imagined, she was not there as a passenger, but unfortunately more-so for Pamela, it was as though she all her life had been under a vow of silence. The being on a raft of wood for the other character who appeared on the boat, it was all part of a mystique of a kind, a deception, but really it was the sheer deviousness of it all. And a blonde Pamela look-a like on a stage that Judd was watching, and then later the other person appears in a gold dress on a stage in a dress almost identical to Pamela's but now in gold? In the same way that Pamela had been unapproachable at first until Judd sneaked his way in, so would that character become now, Pamela imagined stringing the pair of them up by their ankles and separating them, hopefully, they'll both now, the pair of them be focused on other things. Even if they can neither of them get close to them.

The fact was, Judd wasn't bothered by any of it, his 'screw it all attitude,' his image was being shunted around and in the crap he no doubt deposits, he does not care. So, look at it another way, his wife, if he had a wife, maybe Pamela, let's suggest dear Pamela, didn't want fake boobs or was a plain Jane type and very truthful naturally, not suggesting that others are not, some other females just could not afford fake boobs, or those types of clothing however inexpensive they may become, that person was similar, when after meeting Pamela, that date had probably already been arranged, the Wednesday thing, after Judd met Pamela initially, the person he met on Wednesdays after, had to work very fast, that was where he picked it up from, because it wasn't like that between Pamela and him. And to create something that would allow her to create and develop his interest. Some could say they deserve each other. They got off luckily, but not lucky. And before they are strung up, their phones are switched off, and because they only care about themselves no-one will know where they are, and their hands, tied behind their backs, tightly. Yes, despite it all, and quickly remembering Judd's very bad back. Yes, Pamela wanted to think.

Her uncle did say something more then, yes, the uncle in the lair, he said, "Judd, don't think you can call out to the animals either, I'm sure you would consider anything right now, if you understood anything ever, she really has got that covered too." One thing to consider though, must be, not so much the panic that for some, a situation like Covid-19 brought with it, but the fear, like those soldiers in that chateau, before the forest went up in flames, were they first world war, second world war, not involved in war, what type of war? Just trying to make a point, or was it real, and they were truly scared after, had so much pure fear, prevented them from starting a war, or commencing with, and when was it, it wasn't as though they exactly had time to say?

Considering Pandoras box, arc of covenant, attention deficit, attention seeker, full of secrets, mystique, lies, Pamela had construed that whether he was aware of it or not, he was if attention deficit and an attention seeker, and with him being a hotel manager too, just doing what he knew, seeking every easy gap, to potentially go in there with his little mop bucket, and told never to seek medical attention by those who gave him a very different type of attention at weekends, different because he could not attain that from anywhere else, he would never want to, he could not. So yes, even if no wedding ring, in his mind, he was very married. It proves then that there must have been another reason for him having blocked Pamela then, it can only have been that he was either caught out by Pamela or that someone else caught him out, because his actions in behaving as he was, supported it all, the blocking could have been like an attractive man walking around trying to gain attention of others by funky kind of moves to music being heard through headphones he had on, to create that mystique. How sweet you might think. Yes, and rightly so, nothing wrong with it, it's normal for some. And unavailability. When all the time as though just waiting for the right convenient opportunity, not even the right moment to strike, as viruses do. So, was he visiting and staying in contact with those he did not want to see saved if not having him around was to become the best and by far the safest option? Him trusting Pamela, was it just about Covid-19 or was that meant to encompass all the other diseases he might pick up along the way too, and spread En route to very willing and eager supplicants, it would be for him and those diseases like an open door. In Pamela's last dream of him, he was with two girls, one of those and the one saying the nicest things to him comparatively, a person of colour. Had Pamela's catching him out, when he realised, the sudden-ness of it all, he knew it instantly, hence his reaction, just as Pamela had, and he knew that his deceit he could not hide it from her, so effectively, it ruined his whole plan. 'All' of it!

When Pamela had set up that bogus account because she had doubts, or concerns, it pained her, to have to do it, and with every moment of it, pain unimaginable, to see him and hear his working and especially as she knew she could love him, with all his issues, even if diseased to the hilt. One of the questions she asked him albeit behaving as someone else, when it was confirmed at that point he was married, and he had said that he'd split up with another person who was 'his ex,' and the dates coincided on that matter, with the last time he'd then, visited Pamela, If any man would stand in front to of his wife, unless their relationship is destructive of the lives and mentality of others and possibly vulnerable, and for personal gain or greed or sexual gratification 'of any kind, or had the spice simply ran out and they decided, ok, we can take care of some desperados who don't and habitually eventually, or now, either don't or wont or are unlikely to know better, especially if dealing with disease, or unbeknown to them totally, what if they are simply trans people, take theirs? If a wife were to say to him, "you are having fun," and his reply, "what fun do I have, working all day, long hours really," then he drives away with that wife for that day, or two days. Then when he, on other times or during any spare moments, goes to meet women to win them over, and then push into obscurity those he'd met before, and if he'd left with what was her asset on his back, then complains of having a bad back to them or the next, was it always about resilience really? Or off-loading his crap on others and escaping with the goodies. And that she enjoyed being beaten, because "she was asking for it," makes it all ok. An because they are dirt, certainly now anyway makes it somehow 'acceptable.' Then he says to then, "call me," I will be there, as he rolls out the carpet of conquest. So, you walk along that carpet, that lovely red carpet, yes it was red, and feel that he did this for you, the red carpet etc. Then others, bigger than he, see this, it makes him bigger, and you feel bigger too, and special, but not the same special you remembered some saying you were as a child maybe, yes, although still in a perambulator with a frilly hat and knitted lemon-coloured booties, you never forgot those words; isn't she 'special.' It might make you feel like nutcase now to remember it, but it was like that then. Anyway, you walk along that carpet and down some stairs feeling so amazing, and not in any way that it would happen, because you are healthy, then just as a special surprise, look at it as a picture behind very thick glass hanging on a wall, if then, you find yourself with all of those women he'd slept with before, every one of them. Then you call his name, oh, then appears, only to walk past you with another woman in full view of the others. Anyone with a true and meaningful desire or heart or good wish for a better life and future, for themselves and whatever diseases lurking waiting to pounce within that crowd, are better off away completely from that situation. You, having been isolated was not of his doing, he will abuse it, as will others like him. Your own action to, 'get out' is you being good to 'you.' What if by their actions they are creating something worse than even Covid-19 and because some of them, just as Judd is, have never and would not have or could not have a medical check-up. For certain, this means that there is no need to panic, early intervention, even those such as that are happening regarding Covid-19, should also help to win the day there too. Was dear Judd aware that it was not all based on him trusting dear darling lovable Pamela? What a fool. He abused and continues to then, or is it abuse if he is unaware, and whilst surgeries continue to be placed on hold because of Covid-19. He is on a one-way trip to potentially ruining Pamela's life, but although she still gets imagery, to encourage her to 'engage,' she does not. Or Pamela believes that he does. He knows that something is affecting him, but he doesn't know who or where from, because there have been so many in the meantime. Pamela does not call for Judd or think about him, he is not her 'centre of attention' or of any of her focus now, if he tells his own captors what is happening, and explains, they would be angrier to him, not that he was undeserving, but because Pamela didn't want to give to him. He wasn't good enough, however he seemed to some that Pamela no longer were concerned about or with. Then you or dear Pamela look back and you or Pamela sees, him kiss another woman, and you are so happy that you never did ever let him kiss you. Even if you wanted to and got that close.

#

Pamela, still a girl who'd never been kissed, she tried it once, but ','the motion wasn't on the ocean because she knew he had lied to her before in the past, he loved it, you could feel it, you knew it with every grain of your entire body, certainly your mind, that he enjoyed it, but you also knew that it was nothing at all, nothing. It was just so he could discover why he should never have lied in the first place or believed that Pamela was not aware of it. To be happy for the person Judd was kissing, he wins, because you can guess the outcome for them both, it doesn't even require thinking or concern or effort. You win because he'll never know now. Years earlier, yes as a child. Pamela, possibly because of her own perceived inadequacy, when her girlfriends were meeting boys and she couldn't understand why she could not, when the boys she thought she knew went off with her friends and she was somehow pushed to the back out of the way it seemed, had dreamed one day of meeting an ugly man, maybe she felt deserted by them all, but could never say, she just had to accept it, she wasn't like them. She'd dreamed or cried too hard. Some may always need fun of certain kinds, to help then believe what they may believe they are. And she would see in that photo he sent, and recognise it in some now, but say nothing, the ugliness that he was running from, stays with him. It was his decision, not mine, a problem then, or now might be, and not dependent on surgery to affect certainly the outcome of the decision Judd made and to think he can play with Pamela like that? Pamela was now just sitting in her room with a white sheet over her head because she often did this, sometimes even with a hat on too, on top of the sheet, she removed the sheet and stared at a Bonsai Tree in a green pot, not a Jade, nor white pot, Jean had given it to her, she'd said to her when she gave it to her, "something small and perfectly formed." She thought about that, and it made her feel sick, had Pamela now become "all grown up" too grown up? Just as Judd had to his Saturday meets. Pamela would have realised that potentially they or he or she, by their actions had created a love story of the most crazy kind, she would have thought, "what point is a story if it cannot be read to children, she might have thought they because she could now not have them because of the delays in her surgery because of her commitment to work, that initially delayed her request to have it sorted out, but she always knew that, and was happy that others could, where possible. So, if it was a love story of a kind that could never be read to children because of some of its content, was it about how stories are told, so therefore, the cleverness or wisdom, or both, if it's applicable or relevant, of a storyteller. And now, as yesterday, news that the Laptev Sea in Russia has not formed sea ice for the first time since records began. This means that there will be nothing for the sun's rays to be reflected into space by, where usually the ice would do it. Pamela wondered 'why on earth am I or have I even been bothering at all to waste my time and energy on a jerk who obviously doesn't care now anyway. So as though a gale blowed once, and an engine room seemed to have been flooded with sea water, was it Judds, or Pamelas trawler that had run aground with the crew having since thankfully been rescued already. Were they both ever really in the same boat? Probably not.

What might she throw into that cell where that little package is? Nothing.

Would she, did Pamela realise yet? Who knows, maybe we never shall, or it was as Pamela had said, and regarding her ever now wanting to meet a partner after her operation, had he destroyed Pamela, are there are some things we are just not meant to know?

The newest person he had met, had just had a bad experience. Had he done exactly that, had he saved her, had he, or they, created a reason, or they, a reason for her and he, to remain, in some ludicrous way. We'll never know and some things we oughtn't ever-ever, however disgustingly want to.

#

'Basing on Ethics.'

Whether Judd had tried or believed he wanted to, or had any odd misconception of any kind as to his desire to do 'whatever,' to Pamela, Pamela received a call from the Manor House, Lady Broadley had ventured into the garden to the trees, on her small two wheeled scooter, she hadn't fallen, but she must have got a part of her mop slipper somehow caught on a blackberry bush stump or something and was in shock, it was probably more that she did not partake of alcohol these days, not even a tipple on medicinal grounds, she'd said that she now 'personally couldn't.' Under the illusion that somehow the woodland was trying to "pull her in," by her slippers, they are basically very similar to mops, but worn like you might wear short socks on your feet, hers and vivid pink, the message was, "it was at that darned clearing Pamela." Pamela has misinterpreted, but she said to her aunt not to worry and if it had pierced the skin or had her joints been affected mobility-wise, to just contact the local GP. Everything seemed normal. Thinking of the clearing that day when she'd visited, she was reminded of school and of how names change over time, as families grow or develop, for example, Nanne 'Fitchurch,' she thought of the alpha and omega sign, or the 'A' and the 'O' that, to her had appeared on their family crest. She remembered suddenly how one of her teachers at school often used the term, a Bradley in the trees, meaning a clearing. And of the name 'Broadley,' and of other derivations.

It was November and December 2019 when all the various fires seemed to be happening in the Amazon Rainforest and Australia, so much was on the news about it, as though it was an invitation to become involved, "pulling the viewer in," and for good reasons, certainly in January alone, apart from two very sad fatalities where a couple had tried to protect their home, their first home, forty thousand fires there, just then, had burned 2,240,000 acres of 'agricultural development' land. Pamela would be horrified at the losses and not just of the two who very sadly lost their lives. As for the fires though, as bad as they were, they were not the worst fires there that had ever actually been recorded. Pamela wasn't aware of that though, 'caught up' in the whirlwind of reports and furore, granted it made a lot in relief funds and donations from so many wonderful thinking careful and thoughtful people and no doubt helped to carve out new destinies and futures for some too, possibly where there might not have been before.

Some earlier reports PPamela recalled seeing, suggested then, that Covid-19 had first been noticed in October 2019. And yes, that coincidentally was the same month that Jean's book had been published, Pamela remembered her saying that too. In January 2020, Wuhan, China shared sequence of coronavirus, termed Severe Acute Respiratory Syndrome SARS CoV2. Its own ancestor of course, could be placed back as far as more than fifty million years, yes it was a coevolving, potential 'problem.' Pamela wondered whether the different backgrounds that so many had, yes, often based in myth and legend, and very normal even if forgotten about by some, forced maybe to accept different doctrines, yes often necessity based, rather like 'praying for rain that never comes,' who then would have got, or gets the blame when the public might demand it and often of the very leaders, those great people whether you like them or not, 'they' place themselves. How much could the regular normal histories of basically everyone really, possibly, play or perform whether directly or jut by some forgotten habit somewhere in the subconscious mind, forgotten maybe because everyone was too busy trying to chugg along through the malaise of it all, and others content to simply believe and hope and kindly caringly seem to be disinterested when all along they just didn't want to interfere. Maybe because they had confidence in you, even if a confidence you could not realise yourself or that they knew eventually you would find, however those many fables, fictional, mythological, or indeed any of those characters manifested, whether light or dark, may have been presented. Surely then, the most logical and acceptable to 'everyone' therefore by default, should have become, about the recent outbreak was and is, to believe in scientific fact, for and although, 'not,' to over-rule or outdate the beliefs of others or anyone. But to deliver an understanding, not necessarily of compliance, but of reliability and amidst the fumes of fires and haziness of hurt, doubt and mistrust, trust. And surely for everything, everyone was and had come to learn about lifesaving, and even if as with Pamela's own birth whether there were issues or not, as with many others, and from way back, the emphasis is always on saving life.

#

Just as there is in folklore, a creature so terrifying, that lives on the outskirts of civilisation, known so readily to some faerie types, and is said to be a larval form of the Fuath, the son of, amorphous Brollachan, it still has webbed feet and were said to 'inter-marry,' with some humans, usually female, it's also known as a water-spirit, and Judd not keen on water, oh he was trying so hard as a human, to "inter-marry," everywhere and in any place he could, the sneaky individual he was. It was difficult because the brollochan is such a scary character to not say, 'had Pamela not been Pamela,' she knew 'exactly' how to torment it into submission,' or certainly unconnected Judd, should he persist one moment further, unconnected only and purely because he never married Pamela and had no comprehension of her ancestry. True, children should stay away from water, and woodlands at night or if alone as Pamela knew Judd should, as she felt the very kilt covering her legs, now certainly stay completely away from her. Certainly, in folklore there would have been myths and beliefs that Judd had grown accustomed to, even by disrespecting by ignorance because of his situation the merit of some others. It was important that whilst he may 'mingle,' that he'd never actually know and that he did think he knew would never be now of consequence.

Pamela recalled how, when she was a child, her father painted things around their home gold, she knew exactly what clan her father and his family are from, some laughed then, but kindly, Pamela thought it looked nice, her younger siblings would have been either too young or not yet born to have remembered it. Only recently she discovered when looking into gold leaf, that the paint was of an extremely high and expensive quality. Gold, her parents would have only had wedding rings of their or their own, if you need to think gold, not fool's gold, nor real gold, not scientifically anyway. There is no doubt, that Pamela although not afraid to mention the brollochan, because she had incorporated a safety, not to defeat, just because, it had to be slightly different for reasons of safety, because it is extremely scary, a safety precaution in her disguising it that should anyone work it out, even they would never really be able to mention it anyway, neither ethically, morally or even jokingly, or in any way, neither could such knowledge empower them, but only because of the risk. Maybe she also understood too now, in those brief moments when she stepped in, to fill only those mop slippers, why her aunt Lady Broadley no longer drank alcohol, but don't let that be a concern to you, oh no, not at all, it's with the interests and the safety of those who do too, very much at heart. Pamela's understanding of what was actually real, had become scientific, however for her briefly, although for the correct reasons, so effectively, to clear the smoke, where Judds sperm count was way too low for him anyway, to have been creating mini versions of himself, as sad as it was, he had not so much learned, but by cause and effect realised that his own reputation albeit with females most of whom believed he was meeting no-one else but them, unless party fodder, he'd realised that getting 'beneath the skin' by getting into the mind-set of others, he must have heard the phrase being used "hearts and minds," on the television news or something at some point, it somehow resulted in giving him a feeling of his own head now, constantly above the water, this was how he was able to 'seemingly 'resurface so often? And the person he'd visited, the fears and worries of unsettling also caused by the mind-games, would put them at unease, creating a void, an access point for those fears and concerns even if because they believed they wanted him, or were led to believe there was a relationship of a kind, to manifest, but it was all a lie. So yes, as the lid and as a new lockdown started in the UK so the news stipulated, Pamela wondered if he would be furloughed again, but it didn't matter. As the haze, started to clear, Pamela was spreading just a very thin, the thinnest layer of jam on some unbuttered toast to have with some black coffee, science is science and nothing else but science, and that's one flavour he'll neither comprehend, guess, or know of, understand, or have time to. She'd trimmed the edges from toast beforehand but left them on the side plate to just eat much on them as they are, if brown bread, she might have given a piece of it to birds so they can sharpen their beaks, but she'd given them some seeds and mealworms a day or so earlier, a very good discount shop gets them in, it's unusual that she can travel that far but at certain times of the year, she attempts it, she stared at the toasted cut off edges and thought, even whilst clearing debris and any deadwood, we of course must continue too, appreciating the many bugs and insects that would feed upon it.

And although, she didn't hear her uncle say it, he'd remained quiet for quite some time, as though asleep, she imagined him saying to her, "she's like her aunts before her, and no doubt like her own Mother, for sure, always something nice of the table even if a little crunchy, but you'll never go hungry dear with Pamela." Pamela was unable to consider even thinking about responding to that.

Jean, realising that she had acted way too slowly, and should have written things down, but was totally unable to, but how could she if she'd been asleep, it had been as though she'd slept so very deeply and even wondered whether she hadn't simply over-eaten some home-made experimental soup too quickly, she had the most awful stomach cramps, to the point where she at one point could not stand at all, instead she was hunched over as though a very old lady indeed with a crooked walking stick as she would have certainly appeared to have looked crippled had anyone seen her, she could not stand up at all and hung onto furniture just to prevent herself from falling to the ground and to desperately attempt to push herself up, but the pains, it was awful. She said to herself, "I wouldn't wish this on anyone."

She must have been totally knocked out, to the point that when she was trying to push herself up, she even wondered if she hadn't had a blackout, it was normal for Jean with the condition she had, she also realised a while after that she hadn't brushed her teeth the night before, so obviously something had happened. She said to herself, but why did I not choke on my teeth and why is it so cold, it was as though she was frozen stiff. She brushed her few teeth and popped her denture plate containing her two front teeth into a glass in her bathroom with some denture cleaner, then went to check the weather and what day it was, it was 6.0c and it was a Saturday, she heard neighbours in the hallway and thought 'I recognise them but where from,'? She asked herself, surely nine months has not passed, she cried and asked, 'where have I been'? She'd remembered experiencing pains the last time she was awake, it wasn't then conceived that it could be a Covid-19 symptom, because she was very certain that it could not have been, it was very probably not, she thought, because it was all quite normal, these issues, for me. She heard someone say, "what are you doing," It was the voice of her Father, and it would have been now ten days before the anniversary of his death. She was startled and thought of an aunt of hers who'd died too and asked, "who me," as though she was her aunt Annie, that same almost surprised tone that she always had, it was as though she was delirious, and she dozed off again, only to wake again moments after it seemed, her lips again pursed and dry as though totally dehydrated, it was all very strange indeed. It was as though her lips were totally stuck together, Jeans jaw would not move, and all the inside of her mouth was sore, her tongue had become so stuck to the inside of her mouth that it felt like it was not going to be easy to tear it away and throat so parched, she wondered whether she shouldn't have made for herself a drink after she'd struggle to find the bathroom before, but she didn't think to. It was not on her mind to think like that, and she just couldn't have anyway. She felt dazed and was aware that she had again scrambled into the bathroom and that she, unable to stand properly had been bashing into things. She shoved the toothbrush into her mouth with some toothpaste on it and cleaned her teeth and mouth as best as she could again. Her tongue it seemed had indeed been glued by the dehydration to the side of her mouth, that she had to push the toothbrush between just to feel assured that she was cleaning, it felt as though the skin had been damaged. Then she got into the kitchen and got a glass of lime cordial, then she pulled back the blanket on her bed and the sheet and clambered back into bed with her yellow metal rimmed fisherman's hat on and her long floor length blue dress on. She must have been thinking too loudly to herself because she was saying to herself in thought, 'I wonder why my mouth was just and before it was cleaned, it was like the mouth of a cave.' She then rested her head on the two feather pillows that even though they had covers on them seemed to be covered in feather anyway, she wondered where they all came from. Then she noticed where the lamp was on that a spider, or spiders had created webs from her bookshelves to her headboard, and where dust had accumulated, they'd become even more noticeable that they might otherwise have been. 'Oh my,' she said to herself, 'always the bridesmaid, never the bride.' She thought to herself as she stared at the back of a hardboard cupboard by the side of her bed, so those voices, my father had died a few years ago, so if from within that orifice, if my mouth was so dehydrated that it had become like a cave, was that me? Jean then dozed off and dreamed of others she knew and had known, as though it was all normal, and it was, she even conversed, but there were some questions that none of them could answer. Soon she would have a greater understanding as to why. When she woke up again, the first thought on her mind was 'caring for and the care of angels,' she'd not heard it before and it seemed odd, the question there had somehow been answered after all. It was weird and although Jean could accept that, or the very real possibility and potential, although she was very aware, that although she'd conversed and at great length it seemed, that only one of those in those many conversations in that more recent sleep certainly, was still alive. Whether any of it all, however free now from the intensity of it, was it of love, or abuse, certainly Jean could not decide on that.

Before Jean awoke, she in her dream wondered if Pamela might be dreaming, it was a strange dream for Jean to have because dreams are very private. Pamela was dreaming, she'd been contacted by a person who must have obviously kept her contact details, because there was no way that they were now accessible online, not that account, unless you knew her well, or via a designated address. The message said, "we are two guys, friends, and we would both like to come and visit you, or if you like, because we drive, we can have a nice little chat in car and get to know each other better, if you want." Pamela was surprised by this, but her immediate thought I the dream was, with what I have just been through over the past ten months, I am certainly not going to consider taking on a further two. Although she did wonder whether it might be somehow destined so was not as curious as surprised and certainly not intrigued, or she would have responded? Should she have been surprised that they did not send photos of themselves, or was that an invitation to request them? Had she done, so, she'd surely have been back on a treadmill of a sort she thought, plus, there was a lockdown in place, so maybe it said more that they would ask. She imagined the mausoleum and the doors flying open and the light although not disturbing those resting, as it was by their design that the mausoleum be created how it was. She saw all that was obviously not so good, being sucked into it, although she herself had seen nothing bad when she visited there. As it was happening thousands of leaves that had fallen from trees formed to her right, so tall, way taller that even those she believed she remembered from as being of the sea, it had a kind face, and even something like a laurel leaf crown made of leaves of the same brown shade, it was Autumn after all, or they would not have been there then, a huge right arm came down and it picked her up and just moved her to safety. She didn't understand what was happening exactly because it was as though somehow that location was changed from dangers that others saw that she did not, and to how it was when she was there. She did not respond to the message from that person who contacted, not even to enquire. When Pamela woke up, she imagined three brown unicorns, they were not dark like a beetle Jean had seen once that hit her window with such force in the garden with the red spider and the golden locust, but the lightest shade of brown she thought she'd ever seen, at first she wondered if they would overheat because the light was shining on them through then exceptionally tall green leafy trees, she couldn't work out what colour their horns were, whether they were the lightest shade of a beautiful green interwoven with what looked like silver glistening but very subtly and even such, the palest of light gold colours too, as though the finest of strands, then she realised they were the exact same colour as those of white unicorns. They stared at her, and then shyly, they shook their heads slightly and then ran off very happily. Jean then woke up, she thought about why her cheeks sometimes look slightly drawn, although they were when she was quite young too, and of how her wisdom teeth had been extracted, that surely would have impacted she wondered. Then she thought, at least it's not an eyeball of any kind nailed to a tree, certainly not in Pamela's forest. She imagined how she might have been hanged for having withdrawn cheeks at one point, then thought to herself, 'oh well, that's not too bad then.'

One final thing to remember of course, was that although it had been such a long time it seemed since Pamela touched alcohol, and certainly one of the main reasons why she wouldn't now, was that the last time she did, she'd got a little bit too tipsy. She arranged for a person she knew to collect her from the club she'd visited at losing time, unfortunately he got walleyed and as she didn't have her phone, she couldn't phone him. Presuming, because she was slightly intoxicated, that he wouldn't turn up. When a car did stop and offer her a lift home, she thought it was a mini cab. She said to the person driving it, do you know Braithfurling, he said yes, and she got into his car. She must have dozed off because she woke up not knowing where she was, she thought she was in front of a beach in Spain. She asked the chap, "where are we," this is not Braithfurling, he replied with, "we're on the other side of the river opposite Matlin Town. She said to him, 'but that was not where I wanted to go, that's not where I asked you to take me, it's in the opposite direction to where I asked you to take me to. He said to her, "shut up," I'll drive you home. Pamela was very scantily dressed, in fact she has a dress on that was see-through, just her underwear underneath and no bra. The man started driving, she remembered seeing bushes on either side of the road and the road was very narrow. He was driving quite fast and was speaking on a telephone held in his hand, that was why she was alarmed at the speed he was driving. The conversation he was having seemed strange too, he said, "four of them came up to the car and they were all looking in the window, she was just lying there in the front seat, but they were only looking.2 Pamela closed her legs quite tightly horrified and that any of them might have touched her. She felt horrified. He then tried to make it seem as though he was chatting to police on the phone, she said to him, 'you're a liar,' the car sped up and he said to her, "you're drunk, get out of the car. There was a steely look on the guys face as though he was aware that she guessed that she may have been touched although, could never prove it, so really it never happened because of that very reason. He may have got angry and still holding the phone said to Pamela, 'get out of the car.' She responded quickly, it was near 04.00am, she said to him, 'if you stop the car, I'll get out of the car.' He stopped the car, and she noticed a medication Dossett box near the seat, she picked it up and stood outside the car, he would the window down and said, "those are my pills, I need them." She told him, "I'm not getting back into that car and until I work out where I am exactly, you'll follow me in the car with your headlights full on. Not realising of course that would have turned him potentially and truly quite on, especially with her in a see-through dress. She walked a fair way, stopping to look back or check his distance from her, it seemed as though he was testing angles, because he'd moved quite a way behind her, then it was as though she thought he was going to run her down. She jumped over a low wall in her heels and felt safe hiding amongst the bushes. Then after a while she found another way out of there, it meant her climbing over a gate. As she climbed over the gate, she found herself on the main road and knew where she was because she had time to rest a moment. She looked behind her and saw his car travelling toward her at a quite fast speed, she didn't move. She just stood in the road then directly in front of the car and held his pills in the Dossett box up in the air. He stopped withing about two feet of her. She walked across to the passenger side of his car and to the rear wheel of the car and gently placed the Dossett box in front of his car tyre. Of course, from inside the car he could not see whether she'd out it in front or behind his tyre, so he'd have had to get out of the car to recover it, even in heels, this would because he wasn't a small guy, have given her enough time to make a run for it because she knew the area and he didn't know where she lived. She'd said to him beforehand; one move and they go over that high wall, don't test me on it.' She turned and so very casually strolled around the corner, she could hear him get out of his car to recover his Dossett box, then she ran fast down a side street and got home.

It would be sometime after that she met Judd, in one of their conversations, she mentioned the situation about the "guys standing by the car watching," and what he said to her about get out of the car and when it was still moving. It was strange, because Judd walked to the window, shouted at the sky, and said, "don't worry I've got this."

A stage had indeed been set, somehow, certainly not destroyed, and whether he remembered her address or not, that he somehow had, 'got this.' Or should she not have bothered. Did she care? Very, and quite possibly, 'not.' But to be quite honest, some of them he was going with, were quite obviously believing themselves to be so very bitchy with their insidious comments and because Pamela needed surgery and therefore could not do as they'd so often done, and because Pamela wasn't prepared to 'fake' anything of it, if ever she did. It wasn't as though she'd twisted Judd's arm or told him to do anything at all, not ever. They make their beds; and they can continue to lie in them, hoping.

As for Pamela's surgery, those who might still want to 'jibe,' they can pick up their little telephones and dial Pamela's Lawyers phone number, but not without requesting and being given permission, from Pamela, would Pamela's Lawyer legally discuss it, and such permission Pamela was not giving. It would be after waking up early at 02.49AM on the ninth of Novembers that Pamela thought 'my own path and that of Judd and any of his exploits shall never cross again,' You see, yes, he trusted her and was not wrong to, Pamela knew that he could trust her in his work, and could continue to, but she no longer wanted him. Yes, a line had been drawn on the ground between them in Pamela's mind, and just as he'd 'so conveniently,' closed the door on her, Pamela had now closed and bolted that door on him, she 'almost' felt him squint. It wasn't as though he could be seen or viewed as the older Judd or the horrid character, the sexual deviant, not if he'd been married anyway surely, his wife would have seen it as it was reflected upon her surely, Pamela thought. So yes, she was glad that Judd had at least got a holiday out of it somehow, and as honest as Judd suggested he was, that was a lot more than Pamela then or at any time during, resulted with, certainly as far as he was aware, or that he or any of his, 'colleagues would ever then or certainly now realise, there were no means that they could, as Pamela had secured it all. What they believed was only what they believed or would guess at, but they knew absolutely nothing.' It was sometimes debatable as to even whether Pamela herself did, often comatose and in and out of blackouts anyway, and utter dismay.

But what of the welt-like marks scars across the front of his shin bones and across the whole of his back, she wondered, surely his wife didn't do that? He didn't say when she'd had that opportunity then to ask him, even when it had seemed that they were more than they had been before, he just said, "oh nothing." Surely not flagellation, or something done out of the displeasure of her company over preference to whatever threw their legs open to him, how totally pathetic she thought. Pamela then stared at her nails, they might not be falsies and it didn't matter anyway, she liked those too, but Pamela thought 'Juk,' you are welcome to it 'babe,' quite welcome, now take all your decrepit baggage truly back and keep it.

#

It would be a week after, Pamela had to go to a hospital appointment, she decided what to wear, it seemed like an odd combination, whenever she went to hospital she had to walk past where a Princess had once lived, before getting to that point she looked at the ground and was almost hopping when she noticed that the leaves that had fallen from young sycamore trees were across the length of the street in her path, they were the exact same colours as the clothes she had on, she was amazed. Then on the opposite side of the road because you turn into the road to where the Princess had lived, on that side, she walked past and went to hospital. The appointment was a routine appointment, and then she headed back to her home, she passed beautiful roses in gardens of people and admired their choices of trees and when she was halfway along that road, she stopped outside where the Princess had lived, the sun shone through the leaves on a young sycamore so beautifully she saw, that she was a gasp, she looked across the road at the trees on the side of the road she'd earlier walked, they were maybe eight trees of the darkest green leaves and with bark incredibly dark, that they stood out from any others even near there, Pamela said to herself, how very clever the designers are to have chosen such stunning trees and with their bark so unusually dark, she stood there a while and just admired them, then moved on.

Two days after, news she read said that a vaccine against Covid-19 was likely to be phased in at the end of the year and into the following first six months of the next year, it pleased her, but she hadn't put herself at risk, but she was pleased for those who had, she even sent a message to a friend of hers at one of the hospitals and despite that fact that her surgery would probably be delayed yet again, she was no longer able to be affected by it. And thought it quite selfish to think that she could. She felt very let down, although it could never be proven that she had been, because of the situation, let's face it, she thought, 'they were all only following orders anyway.' The cut off point for her surgery to happen before Christmas was that very day, because of preparations she'd have to make, she also was aware that in only four days would be the anniversary of the day her father had died and the following month the anniversary of when he was buried. It had all cut straight through Pamela's grieving process like metal trimming scissors might cut with ease, their way through an aluminium or tin can. With her feelings now raw and exposed to the elements, there wasn't anything she could do, so Pamela lay on her bed and rested with a blanket pulled up to her chin. She could see the photo Judd had stared at of her as a baby with her father holding her in his arm and next to that another photo of them both and next to that, a religious picture of one person with two rosaries placed upon on it. She'd that day said to the friend at the hospital, 'this has all not been a test in any way of my faith, but I'll not pray again." Two days before, she'd sent him a message, realising that the time for to be advised of surgery was due to elapse saying; "May God forgive you if I cannot." She stared at er white hands and long nails, and thought how pale they looked, although in her mind they were more like a statue, she though it was all very odd and even managed to think it was slightly funny, she became as rigid as rigid can be, unable to move, she thought she was about to die. Her breathing slowed down and she even though she heard a person say, "you'll remain there until your heart stops." Then another saying, "she's got problems." Presuming the person who spoke after was referring to the first person to have spoken then, Pamela ignored it and put it all down to experience, she thought she'd heard them hoovering earlier so hadn't been exactly surprised. It in fact had been the same kind of abuse she'd suffered before at two places she'd lived at, and the circumstances identical, so Pamela was accustomed to it even when it first started weeks before although in total disbelief that it might be happening again. But, if the person has mental health issues, she told herself. But hadn't Pamela already had a good dose of all of that? Thinking of the resolution of how the Clara Gringold situation had seemed to 'balance itself out,' she let it pass and attempted to remain calm. Pamela must have been affected by it and was hallucinating and thought she saw Jesus Christ stray from the picture and then to close to her, she also saw an image of Judd from another direction come close to that. She separated in her mind immediately, for fear of cross-contamination, and because not of her belief, but what she believed she knew. Judd was returned to Judd how he was when he first met Pamela and he left. Then an image of the princess came and stood to her right side, she held a child, it was the younger of her children, she almost urged him to go close to Pamela who was still quite motionless and unable to speak, she smiled though and rather than have the son of the Princess so close to her, placed their hands together, as if holding each other's hands. Then they left. She then imagined her aunt who had died and members of her own immediate family on her father's side, who had died, they had come to collect their brother, her uncle from the lair, Pamela called to them as they dragged him along, "don't harm him," then they disappeared. She also heard some voices, she did not recognise apart from their accents, she thought of them smiling, unmistakably possibly, almost as though they seemed content, or understandingly tolerant, and as though they had become more a part of her now, and whilst thinking of her maternal family too, that they would not be excluded, after all, she did think she was dying, it was all normal for Pamela anyway, she then woke up. She even had to, or was made to think, again, would all about how Pamela was somehow be lost with her having surgery. It seemed a cruel fate to have to again question this, especially after such a long time, or were others keeping her like it, or were others slightly fearful that she might not survive the surgery, especially if somehow it has all been however stupid I seemed to Pamela, destined, or even constructed by hopes or thoughts of others at her birth, hopes that however she turned out, she would just survive, and were now an odd reality.

Pamela made some calls and because everyone was in lockdown, decided to get a blanket, and sleep through somehow, she slept the whole day, and woke up at 22.30hrs, she had on her mind, some turned leg table furniture made of dark brown wood, the legs on the piece of bedroom furniture were very thin but quite lovely too, also there was a deep set single bed with four posts made of the same wood and with the same candy-twist style and in the same colour as the other piece of furniture. The bedlinen was all a crisp white, with lovely obviously laundered bedlinen, the room looked stark but so clean, she really liked it. She saw a person, it was Pamela, she very much thought it was, the person had the same or almost pretty much identical dress to that Pamela had on that day and still actually had on, the person had no make-up on, precisely too, as Pamela hadn't either, although she wondered if the shoes didn't change, because Pamela had flip-flops on, the person stood then in front of Pamela was a naked Judd, Pamela sat on the bed and put both hands to her sides on the mattress, then she stood up to withing six inches of Judd and wondered, what was there? There was no reason to fight anymore, it was as though she even wondered whether Judd had anything to offer her at all, neither did it matter. She didn't want sex, although she knew he'd have certainly not refused if she had, but there was no need to even attempt to rush or do anything. Then Pamela, presuming it was, gave him a set of keys to that room, then she left. As she left the premises, she thought of her uncle who'd been in the that cell, or his lair, she stared up at those trees with their almost black bark and smiled, she really did smile. And thought to herself kindly, a room with a view; fete accompli. Whoever owned that property had given to Judd yet again, something that Pamela never ever could, whatever Pamela's own background was, or had become regarded, by some as, however ludicrously crazily in Pamela's own opinion it all sounded or was. Pamela looked at photos that day of how she'd changed in only five years during the wait, it had destroyed her anyway, she couldn't even contact a lawyer, all she could do was wait and face the prospect of the further damage the wait would actually do to her, and whether she would survive it, so that which was by default charged with preserving life when she was born, was now under orders whilst the pandemic was till presumably at large, or so the news certainly indicated, to by default, so no fault of its own, potentially destroy her anyway, whether or not she eventually get to the operating table.

Pamela would never pray again, although she appreciated kindly of those who by their own devotions did, and for their own reasons, neither would she accept counselling from do-gooders who were better off stacking shelves in a supermarket rather than stocking their own bookshelves through her continual suffering, or "frustration." She remembered how days before the last person again aid to her at the hospital, "you tell us about Covid-19." To then be expected to visit that same person after and discuss further her anxieties when they knew so little about how she was, she or what she'd been through and because she was not able to tell the about it, she saw it as perverse and insulting and offensive to her, however it was to her, dressed up, disguised, intended to present, or presented.

She did at least and would attempt to continue to remain hopeful, so that was why they'd said to her, "we've arranged some post-operative counselling sessions at our clinic for you." With all due respect, she thought, it was one of those who'd also told Pamela that her thoughts of Judd were not real, and that she deserved better. Pamela thought it was an unkind thing to say, especially as the person a professional, but they had a closeness and under usual circumstances, that person would not have said something like that to anyone else, she was certain of it or he'd have raised a complaint there and then, it was not in any way intended as a harmful response, Pamela was aware of it, it was a normal thing that unfortunately some say to be kind and sometimes it is sufficient, or they wouldn't say it so readily. She said to them in response, "next time you land yourselves in that much muck, I'll send your boss a spade. Meaning the recipient of, and his, or hers, could be seeking some new employment. But first, a refresher course in counselling, should they have become themselves affected too much, by Covid-19 and its 'range' of situations.

Fortunately, too, for all concerned, Pamela had seen photographs of the interiors of those properties where Judd now had lodgings, she knew precisely, not only what they did look like design-wise, and they were all very uniquely uniform in that, but more to the point, what they did not and because of their structural plan and design regulations, could not ever, irrespective of what style of footwear? Fete accomplii. Unless of course it was a penthouse flat with almost panoramic views, oh my goodness, she thought. Goodbye Judd. xxxxx

Pamela wanted to say something to me, I could feel her hurting across my own chest, I could see her tearful eyes, but she could not cry. Then she said, "I'm a big girl now aren't I, it really does hurt a lot, but please, do not worry."

Whether Judd and accomplice/s had basically just been digging up their allotments whenever they needed, or not, maybe those Pamela knew, including the health worker who said whatever to attempt to appease her soul, or Bernadette, regarding her not knowing what love was, or maybe it was all somehow just to test whether her heart would hold out in surgery, surely it hadn't, she said to herself, and what a conceited notion she thought, and maybe those who knew her had never seen her quite as happy during those times, or as different as during the initial months when she had met Judd, although she kept it quiet. She did dismiss immediately the idea that it was to test her heart capacity, should it upset her. She thought of a distant mountain, not so much with ice now, but with rocks and pebbles and a Stoney bridge with three arches that ran over the smallest of a trickle of the remnants, or the beginning of a stream in an expanse of wilderness, low walls had been built too, and the bridge veered off to the right, just as it had at the entrance to Lady Broadley's home, but there were no buildings there at all. Was she seeing what had been, or what might be to come, or something else, the location although no trees now either, apart from the bridge and the mountain looked the same, mustard-coloured heathers scattered like rugs amongst clumps of dry grasses and should she cross that bridge that seemed as though it went nowhere although it must lead to somewhere, she thought? What was obviously more of a stream once, now looked somehow a faster current or was it where there was less water flowing along it and the light caught the tops of the splashes as they now hit and sticked and splashed over stones. Or the shadowy figure straight ahead, along that path, with a dog, he had stopped and was staring back at Pamela as though beckoning her to follow to the mountain, however far away in the distance and whatever the twists and turns were to get there. To wherever, or as he had a dog, to where he called home maybe? If she thought it was Judd, would she follow? Would she cross the bridge to see where that bridge led to, what was on, or at the next turn after? She even wondered whether it wasn't her uncle, now with a dog, she smiled, oh and she really did, but tearfully too, happily, and sad because the image was so very desolate, she wanted to say, 'bless you,' but although she must surely have resembled a Cheshire cat, was unable to speak. Hours later, the crest that had been on the door of the lair, Pamela saw opposite the home where the Princess once lived as though facing it, not that it required protection, or was it to protect the trees themselves. Pamela thought of the image with the dog and of her uncle and felt sad, she said to it, 'if you are my uncle and if you'd prefer to come back to here, if you are happier in the lair, you are welcome, but I cannot permit you to bring the dog there too. Then separately Judd was seen to clutch the crest as a shield and hold it as though against her, even with a sword in his hand, she stared at the shield and said, that will not protect you, the crest fell to the ground in two pieces and Judd vanished. Then her uncle responded, he said, "you wouldn't do that to an animal would you, but your own flesh and blood." She knew he was okay, then almost at that same point as he turned to walk away, and as sad as he was to, she thought she one of her paternal aunts say, 'he's a real blaggard to have ever spoken to any of us like that, especially you or his sisters,' then she said, 'it started with blasphemous things, but it didn't last for long, he wasn't ever going to get away with that and we knew it, there was many a time he nearly got a clip around the ear from me, then when he couldn't get away with blaspheming, he'd say horrible things about our hair when we were growing up'. She said, sometimes he'd have my sisters crying their eyes out, let the cheeky rascal go, he'll get home eventually, it was always how he was, she said, he's out of harm's way there now too, by the time he does get home he'd have learned to be more polite.' Pamela had to really think about that so carefully. How cruel, Pamela thought, how very cruel.

The following week, Pamela received a phone call indicating that there could become soon an opportunity for her surgery to be conducted, there were a few things she had to do in the meantime, also it was coming up to the anniversary of her Father's death, on the day before, there was a news report saying that, "Black people were twice as likely that those white to get Covid-19 although their risk of dying was the same, although Asian people had a greater risk of dying should they catch it. This distressed Pamela, now thinking about the person who'd been on the boat that day, the person who'd been Judds Wednesday meet. She'd recalled how he turned up with a snake around his neck and those biting his arms and that understanding was of course that some male snakes when exposed to oestrogen, become almost androgenous and a sexual frenzy can occur when they become the arousal point to other male snakes, and that oestrogen is known to be passed to a male during vaginal intercourse and that traditionally whilst testosterone and oestrogen have been considered to be male and female sex hormones, oestradiol, the predominant form of oestrogen also plays a critical role in male sexual function, and particularly libido, and that generally oestrogen is lost or reduced vaginally in females by the female during sexual intercourse. Also, in Australia, in a person's garden on that very same day, a five feet long male 'eastern brown snake,' a deadly snake too, had been found trying to make love to a garden hose pipe, the snake catcher said that there was a much smaller snake in the garden with it and they must have been so confused, it seemed they were both mating with the hose.

Pamela saw her family crest again, that had dropped into two pieces when Judd attempted to use it on her, she placed it again on the handles off the door where her uncle had been, the older Judd and the horrid looking Judd were still locked away, so the younger Judd stood to her left holding a sword, she removed it from him and placed it behind her family crest, she said to him, "you'll not be needing that," she also told him that the cell was ready for him should the piercing of his own heart by his own hand become more prevalent should he continue to provoke under any guise. He then stood next to Pamela's right side, they faced on the same direction, there were two others, a man with headphones and a dark-haired female-looking person standing to Pamela's right, all four-facing forward. Pamela said, 'none of them should die, none.' In order that they would not 'mix,' Pamela thought of a medal ribbon and of four colours and of a particular design and to include black and white also. The thought of the earlier suggestion that "he deserved a medal," They all did, Pamela thought. Then her father appeared to her, the time was 01.11am he was dressed all in black and dark gray and was himself, although Pamela recognised him very easily, as a warrior, with fur around his shoulders and what looked like a skirt of tough dark leather thick straps to his knees, but a very fearsome person with a sword that you would not argue with, to the point that he would only raise it as a gesture, when Pamela heard, "he's my son," thinking that he could not possibly be thinking about her, but who knows really she thought, particularly as she had a deformity on just one 'out of the way,' unseen part of her anatomy? Thinking of the image of her uncle with the dog, and that although the voice she heard was so like here fathers that it could have been, she was sure it was, similarly it may have been his ancestors calling him, and his older brother there already on the journey, so he'd somehow waited, or somehow stayed with Pamela too, until she received news about her surgery, then he would leave to follow his elder brother who would lead him home too. What an amazing thought!

And of the medal, or the medal ribbon that would prevent them from 'mixing,' or blending together that they could each with individual identities and strengths unweakened, take on any enemy that may be thrown at basically everybody or anybody in times to come, just as the rosary broken, had not been 'deliberately' broken, none of them would ever have done that, it was changes of time, a testament of and to, changes over generations. It was nether changes of faith, nor mistrust of anyone's interpretations, or ever lack of faith. Were those changes to prevent a medal or ribbon being created, or had the amulet that Judd put on the table been that medal, all that was required was a ribbon. In exactly that same way that the ribbon with its unification although colour- wise of it would seem 'unblended' primary colours could seem quite appropriate, where she was not able to provide such, maybe as she thought of a rainbow across the sky as she might wave her right hand with her thumb pointing toward the red, might suffice. She did think also, how very typical it all was, that Judd would end up with a holiday and new accommodation and a medal too? She could almost feel him saying to her, 'keep your mouth shut, don't speak, just please, stop moaning ungrateful bitch.' What a horrid man, she thought, horrid, abhorrent, and no, he did not deserve a medal, and neither was he ever to get? She said to me, that if she had Judd here right now, not that he would get that close, she'd tell him he was a conceited fool.

The continuance of consideration, its degrees, and achievement, is always, or often as reciprocated as encouraging, and fortuitous, when the circumstances are precisely and honestly correct, for every party involved, at such times afforded.

Pamela also knew that however, sad things were or had become, whatever was being played out, that things could have been so much worse than perceived. Would she ever be able to mention why? I doubt that. Was it between them more a battle of will, rather than as she'd considered it, a battle of inheritance, whether what he'd gleaned or gained from having met Pamela, or not, floated his own boat or not, she hoped that he enjoyed the fun of the water slide on his way down to Pamela's level, and he did seem to have held her hand somehow, whether she liked it or not, albeit though they had remained apart? Or was its Pamela clinging on? Obviously, he had some steps to climb to get there first. Pamela watched him go down on the water slide, and her now knowing that her surgery date was within only weeks. Would they ever meet again, Pamela was still blocked by him on her phone, so she knew that he was not saying anything to her or pulling her or holding her hand, so she was hanging on, not even hoping now. Had her weakened will where he was concerned, permitted him to abuse her structurally by invading her imagination, although not her core, because her own defences and defence had swung into action, Pamela had to be strong now, so yes, she watched him go, and now he was gone. She stared across at her new crucifix that she'd purchased recently and almost bowed her head, she'd been wearing it for two weeks, thinking more-so of her imminent surgery and the various medical appointments in between, and about Judd, she then thought, 'are we quite done here now.' Then took a very deep breath and went to make for herself a coffee.

As sickening as it was for Pamela, how far might Judd really attempt to go, he knew that Pamela couldn't because of her surgical need, so he sought after those of a seemingly presumably virtuous likeness. They are not Pamela, he knows that, however he might try. Should Pamela age after her surgery just to put Judd off? Or does it not matter now, because he found another "like that." Or is that why he aims so deeply? Your very soul if you are not careful. There was forming too, a cut off point for dear Pamela in all of this. Or should we, as Pamela is, be just so thankful that we have structure, and Churches, organisations and health services and authorities and governing bodies that run them. Maybe he would say, "we might get lucky," maybe it's not about you, or you, or you, or you, or you, as billions are continually spent on rising sea levels globally, on flood barriers and defences, should we all grab one of those small pieces of wood now that Judd seemed to dish out, in poorer parts of the world, people are even moving further inland where the coastal regions are being lost or are further at risk, or is it about the trees that would be required to produce all of those very small pieces of wood? Or should Pamela eventually just bite the pillow and grin and bear it as many seem to, would it make you feel safer? Would she do it if she thought it would help, go with a man who potentially is full of every disease known, and knowing that because of his own 'unprotected' habit, that because of her other pre-existing health condition, it would probably kill her to do so. Or is she better just holding her crucifix as she does, both hands too! Or praying and thankful for not what we do not have, but maybe what you do.

Judd hasn't been told or contacted, to say that her surgery is happening within weeks, do you think he would know anyway? We doubt that, despite how things could seem, no visitors are allowed, or are still allowed at the hospital. Would Judd survive it though if he knew? Was it always about only that anyway? Oh, my goodness Pamela herself then thought, though strangely sad and happy at the same time. He can thankfully always contact a GP she thought then, or why not just arrange to have a medical check-up. She was thinking of some, how they might get angry with Polar bears and the likes of, should they roam into towns, but it's not their fault, she'd think, their habitat is being lost too. But then she'd be reminded again of dear Judd but only because of thinking of him angry, if he did know, and very probably saying, "who cares you bitch." Then as she would know he could say things exactly like that to her, in recent times she'd been so afraid that she even for some odd moments thought that he was having sex now with someone else in the same building where Pamela lives, there are only a dozen apartments. Soo she would have to go for her pre surgery Covid-19 test, had Judd been just vengeful as she'd wondered, or so vicious or cruel or hateful, or even somehow jealous of Pamela? Would it then have been in his interest to do whatever possible, to actually cause as much havoc as possible, to, in such circumstances, prevent her surgery. Even if, had he been so very jealous really, or angry with her, especially having not got from her what he'd set his hear then on, 'duped, 'that it under usual circumstances could have prolonged the agony for Pamela regarding her getting over him, would it not have been like putting money into his account for nothing? Surely if he himself hadn't been aware, there would have been some he'd visited who would have presumably put him straight, someone would have told him. I didn't want to say anything to Pamela because all the other apartments are above hers. If you know that Judd. Please don't mention to him that for Pamela, the problem now is, how can she carry on after her surgery, post-operative, but secretly from him. Very secretly she would no doubt, or want to say, the end

This, these roman numerals, intended to be a paragraph heading, in Pam's notes or a diary entry somewhere, or similar, because something important happened at this time: **V1:X1X:X1X. XL**. Why though, maybe we'll never know? If only I could remember presently what it was?

Anpu Jaffa 11 (2) is also available, book 11 (2) is slightly thicker than this, this has 203693 words, and the second book, an excess of certainly 240,000. Yes, the concluding part of this extremely surprising story, as hopefully you shall indeed discover.

Apologies that this book could not be presented as one book as in one-part, but because of the size, it became impossible to download for some on some devices.

A few pages from the start of Anpu Jaffa 11.

Anpu Jaffa 11.

Chapter Three

Rhododendron on My Pillow.

Motivation, Aptitude and Rigour

It was February 1st then, seven weeks past Pamela's surgery, and one week since her quite 'unusual' accident. She was meant to recuperate for twelve weeks after her five hour long vaginal surgery, but things didn't go so right for the dear girl, not as well as she'd hoped. Much of the time she was so exhausted, it was debatable whether to bother trying to get off the bed at all. Certainly, for the first six weeks she was immobilised, unable even to sit in a chair properly, hoping that during those past few weeks' then, things might have calmed down somewhat, she was only to become further dismayed as it was so obviously, she'd presumed then, just not meant to be. Even a three feet tall Lloyd Loom lamp that had been gifted to her by her friend Jean, who too had been gifted it beforehand by a friend of hers 'Ranjara,' had mysteriously that day, dropped from a shelf where she'd put it for safekeeping, just before it hit the carpeted floor, the sound of the top of the lamp tearing through the back of a small Victorian oil painting of two fluffy looking cats, permanently destroyed that particular painting forever. It was quite weird because she loved that painting despite her always wondering why the fur on the cats was painted quite so very fluffy, there was also a peculiar look on the faces of those cats, as though they were afraid, terrified actually, this was why she'd turned the painting around, it was sitting on the floor because she'd been moving some things anyway, and attributed the style of that painting to Victorianism and was still glad to have purchased it. There was more to it, but of course, Pamela didn't see that, neither did she realise the ease with which she tore from the frame and then disposed of the pieces of painting to retain just the frame. She stared at it and thought, it was sad, but it was however, a nice frame.

Whilst immobilised, a Wiley-Eyed Stickle-Fincke, Pamela noticed it, strangely and as was often the case with darling Pamela, but and even although she hadn't seen one before, neither did she know what to say, think precisely, or whether she should attempt to by questioning as though adjusting the screen view on a television with a remote control, it looked calm as can be, so she just looked at it without directly staring so as not to scare it, for a while. It had propped itself comfortably on top of some of Pamela's clothes that were on top of a metal clothes airer, (it's long legs and larger than average looking feet dangling down). She didn't need to question what it was; she knew immediately from tales presumably although from where she could not then recall. Very short brown hair and not much larger than an average sized cat, a long nose and skinny pointy ears, the hair like small twigs, although they were not, it had two eyes that she could notice, and its long nose pointed downward.

It was as though although it didn't open a mouth to speak, she heard it say to her, "Don't try tempt me with tales of lore." It would chase wid dear," it said, "and journey on their backs so quietly, just to tame them down a little, or certainly to give the impression that they were. "She wasn't sure what to think of that?

Pamela had wondered about putting up some Christmas decorations, or having been outside and seen some, certainly at least a string of lights in the window of her flat. It was difficult because she had just returned from hospital and just wasn't up to it, then although it seemed then, the last thing she might want to hear, the Stickle-Fincke said to her, "don't be such a meany and get up the ladder and find some lights." So, it knew she had a small attic, it made her smile, however reluctantly and barely able to walk at all, it was the nineteenth of December at 01.42AM precisely, it was also, the anniversary of when her father was buried. When she noticed the time, she thought it odd too, because her father was born in '42.' But it was the very anniversary, to the day of when her father had been buried. That he'd been buried in an unmarked grave had been a concern for Pamela, she did not understand it at all. But whenever she thought of him and his final resting place and because she knew that exact location so very well, even or at that very precise spot, she would only ever think kindly, and of all who shared the space at that location to even as far as the walled perimeters. Pamela thought to herself, 'before I can put up decorations, first I must locate the ladder, it was tucked behind a door because she'd moved a brown leather satchel and then pulled the ladder out from where it had been placed. Then she noticed a ream of paper, she'd been writing notes and reminders on the back of a letter from the hospital to save paper, so was pleased to discover that she still had some. She located four carrier-bags of decorations and her wicker twinkling light–up red and white scarved owl, and greeted him, she laughed and said, 'no, no, no, I can't climb up to the top of that tall window on any ladder, not this year, and imagined that the Wiley-Eyed Stickle-Fincke would be happier or understand anyway, and even if it would have made him happier if she did, as though she would have possibly tried then much harder, despite the situation, to climb the ladder to the top, she just could not, her tummy was just way too sore at that moment, that year.

Regarding the Stickle-Fincke, it would be difficult to describe what they looked like too much, because nothing and no-one ever had seen or saw them, you'd know they'd been and the second could last sometimes if you could keep your eye open for, if one eye was closed. Whereas some more horrible children might be naughty and pull the legs from spiders, and cruelly too, they'd stick them back on again quietly, and if you'd had an operation, you'd feel them working on, checking your stitches, if you were given the space to remember, and what to become of those who might deny that, yes, they'd so gently tug on stiches, gentle tiny little pulls, as they tested and cleaned. Everything would be more organised, even if to you it seemed as though nothing was any different at all, and you could begin to start to remember and find things you'd lost, or depending on your motives, your actual honest motives, like meat falling from a bone for them, to coin a phrase, however distasteful to some it could seem, or a key that just wouldn't fit, if not of true and fair, you actually might not find even one thing? But for sure, they were as fast as creative, and so very ancient, not something you could ever conveniently even consider scooping up, or know how to, with a JCB, or even an ice cream spoon. Not as fast as a wind could be, or the tail end of a whisper could seem if on even a dark night in a very silent room though. There was no other way to explain it, they were just fast, not like a runner or a swimmer even, you'd have had to have been there at that moment, or after, to understand. If you'd spent time in hospital, or were feeling poorly, they were just harmless and fast, they'd give you gently tugs to remind you of what suits you, to get you better quicker, certainly it was the case for Pamela, was it all too, to make her more appreciative of the work of those who care and of their struggles and where some might seem so selfish never to consider such, unless it was them or theirs in those situations? What if it were unbeknown to dear Pamela then, a kind of charge, to determine just how she might deal with such situations personally, the selfishness, and effects, the cruelty, and effects, the ignorance, and effects, the hate, and effects, just how good could dear Pamela be, how good was Pamela. Would she still be able to look them in the eye, even a wiley-steely eye and smile and say, 'got you,' or would she say 'okay, you got me guys, like a goodun, oh you sure got me.' The problem was, if she failed, she wouldn't be able to, because they would already be gone 'for ever.' And what if it would be on March 28th, when the first stages of the Covid-19 lockdown that had affected the full year before, were being lifted, that she would realise this? They'd certainly helped her where she'd been so dizzy and unable to stand, to attempt to mimic or become them would be your fate sealed, had many been foolish enough or mischievous, or too young in mind, to have tried? Pamela knew only then, that as brave as some could believe they might be, it made her laugh, she thought, 'ok you try it.' At your own risk, and the risk to yours and those you know very personally. They even reminded her to think of the portion sizes of food in hospital, and again of how grateful she was to them all, quite 'unusual' accident. She was meant to recuperate for twelve weeks after her five hour long vaginal surgery, but things didn't go so right for the dear girl, not as well as she'd hoped. Much of the time she was so exhausted, it was debatable whether to bother trying to get off the bed at all. Certainly, for the first six weeks she was immobilised, unable even to sit in a chair properly, hoping that during those past few weeks' then, things might have calmed down somewhat, she was only to become further dismayed as it was so obviously, she'd presumed then, just not meant to be. Even a three feet tall Lloyd Loom lamp that had been gifted to her by her friend Jean, who too had been gifted it beforehand by a friend of hers 'Ranjara,' had mysteriously that day, dropped from a shelf where she'd put it for safekeeping, just before it hit the carpeted floor, the sound of the top of the lamp tearing through the back of a small Victorian oil painting of two fluffy looking cats, permanently destroyed that particular painting forever. It was quite weird because she loved that painting despite her always wondering why the fur on the cats was painted quite so very fluffy, there was also a peculiar look on the faces of those cats, as though they were afraid, terrified actually, this was why she'd turned the painting around, it was sitting on the floor because she'd been moving some things anyway, and attributed the style of that painting to Victorianism and was still glad to have purchased it. There was more to it, but of course, Pamela didn't see that, neither did she realise the ease with which she tore from the frame and then disposed of the pieces of painting to retain just the frame. She stared at it and thought, it was sad, but it was however, a nice frame.

Whilst immobilised, a Wiley-Eyed Stickle-Fincke, Pamela noticed it, strangely and as was often the case with darling Pamela, but and even although she hadn't seen one before, neither did she know what to say, think precisely, or whether she should attempt to by questioning as though adjusting the screen view on a television with a remote control, it looked calm as can be, so she just looked at it without directly staring so as not to scare it, for a while. It had propped itself comfortably on top of some of Pamela's clothes that were on top of a metal clothes airer, (it's long legs and larger than average looking feet dangling down). She didn't need to question what it was; she knew immediately from tales presumably although from where she could not then recall. Very short brown hair and not much larger than an average sized cat, a long nose and skinny including some of the nurses who made her laugh so very much. Only because Pamela rarely did laugh, those professionals' incredibly special intuition saw that. Everything too, so accurate and time, and where a tweed skirt she loved but had bought the wrong size, brown and beige in colour, where she'd lost weight to go for surgery, the three-inch gap to close it where she'd wear a belt before and a jumper or coat, was no more, actually fitted her that day, she had wondered about sewing a piece of ribbon with a hole in it, or string attached to the ribbon in a loop, on one part of the waistband and attaching a button on the other, but hadn't got around to it by then, but then quietly, in that silent room, she was glad that she hadn't. She'd travelled to hospital with her clothes in a shopping trolley because she was afraid to let some of her neighbours know that she was going to hospital, or when, because she'd heard some say that when she was in hospital, where they'd overheard a conversation, that they were going to have a sex-party, Pamela knew too what that meant, and if her ex was in any way because of how things had been, involved. They actually said that they would plan to have such a party on the very same day she left her home for hospital so yes, she deliberately lied and said she was going to hospital a week after, Pamela was really so very afraid of their threats, those kinds of threats, where they involved her so called by them ex-partner, however they came. At 04.00AM two days after she'd returned to her home from hospital, she made a coffee and dilated, then she heard at that precise moment, just as she pushed the dilator into her, someone leave the premises via the main communal door, it should have been an indicator for her then, but this was not to be realised. She'd heard some people arrive just before midnight, but she was so dosed up when she could remember to take painkillers, it was all somehow a little vague too, it was at that moment she glanced across her room and on a seat, she was staring at a jumper, maybe she was tired, or was it to be a sign, and as she hadn't noticed any romanticism regarding his leaving the premises and when, she thought she saw the image 'The Scream' by Edvard Munch on her yellow and pink fluffy jumper, she dismissed it and thought how she would not be fooled again and that possibly, her former partners presence a day earlier, was maybe a pre-cursor. She'd been beaten savagely, and her morals and standards thrown to the floor and stamped and then spat on recently, as rules that she always believed she would want to live by should she meet someone were obviously unimportant to others, or would be then, although Pamela unaware, she was unaware of how dirty some might play and even when March 28th would arrive, with the clocks having gone forward an hour that day and the start of Springtime, had they failed or gained, had Pamela lost, what had Pamela lost by then, what had she retained? Was 'why' to play. any part in that? And why at all?

No longer, certainly back then was Pamela thinking of them as, 'prying,' but more, 'guttersnipes? And of all of them then it seemed. A weather report came through to her phone at that moment saying it would rain at 04.00AM, It didn't. It must have been 02.20AM, she'd woken up, because although she hadn't messaged him for some days, at 02.40AM she did, the message said "soon xxxx," it would then be at 04.07AM she checked her phone and realized it hadn't rained at all. The light cast from the open curtain then, in that reasonably dark room seemed to reflect on the back of a cupboard, Pamela, never the type of girl who'd think of herself as nutty, was to think then of three giraffes, with another or the shadow of one of them tucked behind, although only glimpses, teetering on her mind, or impressions of, although one of them seemed more noticeable slightly than the other two. Pamela liked Giraffe and imagined them chewing away, on leaves from tall trees, it was winter, and the trees were bare though, she thought, or she did a couple of months after, but by then was damage already done and would it be too late? She thought of her ex, although really, he'd wanted her to believe he wasn't, it was what they'd been telling her, or what she'd been overhearing too much, he was missing Pamela too though, or maybe it was just, that he "enjoyed mince pies with them"?

At 11.56AM the church bells pealed as they usually did, it was a Sunday. Pamela herself had just got outside and back carefully, having put some food out for the birds, she noticed that there was an odd feeling in the air although only four days before Christmas. 'It was as much about mince pies as it was kuchen treats,' something was telling her from somewhere, 'stick to conventional and the wonderment of it,' She would not understand why, such was Pamela though, and for particularly good reason too. 'It's safer,' she then heard, but why, she thought? How Pamela could have been compromising herself was never a question for her, or an option, and certainly no-one else. 'Appreciate the Church Bells,' they certainly did sound nice she thought, and their certainty too, very appealing. She did like the sound of the church bells, and as of that there was, and would be no doubt for her, no doubt at all.

#

In the very back of her mind though, there was another thought, that something was 'kicking off,' or about to. She didn't like it and as she'd only been out of hospital for a few days and had medication to take four times daily and also had to dilate using two glass eight-inch long dilators, a thicker one and one not so thick, and to top it all, possibly because of the stresses, she'd dropped haemorrhoids and seriously had to question whether or not she had experienced a prolapse even where, because she had been to the shops when she was supposed to have remained in bed? Fortunately, she hadn't suffered a vaginal prolapse or anything associated to it, she even wondered too, whether the increased blood flow because of the dilation had caused the haemorrhoids to drop, for most people though who did, if not diet, it can be just stress, but these were vast and horrid, for some it might have seemed like Pamela was somehow totally in the dark, but what if maybe she had an understanding of dark somehow anyway? It was all a horrible mess; she'd had to go to the shop because she'd ordered haemorrhoid cream online and wanted to be sure that should it not arrive by Christmas, she'd have some to use and if the situation were to worsen even more. She'd never seen or felt anything like it, it was genuinely as though much of her insides were hanging out, not like a small treatable bobble or two as some normally infrequently could have been accustomed to. She could push them all back inside, but would they shrink back to normal really, it seemed doubtful? And then to dilate? It was, all of it, just too disgusting a thought, but too, it had to be done or tended to somehow. She found a rubber ball not much smaller than a tennis ball although as hard as a snooker ball and placed it by her rectum after applying the purchased cream. It would serve well and seemed to hold everything in place, Pamela briefly thought of the crawss, or 'cross me palms with silver,' scenario of years gone by and smiled, not cautiously, but knowingly and kindly indeed, and kindly of The Heathers too, all amazing friends of hers. She thought it seemed funny at times laying on her back with her legs wide open and her anus propped on top of a solid rubber ball covered in cream, especially when she felt it moving, as though making its way inside her, she giggled to herself but really it was just so not funny, not at all.

There had, she'd noticed, been a blind spot days before Pamela went into hospital, - so now, looking at the sparkling gold glittered reindeer, had been or became an indicator of the blind spot as she perceived it, that somehow she'd missed out somehow, maybe too, of equally a destiny as that which led her to there, certainly if looking at that reindeer and that scented candle, had something blurred into a significance, were Christmas or festive bells about to chime and ring out, and the sounds and smells of Christmas, a season, about for some, to overwhelm.

DEAR READER........

Grateful that I have been able to get Anpu Jaffa 1 & 2 printed, unfortunately, the scale page-wise is 773 pages per book. Book 11 was 779 pages, In order to balance this, some of the first pages of Anpu Jaffa 11 have been placed here, hence the rest of the story being in Anpu Jaffa 11.

Thank you!

P F

Printed in Great Britain
by Amazon

21066645R00220